CREATING LOCAL ARTS TOGETHER

REVISED AND UPDATED

A MANUAL
TO HELP COMMUNITIES
REACH THEIR KINGDOM GOALS

Brian Schrag

www.clatmanual.com

visit us at missionbooks.org

Creating Local Arts Together (Revised and Updated): A Manual to Help Communities Reach Their Kingdom Goals
Copyright © 2013, 2025 Global Ethnodoxology Network, formerly International Council of Ethnodoxologists

No part of this book may be reproduced, stored in a retrieval system, or transmitted in any form or by any means—electronic, mechanical, photocopy, recording, or otherwise—without prior written permission from the publisher, except brief quotations used in connection with reviews. This manuscript may not be entered into AI, even for AI training. For permission, email permissions@wclbooks.com. For corrections, email editor@wclbooks.com.

William Carey Publishing (WCP) publishes resources to shape and advance the missiological conversation in the world. We publish a broad range of thought-provoking books and do not necessarily endorse all opinions set forth here or in works referenced within this book.

The URLs included in this workbook are provided for personal use only and are current as of the date of publication, but the publisher disclaims any obligation to update them after publication.

All scripture quotations, unless otherwise indicated, are taken from the Holy Bible, New International Version®, NIV®. Copyright ©1973, 1978, 1984, 2011 by Biblica, Inc.™ Used by permission of Zondervan. All rights reserved worldwide: www.zondervan.com.

Scripture quotations marked ESV are from The Holy Bible, English Standard Version® (ESV®), copyright © 2001 by Crossway, a publishing ministry of Good News Publishers. Used by permission. All rights reserved.

Scripture quotations marked NLT are taken from the Holy Bible, New Living Translation, copyright © 1996, 2004, 2007 by Tyndale House Foundation. Used by permission of Tyndale House Publishers, Inc., Carol Stream, Illinois 60188. All rights reserved.

Published by William Carey Publishing
10 W. Dry Creek Cir
Littleton, CO 80120 | www.missionbooks.org

William Carey Publishing is a ministry of Frontier Ventures
Pasadena, CA | www.frontierventures.org

Cover and Interior Designer: Mike Riester

Front cover photos (from top left moving clockwise): Daniel Dama leads group at Africa Sings, courtesy of James R. Krabill; Guatemalan woman teaches traditional weaving to ethnoarts worker, Caitlyn Christie de Hernández, courtesy of Robin Harris; Children perform at a cultural show in Chiang Mai, Thailand, courtesy of Elyse Patten, Wycliffe Global Alliance Contribution; A man carves a wooden Russian Orthodox cross in Georgia, courtesy of Marc Ewell, Wycliffe Global Alliance Contribution; photos used by permission.

ISBNs: 978-1-64508-576-8 (paperback)
978-1-64508-578-2 (epub)

Printed Worldwide

29 28 27 26 25   1 2 3 4 5   IN

Library of Congress Control Number: 2024950352

Creating Local Arts Together helped me tremendously in my ministry in Africa. This manual helped me guide Fulbe and Hausa people on how to redeem their indigenous musical instruments such as the *googe* (violin) and bamboo flute. I have equally used the *CLAT Manual* to facilitate the crafting of local hymns which helped to decolonize Fulbe and Hausa hymnodies. Christians have crafted and performed songs that were not only for worship but for peacebuilding, reconciliation, and Christian witness. As such, this volume is not a mere manual but an instrument of life transformation.

Daniel Dama, PhD
President and founder, Africa Sings Ministries for Peacebuilding and Christian Witness
Parakou, Benin Republic, West Africa

In 2012 my wife and I found ourselves up in the mountains of northern Philippines conversing with the believers of a tribal group, introducing them to the possibility of using their indigenous musical forms and instruments in their worship. When they said yes to the idea, I began wondering, "How do I start the process?" *Creating Local Arts Together* is God's answer to that prayer. I am a musician with little training in ethnoarts, but this material empowers me to do the work of the Lord in ways that will be meaningful and productive.

Roy Fabella
Philippine Ethnoarts Community of Practice
Ministry director and missionary, Windsong Worxtations

The Creating Local Arts Together (CLAT) model has been a great creative research tool for both our undergraduate and postgraduate students at All Nations Christian College in the UK. Students have been able to develop meaningful creative projects for a wide range of communities and differing contexts. In particular, through teaching and hosting the Arts for a Better Future course each summer, we have been able to adapt CLAT for use in intercultural churches and communities in the UK, which has helped foster culturally conscious worship, diversity of creative expression, and deeper unity within the church.

Jill Ford, DWS
Lecturer and Programme Leader for Arts, All Nations Christian College (UK)

The publication of Brian Schrag's first edition of *Creating Local Arts Together* led to students deeply engaging with the material through our graduate courses in World Arts here at DIU and through Arts for a Better Future workshops all over the world. The results of these students' projects attest to the usefulness and brilliance of the CLAT method. Its deep insight into how to humbly work with communities toward their goals has led to fruitful and powerful outcomes in a wide variety of cultural contexts, including urban and multicultural communities. In this revised edition, Schrag has incorporated user feedback, lessons learned, and additional stories of real-life use of these principles over the last decade. The result is a significantly updated and improved version—likely the most important book you'll own for your ministry in the arts.

Robin Harris, PhD
Chair, Center for Excellence in World Arts at Dallas International University
President, Global Ethnodoxology Network

The *CLAT Manual* was instrumental in helping my small group take steps toward cross-cultural understanding and reconciliation. The *Creating Local Arts Together* conversations helped us identify our collective strengths and leverage local resources to find creative ways to move toward a common vision. This manual was an invaluable and very practical guide as we created and improved original artistry to benefit our wider community. No resource has been as essential for creative, grassroots, kingdom-oriented collaboration in my arts advocacy work. Its proven methods and foundational insights are excellent for the work of building and sustaining flourishing communities.

Melanie D. Henderson, PhD Candidate
Board Secretary, Global Ethnodoxology Network

Working among diverse people groups in the creation of contextualized audiovisual resources requires a flexible and adaptable approach. The CLAT method has been an invaluable tool in our journey with others towards realizing the Kingdom Goals of these communities. By encouraging deeper exploration of culture and Scripture, CLAT equips us with the know-how to empower communities to make informed decisions that align with their vision of reflecting the Kingdom of God. In my experience working with the people group in the Sahel, the CLAT method has provided valuable insights and guidance. The stories shared in the book have served as a roadmap, offering invaluable lessons on what to do and what to avoid. By learning from the experiences of others, we are equipped to navigate our path with confidence and avoid repeating past mistakes.

David Oluseyi Ige, MA
Director, Declare Global Outreach Mission, Worship from the Nations Initiatives

The sheer breadth of this project speaks of the multitudes of peoples around the world longing to offer worship and witness drawing from their cultural wealth in ways that bring glory to God. Especially significant is how the dual volumes—an *Ethnodoxology Handbook* with a companion "make-it-happen" practical guide, *Creating Local Arts Together*—offer opportunities for continued growth in the ministry of the church worldwide.

Roberta R. King, PhD
President, Servant King Resources, Inc

We cannot do without this! The *CLAT Manual* is the core resource of the World Arts program at Dallas International University. Most of our courses are built on its seven-step structure, making it an effective tool for ethnodoxology practitioners and scholars who want to see communities engage with God to the fullest in their local cultures. This book crystallizes decades of Brian's ministry and academic experience: theologically sound, intellectually rigorous, and practically applicable to a vast variety of contexts. These cocreation principles facilitate kingdom transformation not only in the communities we work with but also in my own life.

Hsiang-Ning (Dora) Kung, PhD
Assistant Professor, Dallas International University

The first edition of this book was a great resource to me for at least two reasons. In 2016, I was invited to teach a course on Worship, Arts and Culture. At that time, the only resource that seemed relevant to such a course was *Creating Local Arts Together*. Since I work in a French-speaking context, I could not use it as a textbook. However, I used it in my preparation, especially the first section: Foundations. More recently, in 2023, I went to Guadeloupe and organized Scripture-infused songwriting workshops. Once again, the CLAT method helped us in this process. At that time, a French translation of the abridged CLAT guide—*Community Arts for God's Purpose*—was produced. What a joy to see how Christians get to connect to God in a deeper level by creating their own prayers using their own local artistic expressions (poetry, songs, storytelling).

Dr. Ruth Labeth
Professor of Practical Theology, Dean of Undergraduate Studies,
École de Théologie Évangélique du Québec (Canada)

The first edition of this book is an invaluable resource for anyone nurturing local arts anywhere worldwide. Its practical tools and lively tone made it both accessible and inspiring, whether you are an artist yourself or passionate about encouraging artists around you. I've applied its principles alongside countless communities in my work, and they are the foundation of my organization's methodology for working with local arts. Brian Schrag pioneered this community-centric approach and has continued enhancing and improving these concepts over the last decade. I have long anticipated this revised edition to refine an exceptional resource.

Matt Menger, PhD Candidate
International Ethnomusicology and Arts Coordinator, SIL

The book you hold in your hands is the result of great effort by many people who have worked in the area that most deeply touches the heart of a people—the arts. Its seven conversations allow anyone, beginner or not, working in a cross-cultural context to integrate arts into his or her ministry. The gospel message is too important to be misunderstood; local arts allow everyone to hear God speaking directly to them. Studying and applying the *CLAT Manual* will help you tap into this powerful component of the spread of the Kingdom of God.

Héber Negrão, PhD Candidate
Ethnoarts Coordinator, Evangelical Missionary Linguistic Association (ALEM)

I have known Dr. Schrag for years. His love for people in general and Africa in particular has always touched me. This love is so intense that it pushes him to share all that he receives from the Lord. In this season—characterized by a growing awareness of African identity in African churches and in Cameroon in particular—this book is like a bulldozer, paving the way for the enrichment of our arts. I strongly recommend *Creating Local Arts Together* to worship leaders, theology professors, musicians, and all who crave to see peoples of all cultures give the best of themselves to the Lord.

Roch Ntankeh, PhD
Global Advisory Council, Global Ethnodoxology Network

Creating Local Arts Together is the perfect companion to field workers wishing to encourage a community in reaching their Kingdom Goals through the exploration and power of local arts. The painstaking efforts of the author combined with their years of field experience provide one with practical tools to apply in research, analysis, and "sparking" of indigenous art for the glory of God and the blessing of his people. This manual is number one on our resource list as it contains in one thorough, yet convenient place so much of the practical wisdom we've received from various books, lectures, and presentations.

Justin Randolph, MA
EthnoArts Consultant, SIL Global
Bethany Randolph, MA
Expressive Arts Therapist

The Creating Local Arts Together (CLAT) process provides a practical framework for anyone seeking to encourage arts among global communities and churches. Arts for a Better Future (ABF) workshop participants from around the world engage with each section of the *CLAT Manual*, practicing and applying the tools among diverse communities. They leave ABF empowered to encourage artists, value cultural identity, and creatively work toward God's Kingdom. This edition incorporates many new stories resulting from those applications. I am so thankful for Brian Schrag's labor of love in gathering these ideas and sharing his vision and wisdom for this exciting work of ethnoarts.

Laura Roberts, PhD Student
Dallas International University
Arts for a Better Future Global Coordinator, Global Ethnodoxology Network

CLAT method conversations keep me grounded in the local communities I've encountered, their artistic riches, and ways of doing things that work for them. As I've traveled among communities and researched their arts, the CLAT steps have offered me firm handles to process methodically through the sea of dynamic artsy data all around me. The lenses focus me on the component parts and enrich my understanding of the whole artistic picture in its cultural context.

Becky Robertson, PhD Candidate
Adjunct Faculty, Center for Excellence in World Arts, Dallas International University

Creating Local Arts Together serves a wide range of purposes for those exploring artistic communication within communities, whether cultures close to home or far afield. For experienced researchers it is a compilation of ideas and comparative perspectives, while for those newly starting out in the world of arts, the steps or "conversations" serve as an invaluable guide and assurance. Merging God's truth with artistic expressions is never predictable, yet the global church is crying out for such an experience. May this revised edition of the *CLAT Manual* continue to help his Kingdom to flourish!

Julie Taylor, PhD
Senior Ethnomusicology and Arts Consultant, SIL Eurasia

In 2020, I facilitated the CLAT process for the core team of a new church plant near the Texas-Mexican border. "Knowing and living out sound doctrine" within their community was a top priority for the group. Over seventy art forms filled the white board! "Fiestas!," they unanimously declared, best embodied their Kingdom Goal. Fiestas served as a platform to showcase faith, connect with the community, and cultivate a welcoming atmosphere. Today, fiestas remain woven into the very DNA of this church.

Matt Taylor, MA
Director of Cultural Engagement, To Every Tribe

As soon as you get ready to open this book, put everything else aside and read it carefully. In the past, Mono traditional instruments were used only for ceremonial rituals honoring ancestral deities. But in 1992 Brian Schrag moved to my village as a Bible translator and started learning to play traditional Mono songs on the *kundi*—a local harp. Eventually a small group joined him and began composing Scripture-based songs. Today, in all the Mono churches, we see a radical change in how Christians live, because God's message communicated through *kundi* songs directly touches their hearts. Many declare by their actions that the Spirit has used this to bring them back to the foot of the cross of Jesus Christ. We hope this manual will inspire those who read it. Even more, we declare to our Christian brothers and all of God's servants in other places that this manual is truly useful in bringing people back to God.

Rev. Gaspard Yalemoto
Director, Mono Bible Translation Program, Democratic Republic of the Congo

CONTENTS

Preface	ix

FRAMING THE SEVEN CONVERSATIONS

Always toward Heaven	1
All the Arts from All the World for All of God's Purposes	2
From Creation to New Creation	4
Foundations	6
Jesus's Incarnation as Our Model	12
Three Approaches to Arts in Mission	13
Ethnodoxology	15
Ultimate Motivations: New Creation and Its Distortions	15
Preparing for Conversations	16
Starting—and Sometimes Ending—Small	32
Some Advice and Encouragement	35

CONVERSATIONS

Conversation 1: Meet a Community and Its Arts	39
Conversation 2: Specify Kingdom Goals	63
Conversation 3: Connect Genres to Goals	101
Conversation 4: Analyze Genres and Events	117
4A: Look through Seven Basic Lenses	129
4B: Identify Artistic Domain Features	147
4C: Discover Deeper Community Connections	159
4D: Encourage Churches to Integrate Artistry More Holistically	175
Conversation 5: Spark Creativity	203
Conversation 6: Improve Results	253
Conversation 7: Celebrate and Integrate for Continuity	263

CLOSING MATTER

Closing 1: Quick Reference	271
Closing 2: Sample Community Arts Profile (CAP) Outline	273
Closing 3: Global Ethnodoxology Network's Core Values	277
Closing 4: Index of Artistic Domain Research Activities	281
Closing 5: Index of Sample Sparking Activities	285
Glossary	287
Bibliography	291
Scripture Index	307
Subject Index	309

FIGURES

Figure 1.1	Creating Local Arts Together model	18
Figure 1.2	Real Life CLAT: An example from India	22
Figure 2.1	A few participatory methods	95
Figure 3.1	Draft plan to connect community artistry to Kingdom Goals	105
Figure 3.2	First-glance genre comparison chart	108
Figure 3.3	First-glance genre comparison chart for urban Yeshu Bhakta communities	109
Figure 3.4	Components of an artistic communication enactment	111
Figure 4.1	A complex artistic enactment seen through several lenses	119
Figure 4.2	Three-pass artistry research process	120
Figure 4.3	A top-down, hierarchical description of an artistic event	120
Figure 4.4	Categories of insights	125
Figure 4.5	Create a hierarchical segmentation timeline from a basic level outward	138
Figure 4.6	Creativity components of young Congolese churches	164
Figure 4.7	Artistic dynamo: Song form in the *kànɔ̀ɔn* genre	167
Figure 4.8	Artistic dynamo: Rhythm in the *kànɔ̀ɔn* genre	168
Figure 4.9	Artistic dynamo: Community values in the *leneŋe mboŋ* genre	168
Figure 4.10	Same instruments used for both godly and ungodly purposes	186
Figure 4.11	Results of Christians' approaches to artistic forms	192
Figure 4.12	Graphic presentation of contextualization process	193
Figure 4.13	Worship wheel	196
Figure 4.14	Sample schedule for Arts for a Better Future	200
Figure 5.1	Drafting another plan connecting events to Kingdom goals	203
Figure 5.2	Steps to designing a sparking activity	205
Figure 5.3	Sample corporate worship workshop schedule	239
Figure 6.1	Sample intertwined artistic features in an enactment	254
Figure 6.2	Examples of evaluation components	260
Figure 7.1	Creating Local Arts Together idealized model	271

PREFACE

HISTORY AND ACKNOWLEDGMENTS

Like its first edition, I've tried to craft the revised *Creating Local Arts Together* manual into a friendly, rigorous, useful, aesthetically informed compendium of wisdom steeped in centuries of ideas and events, geared toward understanding the present, and invigorated by a vision of the coming New Creation. Members of rapidly multiplying diverse networks contributed their gifts, passions, training, and expertise. We've drawn on historically robust discoveries and methods of academic disciplines like ethnomusicology, folklore, performance studies, anthropology, biblical studies, missiology, and ethnodoxology, inspired by artistry enlivening the church throughout its 2,000-year history. And we've plumbed depths of experiences with the first Creator, inexplicably Lord, friend, and unrelenting lover.

The nascent form of this manual consisted of limited resources we assembled to teach a new curriculum at the Graduate Institute of Applied Linguistics in 2008 (the name changed to Dallas International University in 2018). A core of SIL Global and other Christ-following ethnomusicologists was responding to two realities. First, many of us were frustrated by our incompetence in interacting with the elements of dance, visual, drama, verbal, and other arts that almost invariably went hand-in-hand with communities' musicking. Second, we realized that artistic forms of communication have a much wider range of benefits than those emerging from the church-based songwriting workshops that constituted the majority of our work. So we read experts in other domains, sometimes gathering them for discussion and debate, taught classes, asked for feedback from our patient students, and the material matured.

Concurrently, the Global Ethnodoxology Network (GEN, founded as the International Council of Ethnodoxologists in 2003) had been noticing and nurturing interest in this new approach in other Christian organizations. William Carey Library agreed to publish a two-volume project coordinated by GEN in 2013: a *Handbook* and *Manual*. I was in charge of this manual and soon realized I needed lots of help. In the end, I wrote or edited most of the content, integrating contributions and feedback from dozens of people, trying with mixed results to create an organic, one-voiced whole. It's important to note that when we lacked experience or knowledge in a domain, we called on experts. This is especially true of content in this manual (and the new *Creating Local Arts Together Companion*, available at www.clatmanual.com) related to artistic domains like visual arts and dance.

The first edition has enjoyed a rich life. Over 1,200 people from five continents have taken Arts for a Better Future (ABF), using this manual and its derivatives as primary texts. Dallas International University now offers graduate certificates, an MA, and a PhD in World Arts based on the Creating Local Arts Together approach. Increasingly diverse, brilliant, and untamed students and instructors have discovered inconsistencies, errors, and omissions, developed tools, teaching aids and new materials, and revealed fundamental insights. Much has emerged by living in a world of rapidly changing global and local social dynamics, technologies, ideologies, mission organizations and priorities, heightened awareness of neglected human and environmental tragedies, scholarly exploration, the growth of ethnodoxology and ethnoarts as disciplines, and so on. In response, with much indispensable help, I've attempted a second gathering, reconceptualizing, and winnowing of an unwieldy aggregate of what's become an important touchstone of a thriving movement.

Unsurprisingly, this manual's revised edition's content has outgrown the capacity of one book, filling new publications, web-based ecosystems, curricula, and human networks. Given all this, acknowledging each person's and organization's particular contributions is impossible. So I've made an alphabetical list of everyone I can document or remember who played a role. Please forgive my lapses of memory or attribution. A community truly produced this bit of written artistry.

My deepest gratitude goes to each of you (in alphabetical order by last name): Beth Argot, Wendy Atkins, Tom Avery, Michael Balonek, John Benham, Harold Best, Kevin Calcote, Vida Chenoweth, Geinene Carson, Mat Carson, Duane Clouse, Ian Collinge, Peggy Connett, Matt Connor, Neil Coulter, Cory Cummins, David Dargie, Anya Ezhevskaya, Dan Fitzgerald, Frank Fortunato, Katie Hoogerheide Frost, Chris Gassler, Sue Hall-Heimbecker, Michael Harrar, Holly Harris, James Harris, Robin Harris, Mary Hendershott, Melanie Henderson, Valerie Henry, Harriet Hill, Margaret Hill, Ken Hollingsworth, Debbi Hosken, Lydia Hreniuc, Arthur Morris Jones, Eric Jones, Brad Keating, Pat Kelley, Roberta King, Joy Kim, Younhee (Deborah) Kim, James R. Krabill, Hsiang-Ning (Dora) Kung, Megan Larson, April Longenecker, Chuck Madinger, Roce Anog Madinger, Cathy and Paul McAndrew, Matt Menger, Héber Negrão, Kwabena Nketia, Roch Ntankeh, Jhonny Anderson Nieto Ossa, Steve Parkhurst, Jonathan Parlane, Quynh Parlane, Michelle Petersen, John Pfautz, Hoiling Poon, Elsen Portugal, Evy Pun, Beth Randolph, Justin Randolph, Kristýna Raus Jensen, Scott Rayl, Robert Reed, Laura Roberts, Becky Robertson, Julisa Rowe, Mary Beth Saurman, Todd Saurman, Amy Schmidt, D.P. Smith, Glenn Stallsmith, Julie Taylor, Matt Taylor, Mary Lou Totten, Martie Tracy, Pete Unseth, Susan Walters, Sue Whittaker, Lydia (Duggins) Zumut.

And to the Finalizing Editorial Team: Robin Harris, Laura Roberts, and James R. Krabill, who forged my text into a beautiful, complete manuscript—thank you for this enormous gift! You added case studies and indexes; fixed omissions, inconsistencies, and obscurities; scanned and made every heading and reference conform to meticulous style requirements; and performed other essential tasks that exceeded my energies.

This manual remains an imperfect object that will continue to grow and morph, spawning new objects with different shapes in different places. Hopefully, I've accounted for the complexities of this project in energy producing ways, weaving stable and malleable element interactions throughout. I take responsibility for its current contour and content, including errors and omissions. But now it's yours. Take it, play with it, argue with it, add to it, discard parts of it. Now *you* have the responsibility and pleasure of working with communities as they draw on this manual to create astounding bits of artistry on Earth.

FEATURES OF THE REVISED EDITION

The text of the *CLAT Manual*'s revised edition both follows and differs from the first edition. Here are a few points to keep in mind.

Pronouns and People

Flowing from the history and nature of this volume, you'll notice that I vary in how I refer to the manual's author, audience, and communities. I switch between *I*, *we*, and particular people for the authorial voice, highlighting in turn my individual agency and that of the sodality. Terms for *you* who are reading and applying this book's methods include *arts advocates*, *arts leaders*, *transformation advocates*, *teams*, *community insiders*, *researchers*, and more. Your roles and identities diverge in many ways, at different times, places, and contexts. Finally, I specify our partners in cocreation as whole or subsets of communities, hybrids, *they*, or *we*. So please flow with the profusion of situations we all find ourselves in.

The Transformation Process

When I complete a project, I often think, "This is perfect—now on to the next thing." I inevitably realize that everything needs to keep growing and improving. Those who have read, learned, taught, and applied *The Manual*'s approach have generated new ideas, tools, and obvious points of improvement. People have already integrated many of these into their teaching materials and ministries. I also designed and performed an arduous process of gathering, categorizing, and assessing input from two dozen or so individuals and groups intimately familiar with *The Manual*'s first edition, starting with an extensive survey. All of this has been participant observation.

First Glances, Glimpses, and Activities

Scattered throughout this manual, you'll notice a few types of text: First Glances, Glimpses, and Activities. Because artistic communication is maddeningly complex, it sometimes feels impossible to know how to start. The First Glance tools are designed to give you a relatively quick grasp of the most important elements of whatever the task is. We then show you how to go deeper.

You'll also see Glimpses every so often, marked by a magnifying glass icon. These are short stories that illustrate a topic we're addressing nearby. Many of them have longer versions in the Handbook. Note that only some Glimpses are attributed to someone. The others are stories that seem to have become common property of the Christian ethnoarts community or require anonymity.

Finally, you'll encounter sections preceded by a pencil icon, Activities. These are usually guided research tasks or community engagement tools with steps. In some ways, we want almost everything in this manual to affect your actions, whether by providing principles or specific directions.

From Steps to Conversations

We've tried to highlight the importance of relationships and communities' agency in our engagement. This is most visible in our calling each of the main sets of activities *conversations* instead of *steps*. This change also acknowledges *Real Life CLAT*—application of a methodology is messy, not always following one order.

Core Values

The revised edition reflects GEN's Core Values listed in Closing 3 and their practical implications more thoroughly and seamlessly (see www.worldofworship.org/core-values).

New Features

Readers familiar with the first edition of the *CLAT Manual* may also notice differences like these: We've added a full index; periodic Reflection Questions; case studies from people applying CLAT in various contexts; and updated references and the bibliography to more recent versions and newer resources. We've also changed some key terms, and included more content devoted to multicultural and urban contexts.

More Nodes in a Network

We've been gathering materials that may be critical for certain kinds or places of work that don't fit into this revision. In response, we offer two new resources, each of which should be useful for those using both *The Manual* and an abridged version, *Community Arts for God's Purposes*.

CLAT Companion. This volume contains exceptionally relevant and helpful materials that don't fit in the main text. These include, for example, complete Artistic Feature Research Guides (shortened versions remain in the main text); stories of CLAT applied to real-life contexts; and additional tools.

CLAT Digital Library. This site will grow and change with continual contributions of background documents; more research and application tools; articles (published and unpublished); more stories of CLAT applied; and products and materials developed by practitioners and scholars. Both resources can be found at www.clatmanual.com. The Companion can also be found at www.missionbooks.org.

CLAT Works!

We have over a decade of observing and analyzing the results of people applying this approach in diverse contexts. Things haven't always gone as communities might have hoped, but CLAT has repeatedly proved fruitful. Many stories and testimonies of groups and individuals' lives containing more signs of the Kingdom of Heaven serve as evidence. Also, a number of arts advocates have crafted their stories into formal representations that identify the roles each of the seven conversations played in their results—we include some of these in this manual and the **Digital Library** (www.clatmanual.com). Others are expanding on their experiences in master's theses, articles, oral presentations, books, and doctoral dissertations.

CLAT has proved to be a flexible, community-based tool. We pray that improvements in the second edition of this manual will help generate even more arts-energized bits of Heaven. And we hope that this manual will serve as a central educational and conceptual resource for what God is doing in his church.

WHO SHOULD USE THIS MANUAL?

We wrote this book in a style and level of complexity most appropriate for people at an undergraduate educational level and above. It is not meant to be a guide for a community to use directly; it's too bulky, aiming to provide resources that can be applied to any context in the world. Rather, it helps you craft spaces in which communities make unique plans to produce futures more like Heaven. Another resource, *Community Arts for God's Purposes*[1] guides the reader in the same approach, but in a condensed and simplified form. This shorter manual eases the process of adaptation for local involvement and is being translated into a growing number of languages.

Learning and applying the CLAT method makes you an arts advocate, which we see falling into four primary categories:

Cross-Cultural Workers and Administrators

We originally envisioned the full version of this manual as a tool for Christians working professionally in cultural contexts very different from their own. This could include missionaries, international aid workers, project leaders, administrators, and others. If you or people you manage want to engage with people of a different language, worldview, geography, diet, and social patterns, you may need to expend much effort and use many skills. We provide rigorous research and other activities that will help in this.

---

1 For hardcopy and electronic versions, see https://missionbooks.org/products/community-arts-for-gods-purposes.

Teachers

Second, this manual has served as a text for teachers, professors, seminary instructors and others preparing people for any kind of ministry. A worship leader in a local church, for example, said "I need to do this. I need to first get to know my congregation and encourage different kinds of artists to create new things for God's purposes." Pastors, musicians, liturgists, youth leaders, missional outreach planners, missionaries, mission executives, and others can open doors for God to increase their fruit with a deeper, practical understanding of arts' relationship to the Kingdom of Heaven.

Students

Third, students planning projects, master's theses, and PhD dissertations have drawn on CLAT for community research and engagement resources. Conversations 1 and 4 contain especially rich guides for researching communities' arts in their sociocultural contexts.

Everyone

Finally, anyone can benefit from this approach. As we taught the method to diverse groups, we found that people in many roles and life contexts applied it in situations that we wouldn't normally label cross-cultural. In fact, we've come to believe that the broadest category of who should use the Creating Local Arts Together approach is people in communities. And that's everyone. Every human represents unique relationships, experiences, ideas, neurological connections, physical qualities, emotions, and other characteristics that can never be known entirely by someone else. And every community they engage with can draw on their artistic communication to improve their futures.

You could apply it to people who are very much like you, your best friend, your extended family, or your spouse. In fact, you could follow the CLAT process to learn something new about your own artistic gifts and life goals. You could create something artistic to improve your own future.

Though many examples tell stories of people crossing large cultural barriers, we've included other types of applications, too. Reflect on your own contexts and imagine how CLAT might benefit people you care about.

Brian Schrag
Weathertree Farm
Hamilton, Ohio
July 2024

FRAMING THE SEVEN CONVERSATIONS

ALWAYS TOWARD HEAVEN

We have chosen to organize our activities in the arts in terms of how they can move us toward the Kingdom of Heaven. What is this Kingdom? Jesus taught his followers to pray for the Kingdom of Heaven to come to Earth (Matt 6:10). He described it as centered on himself and his message (Mark 1:15), growing mysteriously but to great size (Mark 4), marked by values contrary to human social systems (Mark 10; 12; Luke 6), and connected in practice to healing and spiritual warfare (Luke 9–11). The Kingdom of Heaven on Earth mysteriously but concretely reflects the reality of life in Heaven, and God wants us to help it expand.

A basic, confounding characteristic of the Kingdom of Heaven is that it exists only partially on Earth now. At the end of time, Jesus will recreate the cosmos—including our bodies—as the New Creation without the all-infecting rot of sin (2 Pet 3; 1 Cor 15). Each community has aspects that are more like the Kingdom, and those that are less. No human culture fully expresses God's Kingdom, but because God created us in his image, there are glimpses of it everywhere, evidence that Heaven exists.

We live and work in the *now and not-yet* phase of Heaven on Earth. This means that we can know and increase Heaven in partnership with God, but the corruption of sin still undermines our efforts. "The creation will be made new from the old, just as happened to Jesus. Resurrection is a vision for both Jesus and creation."[1] Happily, we can nurture rock-solid hope in Christ in us and others based on the certainty of future unhampered relationships with God.

What would a community look like that was deeply shaped by the values and spiritual power of God's Kingdom? It would contain an expanding body of Christ-followers—the church—who worship God in spirit and in truth. Its members would be growing spiritually, socially, and physically healthier in fruitful harmony with their environments. Older members would be passing on God-reflecting aspects of their cultures to younger members. Everyone would have access to well-translated Scripture in the languages they understand best, so that young and old could remember and apply it to their lives. And the whole community would be marked by justice, honesty, health, joy, and care and love for people in their margins.

Until God makes the Not-Yet completely Now, we experience soul-deep pain, exerting every tendon, every muscle, every conviction to find relief and embrace concrete hope (1 Cor 8:18–30). And some of the truest, most fruitful producers of hope touching our suffering cores are our exquisitely, uniquely crafted forms of communication: artistry.

---

[1] Wright, *Future of the World*. N. T. Wright develops a detailed description of this view in *Surprised by Hope*. See also Wright, *Simply Jesus*.

Practically, locally available artistic forms of communication are powerful resources for anyone working toward all signs of the New Creation.[2]

Such systems are embedded in culture, and so touch many important aspects of a society. They mark messages as important, separate from everyday activities; they touch not only cognitive, but also experiential and emotional ways of knowing; they can help us remember messages; they increase the impact of ideas through multiple media; they often include the whole body; they concentrate information contained in a message; they instill solidarity in their enactors and experiencers; they often provide socially acceptable frameworks for expressing difficult or new ideas; they inspire and move people to action; they can act as strong signs of identity; and they open spaces for people to imagine and dream. Perhaps most importantly, local artistic communication exists and is owned locally; there's no need to translate foreign materials, and local artists are empowered to contribute to the expansion of the Kingdom of Heaven.

Our approach is to help you work alongside communities as they explore what aspects of the Kingdom of Heaven they want to see flourish, and the artistic genres and events that might help in the accomplishment of those goals. We then describe activities that spark artistic creativity in ways that meet a community's goals in lasting ways.

ALL THE ARTS FROM ALL THE WORLD FOR ALL OF GOD'S PURPOSES

Important realities shaping our engagement with the arts include the following:

REALITY: Over eight billion people in the world communicate in more than seven thousand languages in innumerable social and geographic contexts. Within this extraordinarily complex milieu, we each belong to specific communities that convey ideas by everyday language, but also through singing, acting, dancing, painting, telling stories, making films, designing buildings, and other innumerable combinations of these and other artistic forms.

REALITY: All communities have nonexistent or imperfect relationships with God. We all struggle with social upheaval, violence, disease, anger, sexual immorality, anxiety, and fear.

REALITY: God gave every community unique gifts of artistic communication to speak Truth and bring healing and hope and joy in response to these problems. Many of these gifts, however, lie dormant, misused, misunderstood, or dying.

The purpose of this manual is to guide your involvement in working toward a new reality, one in which *all* communities are using *all* their gifts to worship, obey, and enjoy God with *all* of our heart, soul, mind, and strength, and to love our neighbors as ourselves (Mark 12:29–31). In other words, it will help you work with communities to inspire the creation of new artistry that increases signs of Heaven.

---

2 To situate our approach to communication among other conceptual frameworks, see Griffin, Ledbetter, and Sparks, *First Look at Communication Theory*.

All?

The title of this section uses the word *all* three times. What do we mean? *All the arts* doesn't suggest that God wants to include every art form in its current state in his Kingdom. Rather, we want to approach every art graciously, not judging its worth or usefulness for the Kingdom until God judges it. All communities and their arts are marred by sin, but God can redeem all things. The process of integrating arts includes a winnowing, a remaking.[3]

For example, not all of a community's arts are equally appropriate for furthering God's goals at a given time. A particular dance might be so strongly associated with immoral or idolatrous activities that its use might pull new believers in Christ back to their old lives. We believe that God will renew everything for himself—see Matthew 19:28—but that it takes insights of local believers and the Holy Spirit to decide what actions are wise at any given point. Communities should not try to force Kingdom change.

From all the world refers to the thousands and thousands of ways people communicate artistically. Because each of us is a finite being with limited experience, we don't naturally recognize arts new to us, especially when they're part of a culture foreign to us. So one goal of this book is to both widen and sharpen our vision to see the myriad potential resources. We want to have a little bit more of a God's-eye view of the arts.

For all of God's purposes helps us remember that God does not limit his use of the arts to our categories. In Scripture we see examples of artistic communication involved in corporate adoration, teaching, warfare, celebration, ritual, correcting, individual growth, healing, confession, remembering, and many other purposes. We've crafted this manual to nudge each of us to think beyond any particular liturgical role of the arts we're used to.

What Are Arts?

In this manual, we treat the arts as special kinds of communication. Like all communication systems, the arts are connected to particular times, places, and social contexts. They have their own symbols, grammars, and internal structures. This means that just as you may have to learn how to ask directions in a language foreign to you, you must also learn, for example, how to move your arms and neck and eyebrows to tell a story in Thai dance. There is no one artistic language that communicates completely across lines of time, place, and culture. So to understand any art form, you have to interact with its practitioners and study it. Whether cultural insider, outsider, or some combination of both, getting to know local artists and their arts is our first job.

Artistic forms of communication differ from others in several important ways. First, artistic communication places greater emphasis on manipulating form than do everyday interactions. Poetic speech, for example, may rely on patterns of sound and thought like rhyme, assonance, and metaphor that a

---

[3] We discuss our adaptation of a long-established approach to winnowing—Careful Contextualization (originally Critical Contextualization)—in Conversation 4D.

simple exchange of information will not. Circling a drum while repeating a sequence of foot movements relies on form more heavily than simply walking from one place to another. Adopting the facial expressions of a mythical character draws on form to communicate more than allowing a person's face to remain at rest.

Second, arts often reveal their uniqueness as bounded spheres of interaction. Artistic events have beginnings and endings (no matter how fluid), between which people interact in unusually patterned ways. Ethnomusicologist Ruth Stone describes artistic events as "set off and made distinct from the natural world of everyday life by the participants."[4]

In this manual we help you use these and other characteristics to discover and describe the kinds of artistic communication in any community you enter, including your own. We keep our discovery parameters broad so that we don't inadvertently miss an important kind of communication that doesn't fit our existing categories. So our view of an artistic act might refer to a performance of a Spanish *flamenco* piece, rehearsals for a Broadway musical, a painting hanging on a café wall, a father speaking a proverb to his daughter, enactment of a *khon* masked dance/drama in Thailand, an expression of hybrid artistry reflecting one church's multiple liturgical backgrounds, or rhythmic wailing at a gravesite. There are tens of thousands of kinds of artistic communication that people use around the world, an amazing and too often undervalued resource.

> Discuss examples of arts in a community you know that outsiders might not understand.

FROM CREATION TO NEW CREATION

The following episodes in God's cosmic story serve as crucial theological touchstones in this manual: God's Perfect Creation → Fall → Waiting → Jesus's First Coming → Now and Not-Yet of the Kingdom → Jesus's Second Coming. At his return, Jesus will recreate the universe without sin. Our final reality, then, will be life in the New Creation that flourishes into infinity.

Our approach places us in the company of a growing movement of churches, theologians, missionaries, and organizations embracing the Scripture-based New Creation model.[5] A foundational tenet affirms that,

> The eternal state is not a heavenly, timeless, non-material reality but a new heavens and new earth, such as in Isaiah 65, 2 Peter 3:13, and Revelation 21 and 22. The dwelling place of the redeemed in that new creation is not in Heaven but on the new earth.[6]

---

4 Stone, "Communication and Interaction Processes," 37.

5 Two publications explain the model particularly well, including long bibliographies: Vlach, *The New Creation Model*, and James, "Recent New Creation Conceptions." Several of C. S. Lewis's fictional works drew me into new creation narratives early in my life, including *Mere Christianity*, *The Last Battle*, and *The Great Divorce*.

6 Blaising, "A Critique," 122.

As we'll develop more fully in Conversation Two, we see Christ-followers engaging with an all-encompassing reality—salvation, relationships, earth, culture, ethnic and national diversity, politics, technology, our bodies, artistic communication, and so on. The frustrations of the *now and not-yet* period we inhabit will give way to thriving in a universe in which sin has been utterly banished.

This narrative and model influence many concepts and practices in the manual. Their implications particularly affect how we define two important words, *kingdom* and *church*. As we'll see, characteristics of the New Creation spill into each, providing glimpses and whiffs of our ultimate home. Also, following some other authors, I often use *Heaven* as a short cut in referring to the New Creation.[7]

Kingdom of Heaven

The first section title ("Always toward Heaven") paints a picture of how Jesus envisions his Kingdom. Historically, however, terms like *Kingdom of God* and *Kingdom of Heaven* have sometimes been distorted to describe the Holy Roman Empire, the Holocaust, the genocide of indigenous peoples, the transatlantic slave trade, and current forms of Christian nationalism. But in the life and teachings of Jesus, these terms mean something profoundly different. They point us to God's action in the world to save humanity and restore all of creation to its intended forms and purposes. For Jesus, this in-breaking of God's Kingdom *is* the gospel! And that is why he launches his earthly ministry by proclaiming, "I must proclaim the good news of the Kingdom of God" (Luke 4:43).

The largely interchangeable expressions *Kingdom of God* and *Kingdom of Heaven* appear ninety-nine times in the New Testament. Always with the what-*will*-be of the New Creation in view, they announce God's triumph over evil, suffering, distortion, and death. Jesus employs artistic expressions in his ministry in part by teaching thought-provoking parables about God's Kingdom values (Matt 13; Mark 4; and Luke 13). He shares mealtimes with extortionary tax collectors (Luke 19), upholds the importance of visits to prisoners (Matt 25), lauds the generosity and healing art of the good Samaritan (Luke 10) and offers water and words of hope with an ostracized woman at Jacob's well in Sychar (Luke 4).

Some scholars point out that monarchies and kingdoms are not as prevalent today and suggest that we substitute new terms like the *reign* or *rule* of God.[8] One Cuban theologian, Ada María Isasi-Díaz,[9] reacted to the hierarchy of king-subject relationships and coined the term *kin-dom*, reflecting reciprocal, family-like relationships. Randy Woodley, a Native American theologian, wants to emphasize the cosmic nature of God's reconciling work (Col 1:15–20), and

---

7 See, for example, Alcorn, *Heaven*, and Alcorn, *We Shall See God*. Wright, in *Future of the World*, reluctantly affirms this practice about 29 minutes into the video.

8 See, for example, The High Calling's daily reflection, "The Kingdom of God Is Near."

9 Isasi-Diaz, "Kin-dom of God."

prefers the term *community of creation*.[10] What all agree upon, however, is that God is doing a new thing (2 Cor 5:17) and offering the world new life, healing and hope through his beloved Son, Jesus.

Church

Jesus's first action after his inaugural announcement of the gospel was to form a community of disciples who would live according to Kingdom values and presence (Matt 5–7). The New Testament provides nearly a hundred different word pictures of such Kingdom communities—as living stones, a royal priesthood, a temple of the Holy Spirit, God's field, the bride of Christ, a city on a hill, an open letter, savory salt, and the light of the world, to name only a few.

One of these pictures—the one that has become shorthand for talking about all of them—is the Greek word *ekklesia*, translated *church*. This term appears 115 times in the New Testament and represents an identifiable group of Spirit-filled, Christ-followers who worship God and are committed to living out his authority in their personal and corporate lives. Such Kingdom communities are God's preferred Holy Spirit home, where Jesus's ongoing presence is celebrated and the Spirit's power to transform individual and community lives—and ultimately the entire world—is made visible (Matt 5:14–16; John 13:34–35). It is, in fact, *through the church*, insists Paul, that God's wisdom is made known to "the rulers and authorities in heavenly places" (Eph 3:10).

To be ambassadors of God's Kingdom purposes in the world is a high calling (2 Cor 5:18–20). Unfortunately, the church has often failed at being a place of grace, forgiveness, healing, and commitment to God's good news in Jesus Christ. Nevertheless, the church is the primary *model* and *messenger* of God's Kingdom reign, and we have the joy and responsibility of partnering with God to make Christ's bride more beautiful. God showers upon the church Holy Spirit power and gifts—including artistic expressions of every kind—to demonstrate and proclaim to all peoples everywhere God's love and goodness in making all things new" (Rev 21:5 ESV). This is the New Creation that will last into eternity.[11]

FOUNDATIONS

Big Ideas

This manual often breaks from historically influential concepts and methods, mostly by integrating insights from multiple domains into a novel contribution to community thriving. Here are a few of the big ideas that have shaped it.

Systems of artistic creativity are more complex than you think

Arts consist of interlocking components, including knowledge, skills, physical resources, social patterns, and people in various roles. It's rare for someone in *any* community to have the perspective to describe their creative systems.

---

10 Woodley, *Shalom*.

11 Eldredge, *All Things New*; and Laurie, *As It Is in Heaven*.

The process in this manual helps reveal the dynamics and details of such systems.

There is no artistic form that communicates intended messages universally
People often say that "music is a universal language." They believe music communicates the same way in every culture. Examples in this manual support the assertion that music and other arts exist universally. However, every kind of artistic communication takes forms and meanings particular to each community.[12]

Every community can benefit from more creativity that comes from within
These benefits include more penetrating, relevant, memorable, sustainable, and engaging communication for education and motivation. Ethnolinguistic minorities whose arts are stagnant or dying may need local creativity most urgently.

Encouraging specific kinds of artistry can help a community reach the goals they choose
This manual describes a method, composed of seven conversations, called *Creating Local Arts Together* (CLAT; sometimes called *cocreation*). In communities that have applied this method, good things have happened.

An arts advocate's primary job is encouraging *others* to make new artistry and events
Someone who understands and implements the approach in this book can have a positive effect on local creativity. This person—an arts advocate—may be a community insider, outsider, or someone with a unique combination of characteristics from both identities. Regardless, their posture toward a community is one of learning, dialoguing, facilitating, encouraging, and engaging in creative processes.

It is vital to learn about insider categories of artistic communication: local arts
The foundation for everything in this manual is understanding the arts that a community identifies with and uses. One of the first research activities we describe is for the community to make a list of local artistic genres and events ("Take a First Glance at a Community's Arts," Conversation 1). In Conversation 4 and the *CLAT Companion* (see www.clatmanual.com), we guide you in finding out if and how some features of Euro-American artistic domains of music, drama, dance, oral verbal arts, and visual arts may contribute to local genres (see **artistic domain** in the Glossary). But our first steps, our starting points are each communities' categories of artistry, each distinct, unique.

We try to capture the essence of such artistry in this definition: **local arts** are artistic forms of communication that a community identifies with and can create, perform, teach, and understand from within, including their forms, meanings, languages, and social contexts.

---

12 Negrão, "Not a Universal Language."

The church urgently needs to embrace its place in God's whole story
Here are crucial events in the narrative of God and his interactions with his creation: Father|Son|Spirit created the universe, including humans reflecting his image; we broke our relationship with God; Jesus became a human, embodied the Kingdom of Heaven, died and rose and ascended to Heaven, restoring our relationship to God; and God will make everything right in the new heavens and the new earth. Jesus will return the way he left (Acts 1:11) to re-make *this* universe, cosmos, earth, our human bodies, the natural world, soil, etc., to return it and us to sinless, Eden-like conditions (see, for example, Isa 35 and 36; Rev 21; Matt 5:5–8; Matt 19:28–30).

Until that moment when Jesus makes everything new, we Christ-followers gather as the church to continue his work. We strive to exist as loving, united bodies, a beautiful bride, the embodiment of Jesus on Earth and ultimately worshipping around the throne in profound diversity (Rev 5). With this certain future, in humility, it is important, yet not enough, for Christian faith communities to develop the arts that their particular history has produced. Rather, we must also be aware of God's artistry and its purposes in the rest of his creation and in Heaven.[13]

How Do Arts and Culture Interact?
The arts may both reflect and influence the cultures in which they exist. Artistic communication reflects the shape of other aspects of culture because it's interwoven with the rest of life. Members of Kaluli society in Papua New Guinea, for example, have a metaphor, "lift-up-over-sounding," that shows up in several aspects of their lives. This idea underlies music-making in which two singers will alternate in taking the lead role, producing interweaving layers of sound. A similar phenomenon occurs in Kaluli conversation when people "interrupt" each other—they are cocreating, lifting-up-over together. So artistic form here reflects a more widespread Kaluli communication pattern.

Artistic communication, however, can also effect change in cultures because of its unique abilities to motivate people to action, inspire feelings of solidarity, and provide socially acceptable space to disagree. As an example, women in the African Apostolic Church in southern Africa can symbolically take hold of time in a worship service to communicate their grievances against men. While they are not allowed to preach to a congregation, women may interrupt a sermon with a song, containing lyrics such as these: "Men, stop beating your wives. Only then will you go to Heaven." Women-led songs provide symbolic protection for their critical content.[14] In this case, artistic communication has the power to change other parts of culture. Arts may also strengthen existing power structures. National anthems are clear examples of this.

---

13 "A Brief History of Eternity" in Conversation 4 expands on this theology. See also Middleton, *New Heaven*, and Lewis, *Business of Heaven*.

14 Bennetta, "Ecstatic Singing."

What Is Creativity?

Since the purpose of this manual is to help you spark artistic creativity that feeds into God's expansion of his Kingdom, it's important to understand how creativity works. We describe it this way: **artistic creativity** occurs when one or more people draw on their personal competencies and their community(ies)' social and symbolic systems to produce an enactment—event or work—of heightened communication that has not previously existed in its exact form. The newness of this enactment varies according to its constituent parts and their degrees of novelty. Each culture values newness in unique ways.

Divine and human creativity

God created the universe *ex nihilo*, from nothing. One part of God's image we reflect is his creativity, but we can only make things from what God has already established. But God also creates new things out of old—like Adam and Eve from the dust. He makes and crafts and creates—always with access to the infinite imagination that allowed him to create the cosmos from nothing.[15] Humans always have to use what already exists, in its *now and not-yet* state. So everything we make has imperfections, will be experienced and used both purely and sinfully, in wholeness and brokenness. God's ventures know no such limits.

Like breathing

Beginning in the womb, human beings are neurologically and sensorially predisposed and equipped to develop complex social concepts, engage in symbolic communication, and be drawn to novelty.[16] These primal impulses constitute foundations for artistic expression that exist throughout our lives and into the New Creation.[17] "Creativity should be an everyday experience. Creativity should be as common as breathing. We breathe, therefore we create."[18] In fact, humans can't *not* create.

Never alone

We can all point to exceptionally gifted artists who have inspired and motivated us. Sometimes these individuals see the world differently and feel compelled to play with and change traditions fundamentally. These are the paradigm shifters. We want to encourage them to create for God and his Kingdom, which should only increase their genius because it connects them explicitly to the Ultimate Creator. Our focus in this manual, however, is creativity on a more communal level, and usually activities that build somehow on existing traditions.

So to understand how people create in a culture, you have to find out who the creators are and what skills, knowledge, and techniques they need to be able to produce something new. In addition, for created works to enter a society's life, we need to identify and include the people who strongly influence

---

15 For a discussion comparing and contrasting the meanings of create and craft, see Manaher, "Create vs Craft."
16 Schrag and Van Buren, *Make Arts*, 12–16; Pinker, *The Language Instinct*; Harris, Negrão, and Ntankeh, "Arts as Validation of Truth."
17 Ball, *The Music Instinct*; Dutton, *The Art Instinct*.
18 McManus, *The Artisan Soul*. See also Fujimura, *Art and Faith*.

a community's acceptance of an innovation (gatekeepers): who influences whether a group values, learns, and passes on a new creation? We also must see if there are taboos or customs the new works might run up against.

Underlying our approach to creativity is an important understanding of tradition. Tradition is not a fixed body of ideas and practices. Rather, people in one generation are constantly passing traditions to the next. Every act of transmission introduces small or large changes. The French philosopher Paul Ricoeur describes tradition as "the living transmission of an innovation always capable of being reactivated by a return to the most creative moments of poetic activity … [A] tradition is constituted by the interplay of innovation and sedimentation."[19] This manual helps you come alongside local creators in their communities, sparking moments of artistic activity that have the capacity to become enduring traditions. Traditions endure when people are continually motivated to transmit them, with the social structures and resources to support their moments of creativity. Tradition is innovation that succeeds.

CLAT and AI

Rapidly developing technologies are increasingly affecting, infiltrating our lives. These include artificial intelligence, extended reality (virtual, augmented, and mixed), 3D printing, human-computer interfaces, gene editing, and many more.[20] I'll address just one of these here: AI.

AI's capacities to produce images, musical compositions, videos, and other works exhibiting novel interpretations of existing or new traditions are deepening and expanding. Will a world suffused with AI generated arts render human creativity superfluous? Historically, technological developments like the printing press, audio recording, photography, and film provoked fears of losing human expressive capacities or being engulfed in an abstracted, mechanistic world. In fact, however, these phenomena have usually sparked new kinds of creativity *without* supplanting the old.[21] Three characteristics of the Creating Local Arts Together approach to creativity add to this likely historical pattern, quelling any angst we may feel.

First, our primary goal is clear: we work toward connecting community artistry with more signs of Heaven, glimpses of the New Creation. This means that our creativity is holistic, touching all conceivable material, social, intellectual, and spiritual elements of our lives, immersed in God's immense universe. It is based on stable|malleable generators of community-embedded newness, not extreme, untethered, sterile novelty. AI and other technological developments already play roles in some contexts we work in, opening new ways the church can bring Heaven to Earth. But our foundation is engaging with real, tangible, human beings who walk, eat, sleep, pray, and commune.

Second, when Jesus recreates his followers and the universe, God will be in

---

19 Ricoeur, *Time and Narrative*, 68.

20 For interesting non-Christian perspectives, see these two resources: Roser, "The Future Is Vast," and Anderson, Rainie, and Vogels, "New Normal."

21 Fiebrink, "Will AI Kill the Future?" See also Coggins, "Response to 'Historical Examples.'"

charge and there will be no undermining sin. Creating for an infinite God will not be merely moving toward a huge, finite number of unique combinations or patterns. Rather, infinity is qualitatively different, an unattainable characteristic of God alone. It's like comparing building a spaceship that takes me 2.5 million light years to reach the Andromeda galaxy to the eight feet altitude my granddaughter reaches when I toss her in the air (and safely catch her). Each represents the same degree of achievement in the context of God's infinitude. We create for a future that knows no limits, no bounds, no matter the means. AI is just a speck.

Finally, we often work with minoritized communities, which popular trends usually ignore.

Making Heaven: a Poem

In the beginning, God created
heaven and earth
day and night
water and soil
plants and animals
man and woman

God created *ex nihilo* (out of nothing)
What wasn't, now was
And it was good

God made us in his image
One way we reflect this image is in our drive and ability to create

We make
cities and dams
houses and shops
clothes and furniture
stories and songs and dances and masks

We create *ex creatio* (out of what God made)

every time we write a letter or message
when we greet or comfort someone
when we cook a meal or play a game or dance
when we paint a portrait or sketch a cartoon
every time we do something in a way that never quite existed before, for a purpose or context that doesn't duplicate a previous purpose or context exactly

We are acting like God. But love compels us to take one more step, to nurture a small group
make disciples of sons and daughters, brothers and sisters
commission someone to write a song or a poem or craft a chair
help someone translate the Bible into their language
tutor a refugee
raise a child

Every time we inspire or prepare *someone else* to create, we are performing one of the highest, most satisfying and enduring acts of love

We are not God, but creativity flows through us
And in that, we are like him

List examples of ways in which you have been creative.

List examples of ways in which you have helped someone create.

Discuss examples of other surprising things God has created.

JESUS'S INCARNATION AS OUR MODEL

This is how Paul described Jesus's ministry on Earth, in poetic form:[22]

> In humility value others above yourselves, not looking to your own interests but each of you to the interests of the others.
>
> In your relationships with one another, have the same mindset as Christ Jesus:
>
> Who, being in very nature God,
>> did not consider equality with God something to be used to his own advantage;
>
> rather, he made himself nothing
>> by taking the very nature of a servant,
>> being made in human likeness.
>
> And being found in appearance as a man,
>> he humbled himself
>> by becoming obedient to death—
>>> even death on a cross! (Phil 2:3b–8)

We learn from this passage that at least three parts of Jesus's incarnation show how we should do mission:

---

[22] Martin, *A Hymn of Christ.*

Be with
Jesus left his "home culture" with God the Father and Spirit and joined humanity on Earth. Our first task in mission is to engage with people in community and make relationships.

Learn from
Jesus learned from human beings in his Jewish community for almost thirty years before he began his full ministry. This included learning to use tools to craft objects from wood and stone in his father's workshop. Our second interaction as arts facilitators, then, is to ask people about their community's arts and goals. We show them love by learning from them. This process may happen over a long time.

Work toward
Only after going to humans and learning from them for three decades did Jesus announce and fulfill his purpose publicly (Matt 4:23). He worked side-by-side with his disciples toward the goals of his Kingdom. Our third missional activity, after going to people and learning from them, is to work toward goals with them. As arts facilitators, we do this by exploring with our friends and colleagues in the community how we might work together to use their arts to meet their goals.

When your work becomes complex, remind yourself of these three basic activities.

THREE APPROACHES TO ARTS IN MISSION

We have found it helpful to divide the church's approaches to spreading its practices into three categories below. Though the three approaches are distinct, they also interact in complex ways, more like three points on a multifaceted continuum. They parallel common attitudes to mission in general.

Bring It–Teach It
People working cross-culturally in the Bring It–Teach It framework bring their own arts to teach to people in another community. In effect, they teach foreign art forms to local communities. Throughout church history, cross-cultural workers frequently adopted this approach, which continues to happen. In rural Democratic Republic of Congo, I could sing the song "Ekangeneli Na Yesu" a week after I arrived. Previous missionaries produced the song by putting lyrics in the Lingala language to the tune of a popular Scottish song I know, "Auld Lang Syne."

On the plus side, this approach can result in common artistic languages that unify people around the world. It also contributes to satisfying and pleasurable cultural blends and fusions, and can inspire a sense of mystery surrounding the worship of God. Bring It–Teach It, however, also poses crucial risks. It often results in miscommunication of messages and emotions, communities that see God as foreign to them, local artists who feel excluded or demoralized, and a sense among local communities that Christianity is irrelevant. Kingdom diversity, witness, and spiritual growth are weakened.

Build New Bridges

Somewhere in the middle of the continuum, you have an approach we call Build New Bridges in which people from one community find ways to connect artistically with members of another community.[23] For example, expressive arts therapists have used local materials or songs to guide suffering children through healing processes. Build New Bridges could also include collaborations between artists of different cultures for common purposes, such as interfaith understanding.[24] Resulting works and events have characteristics of more than one tradition.

The Build New Bridges model often requires a relatively short time before making initial progress, and it can work in communities who are going through trauma and so don't have energy or resources to do their own arts completely. It may also promote healthy interdependent relationships where everyone equally shares their arts. Problems can arise, though, when there is a significant power differential between the missionary and the artists in the community. The higher global, social capital of an outsider can dampen the resolve and courage of local artists. This approach may also produce unsustainable results; new collaborative artistic production that is not deeply rooted in local traditions and social systems will likely fade away.

Find It–Encourage It

In Find It–Encourage It, the arts advocate works with communities to know local artists and their arts in ways that spur these artists to create in the forms they know best. You can think of these activities as catalysts for someone else's creativity, helping give birth to new creations that flow organically from the community. The approach usually requires longer-term relationships with people and an irrepressible commitment to learn.

None of these three categories is untainted by earthly imperfection. We wrote *Creating Local Arts Together*, however, primarily to encourage people to adopt the third approach, and provide a guide for its application. We see Jesus as our primary model, and as King of the Kingdom, he left his heavenly culture to become human. He learned to walk, talk, sing, relieve, and dress himself in an earthly minority society for nearly thirty years before entering his full ministry (Phil 2). Like Jesus, the body of Christ should be with local people, learn from them, and then give to them. Unfortunately, the church has often neglected this calling in its mission strategies. The consequences of this are often tragic.

---

23 OM's Inspiro Arts team identifies three types of bridges: (1) *Show and Tell*, in which artistic enactments serve as foci for missional conversations; (2) *Come and Create*, when an outsider responds creatively to others' arts; and (3) *Come and Collaborate*, when artists from more than one culture create new works with aspects from each.

24 King and Dyrness, *Arts as Witness*.

> Discuss examples you've seen of each of these three types of spreading the Kingdom of Heaven: Bring It–Teach It, Build New Bridges, and Find It–Encourage It.

ETHNODOXOLOGY

The *CLAT Manual* and the *Ethnodoxology Handbook* reflect and have played important roles in the development of the movement, field, conceptual development, and practice of ethnodoxology. "Ethnodoxology," a chapter in the *Oxford Handbook on Music and Christian Theology*[25] traces historical and theological roots, birth, and growth of the movement, mostly through the lens of the Global Ethnodoxology Network (GEN).[26] Since the first edition of the *CLAT Manual* in 2013, GEN and the individuals and organizations it connects have influenced and learned from a growing number of organizations, taught the CLAT approach to hundreds and hundreds of individuals in many institutions, and sparked lively and diverse discussions. This bourgeoning production includes insightful articles in the GEN journal, *Ethnodoxology: A Global Forum on Arts and Christian Faith*.[27] Ethnodoxology's growth has significantly changed the landscape of missional approaches to the arts in Christian ministry. In particular, it increases the geographic, artistic, theological, and personal resources available as you explore and apply the CLAT approach.

ULTIMATE MOTIVATIONS: NEW CREATION AND ITS DISTORTIONS

We have invoked signs of the Kingdom of Heaven as a central motivation for using this manual: we want God's people everywhere to act in artistic ways that result in more evidence of Heaven on Earth. But we have so far barely mentioned the first sign of the Kingdom of Heaven in communities: each human being's existence. God created people in his image, so every child, woman, and man is a fact that points to God's home, Heaven. How should this fundamental sign influence our work?

The answer to this question depends in part on another belief flowing through this manual, that reality exists, both present and future, in two forms: New Creation—the Kingdom of Heaven—and its distortion by Satan for evil purposes. On Earth these realities mingle in excruciatingly complex confusion. Adolph Hitler magnificently developed his oratorical gifts to move people in invigorating, pleasurable ways; his creative skills dimly reflected those of a creative God. But Hitler used his gifts in ways that resulted in violence, horror, hopelessness, despair, and agony; these effects dimly reflected those desired by

---

25 Schrag and Swijghuisen Reigersberg, "Ethnodoxology."

26 See the GEN site at http://worldofworship.org. See also Harris, "Future of Ethnodoxology" and Krabill, "Why Arts and Mission."

27 The *Ethnodoxology* journal is freely accessible at https://artsandchristianfaith.org.

a cruel Satan. We believe that the realities of good and evil are infinitely more extreme and invasive than we can imagine, both on Earth and after.[28]

These truths leave us with a few lessons. First, we must approach every person and his or her gifts as infinitely valuable. I have traveled a lot and sometimes found that new stimuli from clothes, hairstyles, skin tones, sounds, or smells elicit negative or stereotyping responses in my mind. When this happens, I sometimes repeat to myself, "Image of God! Image of God!" Each person carries God's mark, so our first attitudes toward them should always be generous, humble, and expecting goodness and beauty. Second, we should study the realities of good and evil biblically, meditatively, and imaginatively. The more we know about them viscerally, intellectually, and emotionally, the more discerning we can be. Third, we can't allow ourselves to be lured into thinking that the agonies and ecstasies we encounter on Earth are all there is. If we do, we might settle for alleviating hunger without ever caring whether someone connects that satisfaction with the creator of food.

Finally, we should encourage the spread of all types of signs of Heaven, for they are all good in themselves. But we can never forget that people need to know the source of all good, God the Creator: Father|Jesus|Spirit. We can ask God to nurture our understandings of both New Creation and Satan's evil manifestations, so that both can motivate us powerfully.

> Spend some time praying about the topics above. If possible, pray using artistic languages—painting, drawing, dancing, acting, singing, storytelling, or some other form you know.
>
> Listen to God, then respond to him. Communicate with him about the things that excite you most in these discussions, then about the things that frighten or worry you most.
>
> Recall times or events in your life that were important in bringing you to this point in your life, especially as it concerns your involvement with arts in the Kingdom of Heaven.

PREPARING FOR CONVERSATIONS

In this section, we present the Creating Local Arts Together approach in idealized and real-life forms, provide initial guidance on discovering who you and your conversational partners are, give examples of contexts and modifications people have made in applying the method, and recommend ways to start small *before* jumping into the whole process. We want to set the stage for two crucial principles undergirding CLAT: its application differs in each context, and we want to see community agency and ownership of the process and its results everywhere possible.

---

28 We want to help spread the Kingdom of Heaven in contexts still marred at a primordial level by the rot of sin, focusing on what the New Creation will be like. We've chosen to recognize hell's effects but don't explore it theologically. If you are interested, a few treatments include Burk et al., *Four Views on Hell*; Walls, *Heaven, Hell, and Purgatory*; Wright, *Surprised by Hope*, 165–207; and Gray, "Destroyed Forever."

We call each of the seven elements in the CLAT method a *Conversation*. For our purposes, each Conversation identifies a subset of activities that together result in communities experiencing more Heaven. The word emphasizes the relationships and dialogue that we want to characterize every element of the whole process: people listening to each other within communities, organizations … everyone involved.

Creating Local Arts Together: Idealized

Figure 1.1 represents the method that this manual will lead you and a community through: a continuous process of researching and creating together, resulting in more signs of God's Kingdom. We call this process Creating Local Arts Together (sometimes shortened to the acronym CLAT) or *cocreation*. Cocreation reminds us of two crucial truths about Heaven-extending creativity. First, God is directly or indirectly engaged in every act of making something. We can create because we reflect the image of God the Creator (Gen 1:27) and Jesus interacts with and holds together every subatomic particle in the universe (Col 1:15–17; Acts 17:24–28).[29] We can always communicate with God, and he'll know best what to do: "Approach God's throne of grace with confidence, so that we may receive mercy and find grace to help us in our time of need" (Heb 4:14–16). Second, as we'll see, making artistic things that have the effects God intends in communities requires people filling many roles. We want to see as many of those pieces situated in local communities as possible, especially the decisions guiding the process.

We represent the seven CLAT conversations most succinctly in Figure 1.1. Communities and their artistic communication are the focus of this process. This ensures that the community's efforts are grounded in a local reality, based on knowing artists and their arts in context. *Fundamentally, this manual is about helping make space for other people to make new artistic things*:

- **Meet** a Community and Its Arts
- **Specify** Kingdom Goals
- **Connect** Genres to Goals
- **Analyze** Genres and Events
- **Spark** Creativity
- **Improve** Results
- **Celebrate** and **Integrate** for Continuity

---

29 See also Fujimura, *Art and Faith*, 35–36.

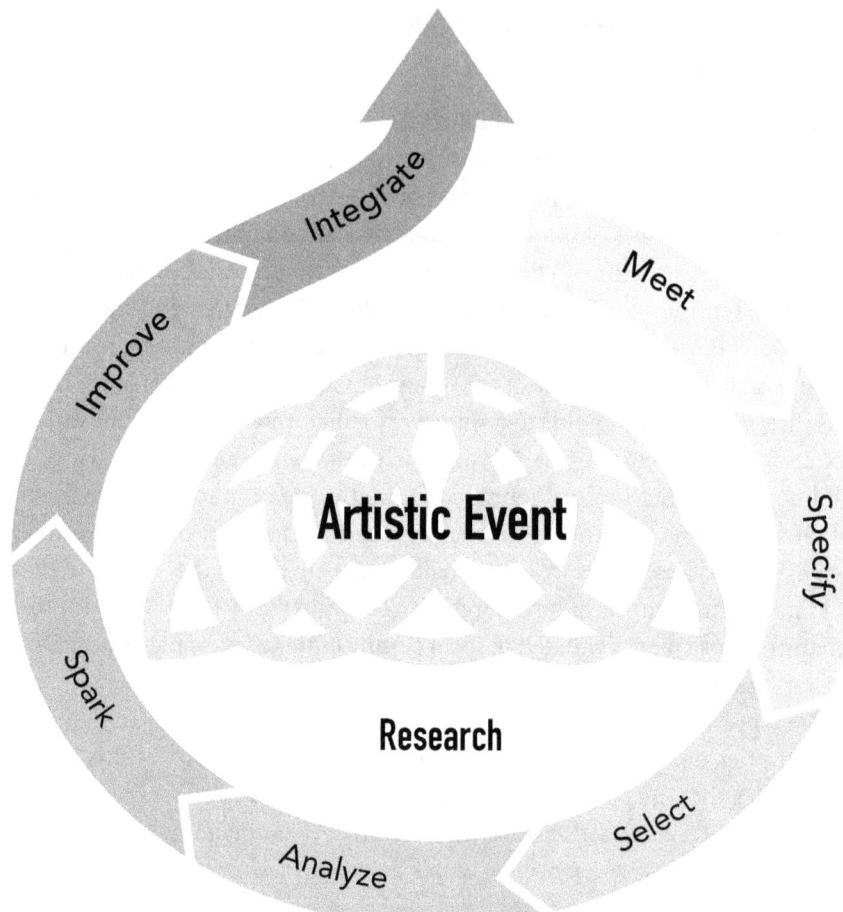

Figure 1.1 Creating Local Arts Together model

We first present CLAT in a linear, idealized, numbered order for a few reasons: This is a logical progression, it aids in teaching the approach, and is scalable. As we'll see, though, real life never looks quite like this.

We now want to whet your appetite for the CLAT process by briefly introducing each conversation with a short illustrative story. In the early 1990s, my family and I lived in northwestern Democratic Republic of Congo (then, Zaire) to help a community translate the Bible into their language, Mono. After describing each component of the cocreation process, I will tell how I saw that component take place (or not) in the Mono community.

Conversation 1: Meet a Community and Its Arts

The **meet** component entails getting to know basic information about a community, first making relationships with people, and listing the kinds of arts that run through the community. We draw on research methods from fields like anthropology, ethnography of communication, and performance studies to help you get to know the community. But most of those fancy research methods ultimately boil down to building relationships with other human beings.

Meeting a Mono community and its arts. When we first moved to the village of Bili in Congo, I noticed that church members sang songs in a trade language, not in Mono. Some of these songs were translations of European and American hymns, and some were composed in a national pop style. Outside of the church, people played and sang very different kinds of music, in the Mono language. Before we could encourage creativity, we needed to know what to encourage. So I asked the leaders of a local church if we could meet under the *paillote* (straw-roofed gazebo) near our house to talk about their art forms and the Bible. We made a list of about a dozen social contexts when Mono people traditionally make music and dance. These contexts include social dances, rites of passage, personal expression, and giving counsel on the *kundi* (a local harp)—a genre called *gbaguru*.

Conversation 2: Specify Kingdom Goals

Which goals for a more Heaven-like life does the community you're working with want to work toward currently? In this manual, we've placed these signs of Heaven into several broad categories: Identity and Sustainability, Healing, Justice, Scripture, Church Life, and Personal Spiritual Life. But this manual is just a beginning—there are thousands, even tens of thousands, of signs of Heaven. So act in freedom: specify new signs of Heaven and new activities that feed into the signs, and tell and write stories of how artistic communication has spread and deepened the Kingdom of Heaven.

Specifying with a Mono community. Still under the *paillote*, the pastor and elders discussed the many purposes of music evident in the Bible, and the fact that God created every person in his image. They said that they didn't use Mono instruments in their church because the first evangelists fifty years earlier had counseled them to burn all physical objects associated with their traditional life. Based on Scripture, the leaders decided that God did want them to reclaim their music for his purposes, including corporate worship. They wanted to relate to God in new, deeper ways. Or at least they were curious about the possibilities.

Conversation 3: Connect Genres to Goals

Once the community has chosen a goal, you can together explore which effects, art forms, content, and events would likely feed into that goal.

Connecting with a Mono community. The leaders wanted Christians to understand Scripture better and value their traditions, so they thought the familiarity of a church meeting would make it the best place for them to first experience something new. They also decided that the best genre to start with was *gbaguru* songs, since much of the Bible is about communicating wisdom. The *gbaguru* genre offers counsel, so the leaders believed they could incorporate *gbaguru* well into worship.

Conversation 4: Analyze Genres and Events

Conversation 4 is about learning—researching and analyzing artistry in its cultural context. Creating something in an existing artistic genre for new purposes requires a great deal of knowledge, skill, and wisdom. Your impressions of an art form are usually wrong and always incomplete—even if you are an insider in some ways. You'll notice that a large part of this manual (and the *CLAT Companion* at www.clatmanual.com) is dedicated to Conversation 4, because it's so easy to assume we understand something more completely than we do. We help you get to the details of art forms and their meanings so you and the community can identify the elements that will penetrate a community for the Kingdom.

Analyzing an enactment with a Mono community. Spurred by my own interests, I had already started to learn about the *kundi*, used to perform *gbaguru* songs. I asked who the best *kundi* player was, and everyone pointed me to Punayima Kanyama. In this case, I analyzed Punayima performing in the *gbaguru* genre in several events: I video recorded him, and transcribed melodies, lyrics, and fingerings. Punayima also taught me to play a couple of songs, which deepened my insights into the forms and themes of the genre. Among many other insights, I learned that *gbaguru* lyrics usually contain Mono proverbs, enactments are usually by male individuals, vocal melodies usually follow the tonal patterns of the words in the lyrics, and composers usually require isolation to make new songs.

Conversation 5: Spark Creativity

One sparks creativity by performing an act that results in a new bit of artistry coming into existence. This can be as simple as suggesting that someone carve a new mask or compose a new song for a celebration, or it may require more complex and time-consuming activities, like workshops, commissioning, apprenticeship, festivals, or developing a new version of an existing ritual or ceremony. In whatever activity is chosen, make sure to include all the people, community gatekeepers, who have an interest in or control over how new works will be integrated into the community.

Sparking with a Mono community. I asked who could compose new Scripture-based *gbaguru* songs for corporate worship. Because the first evangelists told new Mono Christians to burn their instruments, nobody in the church knew how to play the *kundi*. So after some discussion, they decided that they would choose some people from the church to learn from a *kundi* master as apprentices. We met weekly, and Punayima taught us how to construct a *kundi*, tune it, and play some simple songs.

Conversation 6: Improve Results
Checking and evaluation are essential to the cocreative process because we want communities to integrate creativity into their lives that truly results in them achieving their spiritual, social, and physical goals. Evaluation according to agreed-upon criteria helps them make their imperfect artistic communication more effective.

Improving with a Mono community. Unfortunately, we didn't evaluate the early songs that Punayima and others created. They could have been even better. However, we included processes to improve Scripture-based songs that Mono people have composed since then. Bible translators checked for scriptural accuracy and clarity, and Mono artistic experts checked that the enactments were excellent examples of the genres they represented.

Conversation 7: Celebrate and Integrate for Continuity
Our desire is that communities will increasingly integrate Kingdom creativity into their daily, weekly, monthly, and yearly lives. To do this, they need to teach newly created artworks to others and plan for people to keep creating. This means that, at the simplest level, sparking activities like workshops or commissioning should include times to teach new works to other people there. They should also include time to plan for teaching the new works and skills to wider audiences in the future. It may be good to first teach or show them to a small group and get feedback from reflective questions before presenting the works to a larger group.

Celebrating and Integrating with a Mono Community. Somewhere during our apprenticeship, the others decided to form a *kundi* group, called *Chorale Ayo* (the Love Choir). Punayima composed a song about God creating man and woman from the earth. When we played and sang the song in a church service, the normally boisterous congregation was still and silent. I feared that we had somehow made a mistake, making people think of old gods. So after the service I asked a friend why everyone was so quiet. His reply: "What could we do? The song cut our hearts."

The *Chorale Ayo* continued to sing in congregational meetings, and some of the apprentices began to compose their own songs. After a long hiatus because of war and personal calamities, similar *kundi* groups started springing up in other villages. One part of the Mono community—the Protestant church—was beginning to celebrate good parts of their traditions more. But I was looking for ways to include more people. So when we were planning a big *fête* marking the completion of a new house we had built in the village, I had an idea. I commissioned three songs to be performed at the event—two in traditional Mono genres, and one in a church choral style. That night hundreds of people from all walks of life experienced Jesus's parable of the wise and foolish builders (Matt 7:24–27) in forms they had known since childhood.

Creating Local Arts Together: Real Life

We've organized the Creating Local Arts Together process as numbered conversations because each can flow logically into the next. However, though you and a community might plan activities in this order, they often won't happen that way. This is part of what we call *Real Life CLAT*, or sometimes *Messy CLAT*. Figure 1.2 and the following Glimpse represent Laura Roberts's engagement with one community that contrasts with the Mono example. The figure does not completely capture the order of events, but it highlights some of the most important conversations and the repetition of several others. This story exemplifies the complexity of every CLAT-informed engagement and the significance of each of the seven conversations. It also shows the value of the arts advocate's contributions, despite her being a single node in much larger social, spiritual, and local networks.

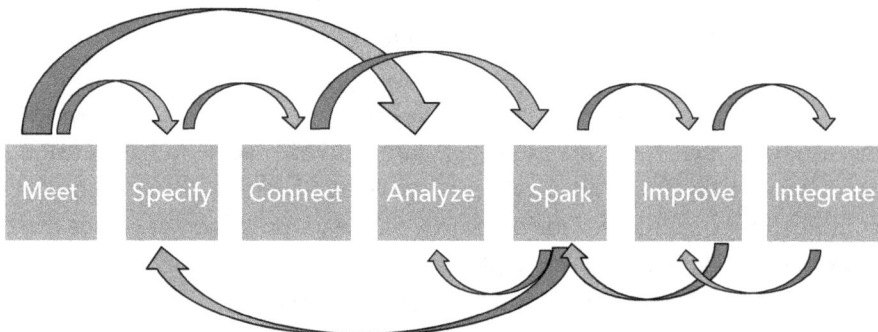

Figure 1.2 Real Life CLAT: An example from India

In India, some communities of people who come from a Hindu background and follow Jesus are finding ways to integrate their cultural forms into their new faith. They began calling themselves *Yeshu bhakta* (devotees of Jesus) and gathering in *satsangs* (contextualized house churches) to worship. They sing *Yeshu bhajans* (devotional call-and-response hymns). Hindu friends and family feel welcomed in this worship gathering with familiar devotional forms that introduce them to Jesus.

As the number of *satsangs* grew, a desire for more *Yeshu bhajans* collected in songbooks emerged. As an arts advocate, I began to meet this community and learn the *bhajan* genre. I quickly recognized their Kingdom Goal—worship and witness through church gatherings—and saw it confirmed through my conversations, observation, and participation in contextual worship. I began learning about *Yeshu bhajans* while living alongside Indian friends and taking lessons from recognized professionals in Hindustani classical and devotional music. New *Yeshu bhajans* were written by both solo songwriters and in songwriting workshops. During workshops, organizers invited experienced bhajan songwriters, musicians, and poets to help guide them through understanding the important details of the form and composition of new *bhajans*. New songs were recorded and collected into a song book for people to use in their worship gatherings, which led to the production of more recordings and other Yeshu bhajan songbooks and mobile apps.

I walked alongside songwriters and community members to encourage this process of gathering *bhajans* and producing a songbook. Many discussions about goals and the chosen genre happened before I even arrived. Some of the conversations happened sequentially, and others happened simultaneously with multiple conversations taking place at a gathering or event.

Viewed as a CLAT story, I began by meeting the Yeshu bhakta community and learning their arts (Conversations 1, 4). I then heard their goals for worship and witness in church life (Conversation 2), which almost immediately connected to the bhajan genre and songbook (Conversation 3). This led to lots of sparking creativity, evidenced by new *bhajans* by individual composers and in group songwriting workshops (Conversation 5). During workshops and the process of recording *bhajans*, Yeshu bhaktas analyzed the bhajan form and specified goals for new *bhajans* (Conversations 2, 4). They also worked together to improve those *bhajans* and create the songbook (Conversations 5, 6). The songbook opened doors for the *bhajans* to be integrated among many Yeshu bhakta *satsangs* around the country (Conversation 7). This in turn led to newer *bhajans* and revised songbooks in the following years (Conversations 5, 6).

—Laura Roberts

You can approach each of these elements as an emergent conversation, a step toward a goal, a tool in a tool bag, a floating resource, or a plant in a vegetable garden that you harvest depending on what's needed for a recipe. We keep Real Life CLAT in mind throughout this manual for several reasons. For one, each conversation might reveal a need to do more of one of the others, because each is related to all. To *Improve* a newly crafted story, for example, a community may need to go back and do more research on the poetic features of good local stories, using guides in the *Analyze* conversation. Ideally, you and the community are trying ideas, learning from what happens, doing more research, trying again, and continuing the process: act and reflect—reflect and act. This pattern results in healthy, growing creativity. Also, God may already have given someone a vision of a Kingdom Goal or prepared a key gatekeeper or artist. Think of the conversations as a reliable, solid framework you can refer to, but not one etched in stone.

Another caveat to our ordered presentation is that some conversations include elements of others. Most importantly, we'll describe some activities in Conversation 5 that spark the creation of new works that are bundles of several conversations. A workshop to produce woven cloth with scriptural marriage advice, for example, may include *Analyzing, Sparking, Improving,* and *Integrating*. As another example, the activity "Help Organize a Festival Celebrating Community Art Forms" includes a larger group in examining and choosing which of their art forms to celebrate—regardless of what genre(s) they choose in Conversation 3. *Our emphasis is not on rigidly defining and requiring separate conversations, but proposing that a community consider each component somewhere in the big picture of their lives.* Please see the Digital Library (www.clatmanual.com) for many more examples, guides and resources to help navigate these complex processes.

A CLAT Story: Songwriting in a Multicultural Community

The following story illustrates the CLAT process applied in a multicultural context. It demonstrates how the approach can be flexibly applied where diverse cultures meet, demanding border-crossing for musicians to cocreate and collaborate artistically.

Conversation 1: Meet a Community and Its Arts

Joy Kim met several diaspora musicians in Clarkston, Georgia, "the most diverse square mile in America,"[30] through Proskuneo School of the Arts. When Joy first visited this multicultural community, she listened to their life stories and their musical journeys. Joy invited them to a songwriting workshop to compose Christian worship songs for a multicultural congregation, where she learned more about their musical backgrounds, unique vocal qualities, and instruments.

Conversation 2: Specify Kingdom Goals

During Joy's initial visit, she met with gatekeepers and community leaders to discover the needs of this diaspora community. She heard their desire to see different ethnic groups in Clarkston not only coexist, but also develop meaningful relationships with each other. The workshop was an initial attempt to bring people from various cultures together to write songs for the whole community, experiencing unity in diversity through creating together.

Conversation 3: Connect Genres to Goals

Joy and the participants decided to create a new fusion genre from all the cultures represented. Each one brought their own sounds, forms, languages, genres and instruments into collective songwriting. The hybridity of this experimental artistic production served as a defining and connecting factor, reflecting each individual and community identity.

---

30 CBS News, "Most Diverse Square Mile."

Conversation 4: Analyze Genres and Events
During the three-day workshop, participants wrote songs in several groups. They contemplated Scripture verses, then discussed the meanings in different languages and cultures. These discussions sparked Scripture-infused lyrics and musical sounds, which set the tone for the songwriting process. Each participant shared musical genres and lyrics in their language, resulting in multilingual and multicultural songs reflecting the diversity of the group. They fostered an environment where each person in the group trusted the others' analysis of their own musical sounds and genres as they chose appropriate forms to communicate the content of the songs.

Conversation 5: Spark Creativity
The highlight of the workshop was sharing each new song with all the participants at the end. The excitement and awe of the cocreation process led to great joy, connection, solidarity, and celebration. The participants affirmed each other in their identity, as each language and artistic expression was honored and celebrated. The cocreation process demonstrated unity in diversity, accomplishing the original Kingdom Goal.

Conversation 6: Improve Results
Workshop participants prepared a community event gathering various ethnic congregations. They worshiped together using the newly composed songs, and other meaningful songs from each congregation. A Syrian group brought their communal circle dance (a wedding dance) to teach everyone together in worship. They also included their Arabic keyboard and traditional string instruments when playing their newly composed songs. During rehearsals for the event, participants learned how to perform the different songs and worked together to refine the presentation of these songs.

Conversation 7: Celebrate and Integrate for Continuity
The night of worship concert was meaningful for both the songwriting participants and other community members. In post-event interviews, attendees said the hybrid, multilingual songs were unfamiliar and new, but helped them engage in worship. The songwriters and community members demonstrated and experienced unity in diversity throughout the whole process. One participant said, "When cultures come together, it's a whole new game changer. We all praise God in our own ways, and we are not judged. There is no judgment in what we can do in the presence of God. When we are all in the presence of God, we are one in worshiping."[31]

This story was just the beginning of Joy's long-term engagement with the diaspora community of Clarkston. She continues to cultivate spaces for diverse people to come together to worship, share, and cocreate through different art forms and expressions. She continues to witness the integration of new hybrid songs and new intercultural ways of worship in her own community in Clarkston, which was demonstrated and inspired through this project.

---

31 Kim, "Diaspora Musicians," 120.

How to Learn CLAT

Arts for a Better Future (ABF) is the most complete, immersive way to learn CLAT.[32] In its prototypical form, ABF consists of a five-day workshop in which participants engage with the CLAT method three times, each increasing their personal mastery and engagement with real communities. The course is bathed in opportunities to engage with God through multiple artistic forms, making it also a spiritually revitalizing retreat. See www.artsforabetterfuture.org for locations and times of ABF workshops.

Institutions and programs also integrate CLAT or closely related approaches into their curricula in various ways. Examples include the Center for Excellence in World Arts (Dallas International University), Payap University (Thailand), All Nations Christian College (UK), Liberty University, and Associação Linguística Evangélica Missionária (Brazil).[33] Though you may be able to learn CLAT by studying this manual by yourself, we've found that practicing the skills along with others enriches and hastens the process.

Conversation Partners

Our first priority is conversations that treat others and ourselves as whole human beings, not just artists or researchers. So build relationships; get permission to do things; earn the right to pry; and be respectful of local limitations on what you can do (e.g., don't expect to study female initiation rites if you're a man). Most of the time, it will be your authentic, reciprocal relationships with people that will allow you to enter their lives. Other times you will benefit from others' long-term relationships with the community to make connections. In any case, always remember that we care deeply about the artistic life of people, but they and we are people first.

Remember also that any particular person, community, and the relationships they form are unique. However, there are also always commonalities to lean into and ways to learn more about each other, even to become more like each other.

You

We wrote this manual primarily for you, an *arts advocate* working by yourself, with a partner, a team, or as member of a local Christian community. You want to help a community—perhaps your own—integrate artistic action more fully into their lives. You want their temporal and eternal futures to be better. *Your primary job is to help others make new things in genres and events they already know.* If a particular artistry is already important in your personal life, finding outlets to express your own gifts may be crucial to your well-being. Your primary job, however, is to help *others* make new artistic things.

We suggest three criteria to help you in your decisions about how to invest your unique but limited gifts, time, and energies in a community:

---

32 For more on ABF, see (especially the ABF Home and About tabs) and an article available in the GEN Virtual Library: Harris and Schrag, "A Practical Approach to Arts."

33 For a more complete list of training institutions using CLAT, see Schrag and Swijghuisen Reigersberg, "Ethnodoxology."

First, ask God to show you where he's working. Remember that his voice might not be the loudest, most obvious voice.

Second, enter a process of discovery with members of the community. Together you'll be wiser in knowing how and where to work. Your background and the approaches in this manual provide you with valuable knowledge and experience. If you have submitted yourself to a locally led decision-making process, don't be afraid to humbly speak the truth from your perspective.

Third, reflect on your own identity(ies). We all present ourselves and interact differently depending on the people we're with, and you are different now than you were five years ago. You may also have a complex, sometimes confusing inner life. This may especially be true for people moving between multiple cultures and generations that are themselves changing: you may be wrestling with deeply hybrid internal identities.[34] As people have migrated, moved, globalized, urbanized, and reflected, this is more and more common. If you are juggling multiple identities, be kind to yourself as God and you craft your unique self. You may also find points of connection with communities who are themselves increasingly navigating hybridities.[35]

> What identities, experiences, and gifts do you have that you can apply to this process?
>
> What experiences and gifts will have to come from other people?
>
> What might your role(s) be in a CLAT process?

The community(ies)

We define a community as a social group of any size whose members share a story, identity, and ongoing patterns of interaction, and whose identity and social practices are constantly in flux. We explore these characteristics in more detail in Conversation 1, but we want to make a few preliminary comments here.

Just as most people in the world speak more than one language, they also perform and experience music, dance, stories, and other arts from multiple traditions and geographical locations. Each community—and each individual within a community—has a unique, changing blend of local, regional, national, and international artistic activity. Fortunately, we have tools (mostly in Conversations 1 and 4) to help discover the patterns and lifeways of any community.

Since 2012, CLAT has been applied to a growing, diversifying set of communities. Though not all fully implemented, these include multicultural churches, extended families, a drug rehabilitation center, video gamers, a guest house, visual arts class, church planters, preteen girls and adult women, a hostel for female sex workers, Christian artists in a country region, a missions agency,

---

34 See Kim, "Diaspora Musicians" and Jones, "Hybridity and Christian Identity." Note that each article in the volume addresses hybridity.

35 Hybridity, syncretism, and contextualization will also enter further discussions in the process. See, for example, Shaw and Burrows, *Traditional Ritual*, and Connor and Menger, "Strengthening Christian Identity."

international college students, a neighborhood, schools, refugee camps, and a number of ethnolinguistic communities.[36]

Relational Dynamics

Every relationship between an arts advocate and a community is unique, but there are always points of connection, degrees and characteristics of insiderness and outsiderness. As you reflect on features of your own history, skills, and personality traits, try to identify commonalities with a whole community, a subgroup, or individual. For example, you may appreciate a particular art form similar to one in the community, or you may have grown up on a farm and so can understand activities and concerns of an agrarian society. If you're working with Christians, you always have Jesus as a central touchpoint.

In addition to evident similarities and differences, you must also reflect on histories and invisible systems that affect your relationships with a community. Your country of origin, education, or race, for example, may trigger certain ways of interacting, perhaps due to lingering effects of colonialism and neocolonialism. If you inhabit an elevated category in such a social system, people in the community may defer to your choices, statements, actions, and priorities. And if this social system is deeply embedded in multiple domains of life, this will take time, wisdom, and humility to overcome. CLAT inherently favors local agency and choices, which we try to emphasize throughout this manual.[37]

How to Apply CLAT

Overview

Engaging with a community using the *CLAT Manual* requires two steps. First, draw on it to craft plans with and for specific communities. These plans must each conform to the unique contexts and characteristics of the group. Second, use the plans as starting points and initial guides to community interactions and activities. This may include modifications of curricula and presentation of materials like those used in workshops like Arts for a Better Future (ABF). Or actual engagement with a community may be completely oral and include only a subset of the seven conversations. Each plan and its application will be *sui generis*, one of a kind, emerging and morphing through time.

During this process, we promote a posture of humility. We want community members taking the lead in as many parts of the approach as possible. Who ultimately decides the Kingdom of Heaven goals? The community. Who connects artistic genres and events with goals? The community. And though most of the research activities follow an anthropological tradition of systematic discovery, we also include some that can be performed by general community members. In any case, we want to follow the community's lead as much as possible.

---

36 Gathered from ABF projects, master's theses, and ethnodoxology networks.

37 For more on systemic barriers and injustices, see Achebe, *Things Fall Apart*; Crouch, *Playing God*; Corbitt and Fikkert, *When Helping Hurts*; Darko and Snodderly, *First the Kingdom*; Liew, Segovia, et al., *Colonialism and the Bible*; Lupton, *Toxic Charity*; and Pacheco-Vega and Parizeau, *Doubly Engaged Ethnography*.

Embracing this posture of humility raises an often-unsettling question: Why are arts advocates—who are often outsiders—even involved? In short, we have access to unique ideas, tools, and perspectives that allow us to be sensitive, wise encouragers and facilitators. Christianity's growth, theologies, funding, and wisdom continue to originate in more and more places. People sometimes call this phenomenon polycentrism, or "from everyone to everywhere."[38] We can all learn from each other and work side by side, always emphasizing the importance of local agency.

The whole process of artistic cocreation requires people with many kinds of competencies, knowledge, and skills, including these:

- artistic sensibilities and abilities
- ethnographic and form research
- relationships with all parts of local, regional, and national communities
- planning and organizing
- communicating well in modes appropriate to different contexts
- technical competencies for recording and production

No one person or type of person can do everything required for Creating Local Arts Together. That's why we put plural terms like *together* and *we* in as many sentences in this manual as possible. We guide you through what needs to be done but don't say who should do it.

We also assume that the community has access to people, resources, and organizations that can help them meet their goals. We don't, for example, develop a theological framework or methodology for starting new churches. Instead, we lead you through a process of getting to know local artists as they incorporate their insights and skills into existing church-planting efforts. As another example, we don't include detailed instructions on how to make a primer for a literacy program. Rather, we show how you can use the lyrics of a local song style as an aid to teaching reading, how local dances can play important roles in motivating people to learn to read, and offer tools to understand local visual patterns that could be incorporated into primer drawings.

In an encouraging development, people have begun producing more comprehensive materials that apply CLAT or CLAT-like approaches to particular domains. Foerster and Saurman, for example, demonstrate how arts can be integrated into literacy and other language-based development.[39] For other examples see the Digital Library at www.clatmanual.com.

---

38 As described, for example, in Yeh, *Polycentric Missiology*; Fung, *Cooperation in a Polycentric World*; and Sanders, *Embracing Winds of Change*, 208–18.

39 Foerster and Saurman, *Producing Language Development Materials*, and Cuthbert, "Church-Based Curriculum Integrating Literacy."

Postures and approaches

Historically, applied ethnomusicologists like Vida Chenoweth and Tom Avery practiced and promoted analyzing a culture's melodic system well enough to make new works in it, which can motivate people within a community to create.[40] Though we provide the seeds of such an analysis in Conversation 4B, our primary focus is to help you enter into relationships with people in a community in ways that result in a panoply of possible goals and methods. A few comments about the diverse ways CLAT has been applied may help you flesh out your own relationship with a community, which will evolve over time.

CLAT menu. Arts advocates have developed CLAT presentations that vary by available time and audience, focusing on teaching the method as completely as each context allows (see the Digital Library at www.clatmanual.com for fuller outlines). These range from the 30–60 minute "Getting Along with the Arts" and "The Big Picture" to presentations and workshops from 90 minutes, eight 60-minute sessions, and the full 35–40 hours Arts for a Better Future (ABF) workshop.

One compact CLAT workshop that has proven especially portable and effective we call "Show One, Do One." In it, we present the seven conversations in a CLAT story we know well, each followed by participants sketching a plan to apply that content and activities to a community they know.

Systematic ⟷ Therapeutic Continuum. Any instance of community engagement varies in its emphasis on systematic or therapeutic interactions. A more systematic application of the model integrates explicit references to each CLAT Conversation and its purposes. Practitioners and communities rely on the insights and principles giving rise to the mindsets and methods aggregated in the approach. Systematic CLAT engagement likely includes earlier crafting of plans drawing on Conversation-informed analyses. A primary goal is that communities will make their plans aware of as many art forms and their characteristics as possible, the extreme breadth and diversity of possible Heaven-shaped goals, and the spiritual, social, intellectual, and physical dynamics in which they live.

A more therapeutic model has its roots in Rogerian psychotherapy, which emphasizes the client's capacity to solve their own problems, with the therapist serving primarily as a facilitator.[41] In our CLAT context, priority is given to waiting for communities to choose discussion topics and actions that emerge organically, responding to community member-directed interactions. Such engagement focuses on the one-of-a-kind characteristics of every group, and their capacity to discover much about themselves with as little input from the facilitator as possible. It often includes multiple meetings over long periods of time—perhaps years.[42] Todd and Mary Saurman report short workshops

---

40 See Chenoweth, *Melodic Perception and Analysis*, and Popjes, "Now We Can Speak."

41 For background on person-centered psychotherapy, see Rogers and Farson, *Active Listening*; De Sousa, "Client-Centered Therapy"; Hopper, "Introduction to Rogerian Therapy"; and Margolin, "Rogerian Therapy," which explores the complexities of power relationships in such therapy.

42 Saurman, *Hmong Songs in Education*, 307–15.

with hundreds of Asian communities over more than twenty years that have resulted in a plethora of signs of Heaven; Mary Saurman sometimes calls these "auto-actionary outcomes."[43]

The therapeutic model reminds us of the imperative of local agency and community ownership of the whole process. It also nudges us to explore options in which community members wield and control the application of research tools.[44] Todd Saurman argues that outsiders should have "less involvement (but the most essential involvement) [so] people can feel more empowered to do their own discovering, make their own decisions, and develop their own plans to success, thereby taking the most ownership and becoming the most sustainable in the process."[45] Connor and Menger provide an apt example from Indonesia of how the "intersection of local agency with autogenic research …" can lead to a "self-directed, self-motivated, and sustainable localization movement."[46]

Note that both emphases rely on common (often implicit) theological foundations: every person and community reflect God's image in unique ways; Christ-followers must adopt attitudes of humility and a posture of learning; and though the particulars differ in each context, God has defined *good* as the presence of his Kingdom. Also, any given community can choose to adopt elements from anywhere on the continuum during the process.

Paradigm shifts. The ethnodoxology movement arose in the late twentieth century in large part as a reaction to theological frameworks rooted in colonialist ideologies that led to churches either denigrating or ignoring local artistic creativity.[47] Stories of emotion-laden moments in which someone's conceptual frame changed dramatically from these excluding beliefs have energized the movements' proponents. For example, VIPs attending the dedication of Scripture translated into their Kenyan language, Sabaot, feared such "… efforts would undermine their culture. Near the end of the ceremony, two of the translators sat down to play the *bukantiit*, a six-string wooden lyre with ancient roots among the Sabaot. As they accompanied words from the Gospel with a traditional tune, the guest elders spontaneously stood and began to sway in Sabaot style … singing the words of the refrain: 'God is good, God is good.'"[48]

---

43 Saurman, 300–302.

44 Saurman, *Singing for Survival*. Explore also collaborative research, in which researchers and communities use "collective research methods to generate research results together" (Harrison, *Value Alignment*, 75). See also the following resources: Lassiter, *Collaborative Ethnography*; Chang, Ngunjiri, and Hernandez, *Collaborative Autoethnography*; Pauwels and Mannay, *Sage Handbook of Visual Research Methods*; and Dossa and Golubovic, "Community-Based Ethnography."

45 Personal communication, 2013.

46 Connor and Menger, "Strengthening Christian Identity," 10.

47 Schrag and Swijghuisen Reigersberg, "Ethnodoxology."

48 Tapia, "Musicianaries," 52. For more examples of such paradigm shifts see "Section 2: Stories" in the *Ethnodoxology Handbook*, 184–357 and Fortunato et al., *All the World is Singing*. Christ followers in every community must also guard against syncretism with religious and ideological belief systems, a topic appearing periodically in this manual.

What if They Don't Want It?

Even if you do everything in this manual perfectly, humbly, and respectfully (which nobody can do), you will almost certainly run into resistance. Resistance could come from several sources: a community's low opinion of artists and themselves, theological or ideological arguments against certain kinds of arts being used in certain contexts, previous negative experiences with trying to do new things with arts, inertia from long-standing traditions, underappreciation of the importance and transformative potential of artistic communication, loss of local arts because of dramatic events or broken systems of intergenerational transmission, and spiritual warfare. Our whole approach of creating together within a community should lessen much of this, but it won't remove all problems. The following bits of counsel may help you navigate your way with more success and peace.

First, protect, pray for, love, and encourage the artists you work with. Whenever they create something for a public space, they become vulnerable to any negative cultural forces that exist. Second, as much as possible, work through existing authority structures. This may not always be easy, because arts sometimes speak uncomfortable truth to power. However, there are many benefits to sustainability if leaders in a community are willing to listen. Third, as we discuss below, you may want to start small with a pilot project. Working to help create a few examples of local artistic genres for Kingdom purposes, then presenting them to community leaders, can be a crucial step in them opening the door to further creativity and self-research. Fourth, be both winsome and persistent in your relationships. Fifth, don't be afraid to try and fail. Nurture your own humility, knowing that God's plan for you and a community will never be exactly what you think. Sixth and finally, talk with God a lot. He'll tell you what you need to know because it's his Kingdom. Remember: "If any of you lacks wisdom, you should ask God, who gives generously to all without finding fault, and it will be given to you" (Jas 1:5).

STARTING—AND SOMETIMES ENDING—SMALL

Almost every potential CLAT application will benefit from explorations and activities *before* trying to work with a whole community.

Preliminary Exploration

At a most basic level, what if they are not ready yet? What if the community is amid trauma, or hasn't recovered from past difficulties? What if you encounter broken relationships, unhealthy churches, or hopelessness? Sometimes the community will struggle to create until some issues are resolved. Be sensitive and listen well—maybe the community needs healing and restoration before they are ready to create.

It's important to note that the CLAT process itself sometimes exposes and provides space for healing and restoration. During one ABF in Alaska, for example, some of the Native Alaskan participants were offended by a flippant remark I made about colonialism. I eventually asked for forgiveness on my knees, both for myself and my missionary forebearers. This led to an emotional conversation in which one of the Native Alaskans shared that he had been publicly and authoritatively forbidden to engage in traditional dances or drumming by his church pastor. What he learned at ABF, however, created a sense of profound freedom in his heart. Later that year, he was granted the honor of representing his school as he performed on stage with a *cauyaq* (Yup'ik drum) at the Native Musicale in Anchorage. It was the first time in the sixty years of that monthly gathering that a Native drum was heard at that event. He has been performing on the cauyaq ever since.[49]

In another case, tensions between four subgroups during a particular ABF in East Africa reached a high pitch, revealing schisms originating in historical dynamics related to slavery. In response, ABF leaders set aside the schedule, modeled, and made room for open, humble discussions. Each group ultimately asked for and gave forgiveness as appropriate. Heaven-spreading creativity ensued.

Pilot Projects

Gatekeepers and community members sometimes assent to the idea of integrating local arts into their lives, but do not change patterns of its exclusion. We have found that frequently people need to *experience* innovations before they will embrace them wholeheartedly. Working with just one or a few people to create local arts that integrate Scripture or other Heaven-focused content—a pilot project—can produce such paradigm-shifting artistry.

As an example, I asked a few friends from a minority community if they could compose a few songs in three traditional genres with Scripture-based lyrics. They did and we made a rough recording and put the songs on a CD. I gave the CD to a Christian leader in the group who was influential in producing church song books—until then containing mostly translated Euro-American hymns. The next Sunday, he called me at 6 a.m. with these words: "My family and I listened to the CD again and again, dancing in the house! These were rhythms that we hadn't wanted to hear again after becoming Christians, but it's as though the lyrics blessed and sanctified them. Now *everyone* can come and have a place listening to the truth. All we need for evangelism is to accompany these songs with people who will challenge people verbally and explain things. How can I get more copies?" This kind of creation of, and engagement with, artistry draws interest and produces energy that can lead to more community involvement and commitment to projects.

---

49 Eugene Stevens has given permission for his story to be told here. Another Native Alaskan, Harriette Slwooko, reflects on that same apology and the effects it had on her life: https://youtu.be/r5q5hvSSj10 (see at 1:25).

Identity Affirmation

A majority of the communities in ABF CLAT projects choose nurturing positive self-identity as a crucial step in becoming more like Heaven, pointing to an overwhelming, near ubiquitous need. Among other causes, certain theologies and colonial ideologies embedded in the spread of Protestant Christianity since the 1800s have played significant roles in the sense of inferiority and loss of traditional arts.[50]

Because a God-based identity is foundational to so much local creativity, addressing the issue even before going through the whole CLAT process can help. You can do this by choosing one of the identity-related activities in Conversations 2 and 5. Another idea comes from Todd and Mary Saurman: a study of 1 Corinthians 14:7–19. Matt Menger, Matt Connor, and others have adopted and adapted this activity for many contexts. Menger reports that they have "seen Christians from hundreds of indigenous groups in Asia freed to start creating their own local art forms by simply studying 1 Corinthians 14:7–19 and answering the questions of what these verses say about language, what they say about singing and music instruments, and how they might respond to what they understood (while also having them explore their culture through the senses)."[51] You can find a guide to leading such a study in Conversation 4D.

If You Don't Have Much Time

To get started, it helps to look for natural connections you may have with local artists. One connection could be that you are intrigued by a particular art form—you just like it. Or you may have experience or skills related to one of the art forms, such as dance or weaving. Or you may have a personal affinity with a practitioner of an art form. In any case, remember that ultimately you want to get to know and encourage people involved in local arts. Look for ways to make relationships. And if you can only do one thing, ask an artist to teach you something.

Here are some simple arts engagement activities for any kind of community:

- Make an initial list of local art forms using the "Take a First Glance at a Community's Arts" activity in Conversation 1.
- Attend an artistic event and describe it in a notebook.
- Make lists of types of song, dance, drama, visual storytelling, or proverbs.
- Ask questions about an instrument you see.
- Ask someone to translate the lyrics of a song.
- Spend relaxed social time with artists, asking about their hopes and concerns.

---

50 There may be points in your interactions with a community when you don't have the time or resources to commit to the thorough process we describe in this manual. Or maybe you're just not sure how to begin. If so, this brief section contains suggestions for arts activities that you can start without much preparation. These will get you going and will feed into more complete actions you may do when you have more time. No artistic exploration or encouragement is ever wasted. And remember that you want any engagement to support mutually beneficial relationships, friend-making. Schrag and Swijghuisen Reigersberg, "Ethnodoxology."

51 Matt Menger, personal communication.

- Make systematic audio or video recordings of an art form according to song categories, composer, events in a village, or proverbs.
- Ask someone to teach you a basic skill in playing an instrument, singing, dancing, acting, weaving, or telling a story in a local genre.
- Talk about these things with local friends and colleagues:
    ◊ How did the kinds of arts in the community come about? Who created the things people use or perform?
    ◊ What are people's general attitudes toward people involved in different local art forms? Positive? Negative?
    ◊ Are there parts of an enactment that have special symbolic significance? For example, colors, shapes, instruments, or clothes?
    ◊ How does the way people do local art forms now from how they did them in the past? Are young people learning how to do them? How does someone get good at them?
    ◊ Are there certain art forms that only men or only women or only children can do?
    ◊ How do people feel when they're involved in different local art forms? Do they ever enter ecstatic states?
    ◊ How are local art forms connected to religious beliefs?
    ◊ What artistic expressions in the culture are not currently being used in the worship of God? Why?
    ◊ How might God want to redeem one for a purpose in his Kingdom?

SOME ADVICE AND ENCOURAGEMENT

You Don't Have to Do Any of This

People have been integrating arts into their communities in astounding ways since the beginning of human existence … without the help of this manual. Individuals and communities sometimes create arts with no explicit purpose in mind except "I really want/need to do this!" And sometimes those bits of artistry spread and enliven the Kingdom of Heaven in completely unpredictable and positive ways.

Or you may be an exceptional communicator-artist who naturally knows how to listen, learn, and lead. You may work more good for the Kingdom by just going and meeting people and learning how to dance or orate on your own. Really.

So you may not have to do any of this. Most of us and our communities, though, will benefit from the reminders bound up in the structure of this book.

Nurture a Learner's Heart and a Listening Posture

Learning to know someone else deeply is a fundamental act of love and necessary for success in everything else you do. So whenever you're not sure what to do, go ask a question, practice a dance, observe an event—anything that helps you learn. **Research = learning = love**. When we research a community, we learn about it and demonstrate love for its members.

Sometimes your research will take you into realms of belief and practice that contradict your Christian faith. In these cases, whenever possible, adopt an attitude of "temporary suspension of disbelief." Do not act counter to what God wants you to do, but try to identify with your friends, at least for a moment. This can be a thorny issue, so pray fervently.

Community Development (CD) lore contains stories like this:[52]

> A CD worker was assigned to a village exhibiting many apparent needs. People in the village had rebuffed previous attempts to help, so this expatriate wondered if he would have any success.
>
> He called a meeting and a large crowd showed up. He asked, "I'm just an outsider, you know better what you need here. What are your ideas? I'm sure you have some." The reaction: total silence. 20 minutes passed, then 30 and 45, and the professional became more and more uncomfortable, sweating, but determined to wait. Still no response at 55 minutes, but when an hour had passed, the tense audience cheered: "You really, truly are interested in what we want? You don't have your own pre-scheduled agenda, all those fancy ideas of your own? You really care about what we need … well!" And their good ideas came thick and fast.

Listening deeply and repeatedly requires commitment and patience, often challenging for people like us, those who want to see more Heaven everywhere. Whether you're more of an outsider or insider to a community, you need to continually nurture a posture of learning and listening, following community members' leadership, sometimes applying your skills and knowledge to help in ways you would never have predicted.

We suggest many tools and concepts to help you connect to and understand a group as deeply as possible. But remember that we are motivated by a self-giving love that puts others' interests above our own (1 Cor 13). We are eager to discover how God's image reflects uniquely in someone else, which underscores the benefits of community members taking leading roles in every conversation in the CLAT process. When you feel yourself taking charge of something, reflect on whether you have truly listened in the process that led to that point.

You Can't Do It All, But You Can Do Enough

Every community and its artistic forms of communication represent an unfathomable degree of complexity and variation. Even the most accomplished master of an art form can learn more and increase his or her skills. To make matters more difficult, the physical and social contexts of these communities are in a constant state of change, sometimes dramatically. In short, there's no

---

[52] Thanks to Marian Hungerford who told this story during an African Orientation Course I attended in Yaoundé, Cameroon, 1992.

way you could fully perform all the activities we describe in this manual in a definitive way for just one art form, even if you had nothing else ever to do.

But you can do enough.

Insights from academic fields like ethnomusicology, performance studies, anthropology, linguistics, missiology, and neuroscience show that we can understand the important patterns of human artistic communication. In addition, God's view of his final Kingdom encompasses every language and nation (Rev 7); we *can* know each other. But because of the complexity, our interactions with communities are more like explorations and adventures than scientific processes. Use this manual to sharpen and broaden your understanding of artistic communication in the Kingdom of Heaven, but don't try to do everything. Follow the streams of exploration and creating together that seem most relevant and fruitful.

Whenever Possible, Help Local Leaders Plan for the Arts

One of the most common reasons that communities and organizations don't integrate the arts into their work is that they don't plan for it. You can help solve this problem by learning the processes through which leaders in churches, nongovernmental organizations (NGOs), and other groups interacting with a community make decisions. Then graciously ask to join those processes in appropriate ways, at key moments. Prepare yourself well, being ready to offer concrete suggestions for how people can draw on the great resources of their community's arts to reach their goals.

Planning can be important for long-term integration of Kingdom creativity in a community. In fact, our seven CLAT conversations constitute a planning method that you can use for sustainable arts development for your community. If you're working with an organization that has adopted a particular planning system, adapt the vocabulary we've developed in this manual to that of their system in your interactions. Conversation 7 contains reflections and resources on continuity and sustainability.

One caveat: regardless of how much you and a community plan, God often works in ways we can't anticipate. So you should plan, but always stay aware of individuals or groups who might be responding to something unexpected that God is doing. Enjoy being surprised.

Consider Engaging with Older Artistry

Consider giving extra attention to local artists who represent older, geographically or ethnically rooted traditions, previous to most of what engages them now. We encourage this focus on local artists because their skills and knowledge are of unique value but often endangered; communities need a combination of deeply rooted traditions and innovation to thrive.

CONVERSATION 1

MEET A COMMUNITY AND ITS ARTS

Communities are the foundation of our approach to creativity in the Kingdom. However extreme a person's originality or individualism, his or her artistic creativity at some point references and depends on others. In Conversation 1 we guide you through a process of initial discovery and description of a community and its arts. You'll learn how to:

- think about what a community is
- start a Community Arts Profile
- learn our key terms
- take a first glance at a community
- take a first glance at a community's arts
- start exploring a community's social and conceptual life
- prepare to use research methods to learn more

THINK ABOUT WHAT A COMMUNITY IS

It is likely that you have already identified a community to engage with. Your connections could exist because you were born into the community or have long experience with it. It could be that you are part of a mission or humanitarian or church organization that has directed you to this group to fulfill its goals. Whether you have a clear idea in your mind about a particular community or not, you will benefit from reflecting on what a community is. We define a **community** as *a social group of any size whose members share a story, identity, and ongoing patterns of interaction*. They are internally complex and constantly changing. We have purposely left the definition simple and loose because real communities can take many forms that we can't predict. As we describe each characteristic, perhaps you'll want to think of how it relates to a community you know.

Communities Share a Story

No group of people exists in more than one point in time, but each sees itself as part of a larger story, a history. On any given day, people may refer to events, characters, ideas, and dramatic elements that have occurred over multiple generations, or that took place much more recently. This shared story provides continuity, connections between the past, and an imagined future, providing impetus to keep gathering. For Christian communities—usually organized as local churches—the story that provides ultimate cohesion is this: God created the universe; the first people made a Big Mistake (often referred to as the fall); God sent messengers to show how to overcome the Big Mistake, but it wasn't enough; God sent Jesus to provide the final solution to the Big Mistake; God is working with his people to grow his Kingdom; this Kingdom will come to fruition in the New Heaven and New Earth, at the end of time.

Communities Share an Identity

People know they are connected by recognizing and valuing common points of reference in each other. Identity markers tie people in a community together and distinguish them from others. Their shared story may provide a primary marker of this common identity. Other signs of a common identity could include a particular spoken language or accent, food, manner of dress, skills, religion, ideology, geographical location, enemies or allies, taboos, or shared needs or struggles. Artistic forms of communication often provide key points of identity.

Keep in mind that the fall has affected all communities' identities. They may include elements like arrogance, worthlessness, inferiority, or hopelessness. Or a community might be losing historically important markers.

Communities Share Ongoing Patterns of Interaction

People in a community communicate with each other in patterned ways, times, and places. Contexts for communication may include these: within a family's living quarters; at meetings designed for rituals, sports, politics, or courtship; during periods of work, business, or education; festivals, celebrations, or entertainment. The communication could be face to face, body to body, or mediated through radio, phones, apps, websites, social media, other audiovisual means, and who knows what people will invent next. Success may be dependent on being geographically close, or proximity may be irrelevant. Whatever the contexts or media, communities depend on common systems of meaning to facilitate comprehension and impact. These systems include spoken and signed languages, visual and video symbolism, movement and tactile sign patterns, and many others.[1]

Communities Are Complex and Changing

Though we've been talking about communities almost as static, coherent objects, they're not. They are composed of individuals who each make their own decisions, enter and leave the community, and respond to external and internal factors differently. Every community has internal variation and changes over time. So beware of saying things like, "Community X sings like this." It may be true for a majority of the group today, but some people may be advocating for a different kind of singing. In five years, things may be very different. The bottom line is that every community displays both continuity and change, internal coherence, and diversity. We hold our ideas about them confidently but lightly.

---

[1] Many of these modes of communication are completely oral or contain oral components. Two important sources of ideas, methods, training and networking in applying orality to Christian mission include the International Orality Network (https://orality.net), Institutes for Orality Studies (https://i-os.org/about) and Orality Talks (https://oralitytalks.net).

Communities in This Manual

The initial spark for this manual came from a desire to engage better with communities that have strong ethnolinguistic identities and modes of communication; they represent some of the richest, most underutilized, and endangered artistic traditions in the Kingdom of Heaven. This remains an important focus. But the world is urbanizing and globalizing, leading to more and more communities made up of people from more than one culture, glued together by diverse interests. We have purposely left the definition broad, because real communities take many, *many*, unpredictable forms. Other examples include nuclear or extended families, multicultural and monocultural churches, towns, clubs, schools or classes, a biome containing humans, a political party, a city or country, Earth, or Heaven. CLAT is relevant to them all.

START A COMMUNITY ARTS PROFILE

Where do you keep what you know? We all store thoughts, facts, feelings, skills, experiences, stories, and smells in our brains and bodies as memories. When we need to drive a car, greet a friend, or dance at a wedding, we call on what we've learned to know what to do. This kind of storage is indispensable to life and artistic action. But memories in the mind and body fade and clutter. Written and recorded data provide a crucial, though imperfect, remedy to this natural loss, especially as you're learning about arts new to you. We've developed a tool to help you keep track of what you're learning, called a Community Arts Profile (CAP).

A Community Arts Profile is a place for you to gather what you and a community learn about its arts. Each community should have its own CAP. It may be in the form of word processing documents, a database, website, or notebook. We have created the outline of such a profile that you can use. In reality, almost everything you and the community do while creating together will lead to new insights into how a type of artistic activity functions, its meanings, and its place in society; you will do well to capture as much of this as possible in the CAP. This information will prove invaluable when you come alongside the community as they plan cocreative activities, spark creativity, evaluate artistic output, and integrate the arts into the community. Our hope is that you will add to and draw from the CAP as long as you interact with the community it describes. Open Community Arts Profile to get started (available in the Digital Library at www.clatmanual.com and a condensed version in Closing 2).

LEARN OUR KEY TERMS

Some of our most important terms were unclear in the first version of the *CLAT Manual*. So after lively discussions with smart and knowledgeable friends, we've defined several foundational concepts more precisely and consistently. You will see and explore them throughout this manual and most fully in Conversation 4. Note also that because we're breaking new ground in some areas, we've adopted unconventional usages for a few terms. You will have to adopt our definitions and their implications, at least while you're reading this book.

Genre

For our purposes, a genre is a community's shared category of communication marked by artistry and characterized by a unique set of formal characteristics, enactment practices, and social meanings. Genre is an abstraction held by multiple community members as patterns and meanings in their minds and bodies.

A few examples, with common locations of ethnolinguistic associations, include *olonkho* epic (Siberia), Broadway musical (New York City), *kanoon* (Cameroon), *huayno* (Peru), *haiku* (Japan), praise and worship (Evangelical churches worldwide, with Euro-American and local roots), *qawwali* (South Asia), graphic novel (international), Bollywood film (India), *jebwa* (Australia), and *güipil* (Guatemala).

Enactment

For our purposes, enactment is a full or partial instantiation of a genre marked by artistry. It's a particular category of communication, a set of ideas made concrete and experienceable during an event. We sometimes refer to enactments as artistry, or bits of artistry. They exist in an identifiable time and place—they happen.

Enactment is the core concept of CLAT perhaps least familiar to English speakers. We made this choice because it embraces not only expressions of genres popularly understood as *performance*—entertainment "by dancing, singing, acting, or playing music"[2]—but also the vast number of genres that produce objects, buildings, food, and the like. In brief, both objects and performances can be genre enactments.

Enactments appear in formal settings, everyday life, with much preparation or little. A few genre enactments I've experienced recently include seeing painted skulls as I entered a church ministering to ex-convicts in Hamilton, Ohio; singing and playing a blues song I composed for neighbors who had helped build our new house on Weathertree farm; I watched members of the Ad Deum dance troupe perform in the rotunda of a building in Ft. Worth, Texas; that same evening, I stood in the rotunda staring up at its stained glass crafted dome.[3] I've attended an Irish dance concert, a community theater production of "Once Upon a Mattress." Our house contains paintings and sculptures and instruments and aesthetically notable rooms we enter each day, and our family has sung at a birthday celebration and watched movies on our television. And then there are God's more direct enactments of brilliantly colored autumn leaves, wildflowers, and dragonflies.

---

2 *Cambridge Dictionary*, s.v. "performance," accessed Nov. 6, 2023, https://dictionary.cambridge.org/us/dictionary/english/performance.

3 These are just a few examples of events I experienced within the last half of 2023.

Artistic enactments we can see, hear, feel, and smell at particular places and times pervade our lives. We provide approaches and tools that help us understand the social, aesthetic, and other elements of enactments and the genres from which they flow.

In the broader academic world, ideas associated with enactment are the subject of lively debate, including this concise definition of the broader category, enaction: "a movement or action made manifest in the world. [A] dynamic process of world-constitution that is always intimately linked to a particular bodily identity and situated within a greater field of interpenetrating relationships."[4] Enactivism as a discipline has roots in cognitive science, but is growing in wider academic influence.[5]

Event

For our purposes, **event** is *something that occurs in a particular place and time containing the enactment of at least one artistic genre*. It is experienced through sensory pathways, divisible into shorter time segments, and related to larger sociocultural patterns of a community. The scope of an event can vary widely depending how broad or narrow your focus is. Examples include festival, church service, birthday party, rite of passage, watching and listening to a music video on an electronic device, studying a museum painting, carving a sculpture, or an ice-skating competition.

Shorthands

Enactments, genres, and events don't necessarily include artistry. However, since almost everything we refer to in this manual contains at least some artistry, we usually remove the modifier *artistic* from these terms. We've adopted these conventions:

- event = artistic event
- genre = artistic genre
- enactment = artistic genre enactment

TAKE A FIRST GLANCE AT A COMMUNITY

The Community Arts Profile includes a place to include the first bits of information you gather about a community, including its geographical location(s), language(s), important identity markers, and modes of communication. We've designed a few First Glances to help you in initial learning you hold lightly, not performing rigorous, thorough investigations. And as in all elements of the CLAT process, research *with* community members, stepping back from leadership whenever possible.

From this you and community members will decide the scope of your activities. Your scope could be very narrow, restricted to one clan in a village

---

4 Malkemus, "General Theory of Enaction," 201.

5 See, for example, Thompson, *Mind in Life*.

or one multilingual neighborhood in a city, for example. Or it could be very broad, such as everyone who speaks a particular language in a region. Scope also refers to how detailed your descriptions will be: you may describe artistic communication from a close-up view (zoomed in), from far away (zoomed out), or somewhere in between.

Questions to Ask

Where is the community and how many of them are there? This includes basic information like village or town or city, province, and nation. It's likely that community members live in more than one geographical location. It could be that they think of themselves as historically connected to a geographical center, with diaspora in other places.

What ties the community together? Answers could include factors like language, geography, ethnic identity, art forms, shared activities, and social structures like churches or families.

How do they communicate with each other and how often? This question points to languages and modes of communication like these: face-to-face, phone, and social media. It may be that they have frequent face-to-face communication with those nearby but also make regular trips to visit members who live farther away.

How do they share their artistic creations? This question points to face-to-face and digital sharing, through DVDs and other media, written notation, or other means.

How did they get there? Identify important historical events and patterns that have brought the community to its geographical location and affected its identity.

People and Places to Ask

Whenever possible, ask these questions of friends, leaders, and other contacts from the community. You can also ask them to point you to other people and resources where you can learn more. In addition, remember that the nearer you live to a community, the more opportunities you will have to learn more.

You can also learn a great deal by reading or watching how members of the community have presented themselves in books, articles, videos, recordings, and other media. Then see how others have described the community through academic research, encyclopedias, or more popular presentations. Note that insiders and outsiders represent communities in different ways—make sure you ultimately get to how communities conceive of themselves.

TAKE A FIRST GLANCE AT A COMMUNITY'S ARTS

A core feature of our approach is that we normally come alongside communities as they create from artistic resources that they already possess. We define these resources as follows:

Local Artistic Genre: *A type of artistic language that a community knows well enough to create, enact, teach, and understand from within, including its forms, meanings, language(s), and social context(s).* Local artistic genres can include those with long traditions in a community, or can be adopted or fused with other genres. Communities usually identify them as their own. We sometimes refer to these as *local genres* or *local arts*.[6]

Note that local genres are our primary focus, and we often give examples from ethnolinguistic groups. The main features of genres in this category, however, are that communities identify with them somehow, and that members know them well enough to create new examples.

One of the very first things we must do, then, is list a community's local artistic genres. We'll show how to make a quick survey, then provide two approaches for making it more complete: *Outside-in* and *Inside-out*. If you are working with a Christian community, then you will also want to consider using the guides in "Discover a Christian Community's Arts" (Conversation 4, Part D). Note that these methods can be important tools even if you are working in your own community—we are often surprised at how much we don't know about our own group's arts.

Make a Quick List of Artistic Genres

A productive way to come up with a list of initial genres is to gather a few people from the community and ask them questions like this:

- When do people in this community sing? play instruments? dance? tell stories? act? carve? paint? use their bodies in unusual ways? play games? build special structures? Remember that each culture divides up and talks about its forms of artistic communication in unique ways, so learn their vocabulary.
- Do people in this community do anything special surrounding the birth of a child? someone's death? someone's passage from childhood to adulthood? For each affirmative answer, ask them to describe what special things happen and make note of the artistry involved.

Whenever an artistic genre comes up in discussion, jot down a few of the genre's basic characteristics:

- a local name or brief description
- kinds of people involved (men, women, youth, children, specialists, a particular socioeconomic group, etc.)
- when it's usually done (events, particular days, seasons, months, times of day, etc.)
- purposes of the genre
- anything else that comes up immediately

---

6   See also *genre* and related entries in the Glossary.

You may find it helpful to distill all this into basic journalism questions like: What, Where, When, Who, and Why, or to consult resources in the Digital Library at www.clatmanual.com. Don't worry about getting all the details while you're making a survey; we'll guide you through much more detailed investigation in Conversation 4.

Extend the List from the Outside In: Research Likely Social Contexts

In the *Outside-in* approach, you begin with an anthropologist's knowledge that cultures often mark important events and transitions with artistically rendered communication. Use the following very brief outline to help identify rituals and special events that may exist in a community.[7] Then explore what arts might be associated with each.

Life-cycle events

- birth (birth announcement, lullaby)
- childhood (funny or nonsense games, teasing, taunting)
- puberty (girl's songs, boy's songs, initiation)
- courting (love, courting, proposal of marriage)
- marriage (wedding, men's events, women's events)
- death (funeral, burial, mourning)

Legendary or historical events

- commemorative (disasters, honors, first outsiders, changes in leadership or government, first road, first vehicles, wars, etc.)
- legend (creation, mythology, epic heroes)
- local news

Activities

- work (cutting timber, hunting, fishing, road making, etc.)
- fighting (preparation for battle, battle, victory, defeat, etc.)
- dancing (male, female, both sexes, social, ceremonial, solo, etc.)
- recreation
- worship

Ceremonies

- religious rituals (planting, harvesting, fertility, power, prophecy, etc.)
- social (greeting, farewell, wedding, funeral, completion of a special community project, etc.)

---

7 Partially modified from Chenoweth, *Melodic Perception and Analysis*, 24–25.

Nature
- animals (pets and wild animals, including birds, fish, and reptiles)
- places and things (mountains, rivers, forests, trees, plants, the heavens—including clouds, sun, moon, stars, and sky)
- time cycles (daily, weekly, monthly, annual)

This is a basic list of artistic genres of the Mono ethnolinguistic group, Democratic Republic of Congo:

agbolo: children's play songs

agidi: dance for god of water

ako'ba: dance of women healers

ambala: malice dance

animation: Protestant church, for offerings and praise

banda: dance enacted during meetings of council of judges (*ngakoala*)

chorale: Protestant church, subgroups for teaching and enjoyment

gaza aga: men's circumcision, leaf dance

gaza mbala: men's circumcision, elephant dance

gaza yashe: women's circumcision dance

gbaguru: proverbs sung to exhort people

gbanjele: social dance to produce happiness

gbaya: celebratory, multi-village social dance

gbenge: mourning song when village leader dies

kowo: dance for victory or war

kpatsha: dance from Banda people in Central African Republic

ku'u agbolo: lullabies, to comfort children

kuzu: death celebration with multiple genres

nganga: protection song for hunters

ngaranja: dance integrated into ritual decision-making by council of judges

Nzembo na Nzambe: Protestant church, translated Euro-American hymns in a book

yangba: celebratory social dance

Extend the List from the Inside Out: Recognize Special Features

In the *Inside-out* approach, you begin with knowledge you have about art forms themselves, often from your own insights as an artist. You'll recognize many of a community's arts because they have characteristics of singing, dancing, acting, carving, or other arts you're already familiar with. Sometimes, though, the surface structures of the arts we encounter are so different from those in our own experience that we may not recognize them as being artistic at all. In this section we've listed special features of artistic expression that may help you think beyond your experience and identify more of a community's arts. As you go about your daily life, train yourself to notice these characteristics and ask yourself the questions we've provided. When you recognize something as artistic, ask preliminary questions, write down what you learn, and plan to investigate it further.

Arts are intimately connected to sensory experiences
People experience artistry in events through their senses—sight, sound, smell, touch, taste, etc.—often amplifying emotions and memories tied to those events. Helping individuals and groups explore each sense has led to revealing more types of artistry.

Arts may have distinctive enactment contexts
Many times—though not always—the occasion for artistic communication is different from everyday interaction. It occurs between recognizable boundaries that set it off from everyday occurrences, and it usually will have distinctive features such as role changes among the participants.[8] An artistic event might occur at a special time of day (often at night), in a special place, use special language, involve the participation of a large group of people, or participants might wear special clothing and behave in special ways. Some groups in Southeast Asia, for example, bundle objects with distinctive meanings—like leaves, twigs, and small stones—to ask forgiveness of someone.[9]

Many enactments are what Milton Singer has called "cultural performances":[10] scheduled, temporally bounded, spatially bounded, programmed, coordinated, heightened (i.e., more pronounced, extreme). You can usually find cultural enactments relatively easily because they require planning, gathering and allocation of resources, and the involvement of multiple people.

> Where is everybody going?
>
> Why are people wearing those hats today?
>
> What marks the beginning of this event? The end?

Arts may expand or contract the density of information
In comparison to everyday communication, artistic expressions often convey a great deal in just a few words. This is often true of poetry and proverbs. Other genres show the opposite effect, such as in Wagner operas, where the dialog and plot unfold almost in slow motion because of the chronological space needed to perform the musical elements. Songs frequently show a great deal of repetition.

> How can those people get so much from that little poem?

---

8 Saville-Troike, *The Ethnography of Communication*.

9 Kristýna Rausová, personal correspondence.

10 Bauman, ed., *Folklore*, 46.

Arts may assume more or special knowledge
Jokes are often very difficult to understand for outsiders because insider attitudes and knowledge are assumed by the tellers. It may be important that the assumed knowledge is not made explicit: it spoils a joke if you have to explain it. The implications of references to other artistic works can only be understood if the audience has knowledge of previous works, often of the same genre. Sometimes terminology or alternative meanings of words are specific to a particular artistic genre.

> What in the world does that mean?
>
> I understand all the words of the joke, but I don't understand what's so funny!

Arts exhibit special formal structure
Artistic expressions are often limited by constraints of form which are not relevant to everyday communication.

> Why did that person rhyme his last comment? (Clue: maybe it's a proverb.)
>
> Why is this building built differently than others?

Arts may elicit unusual responses
Artistic expressions often produce a strong emotional or physical response from people who experience them.

> Why is everybody so excited/upset?

Arts may require unusual expertise
Artistic expressions often seem to take specialized training to enact; not everyone can do them.

> How did she sing two notes at once?

START EXPLORING A COMMUNITY'S SOCIAL & CONCEPTUAL LIFE

Artistic action interacts with its community like threads and themes in an evolving tapestry. To understand an artist and her arts, you must understand her cultural context. This manual helps you understand arts and artists, but to guide you through a broad exploration of a community is beyond our scope. The field of cultural anthropology has developed a trustworthy set of categories and methods for doing that, commonly referred to as ethnography. If you don't have a background in anthropology, we encourage you to take a course in cultural anthropology.

Consulting related materials may also serve you. The University of Pennsylvania publishes a guide categorizing multiple resources pertinent to performing ethnographic research, an invaluable hub.[11] You may refer to

---
11 See Olson, "Guides: Ethnography," https://guides.library.upenn.edu/ethnography/DoingEthnography.

works like McKinney's *Globetrotting in Sandals*[12] or Ferraro and Andreatta's *Cultural Anthropology: An Applied Perspective*.[13] Also helpful are Yale University's *Human Relations Area Files*,[14] Ember and Ember's "Basic Guide to Cross-Cultural Research,"[15] and the *SIL FieldWorks Data Notebook*.[16] Note that there are a few works dedicated to ethnography *and* arts.[17]

For our purposes, we list several important anthropological concepts and research questions to stimulate your thoughts. Remember, we're still in Conversation 1: Meet a Community and Its Arts, and we're taking First Glances. These categories and questions are just to stimulate your thoughts, open your minds to ways you and the people around you might live and think. In Conversation 4C, we extend these ethnographic categories to those most related to how artistry works in a community.

Language in Its Sociocultural Context

> In what contexts do people use different languages or types of language?
>
> How do people use silence in their communication?
>
> What value do people place on different types of speech?

Material Culture and Economics

> How do people use and value objects?
>
> How do people produce, distribute, and use goods and services?
>
> How is labor distributed among genders, classes, and ages?

Kinship

> How do people describe their relationships to other people in their community? What are the named categories for blood relatives?
>
> How do people describe their relationships to their ancestors?
>
> What social obligations are associated with each kind of relationship?

---

12 McKinney, *Globetrotting in Sandals*.

13 Ferraro and Andreatta, *Cultural Anthropology*.

14 "Human Relations Area Files" (http://hraf.yale.edu), especially their ethnographic collections (http://ehrafworldcultures.yale.edu) and Outline of Cultural Materials (http://ehrafworldcultures.yale.edu/subjects).

15 Ember and Ember, "Basic Guide to Cross-Cultural Research" (http://hraf.yale.edu/cross-cultural-research/basic-guide-to-cross-cultural-research).

16 See https://software.sil.org/fieldworks/.

17 Some works that integrate information about ethnography and the arts: Krüger, *Ethnography in the Performing Arts*; Ferro and Poveda, *Arts and Ethnography*; and Goopy and Kassan, *Arts-Based Engagement Ethnography*.

Marriage and Family

How do people define the social union between men and women that results in children? How many men and women are involved, and what behaviors define the relationships between each? Who can marry whom in the community? Where do married partners live?

What constitutes a household?

How do households relate to extended family?

Social Organization

What roles do gender, age, kinship, locality, and shared interests play in organizing social groups?

How are social groups ranked by status?

How do people enter or exit groups?

Power Relationships

How does a community organize itself politically and relate to government structures?

How much power does each smaller group hold?

How do individuals and groups exert, gain, or lose power?

How is power displayed in this group?

Who influences decisions behind the scenes?

What has been the group's history in terms of autonomy and subordination with other communities? With expatriates?

Religion

What sorts of supernatural beings do people talk about or relate to? Do these include ancestral, nature, human, or supreme spirits?

What rituals does the community perform regularly, and for what reasons?

How do people use and control supernatural power?

Worldview and Values

How do people categorize reality, and what attributes does it have?

How can people know what is true about reality?

What do people say they think is important? How does people's allocation of time and resources show what they think is important?

PREPARE TO USE RESEARCH METHODS

Many of the activities we guide you through in this manual require basic research skills. We briefly introduce here some of the most important methods: participant observation, interview, note-taking, audio and video recording, photography, and library research. There are an increasing number of electronic and other tools to aid you in performing these research activities. See the Digital Library for examples (www.clatmanual.com), and do your own research for additional resources. Here's one essential piece of advice: no matter which of these methods or tools you use, especially if it involves equipment, learn to use it before it matters. Practice using a smartphone app, camera, video camera, audio recording device, even writing in a notebook before you need it to capture data. You will thank us if you do.

Also, remember that relationships are foundational to research. And relationships based in love will involve learning about someone else, learning about yourself, and giving of yourself. Your context will determine how formal or informal your activities will be. In all cases, though: people are not containers of knowledge, but human beings God created in his image (including you).

Participant Observation: Learn by Watching while Doing

Participant observation requires moving back and forth between observing and participating, often integrating both into learning activities. For an arts researcher, it might include activities such as: painting, playing an instrument, dancing, taking part in a drama, learning to tell stories properly, watching someone construct a building. In a participant observation model of fieldwork, the researcher lives in a community for an extended period to learn something about how that community functions.

For the arts researcher, participant observation often includes becoming a student of a master artist in the community or joining a group devoted to an art form. Learning to perform and create gives the researcher an entry into understanding the artistic system, the artists themselves, and the place of the arts in the community. This deep involvement also communicates respect and love. Though it has been a part of research for many years, participant observation became widely popular in the late nineteenth and early twentieth centuries, concurrent with the development of the field of anthropology. American anthropologist Franz Boas and his students employed participant observation techniques in their fieldwork. Ethnomusicologist Mantle Hood stressed the importance of acquiring *bi-musicality*—learning about a musical tradition by becoming a part of it.[18] Many ethnomusicologists now consider bi-musicality and participant observation as commonsense approaches to fieldwork.

Participant observation in fieldwork is rarely neat and tidy, however. Becoming a part of a community means adjusting to the stresses and expectations of daily living. The researcher must be flexible and willing to abide by the schedule offered by local teachers and guides. Going with the flow

---

18 Hood, "The Challenge of Bi-Musicality."

and following people where they want to take you is a crucial, yet frequently frustrating, part of fieldwork. Dance scholar Felicia Hughes-Freeland describes participant observation as "determined by a process of planning and intention, which is disrupted by accidents and enhanced by serendipity."[19] Participant observation often yields the most satisfying results when the researcher can spend long periods of time in the field location.

As relationships deepen and develop, community members will share more information. Trust is crucial in the participant observation relationship. Researchers must be committed to being wise stewards of the information they are given, abiding by all proper ethical expectations.

Learning an Art Foreign to You: Learn by Doing

One of the most fruitful and enjoyable kinds of participation in our work is learning a new art form. Putting yourself in a nonexpert role like this helps you build relationships with people, yields insights into multiple aspects of a community, and participating in this new form increases your understanding of the characteristics of the art you're studying.

> I was trying in vain to understand how all the percussion instruments worked together in a Cameroonian dance group. At one of their rehearsals, I played the simplest instrument—the shaker—and moved around the circle with the rest of the dancers. Somehow in the middle of that dance I noticed how one of the men was playing the wooden slit drum, and everything became clear. "Ahhhh! So my foot moves to the right when the shaker goes down and the slit drum hits a repeated pattern." Participating with artists can lead to many insights. —Brian Schrag

Becoming an expert in all the skills, symbolism, and social patterns of most art forms is likely beyond your capacity; artistic communication is complex, as attested by all the research activities we describe in Conversation 4 and the *CLAT Companion*. Each of us, however, can gain something. This may include learning the appropriate ways to show appreciation during an enactment, how to play an instrument, how to sing a song or do a dance, or how to carve a mask. Your research activities in Conversation 4 will give you more ideas of what to learn.

When you decide you want to learn some aspect of an art form, you can enter an existing social context, devise your own system of learning, or a combination. If you want to learn like people in the community learn, first find out how that happens (see "Transmission and Change" in Conversation 4, Part C). Then you can decide whether it fits your life. Local educational systems can range from informal watching to high-expectation apprenticeships. If you decide to figure out your own learning system, here are some things to keep in mind:

---

19 Hughes-Freeland, "Dance on Film," 120.

- Find out who in the community is best at the part of the art form you'd like to learn. It may be that one person knows all the songs associated with a social dance, for example, but is not a respected dancer. Ask a friend or two for advice on how to approach your potential teacher, and whether and how it would be appropriate to compensate them.
- Reflect on your own learning style(s) and plan your activities accordingly. One or more of these types might apply to you:[20]
  - ◊ Relational learner: Wants to relate to people, have variety, and help others develop.
  - ◊ Analytical learner: Enjoys working independently and integrating data into theoretical models and solving problems.
  - ◊ Structured learner: Prefers a systematic and organized approach to learning, a chance to apply concepts in a practical way and have hands-on activities and practical solutions.
  - ◊ Energetic learner: Likes lots of activity and chances to do things with people; lots of variety, adventure, and risk; personal involvement in activities; and hands-on activities.
- Watch, imitate, and practice what you want to learn. You may want to audio or video record an enactment so you can review it as many times as you want privately. You can also use the recordings for memorization or analysis, transcribing texts, melodies, and movements.

Interview: Learn by Asking

One of the most important aspects of your fieldwork is the relationships you build with other people in your host community. You may be adopted into a family, and neighbors may provide for your daily needs. Obviously, it is difficult to learn much about any of the arts without talking to people and asking questions about what you see around you. Casual discussions can lead to profound insights.

Sometimes, however, you need to ask questions intentionally, with particular purposes. When you formally arrange to talk with someone about their expressive arts, you are engaging in ethnographic interviewing. Asking questions in culturally appropriate ways, and that result in the kinds of information you need is a craft you can learn. Despite the formality, think of the interview primarily as a friendly conversation in which you learn what's important to someone in the community.

Primary benefits
- Information gathering: Biographical information; descriptions of events or objects; emotional, ideological, critical, and other responses to artistry.

---

20 Johnston and Orwig, "Your Learning Style."

- Clarification: Confirm or correct information you have previously gathered, or conclusions based on other fieldwork.
- Comparison: Learn the different perspectives various people might have about the same events or objects. What do the differences tell you?

Elements of ethnographic interviews[21]

First, remember that we ask questions of people out of love for them, respecting who they are, not in some cold, detached way.

Preparation. Purposeful interviews require forethought in several areas:

- Ask a friend in the community what's important to ask, how to ask questions, or whether it is appropriate to ask questions at all.
- As much as possible, connect broad questions with actual items or events. This may mean bringing a sculpture, photo, or video recording to ground your conversation in reality and provide fodder for discussion.
- It may be helpful to have recordings ready to play or objects to stimulate thoughtful comments about or reactions. If you later present your interview as part of your field research, consider whether including recorded documentation could clarify the context of the interview.
- Record the interview if the interviewee is willing and your context requires it, and if they can give verbal or written agreement. Practice with any recording equipment you will use.
- Your discussion will be a combination of the kinds of things you've already noticed or have interest in, and following the subjects that your partner introduces or finds important. So create a set of questions you can draw on if necessary, to help guide the interview toward the areas you want to learn about. You probably won't use all the questions, or that order, but it can help to think about where the interview might go.

Questions. It's helpful to think of two types of questions and their uses.

- **Open questions** invite dialogue and present multiple avenues for the participant to explore. These are good for finding out what is important, what the person cares about and knows, what ultimately will be important for success. Examples of open questions include "What are some ways that you prepare for an event?"[22] "What are some other events where people tell this story?" "Please explain what it means to …" Other excellent questions allow insiders to guide your interviews of *other* insiders: Who else should I ask about this? What questions should I ask him or her?
- **Closed questions** allow for a limited set of responses and often stop conversations, so you should only use them for a few specific purposes. They are good for things like getting names of people, numbers, facts, yes/no answers, and as set ups for open questions.

---

21 For expansions of some of these ideas, see Spradley, *The Ethnographic Interview*, 55–68; for arts-specific questions, see Frost's "Questions to Find Arts" in the *CLAT Companion*.

22 That is, "enactment." Use a local equivalent when possible.

Framing the Interview. At the beginning, tell the interviewee about the purpose of the interview, the recording equipment you'll be using, the kinds of questions you'll ask, and how you hope to use the information learned during the interview. Before or after the interview, have the interviewee record a statement or sign a form giving permission to use the interview and the information for your research project. See example permission forms in the Digital Library at www.clatmanual.com.

Miscellaneous Advice. Depending on what's appropriate to your situation: Do background research from published sources; make an appointment; ask follow-up questions; do not interrupt—silence is OK; write a thank you note; plan a follow-up interview; provide snacks or other food, time for breaks; restate what the interviewee has said, which will clarify that you understand and give the interviewee the opportunity to say more or to correct you.

Ethnographic interviews with groups of people are sometimes preferable to those with individuals. Your questions can spark discussion among the participants that unearths information and issues you had never thought of. We have successfully used group interviews to discover genres of artistic communication in a community, identify and agree on community goals, and explore the meanings of an event. Be aware, though, of social dynamics in group settings—sometimes group members will defer to a respected or authoritative leader, leaving you with just the leader's opinion. You may want to become familiar with participatory methods we list in Figure 2.1: A few participatory methods (Conversation 2).

Note-Taking: Learn by Writing

Writing down what you observe and learn forces you to make your impressions clearer and provides a durable record you can refer to later. Two types of notes are especially helpful, and lead to a fruitful approach to analysis:[23]

Jottings: Initial condensed account

- Done on the spot, immediately after or during the event.
- Write short descriptions and keywords and phrases to help you remember the details for later write-up.
- Do not let jotting become offensive or distract you from observing. Initial impressions are very valuable.

Notes: Expanded account

This is a more descriptive account, when you have more time to write and are away from the event. These can be handwritten, typed, or dictated, and the writer is aware of her own perspective, biases, and interpretations.

When writing initial fieldnotes, keep in mind two principles:

- **The verbatim principle.** Record everything in the exact words used by the person you're talking with.

---

[23] From Spradley, *Participant Observation*, 63–72; and Myers, "Fieldwork," 38–41.

◊ Write: "You have to swallow the beat to play that shaker."

◊ Not: "Your rhythm was not consistent."

- **The concrete principle.** Use concrete language.

    ◊ Write: "She looked out the window of the truck and started to take sharp, rapid breaths. After about a minute, she leaned her head back, made a high-pitched, loud, prolonged sound without recognizable words that dropped rapidly in pitch. Tears began to flow, and she soon repeated the vocalization."

    ◊ Not: "She began wailing."

Coding and Analysis: Processing fieldnotes

Read your fieldnotes. Look for threads that identify larger themes. A cultural theme is any principle that recurs in several domains and defines relationships among sets of meanings.[24] Yale's *Outline of Cultural Materials* provides a huge number of possible themes.[25]

- When you think you've found a theme, choose a short word or abbreviation to identify it.
- Do this after you have observed, interviewed, and written quite a lot.
- Look for patterns (e.g., food and warfare).
- You can also code or write about subjects in your fieldnotes when you start to venture and test hypotheses.

We recommend coding software such as ATLAS.ti, Taguette, MAXQDA, NVIVO, or others to save time and reveal themes you might otherwise miss.[26] Analysis of video and audio recordings may benefit from coding programs such as ELAN.[27] While these are the premiere programs available at the time of this publication, more apps for ethnography and fieldwork are being developed all the time, so do your own research for tools that suit your context.

Audio and Video Recording: Learn by Reducing Life to Media

"A picture is worth a thousand words." For the fieldworker this is especially true. Verbal description will never show people what the music sounds like or what the dances look like. Audio and video recording is an important part of every fieldworker's skills.

---

24 See Spradley, *Participant Observation*, 141.

25 Yale's *Outline of Cultural Materials* can be found here in PDF form: https://bit.ly/3yxo7QJ.

26 As of this publication, some other programs include Informer, Quirkos, Hubspot, Dedoose, Qualtrics, Visao, Netsuite, Raven's Eye, Toucan, Grow, Free QDA, Connected Text, Cluvio, Square Feedback, QDA Miner Lite (list provided by Steve Walter). For more information on apps and ethnography, see Collins, "Ethnographic Apps/Apps as Ethnography."

27 See a description of ELAN and how to download it at https://archive.mpi.nl/tla/elan.

History of recording

Documentation of audio and visual data is nearly essential in any field project, and the history of ethnomusicology fieldwork is intimately connected with such documentation. Some of the most iconic photographs of early ethnomusicological fieldwork include ethnomusicologists, such as Frances Densmore, using audio recording equipment.[28] Audio recording and playback began with Thomas Edison's phonograph cylinder in 1877—coinciding with the beginnings of modern anthropology. Audio recording technology progressed from wax cylinders to magnetic tape, and now to digital recording.

The possibility of recording video and audio together developed more recently, in the second half of the twentieth century. Many fieldworkers feel that audio-only documentation is not complete enough; a high value is placed on being able to *see* the artistic enactment (or even an interview), rather than just hearing it. This is especially true of enactments in which movement or dance is a significant element. It is also instructive to be able to see instrumental performing techniques, facial expressions while singing, and body language.

Choosing recording equipment

The pace of change in recording technology makes it impossible to suggest products in a printed manual like this. In addition, smartphones and other mobile devices often include everything you need, are becoming more and more accessible, and provide a gateway to solutions on the internet. When you need more specialized equipment—for example, if you are setting up a recording studio or filming a professional documentary—explore what others in your area are doing or draw on networks like the Global Ethnodoxology Network. Whatever methods or equipment you use, practice using them *before* you need them for essential work.

Purposes for a recording event

Your purpose in reducing live, human activities to static media will determine how you go about it. We present here four common purposes and their implications for how you record: ethnographic analysis, form analysis, preservation, and production for distribution. The purpose for recording will influence how you record. If you want to get a record of an enactment that allows you to later research the meanings of any or all its elements through ethnographic analysis, then you should capture everything that happens. This means that you will do as much continuous recording of an event containing artistry as possible, including non-artistic sounds like chickens and babies. See **Integral recording** in the Glossary.

If, on the other hand, you have a particular analytical interest—you'd like to figure out the melody of a particular song, or understand how weight shifts in a dance movement, for example—then you will isolate these elements from a normal enactment. Benefits of recording sound and visuals in the field is the ability to go back later and look more closely at what happened. Playback

---

[28] See this photo of a 1916 listening session with Frances Densmore and Chief of the Montana Blackfeet: https://bit.ly/4au8M0p.

on a computer allows slowing down the speed of a musical performance and freeze-framing video recordings. This can lead to more accurate description. Recordings also make comparative study easier. Different recordings of the same song, for example, can show where stylistic variation is acceptable. See **Analytical recording** in the Glossary.

The value of audiovisual recording is not limited to your own needs, but also for preservation. With many of the world's indigenous traditions in decline, this documentation may soon be all that exists to show the variety of creative expression. Many—if not all—of your recordings should be properly archived in local, national, and international collections, with performers' permissions for nonprofit and research uses. Future generations and interested researchers will then have access to them. Many archives have high standards for items they accept. Get the best equipment you can afford so you can maintain a high quality of recordings for preservation.

Finally, the community you're working with may want to be the ones holding and controlling recording devices, which can reveal what they see as most important. They also may want to create products from recordings of their arts for sale or distribution. Rely on local skills and technology for this as much as possible.

Other purposes of recordings include helping you learn to perform something or documenting a process, like making an instrument or weaving fabric. You can modify how you design recording events according to each need.

Documenting recordings

A recording without accompanying contextual information has extremely limited usefulness because you will eventually forget what's on it. It is essential, then, to create several kinds of metadata—data about the recording—as you go along. Follow this procedure as much as you can, including as much information as you know at the time:

- Speak onto the medium: If you are working with audio, record "This is *your name*, recording *so-and-so person*, at *such-and-such place*, on *such-and-such day*."

- Make sure metadata associated with the recording is thoroughly documented on the recording itself and in your field notes.

- Write in your field notes: code for the recorded item, date, place, name of the event, participants, types of artistry, community(ies) involved, audience description (size, make-up), context, purpose of event, possible ethical considerations for future use of the recording of the event.

Your notes should have a clear coding system of correspondence with the recorded media and its metadata. Your system may simply consist of the year and recording number. For example, "2025–23" would refer to the twenty-third recording you made in 2025.

Planning a recording opportunity

- Discuss the event with whoever's in charge—figure out permissions, payment, etc.
- Ask someone familiar with the type of event you're interested in what is likely to happen.
- Step through as much of the whole event you've learned about in your mind, writing down what you hope to do.
- Choose, prepare, test your equipment, then test it again.
- Bring backup equipment and batteries.
- Prepare for equipment failure, batteries dying, electricity going out, hurricanes, etc.
- Arrange mechanisms for recording metadata—notebook and pen or pencil always work, and you can back up these physical copies by transcribing or taking pictures of them.
- Prepare permission forms or an audio or video recording of authorization (see "Sample Permission Form" in the Digital Library at www.clatmanual.com).

Photography: Learn by Reducing Life to Still Images

Still photographs freeze an object or scene into a two-dimensional image at a precise moment in time. As in each of these research methods, subjects must give you permission to take photographs of them.

Purposes for photography

Pictures can enrich the research process in many ways, including these:

- Document the existence of kinds of objects, like masks, regalia, props, instruments, paintings, house adornments, ritual aids, and representations of supernatural beings. These could be representations of entire objects in use or in an analytical context.
- Reveal details of objects, especially using multiple shots of the same object from different angles. These can lead to insights into construction, coloring, textures, and other features.
- Document artists, their families, and other community members enacting arts and in everyday life. Photos provide an excellent channel for reciprocity: you take pictures, then give copies back to the subjects.
- Encourage community members to take pictures to tell their stories and document the things about an enactment that are important to them.
- Ask someone to document your presence and activities in the community by photographing you in action.
- Express your own creative impressions of artistry, as a fun exploration.

A few tips for photography

- Becoming a photographer with professional skills usually takes training, expensive equipment, and technical and aesthetic gifts. If this describes you, then go take some pictures. For the rest of us, here are a few bits of advice about taking pictures. Remember, though, that you may need to change this advice depending on the purposes of the photographs.
- Your basic kit: a camera or smartphone, a tripod or monopod, extra batteries, extra lenses if you have them, camera use instructions. Have one or two backup ways to take photos. You may have a fancy camera, but if it stops working (and it will), cheap and lower quality is better than nothing.
- Make sure that the primary element you want to capture is visible and in a prominent place. Many people think that important elements should be off center, and they use the Rule of Thirds (see Glossary). If you can control the focus on your camera, make anything in front of or behind the object be slightly out of focus.
- Make sure that the light reveals what you think is important. Specially make sure that there is no light shining toward you from behind your subject. Force your flash to flash if there is light behind.
- Frame your picture by putting a bit of a wall, tree, or other object at the edge of what the camera captures.
- Keep your horizon lines (e.g., ocean, land) straight.
- Archive your pictures in different places and on different media to be sure that you will not lose them.

Published Sources: Learn from Others

Somebody has probably already written or filmed or recorded something about the community you are working with or a similar group. If so, you may benefit greatly from their experiences and insights.

We use the term *publish* here to refer to anything someone puts into an enduring medium to communicate to an audience beyond one or two people. These could include books, theses, dissertations, articles, films, newsletters, and audio and video recordings. The people who produce these resources could be part of scholarly communities or cultural groups, or they could be individuals like travelers, journalists, or missionaries. You'll find resources in libraries, archives, bookstores, people's personal bookshelves, and on the internet. University libraries, archives, and bookstores in the location of the community often prove a rich source of relevant documents found nowhere else in the world. As with anything you hear or learn, make sure you evaluate these resources in terms of the purposes and credentials of the people who produce them.

Love and Law

We want all our interactions with people to be guided and marked by love. This means that when we're researching a community, we are humble, want the best for them, and don't promote ourselves or our agendas at their expense. So explain your actions and their purposes to your friends and respond to any concerns they may have. In many situations, it will be appropriate—sometimes also legally necessary—to let them sign an authorization form like the samples in the Digital Library (www.clatmanual.com). Sometimes such forms can increase distrust if your relationship with the performers is not well established. In this case, discuss your needs (e.g., to an archive or publisher) with friends knowledgeable of local customs and come up with a respectful solution. Finally, whatever you take, find a way to generously give something back for it. An excellent way to start is to give copies of photographs, videos, and audio recordings to the subjects of your research. The best thing you can do to perform loving research is to be trustworthy, dependable, generous, respectful, humble, and concerned to build relationships that will last into Heaven.

CELEBRATE A COMMUNITY'S ARTS FROM THE START

The overall arc of this manual is to stir up creativity in local forms that meet community goals. But we start with the premise that all people reflect God's image: who they are and what they do now are also inherently valuable. So as you work with a community to document their existing arts, celebrate them. The activities "Publish Recordings and Research in Various Forms and Contexts" and "Help Develop Multimedia Collections of Local Arts" (Conversation 5) are great ways to start.

Our last word to you in this discussion of meeting the community is simply this: keep learning. Nurture your curiosity so you can continue showing this powerful sign of love.

CONVERSATION 2

SPECIFY KINGDOM GOALS

In Cambodia during the 1970s, under Pol Pot and the Khmer Rouge, some of the first people who were taken, tortured, and murdered were the creative people who carried the story and the heartbeat of the land. Even instruments were destroyed during this time, and ultimately an estimated total of 1.7 million deaths resulted from Khmer Rouge policies. Cambodian Christian Arts Ministry School (CCAMS) was started by Noren (a survivor of the Pol Pot regime), and an American lady, Gioia. Former street kids, gang members, orphans, and children being used in slavery and prostitution are rescued into a loving home where they are loved, fed, sheltered, and educated. Alongside its regular schooling, the CCAMS family has an emphasis on the arts (music, dance, drama, visual art, and literature). By teaching the children at CCAMS the arts, they not only give the children incredible skills and a means to express their emotions, they are also restoring something that was stolen from the nation and putting God at the center of it.

    The Ling family could see no other way to survive than to sell their children into modern slavery. But Noren met them at this crucial time and took the children into CCAMS, where they have flourished. One girl became their lead dancer and, together with her sister, earned enough money performing to help their parents build a house in their home village and farm the land successfully. The mother makes many of the beautiful costumes for the children of CCAMS while another sister teaches them to dance. All the Ling family are now Christians, and as others hear of their story they are marveling at the story of God in their transformed lives.   —*Martin and Rebekah Neil*

Many of us experience little visceral anticipation of Heaven because we've never wholeheartedly tried to grasp its astounding richness and complexity. Every good thing we experience on Earth points to something infinitely more satisfying in Heaven. These earthly signs of Heaven are mere glimpses, whiffs, hints, brushes, whispers of that reality. In fact, our story has an even more astounding final step: the New Creation.

Each Kingdom Goal will be gloriously fulfilled when Jesus recreates the universe without sin, as it was in the first creation: "This former wasteland has become like the garden of Eden" (Ezek 36:35 NLT). Consider these Scriptures: "I saw a new Heaven and a new Earth" (Rev 21:1); "I am making everything new" (Rev 21:5); "… the creation looks forward to the day when it will join God's children in glorious freedom from death and decay" (Rom 8:21 NLT); "In keeping with his promise we are looking forward to a new Heaven and a new Earth, where righteousness dwells" (2 Pet 3:13). "How are the dead raised? With what kind of body will they come? … We will not all sleep, but we will all be changed—in a flash, in the twinkling of an eye, at the last trumpet. For the trumpet will sound, the dead will be raised imperishable, and we will be changed. For the perishable must clothe itself with the imperishable, and the mortal with immortality" (1 Cor 15:35, 51–53).

A BRIEF HISTORY OF ETERNITY

Recognition of our place in God's cosmic narrative helps explain what kinds of fruit our efforts may bear. We're using *signs of Heaven* and *signs of the Kingdom* as convenient pointers to this deeper reality: Jesus will recreate everything with the utter absence of sin.

First, before anything, Father|Son|Spirit existed in relationship somehow in ways impossible for us to fathom. Here is one way to express the narrative of God's interaction with us, beginning with creation:[1]

1. **Creation.** Father|Son|Spirit creates the universe, including God-reflecting man and woman in the garden of Eden. God is with humans, in perfect relationship.
2. **Fall.** Adam and Eve sin, corrupting the entire universe.
3. **Waiting.** Sin thrives and humans retain diminished Imago Dei. God forges a special relationship with Israel, a nation meant to embody shalom, be a light to the nations. Israel repeatedly rebels.
4. **Jesus's First Coming.** Jesus physically enters the human mess as a zygote in Mary's womb. His birth, ministry, death, resurrection, and ascension destroy sin in a fundamental way. Jesus mentors, equips, and sends his followers—who become the church—to extend his Kingdom through God's leading. This leaves incomplete bits of the New Creation on Earth that Jesus will bring to fruition when he re-creates the universe at the end of time.
5. **Now and not-yet.** We are in the *now and not-yet* period of the Kingdom of God, the New Creation.

---

[1] Others also argue for the clarity and guidance gained by learning where we fit in the grand Christian story, with similar acts or parts. See, for example, Michael Vlach, *New Creation Model*, 399, and Wright, "How Can the Bible," 7–32.

Specify Kingdom Goals

  a. Jesus provided a way for people to enter the Kingdom and remove parts of creation's groaning.
  b. Jesus inaugurated and energized the Kingdom of Heaven's growth.
  c. The church—Jesus's followers (and others, because of Imago Dei and common grace)—with Father|Son|Spirit instill more Heaven on Earth in many ways. This includes embodying and communicating Heaven (good news) through incredibly diverse artistry.
  d. Sin is in its death throes because of Jesus's death and resurrection, so Satan is active in resisting the spread of Heaven on Earth.
6. **Jesus's Second Coming.** Jesus returns, recreates the universe without sin.
7. **New Creation.** Through Christ, humans live, thrive, become more and more like God in the New Creation forever.

We live and work in the *now and not-yet* phase of Heaven on Earth. This means that we can know and increase Heaven in partnership with God, but the corruption of sin still undermines our efforts. "The creation will be made new from the old, just as happened to Jesus. Resurrection is a vision for both Jesus and creation."[2] Happily, we can nurture rock-solid hope in future unhampered relationships with God.

Our goal in Conversation 2 is to stir your imagination in ways that release aromas of the Kingdom of Heaven, awakening your hunger for the New Creation. You'll then be more able to inspire that same hunger in the communities you're working with.

Consider the poetic explorations of laughter, your body, senses, worship, freedom from trafficking and mental illness, and other realities in Heaven and the New Creation at www.firstmomentsinheaven.org. For a taste, here is the beginning of a poem I wrote titled "God":

> Soul, I think that when you first get to Heaven, you'll immerse yourself in Trinity. The all-pervasive Person of Father|Son|Spirit, moments of utter contentment, trust, love rushing in and round you, scared at first then tentatively soaking in the complete resolution, satisfaction, peace that flows from him. Maybe still not really believing that his all-encompassing love includes you! All of you: every toe, neuron, gift, prayer you said and tried to listen for a response to—He's all there! Hugging, rushing, flying certainty that *it's all right!*

We must also, however, emphasize the *now and not-yet* nature of these signs of Heaven, recognizing that none will flourish completely until God institutes his perfect realm, the New Creation. The expansion of the Kingdom often takes us into enemy territory (e.g., see Luke 10:1–18), so there will be significant

---

2 Wright, "What Is God's Future?" N. T. Wright develops a detailed description of this view in *Surprised by Hope* and a convincing summary in the video, "N. T. Wright on the Future of the World."

obstacles along the way. Reflect on these two broad questions to get a foretaste of the fruit Conversation 2 produces:

> Jesus taught us to pray, "Your Kingdom come, your will be done, on Earth as it is in Heaven" (Matt 6:10). What's one way a community you know *already* looks like Heaven?
>
> What goals does *this* community have to become *more* like Heaven?

We've put extended discussions and examples of the signs of Heaven first, so communities will have fuller understandings of the universal reach of "your Kingdom come, your will be done on Earth as it is in Heaven." The second major section of Conversation 2 guides you through processes a community can follow to identify the Kingdom Goals they want to work toward. Community members might also decide to switch the order of these two exercises or integrate them into one longer process.

In the broader CLAT process, we want enacted artistry to have effects that result in signs of Heaven. Conversation 3 helps communities formulate initial plans that flesh out channels linking Earth and Heaven. Conversations 4, 5, 6, and 7 provides resources to refine, reimagine, and change these plans when necessary.

REAL LIFE CLAT

We've seen several complexities in how we answer these questions. For example, because of low community-esteem or worldview patterns, some communities have a difficult time imagining better futures for themselves. This may mean the process needs to take place informally over a long period of listening and discussion.

Other complications arise related to aspects we've included in our definition of communities: they are internally complex and always changing. As we discussed in Conversation 1, identifying a static, simple thing we call *the community* in the CLAT process is impossible. Which individuals should be involved and what subgroups do they represent? What role(s) should an arts advocate play in deciding who to gather to make decisions? How do personal relationships or organizational requirements affect who chooses a Kingdom Goal?

We emphasize that the community should make decisions and perform as many aspects of the CLAT process as possible. This follows Jesus's model of incarnation and learning in ministry. Practically, such an approach makes it more likely that communities will use their arts to increase characteristics of Heaven now and into the future. Who chooses the Kingdom Goal? The community.

In real life, however, many people influence what happens. Community members and friends all have different features and degrees of insiderness and outsiderness, varying goals and agendas, and unequal capacities to be involved in a process like CLAT.

Personally, I have a particular interest and calling to encourage creativity among people in society's margins, and to inject energy into cultural elements disappearing due to globalization, urbanization, mediazation, incomplete theologies, or other dynamics. In my Mono story in the **Introduction**, for example: *I* asked the church leaders to meet, *I* chose the Scripture passages to study, *I* asked whether Punayima could be involved in teaching *gbaguru* to Protestant church members, *I* commissioned new Scripture-based *gbaguru* songs, and *I* lent whatever cultural capital I had as a white, relatively rich missionary to this innovation. But they increasingly grabbed hold of *gbaguru*-for-Christian purposes, expanding into other villages, adding new genres, and innovating enactment formats, owning the movement more and more. Each context is different, so remember to treat this as a *flexible* guide.

CATEGORIES OF KINGDOM GOALS

Jesus's recreation of everything at the end of time will result in a material reality (1 Cor 15:35–55) and fully functioning societies (Rev 7:9–10; 21:24, 26) unmarred by sin. If we are created in the image and likeness of God, then whatever good, true, or beautiful things we can say about humanity or creation we can also say of God exponentially. "God is the beauty of creation and humanity multiplied to the infinite power."[3] We want to imagine better futures that reach as far and wide into the New Creation as God allows.

The Hebrew word *shalom* describes a community marked by the "as it is in Heaven" bits in this section. Jesus entered human society so that his followers would be able to live life to the fullest (John 10:10) and have peace (John 14:27). Shalom captures much of what he promised: a state of peace, completeness, social harmony, justice, and health. Bryant Myers suggests that the "vision of a shalom that leads to life in its fullness is a powerful image that must inform and shape our understanding of any better human future"[4]—a future that begins now.[5]

Flowing from these spiritual realities, we present six broad, biblically based categories of goals that could indicate that the Kingdom of Heaven is thriving in a community: identity and sustainability, healing, justice, Scripture, church life, and personal spiritual life. In each category we briefly describe some specific objectives that a community could adopt, explain how local arts might help meet them, and give a few real-life glimpses of these goals fulfilled.

The forces arrayed against shalom are formidable: war, natural disasters, sexual exploitation, disease, slavery, hunger, and thirst. A community marked by the Kingdom of Heaven responds to these groanings of creation with healing and restoration. Artistic activity plays crucial roles in increasing shalom because it can point suffering people to hope, instill solidarity within a community, and aid emotional and physical healing.

---

3 Rohr, *Falling Upward*, 110.

4 Myers, *Walking with the Poor*, 51.

5 Note the significant overlap between these signs of Heaven and the concrete, gritty stories recounted by contributors to Lauren da Silva's *On Earth as It Is in Heaven*. The publisher describes this book as "a collection of the dreams and visions heart-centered women have for a better world and the things they're doing to make them a reality."

A TOOL FOR UNDERSTANDING THE VARIETY OF KINGDOM GOALS

Time permitting, exploring these categories will aid people to think more broadly in choosing goals to nudge their community(ies) to be more like Heaven. Here's one way to do this, using the subcategories below: Valuing Identity; Teaching Children; Using Media; Well-being; Reconciliation; Rest and Play; Creation Care; Social Justice; Education; Literacy; Economic Opportunity; Translating Scripture; Oral Scripture; Corporate Worship; Studying and Remembering Scripture; Christian Rites; Witness; Prayer and Meditation; Spiritual Formation; Personal Bible Study; Applying Scripture.

For each subcategory:

1. Read all the associated text. Read the summary statement, like this, for Education: "Where the Kingdom of Heaven thrives, community members learn what they need to succeed in and contribute to their societies."

2. Answer these questions:
   a. What is one example of how this sign of Heaven **might be true** in our community?
   b. What is one example of how this sign of Heaven **might not be true** in our community?

This can be done as individuals, small groups of two or three, or the whole group. You can write ideas on a black or whiteboard, on pieces of paper, or just trust your discussion to memory. This exercise is not meant to feed directly into the Methods to Specify Kingdom Goals below. Rather, it will increase the number and kinds of possible Heaven glimpses in the background of their minds.

Here are the six broad categories of Kingdom Goals, each with a few specific expressions of those goals for communities to consider.

IDENTITY AND SUSTAINABILITY

Valuing Identity

Where the Kingdom of Heaven thrives, communities value their culture.
"God created people in his own image" (Gen 1:27 NLT). Not only does every man and woman reflect God's image, but the cultures they form will continue into eternity: "a great multitude that no one could count, from every nation, tribe, people and language" (Rev 7:9) will stand before God's throne. Until Jesus's ultimate reign in the future, of course, cultures show evidence of both God's image and the brokenness and sin that exist. But it is a right, healthy, and holy thing for people to value the good aspects of their societies. In many places, however, minority groups think more highly of other people than they think of themselves, and so denigrate the usefulness, beauty, or intrinsic value of their own culture. Sometimes other groups—often more powerful—have

overtly or inadvertently taught this. Missionaries and colonizers are infamous for this, despite Paul's planting the seed of affirming the equal value of each culture (Gal 3:28). The groups we belong to are all susceptible to either self-exaltation or self-rejection; neither reflects truth in the Kingdom of Heaven.

People valuing the good aspects of their societies is right, healthy, and holy. We have seen that the more a community appropriately values its own culture, the more the Kingdom of Heaven is likely to thrive. Further, a community's artistic genres constitute some of the most identifiable and valuable parts of their culture. If community members see no good in their own arts, they will not use them to worship God or communicate truth to each other. We explore ways that a community can affirm its artistic resources and create new works that foster strong, godly cultural identity.

> Among the indigenous groups in the Philippines that I've supported in ethnoarts, one Matigsalug story stands out. The story was six to eight years in the making, beginning with the work of the Holy Spirit through Tano, an encouraging mother tongue Scripture translator who was convinced of the power of arts to move people's hearts. He invited me to conduct a workshop with my outsider voice, which can be heard differently. The community went through quite a transformation. After an initial ethnoarts workshop, the church invited me back three times over the years for further workshops. They began to use their own arts and language more and learned to appreciate the role of culture in understanding and sharing the Gospel.
>
> Their worship now vibrantly displays colorful indigenous dress, enthusiastic traditional movements, and the blended sounds of traditional songs in local language with modern instruments. From child to grandparent, the church connects to God, one another, and their indigenous identity across generations. This transformed church now reaches other indigenous communities with fewer language and cultural barriers to cross. We encourage and celebrate this. We affirm this. We want to provide spaces where communities can freely worship God using expressions that are closest to their hearts. —*Roce Anog Madinger*[6]

> Six open-minded, local believers came together as the first Creating Local Arts Together group in our Central Asian country. We gathered and discussed barriers to people coming to faith in Christ. "In our country," they told us, "Christianity is viewed as the Russian religion. By turning to Christ, you're committing cultural betrayal." The group wanted to show how their church can be "Central Asian and Christian." To do this, they picked a

---

[6] Adapted from Robertson, "Seven Core Values," 11–31.

local instrument that strongly resonates with their identity: a five-foot long horn called the *karnai*, which is used in local wedding receptions to announce the arrival of the bride and groom—and to cue the dancing! There was only one problem: no one in the church knows how to play the *karnai*. Our group persevered with this new idea—they hired three Muslim wedding performers to inaugurate Easter Sunday with two *karnai* and a local drum. The Muslim performers did not object to this unusual morning "gig," and for the first time in the history of that church, they kicked off Easter service with dancing and celebration of the risen Savior in a very local way. —*Ryan and Isla (names changed)*

Teaching Children

Where the Kingdom of Heaven thrives, communities teach their traditions to their children.

One telling sign of the health of a community's identity is how much they pass on good parts of their culture to their children and grandchildren. Identifying patterns of what and how each generation is passing on artistic knowledge to the next will reveal a community's health in this area.

> One South Asian language group faced a rupture in their transmission process. This happens with many cultures desiring a move towards national education. This meant there was no passing on of their traditional culture and values. Children no longer worked the fields during the day or sat with elders in the evenings, where transmission of cultural knowledge usually took place. With this shift, a generation grew into young adults who did not have interest in their own traditional songs and dances. Soon the songs and dances would be lost.
>
> Through a participatory workshop, the generations came together and discussed what traditions they valued and what was slipping away from them. Together the older and younger adults interacted and planned how they would actively pass on their valuable cultural wisdom and art forms.
>
> One approach included older expert musicians and artists teaching in public classes about their art forms and cultural knowledge. Books and other reading materials about the creation process and cultural values were also created. The transmission process that was severed was reconnected through a new creative method within the national education system that initially caused the rupture. —*Mary Beth and Todd Saurman*

Using Media

Where the Kingdom of Heaven thrives, communities may contribute to local, regional, and global recording industries.

People around the world are constantly figuring out new ways to communicate with each other. A community with an appropriately strong sense of its value will have a foundation on which to decide how or if they will share their cultural heritage with the rest of the world. If they choose, they may not only receive and learn artistic communication from others but will also contribute to available artistic resources through recordings of their own arts through local, regional, and global media.

> On a bright, sunny, Sahel day, four university students came to visit John (not his real name) while the newly produced Fula song played from his phone. Intrigued, they were surprised to hear this story song. "Where did you find this? This is our song." They asked more about this prodigal son mentioned in the song, and he invited them to learn more such stories from the Bible. Eventually, they became followers of Jesus and are baptized disciples today. —*David Oluseyi Ige*[7]

> In Azerbaijan, the Tat community passes on cultural traditions through storytelling. Many of the older generation are very skilled in telling oral folk literature in their native language, however they are concerned the younger generation will lose the language and cultural identity of their community.
>
> A group of young people from this community discussed how they could share God's Word with their people, many of whom follow Islam. They commissioned an older recognized storyteller to tell a folk story in their heart language. The young people created a YouTube video of her telling the story and concluded with a short verse from God's Word. They shared the video with their community. This local story in their heart language and folk storytelling style allowed people to feel a sense of belonging to their community and hear truth from God's Word in a local artistic form they enjoyed. —*Ellie Asker*

HEALING

Our *now and not-yet* Earth is full of people who are sick, abused, forced from their homes, tortured, violently attacked, starving, divorced from social stability, and deprived of loving interactions. And in real ways, we all suffer from living in a broken world and need healing. Some organizations are

---

[7] Robertson, 11–31.

producing training and tools[8] that integrate arts into restoration processes, trauma healing—especially contexts of extreme suffering.[9]

Well-being

Where the Kingdom of Heaven thrives, communities respond to physical, social, and emotional challenges in healthy ways.

When God remakes Earth unpolluted by sin, no one will be physically sick (Matt 4:23; Rom 8:22–24; Luke 10:9; Rev 21:4). The emotions we experience will flow from the Spirit's nature, like love, joy, peace, kindness, and patience (Gal 5:22–23; 2 Cor 3:18; Rev 21:4; Rom 8:22–24). And our brains' neuronal networks will always fire in ways consonant with the New Reality, without mental or spiritual illness (Matt 4:24; 8:28; 11:28–29; see also 1 Kgs 19:4; Dan 4:31–32). As recognized anecdotally and confirmed by a bourgeoning body of research, acting artistically improves health.[10]

> For many suffering people, the sixty-eight Psalms that are laments—and in fact the whole book of Lamentations—are a good model of how we can be angry with God and lament what has happened to us. During trauma healing workshops, participants are encouraged to write their own laments to God, including the six parts found in many of the Psalms (address to God, past faithfulness, complaint, plea for help, answer from God, vow to trust). They are also encouraged to set their lament to music in local ethnic traditional forms used at funerals and other sad occasions. —*Margaret Hill*

> One birth-mother's heart rate began soaring beyond control during delivery. The nurses refused my assistance to let her listen to her favorite music, even though I had explained how helpful it would be. Finally, in desperation, they consented. I turned on the *heavy metal music* (the birth-mother's favorite) and immediately her heart rate and the baby's (still in her womb) began dropping and quickly returned to a normal state.
> —*Mary Beth Saurman, music therapist*[11]

---

8 See, for example, Dallas International University's Graduate Certificate in Arts and Trauma Healing (https:// diu.edu/gc-ath), which adds expressive arts to the basic trauma healing approaches provided by the Trauma Healing Institute (https:// traumahealinginstitute.org) and its partners.

9 See, for example, Herman, *Trauma and Recovery*; Langberg, *Suffering*; Mollica, *Healing Invisible Wounds*; Nichols, *The Lost Art of Listening*; Schrag and Rowe, *Community Arts*; Yoder, *Little Book of Trauma Healing*.

10 See, for example, Goldbard, "Art Became the Oxygen"; Chapline and Johnson, "Guide to Community-Engaged Research"; Koch et al., "Effects of Dance Movement Therapy and Dance"; Betuel, "Art Therapy"; Saurman, *Hmong Songs*; Rubin, *Approaches to Art Therapy*; Chaiklin and Wengrower, *Art and Science*; Camlin et al., "Group Singing."

11 Saurman, "The Effect of Music," 2.

Specify Kingdom Goals

> In Benin, I met a community nurse who had realized that singing about health can inspire people to change their behavior. Yerima, the nurse, told me that he started to sing about health issues out of frustration. He had noticed that the women who came to his village's two-room health center for prenatal care paid little attention to his lectures on topics such as nutrition and childhood vaccinations. Yet when he composed and performed songs with the same information, he found that his audience became much more interested, and they sang with him in the common call-and-response form of the region.
>
> Given the threat of a cholera epidemic at the time of my visit, I asked whether he could write a new song to communicate fundamental ideas about water hygiene. Yerima disappeared into the back room while the clinic director gave a lecture on cholera, which received scant attention. Five minutes later, Yerima returned and began to shout that cholera causes diarrhea. The crowd responded with sounds of disgust. Yerima then began to sing, repeating a response line for them: *kolera baradarorwa* (cholera will kill you). Gradually, he began to sing lines of information between the response lines, advising the women to boil their water and urging them to wash their hands and those of their children before eating. In less than ten minutes, a new song had been learned and a new message communicated: simple, fast, effective, memorable. —*Matthew Davis*[12]

> We communicate our messages primarily through music, dance, and drama. Counseling on our site is also done through music and drama. When we organize a play or music, we don't just compose any song or meaningless drama. First we recognize the experiences and needs around us. If we pass along those experiences in drama we find that we help people enormously. We can show a drama demonstrating how younger girls acquire HIV because they want to get rich, to become "smart" at an early age. We can show what happens when women go to witchdoctors instead of testing centers. We can pass along some songs in places where AIDS has hit aggressively. Music is our most powerful tool … for affecting change in Uganda! —*Gregory Barz*[13]

Reconciliation

Where the Kingdom of Heaven thrives, communities reconcile with each other and with outside communities.

Human beings don't get along. We fight, denigrate, mock, disdain, undermine, exploit, deceive, and exclude each other. We justify our sickly outrages through

---

12 Davis, "Health through Song," 36–41.

13 Barz, *Singing for Life*, 168.

appeals to self, ethnicity, class, religion, ideology, and pleasure. But God emptied himself to flood us with a unifying love, a God-human reconciliation that models human-human fellowship. Brittle turns to soft. Furrowed brow turns to open smile. "Everyone will know that you are my disciples, if you love one another" (John 13:35). In the Kingdom of Heaven, there are no lasting human distinctions that put some of us above others (Gal 3:28; Col 3:11; Jas 2:5).

Artistic communication can help us open our arms to each other and feel unity that draws on something deeper than our histories. Singing and dancing together require us to mold our individuality into coordinated sound and movement. The joy, pleasure, and solidarity that arts evoke pull us out of patterns of distrust and lift our eyes from our hurt to transcendent truths. Artistic forms of communication can lead to powerful moments of repentance, forgiveness, solidarity, love, and lasting reconciliation.

> In Sudan, RECONCILE facilitators in trauma healing settings use experiential processes to make the material "come alive" and to give space for the participants to share their insights. One of the activities used, after sharing material and biblical passages on the concept of forgiveness, was to have the multiethnic participants write down situations in which they needed to grant or seek forgiveness on a piece of paper, which they then nailed to a wooden cross. Often the situations they were concerned about involved other ethnicities present at the workshop. They then made a procession together, singing as they marched, and brought the cross to an area where prayers of forgiveness were offered, and it was burned amidst jubilant singing and dancing representing each of the groups who had wounded each other.
> —Debbie Braaksma

> A group of five women, part of a larger community from a church in Northern Virginia, USA, gathered remotely to work through a study by Arrabon called "Race, Class, and the Kingdom of God." Ethnically, the group was African American, Caucasian, Filipina, and Latina, but identified primarily as Black or White. After participating in this study, the group continued to discuss Kingdom Goals related to justice and Scripture for the women in their church. As an intentional reconciling community, they chose to focus their creativity on "shalom" or healing. Their vision for healing extended to areas of personal, church, and global healing. The women decided poetry would communicate shalom with hope, longing, and emotional depth to their primary intended audience. They commissioned an artist who was skilled and knowledgeable in the genre of poetry to write a poem of shalom, reflecting on Isaiah 58:8–12 and Revelation 7:9–10. The newly created poem offers encouragement and hope for women experiencing different forms of suffering. They invited more

women from the wider church community to participate as readers for a poetic performance and recording of the newly created work. This provided the community with an opportunity to experience fellowship together in a new vein outside of the standard Sunday morning worship event. —*Melanie Henderson*[14]

The local churches in our Central Asian country have struggled with unity. Not many people have come to faith, and there is often a spirit of "competition" between these churches that is instigated when people change **churches** during conflict situations. As international workers in this setting, we have sought to become agents of peace, reconciliation, and unity. Over 30 local believers from 14 different churches attended our songwriting conference last Spring. Three women, all worship leaders, and all different nationalities, had been previously estranged from one another by conflict and a relocation. One afternoon, we directed people to spread out and spend a few hours writing new songs to address needs in their communities. As the Holy Spirit moved in these ladies' hearts, they gathered during the afternoon songwriting session, reconciled with one another, and wrote a song together in the Russian language (their shared language) about unity in the body of Christ. As they shared their song with us that evening, we saw clearly how Jesus's words are true for the church in our country: "By this everyone will know that you are my disciples, if you love one another" (John 13:35).
—*Ryan and Isla (names changed)*[15]

Rest and Play

Where the Kingdom of Heaven thrives, communities balance productivity with rest and play.[16]

Foundational to Jewish and Christian faith is the fact that God wants everyone to follow his example of integrating a pattern of rest into work. God created in six days and rested the seventh (Gen 2:2). Isaiah connects restoration and keeping Sabbath to delight (58:12–14). God decreed Sabbath for human benefit (Mark 2:27), Heaven will include rest (Heb 4:1–11), and Jesus offered to give rest to weary people (Matt 11:28). God even wants land to enjoy rest (Lev 26:34). So part of shalom is a satisfying mix of fruitful work, rest, celebration, and play. Artistic forms of communication provide exceptional opportunities for playful restoration: they can contribute to reduced stress, heightened hope, and improved emotional and physical health. The world's communities engage

---

14 You may listen to the recording here: https://youtu.be/DN2WfyJzRks. The video begins with a silent scripture meditation [0:00–0:56] to orient the listener/reader. The poem begins about [0:56].

15 Anthony, "Beautiful, Wonderful Gospel," 34.

16 For further study, consult Buchanan, *The Rest of God*; Heschel, *The Sabbath*; Liponski, *World Sports Encyclopedia*.

in an astounding variety of sporting activities that both display artistry in themselves and are integrated into larger events full of arts.

> Games and sport can energize a community, help develop identity, and transmit cultural values in ways that might not otherwise occur. A prime example of such a game is *castells* (human towers). Castells are found in the Catalonia region of Spain and have been in existence since the eighteenth century, generally occurring during festival times. These human structures are visually impressive, sometimes with ten levels of people standing on each other's shoulders with a supporting base of hundreds of assistants. Variations of these towers not only add to the complexity of the tower and success of the *castell* team but also to the visual beauty. As a nonprofessional sport, participants wear specific clothing to indicate their regional identity, and unique songs are played while the *castells* are being built. UNESCO has recognized the value of the *castell* and placed it on their list of the Intangible Cultural Heritage of Humanity. —Cory Cummins

Creation Care

Where the Kingdom of Heaven thrives, communities live in life-giving environments, interacting with their physical contexts in mutually beneficial ways.

God made all his creation good (Gen 1–2), provides the energy to keep it from falling apart (Col 1:15–20), and will restore all that is now decaying at the end of time (Rom 8:18–21). This includes the earth, animals, oceans, air, plants, and humans. He actively engages with us in counteracting creation's groans. For example, God purified a community's water source (2 Kgs 2:21–22); promised to heal Israel's land as integral to their salvation (2 Chr 7:14); and used his people to reduce suffering caused by a famine (Gen 12:10). He cares about restoring the land (Exod 23:10–12) in ways that benefit the poor (Lev 23:22) and other creatures (Deut 25:4).

A vast number of people in the world—mostly poor—live in environments that make them sick, contain poisons, have unfertile soil, were designed to be temporary, or are increasingly vulnerable to epidemics and natural disasters.[17] People cannot live healthfully in harmful surroundings. Many factors contribute to these situations, including Christians' actions stemming from theological errors.[18] Indonesian businessman and philanthropist Anderson Tanoto believes that leaders in mitigating the perils of climate change must come from emerging economies.[19] Local communities can develop solutions, perhaps working with

---

17 *Global Environment Outlook GEO 5: Environment for the Future We Want* (Nairobi, Kenya: United Nations Environment Program, 2019).

18 See Padilla DeBorst, "Living Well Together"; Bonhoeffer, *Creation and Fall*; Two Bears, "Seeing the Whole"; Sutterfield, *Cultivating Reality*; Berry, *What Are People For?*

19 Tanoto, "Tomorrow's Climate Leaders."

governments and NGOs. Acting artistically can contribute to more thriving in the human|all creation relationship, in local, regional, and global ecosystems.[20]

> Northern Hills United Methodist Church (San Antonio Texas, USA) is made up of both Spanish and English speakers. They wanted to use their physical environment to connect with the surrounding bilingual community and encourage discipleship development. So they decided to create a walking trail surrounding their land, connecting parts of it to neighboring properties. Different church members contributed to the project. One artist designed a mural at the trailhead with a painting of a tree and a title, "Beatitudes Prayer Walk." They cleaned up the surrounding land, laid mulch and stone for the path, and highlighted native plants. They crafted eight stations along the trail, each consisting of stone benches, markers with verses of the beatitudes, and QR codes that walkers can scan for prayers and devotions. The church continues to improve the trail, and has been working with the National Wildlife Federation and San Antonio River Authority to develop the area as a wildlife habitat. The "Beatitudes Prayer Walk" provides a wonderful example of expressing love by linking creation care, spiritual growth, and witness. —Abel Stewart

> Art for Change Foundation is a New Delhi-based arts organization founded with the conviction that art plays a profound role in exploring questions of human dignity and the common good. In 2008, in collaboration with the Mukteshwar Mutt and INTACH Varanasi, Art for Change organized a four-day painting residency in Varanasi addressing the issue of pollution of the Ganges River. Eighteen art students from Benares Hindu University joined eight artists from New Delhi to explore the issue of pollution of the sacred river and the role of art for social service. The artists created paintings and visual art based on this theme.[21]

JUSTICE

Social Justice

Where the Kingdom of Heaven thrives, communities love and strengthen the poor and others on the margins.

God has communicated clearly and repeatedly throughout Scripture that he cares for people without power. He highlights orphans, widows, and foreigners

---

20 See, for example, Schippers and Grant, *Sustainable Futures*; Global Environments Network, "Art as Environmental Justice."

21 This story with photographs of the event located here: https://artforchange.in/residencies#/2008-the-ganges.

(Deut 10:18; Jas 1:27), people without enough money (Deut 15:7–8; Ps 9:18; Luke 4:18; 6:20), the politically and socially oppressed (Neh 9:15; Luke 1:46–55), prisoners (Ps 146:7), and hungry and homeless people (Isa 58:6–11; Matt 25:34–40). Jesus made a special point of telling the poor that they could have the Kingdom of Heaven (Luke 6:20–26). And God shows how the lack of justice for marginalized people often—though not always—results from the callousness and sin of people in power (Pss 12:5; 35:10; 72:12–14; Prov 22:22–23; Isa 10:1–3).

In response to these realities, God told people *with* resources to be generous (Deut 15:7–8; Prov 11:24–25; Rom 12:13; 2 Cor 9:6–13; Jas 2:15–17) and kind to the marginalized (Prov 14:31), to defend them (Prov 31:8–9) and break the systems that keep them down (Isa 58:6–11). Communities can work toward Kingdom justice by drawing on their arts' abilities to instill hope, speak unwelcome truth to those in power, and encourage solidarity.

> In September 2022, Russia began to mobilize men to join the war against Ukraine. In the Russian city of Yakutsk, a group of young Sakha women began to form an *ohuokai* circle dance in a public square to protest their husbands, sons, and brothers being sent to war. Older women began to join them, along with their families. They began to chant slogans of protest and a Sakha song of peace was also performed. The police broke up the dance protest after some time. The head of Yakutia's Public Chamber said the protest was a "mothers' blessing so that husbands and sons come back alive! The Sakha people always unite during difficult times."[22]

> In Bogotá, Colombia, a soup kitchen in a community experiencing forced displacement, violence, and generational poverty was transformed when they moved from sharing soup to training people in culinary arts. That soup kitchen grew to become Santa Cecelia Alliance Church. Santa Cecelia's 80 members now serve others through after-school programs, a sewing workshop, and a bakery, in addition to aerial dance classes, puppetry, circus, tailoring, and muralism. Many, like the youth leader, Danny, came from drug use; and most, like Lorena, imagined they would never escape poverty. Lorena now has a degree in social work!
> —*Jhonny Nieto and Ninoshka Gelpi*[23]

---

22 This dance against the draft was reported by Novaya Gazeta.eu (https://bit.ly/4b9gFJu). A brief video of the dance can be seen here as reported by NBC News (https://bit.ly/49T0ONZ).

23 Anthony, "Beautiful, Wonderful Gospel," 34.

"Dancing changed my life. For the first time I felt that I was doing something I liked," recalls Shampa Roy. The eighteen-year-old from Kolkata lived in children's homes from the age of five after her parents died. "I was always angry, I didn't know why. I beat up other inmates at the slightest provocation; people used to avoid me. I didn't respect my teachers or my elders," she admits. And then she discovered dance. Roy realized she could express her inner turmoil through dancing. It was, she says, a discovery of joy. Roy is now an assistant dance instructor, sharing her discovery with other women.

She was trained by Kolkata Sanved (which means sensitivity in Bengali), a local NGO that uses dance to help people cope with mental trauma. A main area of Sanved focus is working with trafficked girls and women, with Kolkata a significant source and destination for trafficked women.

Sanved was set up in 2002 by Sohini Chakraborty, a sociology graduate from Kolkata. Chakraborty first started to use dance as a form of therapy when she volunteered with another NGO, Sanlaap, which works with former prostitutes. Using her background in classical Indian dance, Chakraborty initially taught the girls a combination of classical and contemporary dance movements. However, they didn't respond to the classes. So instead she began to create a series of body movements based on everyday actions, such as making chai or sweeping the floor, and this clicked with the girls. She would ask a girl to imagine that she was a tree. How would she project it? Gradually the girls started to open up and learned to express their emotions through their movements. It was only later that Chakraborty realized that this form of movement is a recognized therapy, known as Dance Movement Therapy (DMT), which was devised in America in the 1940s.

As Chakraborty explains, the women she works with often feel a deep inferiority and have extremely low self-esteem. "DMT encourages them to think, 'I am creating my own body through my own expression.'" By taking control of their bodies, they are able to rebuild their confidence and begin to cope with mental trauma.

Kolkata Sanved has since expanded its work to other groups. Today Chakraborty collaborates with NGOs working with street children, young people living in red-light areas, those living with HIV, and also people with mental health issues. The NGO also helps elderly women living in shelter homes. Workshops are held regularly in rural areas in collaboration with outreach organizations. Sanved also runs projects with domestic workers, including one held on the platform of the main train station where many workers pass through daily.

Indrani Sinha, director of Sanlaap, says, "A lot of pain and hurt haunts these women, but there's a lot of beauty too. We have to look for their wellspring of beauty, try to bring it to the surface, and not treat them as only case studies. DMT helps them to rise above the brutalities they have gone through." —*Ranjita Biswas*[24]

Around the world, Deaf community members are regularly treated as low-caste citizens by the hearing majority. The church is often unwittingly one of the greatest culprits. Hearing ministers and missionaries teach not only the Bible, but hearing culture, forcing Deaf Christians to conform to hearing learning methodologies which tend to frustrate and bore the Deaf. Often Deaf church attendees never learn the story of Jesus Christ because they are not told through their languages and their artistic learning norms.

Upon visiting the Woodhaven Baptist Deaf Church in Houston, Texas, I was pleased to find a church where Deaf culture and arts were central to church community. American Deaf culture celebrates the gift of American Sign Language in all its artistic glory, and Deaf community members often gather for storytelling and poetic performance. Adjacent to the church building is a community center in which stands a large room which serves as both cafe and performance space. A raised stage against one wall stands in the line of sight of all present, including the baristas, who are stationed at the opposite wall. The room is full of small round tables, for ease of signed communication, which requires sustained eye contact within a group. There is extra space left between tables, so that conversants can easily shift their chairs for a clear view of the performance space. In this way, Woodhaven Baptist has fully integrated Deaf artistic culture into their community center. —*Maan Di Thomas*

Education

Where the Kingdom of Heaven thrives, community members learn what they need to succeed in and contribute to their societies.

Communities *not* marked by the Kingdom signs of health and valuing their identity often have weak educational systems. Rapid social change—when new economic and political realities devalue previous knowledge—can also leave people without the knowledge or training to thrive. Because the arts are such penetrating and memorable systems of communication, communities can integrate them into all educational subjects and teaching contexts.

Cherry Faile smiles when she hears villagers singing songs in the Manpruli language about how to properly nurse children or cook nutritious meals. In a place where accurate statistics are tough to

---

24 Biswas, "Dancing Away the Pain."

track, the songs affirm that the public health programs she helped develop at the Baptist Medical Centre in rural Ghana are working.

"You'd hear them singing those songs everywhere," says Faile. "You'd be surprised how quickly those messages spread and become part of the thinking in the community." That's just one example of the unique public health programs the hospital uses to educate and minister to the large local community, most of whom still live in simple huts and have little formal education.

As Faile began putting up a public health building years ago, she realized, "I really wanted [it] to belong to the people so they would feel comfortable coming here." So she invited village chiefs to send villagers to help with construction. Together, they built the traditional huts used as exam rooms and administrative offices.

The hospital offers other special health education programs building on community values. A rustic pavilion beside the hospital provides a place for mothers to nurse their malnourished children back to health. Every morning the mothers sweep camp together, attend devotionals, and learn how to prepare healthy meals using local foods. Each afternoon, with babies strapped securely to their backs, the women prepare the food in giant cast-iron pots. "They come every day until their children reach a healthy weight," Faile explains. "They may stay six weeks."

—Emily Peters

Literacy

Where the Kingdom of Heaven thrives, communities read and listen to the Bible and other literature.

Members of a community marked by the Kingdom of Heaven will be able to access Scripture and other literature through written and aural means, empowering and liberating people.[25] Since many decisions affecting people's lives in private and government relationships involve written documents, the ability to read and write provides minority communities tools to help protect their interests. Literacy goals relate to both technical (e.g., understanding language structure) and social issues (e.g., wanting to read and write in a language, and feeling capable of acquiring these skills). This makes it likely that artistic forms both with heavy language components (e.g., songs, drama, storytelling, proverbs, and riddles) and those without (e.g., dance, visual arts) will strengthen literacy goals.[26]

> Muslims in Dagbani communities of Ghana feared literacy because of a history of school learning leading to Christian conversion. Leaders of a literacy project there asked students

---

25 See https://unesco.org/en/literacy/need-know.

26 Cuthbert, "Church-Based Curriculum Integrating Literacy." See also Walters, "Tell Me a Story" (Part 1 and 2).

questions like these: "Why are you learning to read? Why is it worth the trouble? Make a song about it." Then the songs were collected on cassette and transcribed into a booklet with pictures done by a local artist. The songs were rerecorded for quality in a makeshift studio in the office, and copies of the tape and booklet given to all the class supervisors. They typically used them by writing a song on the blackboard for a class, teaching the song orally or from the tape, and having learners join in, following the text. The songs were a learning tool, but more importantly built community motivation for engaging with the process of learning to read. The students' reasons for wanting to read included being able to write and read letters, becoming "enlightened" so that no one could fool them, being like other people groups locally who had classes, and helping their children with schoolwork.

—Sue Hall-Heimbecker

A literacy specialist in the Central African Republic felt that an alphabet song was needed to strengthen the reading readiness component of the Sango literacy program. She commissioned a local choir director to set a poem to music. It was to accompany a one-page alphabet chart which teachers distributed to learners and posted in their classrooms. A local artist had illustrated it. The chart had a key word and illustration to go along with each letter. The "Sango Alphabet Song" used alliteration, and Sango literacy teachers taught the song to help students learn the sounds of each letter. Here is part of it:

A Bâgara tî âta agä,
   Grandfather's cow came,
B lo buba bongö tî babâ.
   It ruined father's clothes.
D Deku adö dödö tî lo.
   The mouse did his dance.
E Ë te lê tî këkë sô.
   We eat fruit from this tree.

Singing the song fostered group enthusiasm and built team spirit. Churches sang it enthusiastically when certificates were presented to graduating students; students in some classes sang it while passing around an offering cup to collect coins for their teacher.

Six local literacy supervisors trained over one hundred volunteer literacy teachers in Sango-speaking churches. They, in turn, taught thousands of Central Africans how to read so they could benefit from health booklets, cultural materials, and Bible portions, as well as use their new skill to learn French. The "Sango

Alphabet Song" was one of the strongest motivators to encourage new students to attend Sango literacy classes and learn how to read.

One pastor was among the students who received their reading certificates after learning how to read. He read to his church from the third chapter of the Gospel of John and encouraged everyone in his congregation to be in the next reading class. "Don't be ashamed to admit you don't know how to read," he said. "I learned. So can you!" Another student said, "When I didn't know how to read, I was like a blind person. Today I am happy to say I am like the blind man of Jericho. My eyes are opened, and I can see!"
—*Michelle Petersen*

Mary Stringer in Papua New Guinea encouraged teachers to use a different song to go with each week's literacy theme. They made up songs about rats, frogs, women, houses, and other themes.
—*Mary Beth Saurman*

Economic Opportunity

Where the Kingdom of Heaven thrives, all community members can work to contribute to their material well-being.

From God's own crafting of the universe (Gen 1) to putting Adam in charge of the garden of Eden (Gen 2:15), and admonitions to be productive (Prov 18:9; Col 3:23; 2 Thess 3:10; 1 Tim 5:18) and to reward labor (1 Tim 5:18), Scripture shows that humans are meant to work. The members of a community marked by the Kingdom of Heaven have opportunities to engage in meaningful, materially rewarding endeavors. Artists benefit from their activities when people pay for performances or objects. Artistic communication can also grease the wheels of commerce in advertising and can motivate and coordinate people who are laboring. A thriving community will value and reward the contributions of its artists to its material health.

The Wagogo people of Tanzania, Africa, are renowned for their musicality. A British couple under their charity Voices from the Nations have recorded audio, pictures, and video entitled "Sing to the Well" to bring their story of hope in adversity to a wider audience. The CD and DVD were recorded in a mud hut and designed to appeal to a Western audience. The recording is a collection of songs taken from everyday life in a beautiful but harsh environment, where famine and drought are often just around the corner. Through an agreement between the local community, musicians, and the producers, sales of this production have provided water sources, a clinic, and other emergency help to the Mnase area implemented by a local development committee.
—*Martin and Rebekah Neil*

SCRIPTURE

Translating Scripture

Where the Kingdom of Heaven thrives, communities translate Scripture well. A community marked by the Kingdom of Heaven will know what God has communicated through Scripture. To do this, they must first have access to a translation of the Bible that is faithful to the original documents, communicates in ways that are clear to the vast majority of its members, renders texts in the most appropriate and penetrating forms of the local language, is interpretable by various Christian traditions, and can be transformed into oral and visual communication forms with ease. Since the Bible is riddled with artistic forms of communication—parables, proverbs, stories, song lyrics, poetry, and so on—insights into local artistic genres will help a community translate Scripture in ways that feed into their goals.[27]

> I knew that one of the most common features of biblical poetry is semantic and accentual parallelism. Translators often indicate this poetic device through typographical conventions, using indentation and line breaks. In my preparations to help Baka speakers in Cameroon translate the Bible into their language, I discovered that Baka poetic "lines" are not constructed in quite the same way. They do not mark poetic lines through accentual parallelism, but through periodic parallelism; that is, through musically metered lines. This means that Baka poetic lines are primarily bound by repeated groups of musical pulses ("beats"), not by repeated groups of patterned word stresses, as in Hebrew poetry.
>
> Parallel Baka poetic meters may be formed of 4, 8, 12, or 16 pulses per song line, depending upon the song genre in question. The texts of these metered song lines are then grammatically segmented according to generic line lengths. Generic story-song poetic texts, for example, typically include an average of 11 words per line (ranging 7–16 words per line) and an average 21 syllables per line (ranging 20–22 syllables per line). Thus, when preparing the text for the "Song of Moses" (Exod 15) for translation, the Baka translation team knew beforehand that the traditional text load of any single poetic line should contain between 7 and 16 words, and between 20 and 22 syllables. By respecting such grammatical parameters, the translators could be reasonably confident that they were meeting traditional Baka expectations regarding some of the most fundamental rhythmic and syntactic phenomena of Baka poetic texts. —*Dan Fitzgerald*

---

27 For an extensively researched, practical call to connect biblical and local genres in translation, see Katie Hoogerheide Frost's "Why Consider Local Genres in Translation?" The article includes a clear overview, history, conceptual framework, and examples. See also Conversation 5's Scripture section for more discussion and resources.

Specify Kingdom Goals

> The Bible translation team for the Paypa people in central Brazil had recently finished translating the Gospel of Luke. They wanted portions of it in an artform to engage the people with the recent work. To help them achieve that goal, I conducted a series of conversations using participatory activities that would facilitate detailed reflection on this project.
>
> The team decided to create a video of the parable of the two builders (Luke 6:46–49) with contextualized visual art. They illustrated a good and a bad house following the cultural construction techniques. After that, we created a short video with those drawings, narrated in Paypa. In the process, the team also devised other goals for that artwork; they wanted to encourage people to trust God. Finally, they planned to create videos with different stories from Luke to share in villages throughout the region. —*Héber Negrão*[28]

Oral Scripture

Where the Kingdom of Heaven thrives, communities access Scripture through forms familiar to them.

A community marked by the Kingdom of Heaven has access to Scripture in many forms. Local art forms—especially those related to storytelling—can play key roles in integrating Scripture into community life.

> A Tibetan language group completed a full set of oral Bible stories. These stories accurately paralleled the stories from Scripture. People, however, were not embracing them or passing them on.
>
> The believers prayed together, asking the Lord to show them the barriers. They studied the biblical stories in more depth. They then contextualized the stories through cultural lenses.
>
> The believers also looked at their own local storytelling and expressive art forms. They realized that their traditional way of storytelling is not just through words. Storytelling within their culture occurs through poetry, songs, dances, dramas, and visual arts.
>
> With this new awareness, these believers created more relevant Bible stories. These artistically infused stories now emphasize both the needs and the cultural issues within their Tibetan communities.
>
> The story of the prodigal son, expressed through several songs and a dance, contains a song sung by the father. "This will reach the hearts of our people," said the composer, "because a father's expressed care for his children is so important in our culture. Now, people will listen, understand, and grab this story."
>
> —*Mary Beth and Todd Saurman*

---

28 Robertson, "Seven Core Values," 21–22.

> In some cultures, the person who works with the words as a poet, and the one who works with the musical notes as a composer, may not be the same. In Cambodia, a threefold process was used to develop indigenous hymns at United Bible Society translation workshops. The first step was to accurately translate the chosen passages (from Matthew 5 and Philippians 2) into prose; then poets were given the translated texts and "were assigned to turn this prose text into good Cambodian poetry, using their own traditional rhyming patterns and poetic forms." In the third step, musicians were asked to work with the poets to create translations that could be actually sung.
>
> —Howard Hatton and David Clark [29]

CHURCH LIFE

Corporate Worship

Where the Kingdom of Heaven thrives, Christ-followers gather to worship in ways that promote deep communication with God and each other.

In its deepest sense, biblical worship is a life completely sacrificed and given to God (Rom 12:1–2). It is the moment-by-moment choice to live for God's glory and not one's own. But this whole life of worship includes particular times of gathering with other believers for heartfelt adoration of God and communication with him (Pss 95:6; 96:9; Acts 2:42; Heb 10:24–25; Rev 19:10). Local arts provide languages for these moments of worshiping God and listening to him that involve our whole heart, soul, strength, and mind (Ps 100:2; Mark 12:29–30). Jesus taught that it doesn't matter where you worship, as long as it's done in spirit and in truth (John 4:21–24). This opens the door to people from every nation and language using their own forms of communication to honor God.

To express such corporate worship, the Bible urges us to be filled with the Holy Spirit (Eph 5:18–20) and to use languages and forms that are clearly and deeply understood by others (1 Cor 14:6–19). This includes not only spoken words (v. 9) but songs (v. 15) and symbolic forms that are unambiguous in meaning to all culture members (see the analogies in vv. 7–8).

> In Senegal, a group of Wolof believers used songs translated from English or French—but they sang with little joy. One day, they discussed the use of indigenous arts in worship. All of a sudden, a Wolof man began to praise God in a chanting style typical of the way Wolof express joy. Within seconds the whole room exploded in spontaneous praise. After further probing questions about how the Wolof express joy and reverence, this group of Wolof believers redesigned many aspects of their gatherings. First, they decided to sit on mats on the floor (not on chairs), to chat informally outside but not inside the building, to remove their shoes before

---

29 Hatton and Clark, "From the Harp to the Sitar," 132–38.

Specify Kingdom Goals

entering quietly and kneeling reverently to prepare their hearts. These changes provided greater flexibility and expressed biblical worship in Wolof ways. Secondly, indigenous repetitive chants were devised to praise Jesus. Often the congregation explodes in sound and movement. One believer, trained in Qur'anic chant, set New Testament passages to chant. Even those usually opposed to Christ can sit for hours repeating the Bible stories they have heard presented in such an acceptable way.[30]

What makes the worship in our multicultural Proskuneo community of Clarkston, Georgia, somehow richer? The diversity in our gathering, language, culture, generation, and religious background traditions demands a higher and deeper sense of community of those present. When people bring all that they are into the worship space, give themselves to each other and to God, and feel safe to bring themselves, they can fully contribute, listen, receive, and create together. They share leadership and like to imagine what is possible with the wealth of perspective, language, and skill in their group. Our group started with two families gathering for potluck and worship together. From there, it grew organically until we asked themselves, "Is this worship? Are we a church?" We hadn't intended to plant a church, but our relationships, shared context, and our response to each other birthed something special.

Most people prefer to worship within a shared language and culture, not with "others." But our community leaned into each other because they had to. Our differences afforded us no presumptive common ground, except our desire to be together. We brought together the new ingredients, the process became ours and we felt we belonged to it. It's unique, and each week's service brings something new: a song we learn, a new language, nuance, or perspective on Scripture. Our Middle Eastern members are able to highlight rich cultural connections in Scriptures too. Syrian and Ethiopian members bring their ancient church history. It's our special embodiment of unity in diversity. Our multicultural group brings more of ourselves because we are both welcome and willing to. —*Joy Kim*[31]

---

30 Shawyer, "Indigenous Worship," 326–34.
31 Adapted from Robertson, "Seven Core Values," 12–13.

Studying and Remembering Scripture

Where the Kingdom of Heaven thrives, communities understand and remember Scripture.

A community that is coming more and more under the rule of the Kingdom of Heaven will study, remember, and understand Scripture. Jesus marked its defining authority on his life and that of others (Matt 22:29; Mark 12:24; Luke 4:21; 24:45), the early church used Scripture to explain and verify their faith (Acts 8:35; 17:2, 11), and God uses it to regularly guide followers of Christ (Rom 15:4; 1 Tim 4:13; 2 Tim 3:16). The more ways we learn Scripture—including through local arts—the more likely we are to remember it. Studies have shown that memorizing words through song and/or motions involves more areas of the brain. In addition, when people from more than one culture are present in a Bible study, the leader needs to work with people in a variety of ways reflecting the variety of cultural learning styles, arts, and languages of all of those present.

> In Nigeria, Yoruba Christians found that when they studied the Bible in Yoruba song forms as well as in print, they strengthened their memory of the content. Herbert Klem organized Yoruba Bible study groups in which Bible study leaders taught the first six chapters of the book of Hebrews to four groups in four ways. Klem then evaluated the effects of various teaching modalities on comprehension. The four different Bible study groups studied the first six chapters of the book of Hebrews in four different ways:
>
> - Participants in the first group held Bible studies in which they studied the *written text* of Hebrews 1–6 in Yoruba.
>
> - Participants in the second group held Bible studies in which they studied both the *written* text of Hebrews 1–6 and a *recording* of Hebrews being *read* aloud in Yoruba.
>
> - Participants in the third group held Bible studies using the *written text* and a cassette of Hebrews 1–6 being *sung* in a traditional Yoruba song style.
>
> - Participants in the fourth group held Bible studies using the Yoruba Hebrews *song recording* alone, without any written text.
>
> Klem trained a group of Bible study leaders so any of them could lead a group using any of the four teaching styles. Then the Bible study leaders rotated among the four groups to minimize the effects of having different teachers. They wanted to see if the way people learned made a difference in how much they remembered, not just find out if one teacher was better than another teacher. At the end of the Bible study, all four groups had a test to see how much they remembered of Hebrews 1–6. The highest scoring group was the third group. They used both the text and the song of Hebrews 1–6 in a traditional Yoruba song style. The next highest scoring group was the second group.

They used the text and a recording of the text being read aloud. The group using only the song came in third, and the group using only the text came in last for their test scores.

The two highest scoring groups learned in two ways. The two lowest scoring groups learned in only one way. This shows us that the more ways we learn, the better we remember and understand the message of Scripture. Because the group with only the text came in last, we should increase the variety of forms in which we study Scripture, so we can remember it better.[32]

Christian Rites

Where the Kingdom of Heaven thrives, Christ-followers mark crucial events with ceremonies.

Where the Kingdom of Heaven is strong, people mark important moments with intense spiritual events. These could include weddings, Communion or the Eucharist, funerals, rites of passage, and agricultural feasts. Artistic forms of communication mark these events as special, provide historical continuity through unique repertoire and forms, and open up holistic channels of communication with God.

> Pilgrims regularly travel to a special shrine a day's travel from the capital of Ghana, Accra. They bring offerings to the shrine in hopes that its god will make their farms fertile. An arts advocate started a discussion with the small number of Christians in one of the nearby ethnolinguistic communities about how they could express their need to God for spiritual help in their own farming.
>
> They looked at over twenty scriptural references to God's involvement in agriculture. From these they developed a series of vows and entreaties to God, acknowledging their ultimate dependency on him. This ritual has become a seasonal part of this Christian community's life. —*Paul Neeley*

> Dinka believers (Sudan) are experiencing the help of God and the reality of Scripture in their lives. One central result is that they are becoming more able to forgive and heal within their communities, rather than seeking revenge. They are choosing to carry ebony crosses decorated with fragments of metal found on the ground—the debris of the war that has surrounded them for years. These crosses indicate the bearer to be a follower of Jesus, willing to help others in the refugee camps and village communities where many Dinkas have been scattered by the turmoil of the last two decades. These communities are "beating" the tools of war into ebony crosses, fit to articulate their suffering and their trust in God. —*Karen Campbell*[33]

---

32 Klem, *Oral Communication of the Scripture.*
33 Campbell, "God Looks Back on Us," 110–15.

Witness

Where the Kingdom of Heaven thrives, non-believers in communities learn about God.

A community marked by the Kingdom of Heaven will learn that he is their Creator and Savior. Local arts provide penetrating means for communicating truth about God because they are often intertwined with both special and daily activities of life: important life events, social interaction, entertainment, teaching, and the like. Sue Whittaker provides an encouraging, extended example of how a church in Turkey was able to engage socially and theologically with their Muslim neighbors.[34] Here are more stories from other places.

> Most members of the evangelical church in Brazil look askance at everything associated with the annual festival of *Carnaval*, especially its *samba* music; immoral connotations are extremely strong. Christian leader, writer, composer, and performer Atilano Muradas believes that God can redeem even this. He formed a *samba* school of Christians that has more than five hundred members. They prepare all year and perform Scripture-based *samba* songs during *Carnaval* in southern Brazil. Their troupe has won awards not only because of the excellence of the costumes and music, but because people are drawn to their holy, healthy, exuberant version of *samba*. —*Tom Avery*

> As the Ifé churches grew stronger in Togo, they realized that there might be a more communal and effective way of reaching out than sending a lone preacher to a village with his Bible. They called together sixty active Baptist church members to consider how storytelling, song, drama and dance might combine to create a uniquely Ifé way of sharing the good news of Jesus with other communities. They were encouraged by the example of an older, illiterate grandmother who had seen three churches established as she composed new Ifé songs and taught them to children. As they learned to tell Bible stories by hearing others read to her, the participants grew excited about the potential of culturally relevant evangelism. After two days of teaching, experimenting, and polishing their presentations, four teams headed out into villages to put into practice their new ideas. All returned excited about how they were received in communities, with a great deal more openness to the gospel message since it came in a relevant and attractive presentation. Many villagers had been drawn by the music and dancing and had stayed to watch the dramas and hear the testimonies. The group approach to witness left these believers eager to share more of Jesus in Ifé terms back in their home communities. —*Tom Ferguson*[35]

---

34 Whittaker, *Music and Liturgy*.
35 Ferguson, "Music, Drama, and Storying."

What started as a unique ministry in a small reservation church has grown into walking out the gospel of Jesus among Native peoples from Montana to the Zapotec people of the southern Mexican state of Oaxaca. Using Native dancing, drums, flutes, and other instruments to worship our Creator has touched the hearts of many people, both Native and non-Native alike.

All of this has led our ministry to put on an annual traditional powwow in Flagstaff, Arizona. We work together with traditional Native people to make this happen. Through this bringing together of peoples, we are seeing many people touched and healed. We recognize the hurts of the past while working together to see hope for the future. We have seen Native and non-Native people touched by the Holy Spirit through the songs and dances. One woman came up to me after a service where we had some traditional powwow singers sing drum songs for us. The woman said, "Those songs made me want to worship God, is that OK?" From Montana to Mexico and at our Native Christian gatherings in Flagstaff, we are seeing lives changed. The dancing and traditional songs are helping to break down the barriers that keep many Native people away from the Church. —*Bill Gowey*[36]

PERSONAL SPIRITUAL LIFE

Prayer and Meditation

Where the Kingdom of Heaven thrives, individuals have vibrant prayer lives. A community marked by the Kingdom of Heaven will have followers of Christ who communicate with God frequently and wholeheartedly. Artistic forms of communication can help this happen because they are enjoyable and connect deeply to people's emotions and wills.

> Tami Diagne, a Senegalese woman, has had much sorrow in her life. She suffers ill health, her young adult sons are in trouble, and her non-Christian family has treated her badly since her husband abandoned her. Yet she wakes with songs in her heart during the night. And these are not just songs she heard on the radio—they are songs full of passion and yearning for her Savior Jesus, songs pouring out her heart full of sadness to him, and songs full of confidence that he will meet her in her sorrow. These powerful testimony songs are a source of deep reassurance to Tami, and they speak powerfully to Christian and non-Christian Senegalese women as she finds opportunities to share them. These songs begin as a personal prayer to "the God of her life" but overflow into a life that witnesses to the power of Christ to overcome suffering.
> —*Sue Hall-Heimbecker*

---

36 Gowey, "Walking Out the Gospel."

Spiritual Formation

Where the Kingdom of Heaven thrives, Christ-followers experience spiritual growth.

Where the Kingdom of Heaven is strong, Christ-followers grow in their knowledge and experience of God, in their obedience to God, and in godly character traits and habits. Artistic forms of communication can energize and provide structure for formal and informal spiritual training, coaching, and mentoring.[37]

> Nanias, a master carver, potter and painter from Papua New Guinea, learned his traditional arts from his father and grandfather. As an arts advocate, I came alongside Nanias to learn about and discover the needs of his Kwoma community. They realized the lack of local Kwoma arts in the church. Nanias decided he would like to try to reclaim traditional artistic genres for use by Christians for church life and identity. Nanias chose the Jebwa genre of traditional bark painting, and I commissioned him to create a Jebwa painting based on Scripture. Nanias consulted a Bible in Tok Pisin as a foundation for his Scripture based paintings. He created paintings based on the Genesis story of creation, and the Life of Christ. Nanias and I went back to the Kwoma village to evaluate them with the elders, cultural custodians, and leaders of the community. After the elders saw the paintings and heard Nanias discussing them they commented that "it shot their stomachs." The elders said, "These paintings are our story, we understand these." Some of these elders came to church for the first time after this discussion.
>
> —*Peter Brook*

Personal Bible Study

Where the Kingdom of Heaven thrives, individuals examine Scripture accurately and faithfully.

Acts 17:10–12 gives a great example of the importance of studying Scripture:

> The brothers [in Thessalonica] immediately sent Paul and Silas away by night to Berea, and when they arrived they went into the Jewish synagogue. Now these Jews were more noble than those in Thessalonica; they received the word with all eagerness, examining the Scriptures daily to see if these things were so. Many of them therefore believed, with not a few Greek women of high standing as well as men. (ESV)

---

[37] Practical guides, some integrating arts, include Aronis, *Developing Intimacy with God*; Barton, *Sacred Rhythms*; Earley, *The Common Rule*; GEMeDOT, "Soul Connection" (smartphone app allowing user to choose one of six trails for a customized personal spiritual retreat) https://gemedot.com/soul-connection/; Global Ethnodoxology Network, "Arts with God" (collection of devotionals connecting Scripture, arts, and spiritual formation) at https://tinyurl.com/ABF-artswithGod; Hoogerheide and Harris, *Engaging the Arts*; Macchia, *Crafting a Rule of Life*.

A community that demonstrates characteristics of God's Kingdom has community members who examine Scripture accurately and faithfully. When community members integrate artistic forms of communication into their personal Bible study, they remember, understand, and are changed more.

> In South and Southeast Asia, tigers abound in the jungles. People are fearful as they hike through these jungle areas. A traditional way of handling this fear for many groups is to close one's ears with index fingers and sing songs as loud as possible when walking through these areas and feeling afraid. There is hope that this activity will scare away nearby tigers.
>
> Some believers in two different language groups in this region created songs from Scripture passages about not being afraid and about God's protection over his children. These songs helped believers learn these scriptural truths and walk with less fear through the jungle. One believer said, "Now we don't need to close our ears or sing loudly out of fear, we can sing with joy about God's promises to us and walk confidently knowing he is with us through whatever we face." —*Mary Beth and Todd Saurman*

Applying Scripture

Where the Kingdom of Heaven thrives, communities apply the Bible to their lives.

A community becoming more and more like the Kingdom of Heaven will apply the teachings of Scripture to their daily life experiences. Yet the Bible was written to people in different cultures and at different times. How can we accurately apply it to our lives today, in all our various cultures? Local artistic communication can help people connect scriptural truths to their lives in memorable, motivating ways.

> Scripture Relevance Dramas by West African dramatists show stories that apply Scripture to typical life situations.[38] In each of their half-hour weekly radio dramas, they follow the story of a person or a family who develops some difficulty. A friend or neighbor then tells them a Bible story that helps them resolve their difficulty.
>
> The program's scriptwriters think of typical questions their audience will be likely to ask about each Bible story. The characters hearing the Bible story ask the storyteller those questions. Background information they need to make sense of the story is given through dialogue. The difference the story makes for the audience today is shown as appropriate applications of the Bible story are shared by the characters. The Bible storyteller sometimes relates the point of the Bible story to the point of a local proverb, to show that the Bible affirms many cultural values.
>
> As the play's conflict is resolved, personal applications dramatize the point of the story for the main character(s), and

---

38 Petersen, "Scripture Relevance Dramas," 22–31.

the radio audience hears possible biblical ways they could deal with their problems, too.

Christian leaders suggest changes and approve the scripts before they are acted out and recorded by the drama group. Their programs began airing on one radio station and spread to fifty-seven radio stations in three countries.

Like drama, storytelling and other arts can also communicate the relevance of Scripture. Colgate discusses what he calls "relational Bible story telling" as an alternative to simple Bible story telling. He encourages Bible story tellers to first listen to people's stories, then tell their own personal stories, and only then tell Bible stories that relate thematically to their local friends' personal stories.[39] You don't need a radio station to do what the radio drama program did. You too can say to a friend, "Your problem reminds me of something I went through once and how God helped me with this Scripture. May I tell you a story?"

—Michelle Petersen

Methods For Specifying Kingdom Goals

As this whirlwind tour shows, God's Kingdom shows up in incredibly diverse ways around the world. In this section, we describe what a space in which a community explores possible goals might look like. We conclude by outlining a process—one that we've seen work in many contexts—that you and a community could adapt to choose one or more signs of Heaven that they can encourage.

MAXIMUM PARTICIPATION

We want this procedure to be marked by maximum participation of the community. This means that everything we do should demonstrate respect for local knowledge and intelligence; emphasize discussing, listening, and building consensus; help community members become agents of change; and advance sustainable transformation. This mindset plays a crucial role in deciding what goals a community wants to work toward. You may be familiar with some formal methods people use to specify community needs and goals in participatory ways, with names like Appreciative Inquiry, Theater for Development, Force Field Analysis, Stakeholder Analysis, and Participatory Action Research (see Figure 2.1 in the section called "Methods for Specifying Kingdom Goals," Conversation 2, for brief descriptions of a few of these).[40] We present one activity—a "Tool to Help People Choose Kingdom Goals"—that the community can modify to fit its context, but many approaches are possible.

---

39 Colgate, "Relational Bible Storying," 135–42.

40 See Hogan, *Practical Facilitation*; Kaner, *Facilitator's Guide*; Resources: Participatory Methods, http://www.participatorymethods.org, a rich source for case studies and wide range of methods. More information and many examples for facilitating conversations with Participatory Methods can be found at the site.

Specify Kingdom Goals

Be aware also that unless you are working with Christians, the community you're with will not be motivated to work toward goals stated in terms of the Kingdom of Heaven. But because all humans are created in God's image, we all yearn for many of these signs: peace, health, joy, significance, and justice; you may simply call them "Signs of a Better Future" or "Goals for a Better Life." A separate publication, *Make Arts for a Better Life: A Guide for Working with Communities*, will help in such contexts.[41] So when a community wants these things, we can join wholeheartedly in helping according to our skills and calling. If we are working with a local church, then their goals will also naturally include deepening their relationship to God. The ultimate King of the Kingdom of Heaven is Jesus. As we journey alongside individuals and communities who don't know Jesus, our love and words can point them to him.

Creating together will include a continual process of specifying and refining community goals. This section provides a place to start.

> **Appreciative Inquiry.** Provides spaces for people to hope and dream about their future, highlighting their existing strengths and resources.
>
> **Workshops for the Co-generation of Knowledge.** Extremely flexible and inclusive in form and purposes, from planning to outcomes.
>
> **Strengths, Weaknesses, Opportunities and Threats Analysis (SWOT).** A tool that helps people name and categorize the realities that impinge on their planning.
>
> **Stakeholder Analysis.** Aids people in identifying individuals and groups that could aid or thwart accomplishment of their goals. In general, including as many stakeholders as possible in planning and performing projects increases success.
>
> **Participatory Visual Methods.** People use film, photos, animation, games, or other media to create stories expressing their situations, hopes, dreams, and possible paths to a better future.
>
> **Surveys.** Sometimes arts advocates need to get facts, opinions, ideas from a larger number of people. Surveys can be used to gather reliable information when community members participate in each step: exploring the purpose(s) and need (or no need) of the survey, its design, testing, administering, gathering and analyzing data, and deciding how to use what they've learned.

Figure 2.1 A few participatory methods

How Does This Community Usually Make Decisions? One important aspect to note before choosing a method with people is that all communities do not make decisions the same way. Learning and respecting how the community makes decisions will help you determine if the "Tool to Help People Choose Kingdom Goals" in the next section will work well. If the community you are working with has a strong, hierarchical system, the voices of everyone may not

---
41 Schrag and Van Buren, *Make Arts for a Better Life*.

be respected—see the Glimpse below for an example of this. Cycle back to the mindset of Conversation 1 and peek ahead to Conversation 4C's discussion of decision making, observing and asking questions that will help you understand how the community decides. Ask questions like:

> Who makes major decisions in your community?
>
> How open are those in authority to listening to the opinions of others?
>
> Who do most people look up to for guidance and advice?
>
> Whose voices are most important when it comes to promoting change?

Gaining an understanding of how decisions are made, and how change takes place within the community will help you facilitate Conversation 2. The two glimpses below show contrasting results, depending on the decision-making values of the community.

> Between 1986 and 1991, artist-animators from the University of Dar es Salaam helped organize a series of two-week "Theatre for Development" workshops in Tanzania. They led participants through identifying local art forms, elicited problems in the communities, and helped participants address these problems through communication in local enactment genres. Problems often included many particular to women, such as frequent cases of being beaten by men. After listening to concerns and issues in the community, the participants put together a community theater performance, and engaged the audience in discussion of the problems and possible solutions after the performance. This use of a local art form provided a way for women especially to actively communicate their needs and enter into community development conversations. Women were able to communicate their frustrations and protest oppression and ill treatment through song and dance, while finding solutions together as a community.[42]

> I had spent several days visiting each artistic creation group in their different locations. To culminate the visit, representatives of each group—men, women, older and younger, college-educated and those who had never attended formal education—came together to decide how they could encourage the use of local artistic genres within their churches. I led the group through an Appreciative Inquiry exercise, asking the group to identify the strengths and weaknesses in their church arts programs. I encouraged them to dream about how they would like to see local forms of song, dance, instrumental music, and drama used in the churches to communicate the gospel in ways that would most effectively reach people's hearts. The discussion was lively with everyone contributing

---

42 Adapted from Mlama, "Reinforcing Existing Indigenous Communication," 51–64.

thoughts. As priorities unfolded, the group narrowed their ideas down to three. Then the top church leader, who had been sitting silently in the back of the room during the discussion, approached the group. Reaching towards the slips of paper on the table that had the group's ideas written on them, he picked up one of the rejected ideas and laid it down firmly on the table for all to see. Everyone fell silent. I realized that even though the group discussion went well, the local decision-making process of leaving major decisions to those in established leadership positions had surfaced in the end. This lack of respecting the voices of all the members of the community ended up with an agreed-upon decision, but one that was never acted upon. The voices of those who would have enacted the activities were not respected so the activities were not deemed valuable to the community. The proposed plans never materialized.
—Wendy Atkins

A TOOL TO HELP PEOPLE CHOOSE KINGDOM GOALS

One method for specifying Kingdom Goals follows the process described in "Steps for Nine Participatory Tools for Language Programs—Appreciative Inquiry."[43] This process allows the community to imagine how they would like to see changes for the better by identifying their strengths and the hopes they have for the future. We've also added space to talk about challenges they face. You may do this as an event, or a series of more informal discussions over time. If the community wants to follow a method as a meeting, they can gather a large group, making sure everyone participating has an opportunity to share. Or you may divide the community members into groups of three, asking each group to discuss the same questions. After several minutes, ask the small groups to come together to report their responses.

1. Gather Voices

Your first task is to talk with and listen to people. As we've discussed, communities are internally complex, sometimes with subgroups or individuals at odds with each other. If so, ask friends in the community how they think they could overcome sticky situations like this. You may join conversations about goals that people already have in social structures like traditional or government organizations, rotating savings and credit associations, churches, or mosques. Or you may have this conversation as part of an event that's already happening, like a conference or workshop. Work toward including people from as many parts of the community as possible, especially those not usually given a voice.

---

43 These methods are described compactly in a paper outlining their use with the Kamayo language community on the Island of Mindanao in the Philippines (see Hasselbring, "Nine Participatory Tools"). In addition, Keller, "Deciding and Planning Together," provides an extensive overview of the participatory approach.

2. Explore Strengths and Hopes

All communities have strengths and challenges. Identifying strengths and aspirations first gives people courage and may suggest solutions to problems. Identifying hopes for the future allows people to provide positive suggestions for changes they would like to see in their community. Since all people reflect God's image, we expect to find good in every community. Note that the group may find it easier to see good things if they have used "A tool for understanding the variety of Kingdom Goals" in the first half of Conversation 2. Ask people questions like these:

Strengths

> What are some strengths of your community?
>
> What good things are happening?
>
> What are some activities in your community that make you feel proud of who you are and what you and others are doing?
>
> What is your community known for doing well?

Hopes

> What hopes do you have for your community as a whole?
>
> How would you like it to look different in the future?
>
> What would you like to see changed in your community to make life better for yourself, your children, the women in your community, the elderly, yourself?

Encourage the community to talk about these questions. Help facilitate their discussion of those activities that make them feel proud of who they are and what they are doing. Note these ideas in a locally acceptable way for recording ideas: write them down on small pieces of paper; write on a blackboard or whiteboard; jot down each idea on a sticky note; ask individuals to remember them; use local objects to represent each idea; ask people to make drawings; etc.

3. Explore Difficulties and Challenges

To foster more signs of Heaven, we also need to acknowledge, discuss, and account for aspects and forces that may work *against* the CLAT process. Ask people questions like these:

> What issues are difficult for your community?
>
> What challenges does your community face?
>
> What causes you significant worry?
>
> What is worse in your community now than five years ago? Ten? Twenty?

Lead the community to think about those aspects of life in the community that keep them from developing towards a better future. However, try to keep them from viewing these challenges as blockages that will keep the community from moving towards the Kingdom Goal. When the focus is kept on the strengths and hopes, the community is more likely to consider the messages needed to move towards fulfilling the Kingdom Goal.

4. Choose a Goal or Goals

Now that the community members have noted these items in these categories, read through the ideas in each of the categories. As you do, encourage the community to note which ideas they will be able to achieve soon, and which ones might take a long time. Have community members place these ideas on a time continuum. You may find that some of the individual ideas will group together as you process them. That's a good thing! Allow the community to prioritize their hopes by indicating which ideas are most important to them.

Guide the community to look at their answers to the two categories above, then think together how they relate to goals for the Kingdom (or a better future). The community should reflect on what they have discovered about themselves through the participatory engagement process. Which of the CLAT Kingdom Goals best expresses the community's desires to see progress and change? Which Kingdom Goal would best address the challenges the community faces? Here's a reminder of the goal categories we used above:

Identity and Sustainability: Valuing Identity, Teaching Children, Using Media

Healing: Well-being, Reconciliation, Rest and Play, Creation Care

Justice: Social Justice, Education, Literacy, Economic Opportunity

Scripture: Translating Scripture, Oral Scripture

Church Life: Corporate Worship, Studying and Remembering Scripture, Christian Rites, Witness

Personal Spiritual Life: Prayer and Meditation, Spiritual Formation, Personal Bible Study, Applying Scripture

It may help community members match a goal to each strength or hope they chose. List the most closely related goal category next to the strengths or make up a new one. You may come up with something like this:

Strengths	Hopes	Goals for the Kingdom Category / a Better Future
Respect between generations		Identity and Sustainability
Celebration		Identity and Sustainability
Hospitality		Well-being
...		...

As the community looks through the difficulties and challenges that they identified, think together how solutions would relate to goals for the Kingdom (or a better future). List the most closely related goal category next to the difficulties or make up a new one. You may come up with something like this:

Difficulties and Challenges	Goals for the Kingdom / a Better Future
Disease: HIV/AIDS, malaria	Healing
War, crime, violence	Healing
Intergenerational conflict, loss of traditions	Identity and Sustainability
Fear of death	Personal Spiritual Life
Exploitation: slavery, prostitution	Justice
Inability to read or write	Justice
Lack of access to the Bible	Scripture
Lack of spiritual growth	Personal Spiritual Life
Lack of unity in Christian community	Church Life
Some groups left out of worship	Church Life
Inadequate communion with God	Personal Spiritual Life
Poor education	Justice
Hunger	Justice
…	…

Ask the community to decide which strength they would most like to build on, or which hope they would like to work toward with a Kingdom Goal. Or perhaps the community will choose a challenge they would most like to address with a Kingdom Goal. If you are not a decision-maker in the community, your role in Conversation 2 is now complete. *The goal(s) must emerge from and be owned by the community, not inserted from outside.*

CONVERSATION 3

CONNECT GENRES TO GOALS

Priscille Ndjerareou feels that a primary means of promoting solidarity and passing on important knowledge has all but disappeared from her Ngambay (Chad) community; hardly anybody gathers around the fire to sing, talk, and tell stories in the evening (a genre called *tà pòr ndàāl*). She also wants to encourage young Christians to value traditional storytelling and be courageous in their faith. To this end she developed a plan to revitalize the *tà pòr ndàāl* event by modifying it in three ways. First, she would find and invite people who are excellent storytellers to come. Second, she would tell Scripture stories in another story form, and encourage other Christians to do the same. Third, she would commission new songs in the *pa nō gōr* genre with Christian themes. She believes that these innovations will attract people to gather, result in transmission of crucial life knowledge, raise the younger generation's sense of Ngambay identity, and instill biblical knowledge that will lead to stronger discipleship. She is looking for ways to put this plan into action.

Once a community has identified a goal or goals that they want to work toward, it's time to figure out how their arts can help them get there. Each genre is particularly apt for communicating certain kinds of content and producing certain kinds of effects. So in Conversation 3 we explore approaches to help a community solve a complex puzzle: *what combinations of genres, content, events, and effects of artistry on people are likely to help them reach their Kingdom Goal(s)?* You may want to have this conversation with the same people you gathered for Conversation 2, or include others. Remember to pray for wisdom, love, humility, and protection during this process.

In this discussion, we deepen our understanding of two concepts especially important from this point onward: Meanings and Effects. We outline an idealized, linear, logically coherent set of actions that can result in communities producing an initial overview of elements and connections that could help them achieve their hopes and goals. But human beings are complicated, gloriously diverse, and make their own choices. So we then present a few tips for contexts in which things don't happen this way: Real Life CLAT. In Real Life, each of these points should be addressed, but the process need not follow this order. And as in the Ngambay anecdote above, the community may innovate both genres and types of events. As always, we listen to community members and hold our expectations *lightly*.

You and the community will refine, expand, fill out, and improve this draft overview in Conversations 4, 5, 6, and 7. You all may even decide to start over completely.

MEANINGS

On the surface, this part of the Creating Local Arts Together approach may appear mechanistic: find the right people to enact the right kind of arts that make people change to fit in the Kingdom of Heaven more. In fact, everything we propose needs ultimately to emerge from and be integrated organically into a community to be useful in reaching their goals—and God must be involved. This makes it more likely that groups will draw on the meanings they themselves associate with elements, patterns, social structures, and other aspects of their lives they explore. But what is *meaning*?

What is Meaning and Where Does It Come From?

Many disciplines like linguistics, cognitive science, semiotics, philosophy, communication studies, and anthropology have devoted astronomically large amounts of time and energy and research and analysis to understand meaning.[1] We obviously can't benefit from all this thought and practice, so I've developed a flexible working description of meaning that draws on several fields and seems to flow easily and helpfully through the CLAT process. For our purposes, **meaning** refers to ideas and emotions a community or individual attaches to elements of their internal or external experiences. As we'll see in Conversation 4, the field of phenomenology provides helpful insights into the identification and description of experiences.

Making Meaning. Human beings begin searching for and attaching significance to the vibrations and chemical combinations that impinge on their sensory organs even in the womb.[2] God made us "namers" (Gen 2:19–20), sign finders, and interpreters (Matt 16:2–3; Luke 21:7). We are predisposed to create systems of communication, including language in its artistically marked forms.[3] Our goal is to enter into and learn as much as we can about a community's systems of communication, especially the meanings connected to artistic events and genres. The only way we can discover meanings is through research.

As we grow, we each make sense of our worlds through complex interactions between our individual neurological and bodily characteristics and our physical and social environments—often referred to as nature and nurture. Neither of these is static or fixed, but some things are more malleable than others. We engage with our experiences in ways that result in cognitive structures reflecting our communities—like beliefs, worldviews, language, and social structures—and idiosyncrasies: each individual's unique combination of genetically influenced characteristics. Each of the elements in our stories—our upbringing, events—can help growth toward thriving, be neutral, or detrimental (e.g., traumatic events).

Kinds of Input. We try to make sense of three types of encounters. First, an experience can originate outside of our bodies, entering our stories through

---

1 For a summary of several historical approaches to meaning, see Marsen, "The Role of Meaning."

2 See, e.g., Adolphs, "Cognitive Neuroscience"; Delton and Sell, "Co-evolution of Concepts and Motivation."

3 Dutton, *The Art Instinct*; Ball, *The Music Instinct*; Pinker, *The Language Instinct*.

sense organs that respond to certain types of stimuli, like vibrating air waves or chemicals. Depending on our individual capacities, our sensory receptors send nerve impulses to our brains, where we interpret and respond to what has come in. So we assign meaning to elements of our environment that enter through hearing, smelling, feeling, tasting, and seeing.[4]

A second source of input that triggers meaning-making activity is internal: our own thoughts. Mental objects can enter our minds with different levels of control, detail, and welcome by remembering, meditating, praying, daydreaming, or even doing nothing.

A third possible source of input is supernatural. If we are Christ-followers, Jesus lives in us, the Holy Spirit flows on and around us, and Father|Son|Spirit is with us in every communication event. God responds to prayers in all sorts of ways. Remember also that Satan and his coterie may impinge on people's lives destructively and deviously.

How Can We Find Meaning?

In Conversation 4, we offer detailed, rigorous methods to identify artistry's signs and their meanings for individuals and communities. Because we are producing an initial draft plan in Conversation 3, however, we will introduce a few concepts and proceed more casually.

Accessing the meanings a community places on artistry requires identifying the signs that point to those meanings. Thinking about signs, or signifiers, as one of three types—lexical, iconic, or indexical—can help us recognize them. Each rouses or initiates a thought, feeling, or memory, in different ways.[5]

- **Lexical (or propositional).** A conventional *symbolic* sign relates a sign and an object *through language*—propositional, conventional, referential language. The word *elephant* occurring in an encyclopedia, for example, refers to a large mammal with a trunk and usually tusks. The sounds I make when saying *elephant* in my English dialect[6] are together an auditory lexical sign linked to the idea of that animal in my thoughts. The letters *elephant* as printed on a page constitute a visual lexical sign to the same animal.

- **Iconic.** Relates a sign and an object *through resemblance*: the sign looks or sounds or feels in some way like the object it points to. A realistic statue of an elephant bears a strong resemblance to an actual elephant. The statue is a visual iconic sign. Someone mimicking an elephant's trumpeting sound is an auditory iconic sign.

---

4 Note also that some experiences elicit autonomic responses to stimuli, thoughts, or signs, mostly activating the autonomic nervous system. These responses—like jerking your hand back from a hot object—are usually outside conscious control.

5 Also consider this profound assertion: "The Catholic liturgy is the only play wherein symbols actually become the things they symbolize. It sets the (unobtainable) ideal for ... all true art," that which "aspires to be incarnational" (Hernandez, "The Vocation of the Catholic Artist").

6 In the International Phonetic Alphabet (IPA; see https://www.ipachart.com and https://ipa.typeit.org/full/): [ɛləfənt'].

- **Indexical.** Relates a sign to its object *through co-occurrence* in actual experience (i.e., by association). Someone who saw an elephant family group being killed for their tusks might feel anger and a resolve to protect others. A later occurrence of seeing or thinking about another elephant might index her previous experience, arousing those same emotions.

In Conversation 3, lexical and indexical signs help us choose content and genres we need for our initial plan. For us, **Content** refers to lexical meaning—symbolic communication (language). As Jesus-followers who know the profound importance and impact of Scripture, we place special emphasis on symbols, words, and language. Language bolsters people's engagement with complex thoughts and beliefs in their interactions with others and God.

Indexical meanings play pivotal roles when communities reflect on a genre or event's appropriateness in connecting artistry to their goals for a more Heaven-filled future. We focus on a particular kind of association: **Connotation.** We define connotations as *meanings people associate with genres based on their experience of its enactments and community understandings of its purposes as a whole.*

As we'll see, these types of meaning are integral in assessing the effects of choosing and enacting a genre. One confounding factor, of course, is that each person and subgroup makes meaning of all communicated forms. Keep in mind that this may lead to internal diversity, which can reinforce or undercut effects we hope and plan for.

IDEALIZED APPROACH: TRY TO CONNECT EARTHLY ARTISTRY TO MORE HEAVEN

This planning process flows from temporal logical models sometimes used by local and international non-governmental organizations (NGOs) in community development.[7] It begins with goals, then works backward through steps whose accomplishment depend on previous steps, conditions, and resources. Following these steps has a good chance of producing a bundle of elements and activities that will connect genres to goals:

1. Restate the Kingdom Goal(s) chosen in Conversation 2.

2. Identify effects of enactments of artistry that would likely result in the accomplishment of the Kingdom Goal(s).

3. Identify content that would help the artistic enactment have the desired effects.

4. Identify a genre (or genres) whose enactment has the capacity to communicate the content and produce the desired effects.

5. Imagine events that could include enactments of new works in the genre that would produce the effects in its experiencers, ultimately resulting in reaching the Kingdom Goal(s).

---

7 The Logical Framework Approach (LFA) is a methodology mainly used for designing, monitoring, and evaluating international development projects. Variations of this tool are known as Goal Oriented Project Planning (GOPP) or Objectives Oriented Project Planning (OOPP).

Figure 3.1 provides a place to insert tentative results as you and the community work through the rest of the Conversations. It can provide a way of summarizing *one possible path* from a genre choice to achieving the goal. You and the community will likely choose to explore other genres and paths during the rest of the conversations, so hold these initial results lightly. Please note that this template is only meant to capture these very early possibilities, not to replace the important process of doing all the Conversations.

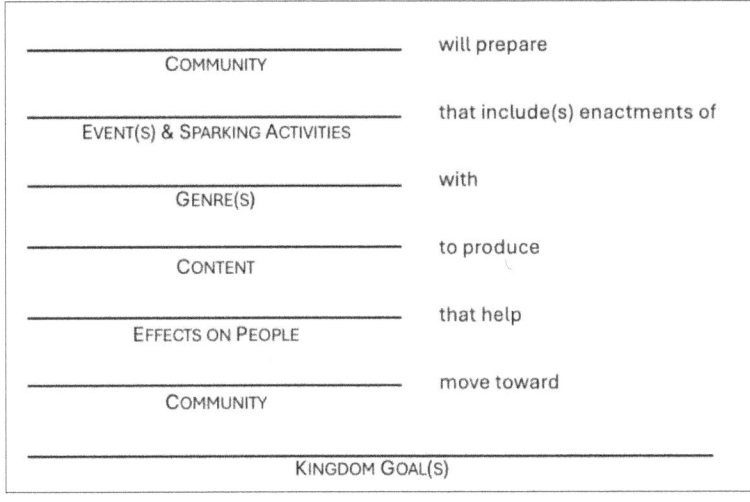

Figure 3.1 Draft plan to connect community artistry to Kingdom Goals

Restate the Kingdom Goal(s)

In Conversation 2, community members chose one or more ways they would like their futures to be better, to be more like Heaven. Write this goal where everyone can refer to it again: on a white or chalk board, pieces of paper, a projected computer file, or other location. Also enter it into Figure 3.1 and the Community Arts Profile.

Identify the Desired Effects of the New Artistry

Experiencing more Heaven requires change. We're focusing on how God can bring about New Creation change through artistic communication he originally created. Specifically, we want to identify likely impacts on people resulting from their involvement with artistry. We define **effects** as *changes in a person or group tied to meaning(s) they attribute to creating, enacting, experiencing, participating in, remembering, or otherwise engaging with types of artistry*. These changes could include the way people feel, act, understand, remember, pray, talk, think, relate to others, and so on.

Think back to the stories we told in the introductory chapter about a Mono church community in DR Congo. Though they may not have expressed them as completely as this at the time, they had these Kingdom Goals: deeper communication with God; fuller understanding of Scripture; affirmation of good arts in their culture; and witness to the rest of the community. To reach these goals, people in the community needed to think differently about their arts, sing new kinds of songs in church and out, and experience Scripture in a communication genre closer to their hearts.

Remember again that artistry acts on and in both individuals and groups, so its effects may not be uniform. It can also elicit strong—even violent—responses to bullies, corrupt officials, armies, abusive family members, cult-like ideologues, and so on. Praying, focusing on constructive effects, and studying Jesus's humility and limited contexts provoking his anger, can help a community navigate complex social and moral contexts. Some situations will require extensive time devoted to potentially dangerous artistry, which is beyond the scope of this manual.[8]

With the intent to act wisely, our next task for connecting Kingdom Goals with local arts is thinking through the effects community members want those arts to produce in their community. These are some common effects of artistry that can move people toward goals. For example, they may:

- understand an important message.
- act differently.
- change an unhelpful or dangerous behavior.
- do something new.
- think differently.
- feel solidarity with others.
- experience emotional, physical, or relationship healing.
- experience hope, joy, anger, remorse, elation, peace, satisfaction, relief, empathy, surprise, or other emotions.
- organize themselves differently, in government or other social structures.
- adjust how they interact with their physical environments.

To identify such effects, community members discuss questions like these:

> How do we want people to change in ways that move them toward our goals?
>
> What do we want people to feel and do as a result of experiencing the enactment?

Enter the results of the discussion in Figure 3.1 and the Community Arts Profile.

Identify Content for the New Artistry

If the desired effects depend on people learning ideas—that is, lexical meanings—through arts, then it's crucial to make sure that those ideas are trustworthy. In the Mono case, church leaders wanted others to hear and understand Scripture, so they needed to have excellent translations available. The lesson is this: study the truth content to be taught so that an accurate

---

[8] For a few examples of arts used for destruction, see Schrag, *Artistic Dynamos*, 144–45.

message is conveyed. If the message is about how malaria may be prevented, make sure you know the facts about how malaria is actually prevented: talk to health care professionals, inviting them into the process. For Scripture-related goals, study the passage before creating a message based upon the passage: talk to Bible scholars and translators. Talk about the content with God, other artists, and leaders. Together the community members should discuss these questions:

> What content do we want to communicate?
>
> How can we make sure that the content is reliable?
>
> Can we invite any experts in the content into our discussion?

Enter the results of the discussion in the CAP and Figure 3.1.

Identify a Genre or Genres that May Have the Capacity to Communicate the Content and Produce the Desired Effects

Every artistic genre has characteristics that affect the messages it conveys and the effects it has. Because one of the effects that the Mono community wanted was that people would understand Scripture better, they chose the *gbaguru* genre for their initial activities. It was a relatively straightforward genre to start with for this purpose because it can include lots of words (that is, signs pointing to lexical meanings), is used to communicate advice that people respect, and doesn't have distracting connotations (that is, indexical signs associated with the genre) like sexuality or ancestor worship. Note that sexual connotations could be appropriate for goals having to do with marriage, but not for this situation.

So together:

- Show the list of artistic genres you produced in the activity "Take a First Glance at a Community's Arts" in Conversation 1. This could be on a big piece of paper, a chalkboard or whiteboard, an overhead projector, or a digital screen.

- Now place some of the genres into an outline like the chart in Figure 3.2. To get started, compare a reduced number of genres that are most likely to have effects: those that are popular, beloved, prominent, valued but endangered, and so on. Together, fill in as many of the cells as you can, noting which bits of information need more research. The process may reveal a need to add, remove, or replace columns with other categories that fit the situation better. Also, this chart contains facts, not opinions.

Genre	Brief Description	Event(s)	Participants	Connotations	Effects on people	Feasibility
...	...	...	...	...	...	

Figure 3.2 First-glance genre comparison chart

For each genre, ask:

> Would a new artistic work in this genre have the effects we've chosen? If not, why not?
>
> Would a new artistic work in this genre communicate the content we've chosen well? If not, why not?
>
> Do resources exist that allow enactments of the genre? For example, are there people who know how to do this? Would the genre's status promote people's eagerness to create in it, or would it be a hindrance? Are there other factors that make using this genre more or less feasible?
>
> Will connotations or associated emotions overpower or dilute the desired effects?
>
> Is the genre associated with organizations or other social structures that could positively or negatively impact creativity?

Narrow the list to one or two genres that would be the best for producing these effects and communicating this content now. Conversation 4 will lead you through more detailed exploration of the genre or genres you finally decide on. Put the results of this discussion in the CAP and Figure 3.1.

Figure 3.3 contains such data for some genres available to urban Yeshu Bhakta communities in India (Laura Roberts).

Genre	Brief Description	Event(s)	Participants	Connotations	Effects	Popularity, Status, Feasibility
Bhajan	Hindu devotional hymn. Call and response.	satsang, bhajan kirtan, temple, home	Lead singer and group, instrumentalists	Devotional, spiritual, traditional, light classical	Worship, adoration, familiar	Easy to sing, spiritual genre for all ages, castes
Lok geet	Folk songs (vary by region)	Home, festivals, village	Anyone, instruments like bansuri	Simple, stories, melodic, during tasks	Nostalgia, accessible	Older people, villages, traditional communities
Ram Lila	dance drama of Ram, Hanuman mythology	Outdoor venue (park, school)	actors, dancers, costume/set design	Stories of gods, cultural pride	Entertainment, impressive	During Dusshera festival season
Rangoli	Colorful designs outside homes	Festivals, special satsangs	Usually young women in the home	Celebration, welcoming, luck	Peace, calm, happiness, joy	During Diwali mostly. Loved by all castes, ages.
Bollywood music videos	Videos of songs from films with dancing	TV, YouTube, home	Celebrities, girls dancing at home	Romance, love, dramatic	Pride of culture	All enjoy, especially young generation
Mehendi	Henna patterns on hands or feet	Weddings, festivals	Mostly women, bride & groom	Celebration, beauty, marriage, community	Beauty, cultural identity	Very popular among women, tourists
Kathak	Classical dance with hand gestures	On a stage	Highly trained solo, duo or team	Storytelling through gestures	Impressive, beautiful	Middle-upper class, on stage

Figure 3.3 First glance genre comparison chart for urban Yeshu Bhakta communities

Remember that all artistic genres have characteristics that can be redeemed for God's purposes, but that not all are appropriate at a given moment in a community's life. In addition to pooling their knowledge of these genres for group wisdom, encourage community members to pray a lot, and listen for the wisdom of the Holy Spirit. Do not try to force a genre into new uses in a community. Be certain that God wants it to happen now.

Imagine Events and Sparking Activities

When an individual or group acts artistically internally, it can be deeply satisfying, cathartic, or healing. This is of great value. We focus here, however, on creativity that looks outward, to pervade a community.

This means that a new dyed cloth, play, poem, or prayer room has limited value for the Kingdom if it remains hidden. It has no effects on anybody else unless it is part of an event where communication happens. The Mono apprentices of Punayima felt that and performed in a corporate worship setting as *Chorale Ayo*.

Events

Before a community starts planning how to create new works in a genre, they should imagine the contexts for their presentation, possible creation-sparking activities, and how enactments work as communication. In Conversation 5, community leaders will refine these ideas or may choose activities related to other events. To start, here are some examples of an infinite number of such communication events:

- Mass, worship service, Bible study, Sunday school, home group, outreach, weddings, funerals, baptisms
- Festivals, harvest celebrations, courting rituals, birth rites, rites of passage, teaching contexts
- listening to an audio recording, watching a video recording, transmitting live audio or video to other locations
- viewing a sculpture in a museum, advancing meditatively through seven rooms depicting the last words of Jesus, straining to see the top of a skyscraper
- concert, rehearsal, gig, awards ceremony, sporting event
- intimate family discussion, smoking a peace pipe, court, war

Sparking Activities

We want communities to design activities that result in more artistry that will likely result in more signs of Heaven. We favor existing stimuli and modes of local creativity because they usually enhance continuity, ownership, and motivation. But CLAT also involves novelty, so we've defined sparking activities with enormous scope and freedom: they may follow local processes meticulously or adopt ideas from someone on the other side of the world; last a moment or years; include one person or thousands; rely on live enactments for transmission or various media; engage with churches or secular global NGOs; integrate the complete CLAT process or just one Conversation.

Here are a few of the types of activities we expand on in Conversation 5:

- **Fostering Relationships**. Creativity can emerge organically from trusting bonds.
- **Commissioning**. One or more people can ask one or more other people to make something for agreed upon purposes.
- **Workshops**. Concentrated gathering that turns training, making, and solidarity into plans for continuing Heaven-producing creativity in participants' communities.
- **Showcase Events**. Exposure at local, regional, or national festivals can lure artists to offer examples of their own expressions.
- **Mentoring**. Someone with substantial social capital or status can open doors for others building their reputations as artists and leaders.
- **Apprenticeship**. Learning at the feet of a gifted artist can result in mending broken transmission mechanisms and competencies for newly redeemed traditions.
- **Publications**. Short- or long-term, printed or online, thoughtful prose, proverbs, and stories can educate and motivate.
- **Creators' Clubs**. Groups that meet regularly to encourage each other and advance in their crafts can serve as fertile, consistent incubators for arts addressing Kingdom needs as they arise in a community.

Conversation 5 and Closing 5 include examples of these and more kinds of sparking activities, with guidance on implementing them in your contexts.

Communication Mechanics in Artistic Genre Enactments

Communication emerges from every enactment containing artistry through systemic interactions between its components. Understanding how communication works, illustrated in Figure 3.4, will help you identify the unique organization and dynamics of your context.

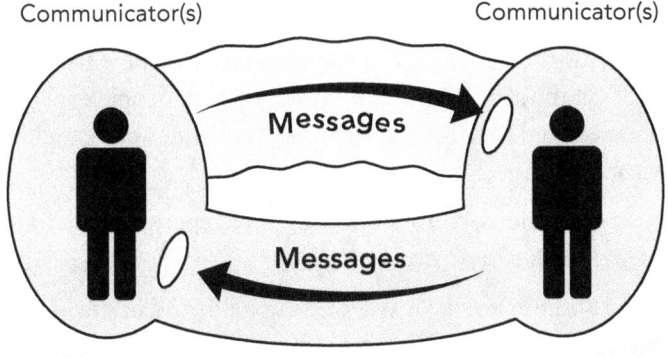

Figure 3.4 Components of an artistic communication enactment

This figure illustrates how people interact by directing messages through various artistic genres to other communicators at particular places and times. The place and time could be one evening in a concert hall or spread out when someone watches a film created previously by someone else in a different location. The people involved in the communication enactment usually consist of at least two individuals or groups who may or may not be physically near or exist materially; humans often communicate with spiritual beings. In addition, individuals can make things for themselves. Creativity leading to trauma healing, for example, often entails one person communicating with God.

We represent artistic genres in the diagram by the tubes enclosing and connecting the communicators. Note that some genres are more regular and predictable than others—these are depicted in the front with smooth lines. Others include more variability or improvisation, which we've shown with the curled edges. Repeating interactions between stable and malleable elements can inject energy into an enactment.[9] Messages are the thoughts or feelings that take form when mediated by a genre. People encountering an enactment may experience this content with their whole bodies when they hear, see, feel, smell, and/or taste whatever other communicators produce with their singing, dancing, painting, cooking, constructing, and the like. Finally, you'll see that communication happens in particular directions (indicated by the arrows) but is always eventually reciprocal. Responses may include verbal, physical, or visual encouragement or discouragement, joining the enactment, and notable silence, among many other possibilities. It's this response that so often feeds back into the artistic expression, resulting in more energy, pleasure, and creativity.

Questions to Inform Event and Sparking Activity Preliminary Decisions
Together with community members:

> Remind yourselves of your choices thus far: Kingdom Goals, effects, content (messages), and genre(s).
>
> Make a list of kinds of events that new works—that is, enactments—in the artistic genre(s) could be part of. Let your minds run free with possibilities at this stage. Include both presentations where participants are physically in the same place, and those in which people experience the artistry mediated through, for example, recordings or virtual reality environments.
>
> During your discussions, consider how different sparking activities might pair well with certain events.
>
> Choose a few of the event types you came up with and briefly describe them in terms of their communication components:

---

9 For examples of stable|malleable dynamos, see Schrag, *Artistic Dynamos*, 145–51; Ezhevskaya, "Russian Bards in America."

- Who are the communicators?
- When and where might such an event happen?
- What senses will participants use in experiencing the content?
- How will the genre(s) enactments affect the messages that people experience?
- When people experience the artistry, will it have the effects you'd like? How will people respond to the original communicators?

Choose one or two events and sparking activities that would be likely goals for cocreative activities.

Make sure you put the results of this discussion in the Community Arts Profile and Figure 3.1.

Glimpses

Here are a few more examples of CLAT summary statements of initial plans made by a community. These statements connect genres to goals identified as important by particular communities, following the steps in Conversations 1, 2, and 3:

1) For the anniversary of the founding of the Dorkas Orphanage in Indonesia, UKIT professors will work with a dance expert to prepare a performance of *maengket* (song and dance for celebrating) helping the children to appreciate their cultural identity and overcome the trauma of being placed in an orphanage, reconciling them to their parents (invited to the performance), and moving the orphans toward the Kingdom Goal of Healing and Valuing Identity.

2) The Deaf church in Barcelona, Spain will prepare a mini-workshop and showcase event that includes performance of poetic, emotive-expressive language with translated Scripture to produce congregants who are able to emotionally connect to Scripture and integrate it into their daily lives moving them toward the Kingdom Goal of personal spiritual life: prayer, meditation, and applying Scripture.

3) The Zande Community in the DRC will prepare a church event that includes an enactment of *kpaningba* dance with Scripture from Isaiah 40:28 to communicate truth in a joyful, engaging manner that helps the Zande community move toward understanding God's power in their daily life.

4) The Kaqchikel people in Guatemala will form a Creator's Club that collects, creates, tests, revises, and records Kaqchikel children's songs about community life and values that will be used in schools to promote confidence that the Kaqchikel language can be sung.

REAL LIFE TIPS

Using Other Methods to Reach Similar Goals

Most of us rarely think primarily in linear, logically ordered ways. Our thought processes may be more circular or take a long time to mature. We often make decisions more organically, holistically, integrating feelings, following unique social conventions, strongly aware of the intricate web of connections between people, events, and genres. So if community representatives you're working with find the approach we've presented unproductive or confusing, work with them to develop a more appropriate process. It may also be helpful to revisit the "How Does this Community Usually Make Decisions?" discussion in Conversation 2 and Decision-Making section in Conversation 4C.

Responding to Requests that Reduce Choices

Sometimes communities find themselves in situations that push a particular art form, event, artist, content, activity, or goal to the forefront. So instead of agreeing first on a common goal, there may be energy and interest in one of the other of these elements. For example, several large church denominations in Indonesia were especially interested in writing new songs in local languages and styles for different parts of their liturgy. They were initially only interested in songs so they could conduct a full liturgical worship service in the local language. Song content and stylistic choices, therefore, were dictated by the needs of the liturgy.

In some cases, these initial requests lead to further conversations about dance, symbolism, and other elements of worship from a wider variety of artistic domains. Meeting this need also allowed arts workers to build relationships with key leaders and lay the foundations for further work with the arts.[10]

In addition, a community might decide to partner with a church denomination, missionary organization, or other group that promotes particular products or methods. Cru's Jesus Film initiative, for example, requires communities to agree to certain partnership requirements and follow detailed recording processes to produce a video representation of Jesus's life dubbed by local actors in the local language. Other organizations might promote unique approaches to telling Scripture-based stories, dramatizing Scripture, developing multicultural musical worship in churches, and so on.

Adopting a goal or other element already chosen from outside the community will change the CLAT process. It may open people's minds to beneficial possibilities they hadn't thought of. On the other hand, there's a risk that the community might not share the goals, not owning them in the same way. This could undermine, weaken, or delay the chance of reaching their most important hopes for a better future.

---

10 For more, see Connor and Menger, "Strengthening Christian Identity."

Intentionally Messy CLAT

Remember that CLAT is a flexible approach, consisting of Conversations that communities will need to visit and revisit according to discoveries, social and spiritual dynamics, deepening relationships, and everyone's growth in wisdom and understanding. We designed Conversation 3 to result in a draft plan, one that will need to be changed.

Conversation 4 will almost certainly result in discoveries that require modifications of the plan. In particular, research about genres and events will feed into our mindset and process of Careful Contextualization, which we've crafted into a tool in Conversation 4D. The community will have a chance to keep, modify, or reject a genre after or during deep analysis. This is part of the design.

CONVERSATION 4

ANALYZE GENRES AND EVENTS

You and the community have stepped through first meetings, explored dreams and goals, and have begun to imagine how their arts might help make their lives more like Heaven. Now you've reached the crux of creativity: the artistry itself—the complex, intricate processes and objects that move us to cry, laugh, dance, resolve, remember, repent, understand, and imagine. Artistic communication affects us because our previous experience leads us to expect certain things to happen. These expectations are sometimes completely satisfied, sometimes pleasurably tweaked, sometimes startlingly overturned, or sometimes clumsily imperfect due to a lack of skill or unavoidable crisis (like a lightning strike or marauding elephant). But it's a communal sharing of artistic skills and anticipations that makes all the good things happen. All this energy is wrapped in extremely complex packages, so Conversation 4 takes up a large portion of this manual, plus you can find more methods, vocabulary, and tools for analysis in the *CLAT Companion* and Digital Library at www.clatmanual.com.

But don't most people in communities already know the information we're trying to tease out in this Conversation? Don't artistic masters know how to subtly modify a vocal timbre to bring a tear to one's eye or a spring to one's step? Yes. And aren't others sometimes able to express this knowledge explicitly, using their own or outside analytical vocabulary? Yes. So why do communities have to put such time and energy into studying what they might already know?

Here are some good reasons to research artistic genres. First, even within our own communities, most of us don't have the perspective or categories to understand everything that's important in our artistic actions. Second, this research will help you enter an artistic practice, develop a common language for exploration, and bring pleasure to you and your friends. Finally, discoveries and decisions resulting from the process will help a community design contextualized sparking activities in Conversation 5, improve new works in Conversation 6, and integrate new creativity in Conversation 7.

To help you access these benefits, this introduction will show you how to:

- grasp a reassuring overview
- think more clearly about genres and events
- understand Conversation 4's structure
- decide what analysis to do (which is not everything)

A REASSURING OVERVIEW

We are convinced that the Creating Local Arts Together approach is nestled securely in God's plan for his creation for two primary reasons: its nature in view of an infinitely comprehensive historical scope, and how it depends conceptually on what's really real about humans—aided by phenomenology.

In God's Story

First, we know our current and future roles as actors in the drama God has scripted for us, which we summarized in "From Creation to New Creation." The narrative flows like this: the triune God creates the cosmos, which is very good; Adam and Eve rebel, corrupting all that God created; humans—primarily Israel—continue their broken relationship with God, with periodic reconciliation and hope for the Messiah; Jesus is born, ministers, dies, resurrects, sends out his disciples, and ascends; God extends Heaven on Earth with us, still impeded by sin, so we live in the *now and not-yet* of Heaven; Jesus will return, re-making all things and people with no rot to overcome. This will result in the utterly pervasive New Creation, where we will thrive and grow and know Jesus without barriers or limits for eternity. So we in the church know the frustrations and pains of the current mélange of the "some but not all-ness of Heaven" now, always knowing our future is final union with God.

Phenomenology

Second, we recognize insights from the field of phenomenology. In short, we base our efforts to increase Heaven on Earth on engagement with fundamental characteristics of particular communities and their environments. This means that we inhabit, are intertwined, with creation that both groans and laughs. We can disentangle the expressions of this tug-of-war peculiar to each community through God-aided experiences. When communities approach their efforts to increase signs of Heaven through artistic events, they need to act informed by as complete understandings of their realities as possible. The study of phenomenology provides especially helpful approaches to identifying and describing these experiences as part of larger events.

The field of phenomenology is historically and conceptually complex, continually spawning many sub-disciplines. To avoid confusion, I draw on Smith's entry in the *Stanford Encyclopedia of Philosophy* to highlight aspects most germane to our work. Phenomenological research and analysis, then, begin by identifying and describing experiences entering our consciousness through sensory pathways like seeing, hearing, feeling, tasting, and smelling. Since our experience is normally much richer in content than mere sensation, phenomenology also addresses meanings, the "significance of objects, events, tools, the flow of time, the self, and others, as these things arise and are experienced in our 'life-world.'" In other words, "phenomenology studies the structure of various types of experience ranging from perception, thought, memory, imagination, emotion, desire, and volition to bodily awareness, embodied action, and social activity, including linguistic activity."[1]

---

[1] Modified from Smith, "Phenomenology."

Engelland describes phenomenology's core contribution to understanding human experience as "… a rallying cry, 'Back to the things themselves.'"[2] Interestingly, he defines phenomenology as "[h]ow truth and essences arise in experience,"[3] dividing its description into these chapters: To the Things Themselves, World, Flesh, Speech, Truth, Life, Love, Wonder, The Method, and The Movement.[4] Recall Figure 3.4's depiction of an artistic communication event, showing how experience of artistry encompasses our whole bodies. We emphasize and provide methods of learning and researching based on experiences we understand—rooted in the *thing itself*—so communities' efforts to increase Heaven will be more likely to succeed.

The Methodology

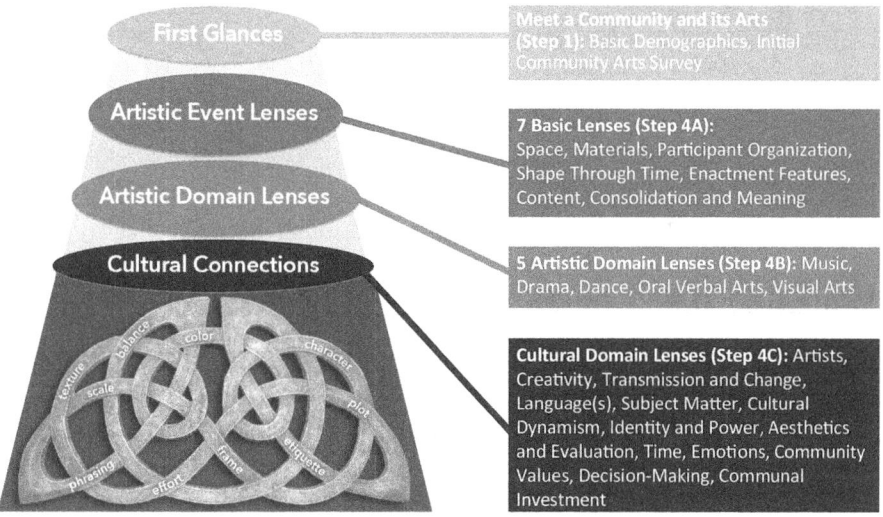

Figure 4.1 A complex artistic enactment seen through several lenses

Figure 4.1 focuses on the representation of an artistic enactment at the bottom, with multiple, intertwined features. First glances in Conversations 1, 3, and 4A provide a backdrop for deeper analysis of artistry. This includes a community's basic demographics, making an initial community arts survey, and comparing several genres through basic categories and connotations. Now we go deeper and in greater detail through a process summarized here:

Primary Research Object: Enactments of genres occurring in space and time.

Process: Sequential research leading to ever-more detailed, comprehensive understanding of genres and events (never complete, but always becoming more thorough with experience and research).

Three Passes: looking at enactments through lenses that highlight three types of features, as seen in Figure 4.2. We expand on each pass in Conversations 4A, 4B, and 4C.

---

2 Engelland, *Phenomenology*, 131.

3 Engelland, 217.

4 Engelland, *Phenomenology*; See also, Grant, McNeilly-Renaudie, and Wagner, *Performance Phenomenology*.

	First Pass: Look Through Seven Basic Lenses [4A]	**Second Pass: Identify Artistic Domain Features [4B]**	**Third Pass: Discover Deeper Community Connections [4C]**
Primary Questions	What are the basic characteristics of a particular genre enacted in an event?	How are shapes, colors, construction, words, melodies, aromas, touch, and so on used in each lens to add more artistry to enactments of a particular genre?	How do the forms and features revealed in first- and second-pass research connect to broader community patterns and dynamics?
Output Summary	Genre Enactment Features, as seen through 7 artistic enactment lenses: Space, Materials, Participant Organization, Shape through Time, Enactment Features, Content, Consolidation and Meanings	Genre Enactment Features augmented by features associated with some larger arts categories	Genre Enactment Features enriched by evaluation through some ethnographic lenses

Figure 4.2 Three-pass artistry research process

MORE ON EVENTS, GENRES, AND ENACTMENTS

In Conversation 1, we introduced key terms that form the conceptual core of the CLAT research process.

One way we learn about enactments of genres is by first describing an event that contains it in a hierarchical way. Lens 4—Shape through Time—provides ways to reveal such structures, including those presented in Figure 4.3. Note that objects themselves can be enactments of artistic genres, independent of or associated with one or more of the other genres in the event. The sections that follow explore some implications of these hierarchical descriptions.

> **Master Event:** Consists of activities over a time frame, including both artistic and non-artistic activities (e.g., siesta, eating). Any particular Master Event timeline could have parallel streams of activities (e.g., a fair, 3-ring circus, festival) all happening at the same time.
>
> **Enactment of a Genre:** Arts-marked activities that occur during a Master Event. If an artistic event contains examples of multiple genres, we can call it a **Composite Event**.
>
> **Sub-Enactment of a Genre:** Arts-marked activities that occur during the enactment of a genre that are from a *different* artistic genre. Each sub-genre enactment may include enactments of sub-sub genres.
>
> **Completing the Analysis:** Keep exploring the event until you're at a point in the hierarchy where there are no more constituent genres.

Figure 4.3 A top-down, hierarchical description of an artistic event

Events often Contain Enactments of More than One Genre
A commemoration of the death and life of a Bamiléké (Cameroon) king may last a month—one event with many subevents. During this time, performers from other kingdoms visit to pay their respects, usually including examples of one or more genres, each with unique combinations of music, dance, drama, objects, and visual features.

Events are almost always longer than enactments of a genre
At a wedding, for example, you may perform a solo in a love song genre. Enactment of the love song genre is just one part of a larger event that includes rituals and other elements.

Enactments of genres may be found in more than one kind of event
Certain kinds of acrobatic feats, for example, may appear both in circuses and gymnastics competitions. Also, for example, blessing songs can show up in weddings, baby celebrations, bride negotiations, lullabies, and so on.

Many events entail strong expectations of what kinds of genres they can include
An Orthodox icon, for example, might offend worshipers in a Baptist sanctuary. There may be an inflexible association between a certain type of event and a certain genre, or participants in an event may have the freedom to switch out elements from different genres. In Conversation 3, you already explored this a bit. We'll help you think about it more in Conversation 5.

Genres, enactments, and events are always changing
Old ones die, new ones are born, creative people innovate. Genres like Christian Kiswahili rap have multiple origins wrapped in unique ways; such fusions are ubiquitous.[5] So don't hold your definitions too tightly. As you describe more events and genres, you will be able to understand their boundaries and flexibilities more and more.

FINDING THINGS THAT MATTER

With a community, we want to discover facts and dynamics related to their artistry that will help them reach their goals. To that end, we weave the identification of two crucial elements throughout Conversation 4's activities: **Patterns and Meanings.** Flowing from phenomenology's holistic approach to experience, honing our senses and conceptual frameworks to expect patterns and meanings in artistic communication will energize every aspect of our Heavenward engagement with communities.

Patterns
Human beings can engage with their communities in part because they learn what they can predict in their interactions. Shared communication systems like languages require the ability of people to know what to expect: Patterns.

---

[5] Schrag, "Motivations and Methods." For ethnodoxology resources on fusions, see Portugal, *Authenticity in Fusion Music*; Troutman, "Crying Ukhai."

For our purposes, a **pattern** is *a repeated or regular way that elements of an enactment occur or is arranged, with differing levels of variation and complexity.* We may or may not be conscious of the underlying systems that result in such patterns, but we usually notice discrepancies. For example, each participant in an Indonesian *angklung* ensemble shakes one or more bamboo instruments—called *angklungs*—tuned to specific pitches. They take turns playing each instrument so that together they produce melodies and harmonies of a particular song.[6] Some genres integrate *angklungs*, dance, and regalia—experiencers familiar with such a genre can detect divergences from expected melodic, movement, or visual patterns.

> **Discover**
>
> Do you notice anything that repeats over time? in different spaces?
> Do other enactments in the same genre always follow the same pattern?

Meanings

Arts Advocates who are not community insiders should *never* assume or assign meanings to artistry or events or social patterns or *anything else*. The meanings our research identifies always refer to meanings that have been discovered. In Conversation 3, we defined **meaning** as *ideas and emotions a community or individual attaches to elements of their internal or external experiences.* We've designed many Conversation 4 research and analysis activities to identify features of artistry and their patterns. Some research activities focus on elements—especially those with words, like stories or dialogue—that are bathed in or consist intrinsically of meaning. Remember to search for and record—in the CAP—ideas and emotions attached to artistic elements. You will integrate what you learn in Conversations 5, 6, and 7.

> **Discover**
>
> Observe and later ask about emotions people express during, before, or after an enactment. Ask about the degree of importance of an element. Sometimes people will not be able to answer a straight forward, abstract question, like "What does this mean?"

UNDERSTAND CONVERSATION 4'S STRUCTURE

Conversation 4 is devoted to exploring enactments of one or more genres in an event that has actually occurred in time and space. We emphasize this so much because we want to make sure that everything you and the community do is based on reality, not only a disembodied idea.[7] So all the research activities require direct experience with or at least recordings of an event and its

---

6 This hocketing technique is similar to that used in a Euro-American handbell choir. See UNESCO, "Indonesian Angklung." For examples including movement and regalia, see https://bit.ly/4bii1lj.

7 We explore and document how people envision, remember, and think about genres. But integrating ideas with actual experiences is crucial to understanding their realities.

enactments. We augment these with secondary research, often in the form of interviewing people with more direct experience. The knotted shape in Figure 4.1 represents some of the possible artistic features in such enactments, each of which can reference research-discovered meanings and patterns.

After the community has chosen a type of artistic enactment to focus on, they and you may analyze them with these four approaches:

Part A: Look Through Seven Basic Lenses
Part B: Identify Artistic Domain Features
Part C: Discover Deeper Community Connections
Part D: Encourage Churches to Integrate Arts More Holistically. Part D includes specialized research and tools for the church that we will explore later.

Here we show you a small example of the kinds of information you would learn by analyzing Barb's and my wedding through Parts A, B, and C. We focus on one genre enactment: singing a love song.

Choose an Artistic Event to Analyze

You may explore anywhere from one to hundreds of events—each will make your understanding of the genre(s) the community has chosen to enact richer. Here are a few guidelines to get started.

Essential elements

You need to be able to witness the enactments firsthand or have a good video or audio recording. Any artistic event at all is better than people's words about something you can't experience. A bird in the hand is worth two in the bush.

- It needs to contain an example of the genre or genres the community has chosen to work with.
- It should be done by people in the community.

Elements that may make your analysis more immediately fruitful

Experiencing the enactments with one or more people who already know things about their artistry may help you focus on important elements sooner.

- A typical example of this type of artistic event will help you understand its normal elements more quickly.
- An example of the genre enacted by artists whom the community states are the most skillful will help you understand aesthetic values.
- An event that recurs regularly will make comparing multiple examples of the same genre(s) more possible. From a purely analytical perspective, the way to approximate the essential elements of a typical, normal, integral, prototypical expression of a genre is to study more than one instantiation.

Part A: Look through Seven Basic Lenses

Take a first glance at an event: Brian and Barb's wedding

The short questionnaire at the beginning of Part A leads you to basic information like this: it's the coalescing of a two-family community; California (USA); May 18, 1985; inside a church building; ornate regalia; kin and fictive kin of bride and groom; stylized walking; organ, piano, voice, oratory; scriptural themes; joy and sadness; affirmation of Christian marriage; much time, money, and activity invested.

Look at the event and its enactment(s) through lenses on forms and their meanings

This section helps you and the community take a closer look at the forms of the artistry in the event through the lenses of space, materials, participant organization, shape through time, enactment features, content, and consolidation and research-discovered meaning. Doing a few of these research activities on the wedding would lead to the following kinds of insights: the front of the church sanctuary was reserved for the most sacred activities; the bride and groom exchanged rings that symbolized love and eternity; the groom's brother had the role of bringing the groom's ring; the event's ritual expectations were followed closely; enacting the love song genre included the groom's three siblings as singers, the brother as pianist; the song emphasized romantic love in the context of God's love.

Part B: Identify Artistic Domain Features

The guided research in this section is divided into five Euro-American artistic domains. You and the community only need to delve into those that the genre in question contains. The wedding event contained several artistic genres: classical organ music; love song; processional and recessional instrumental music; oratory; blessing; storytelling. For this example, we've decided to learn more about the artistic features of one of these genres, the love song. The primary artistic feature domains that this genre draws on are music and oral verbal arts.

From examination of the song through a few of the research activities in "Musical Features in Enactments and Events," we discover a strophic form of verse / chorus / verse / chorus / gentle, floating outro; the groom's brother played the piano (a struck chordophone) and sang, and his sisters sang; they used narrow vibrato at the end of phrases; the chorus was contrapuntal; the song used a divisive meter of ¾; quarter note equals 94 beats per minute; tonal center was G.

From examination of the song's lyrics through some research activities in "Oral Verbal Arts Features in Enactments and Events" (section 4B and *CLAT Companion*) we discover phrase repetition, metaphor, lexical substitution, rhyme, and that overall form parallels song form.

Part C: Discover Deeper Community Connections

This section leads you and the community to connect the artistry in the event with other elements in the community. Applying a few of these research tasks to the wedding lead to the following kinds of knowledge: the performers and composers of the love song are siblings in a family with historically notable singers and instrument players, rooted in Mennonite choral traditions; the performers enjoyed a transiently high status in the eyes of many experiencers during the event, but their skills were not esteemed as enduringly valuable by most; the new love song resulted from collaboration between two siblings; high aesthetic value was placed on new lyrics and melody, with highlighted vocal harmonies; the creativity components—creators, language and other symbolic systems, and gatekeepers—were all within the family; many in the audience experienced a combination of pleasure and melancholy.

Figure 4.4 shows the categories of insights each of these three kinds of research produced in this example. Note that you only have to investigate the artistic domains (music, drama, dance, oral verbal arts, visual arts) that the genre under investigation contains.

Event: Brian and Barb's Wedding

Enactment of Genre 1: Love Song		Enactment of Genre 2: Blessing	
Unique set of relations to broader cultural context (Part C)	Unique form and meaning description through seven-lens view (Part A)	Unique form and meaning description through seven-lens view (Part A)	Unique set of relations to broader cultural context (Part C)
Unique set of musical and verbal characteristics (Part B)		Unique set of verbal and visual features (Part B)	

Figure 4.4 Categories of insights

Each kind of analysis will help you and a community understand what goes on in the others. So let your minds roam from very detailed information about minute features of an event to broad cultural themes and back again. We never know whether a single note, vocal timbre, feather, facial expression, eyebrow movement, color, or any number of other elements could hold meaning that either frees or stifles creativity for the Kingdom.

The more you and the community know the range of art forms available and understand how each one works, the more you can reflect together with God on how to best use them. We provide research activities in this conversation, but they are only a start. If you're not learning anything interesting from our directions, think about these questions: What other questions could I ask? What other ways could I find out about this phenomenon? What is true about this genre that doesn't fit any of the categories here? And remember: **Research = Learning = Love.** We discover meanings from a posture of learning, researching meaning.

PLAN DOABLE AND RELEVANT RESEARCH
General Principles for Finding Foci
Not every research activity we include in Conversation 4 is relevant to the artistry you're investigating. Even if it were, you don't have enough time to do it all. So here are a few ways you can focus your research.

First, always do anything that starts with "Take a First Glance at …" These provide a lot of insight requiring a relatively small amount of energy and time. Second, scan the research activities we describe in these sections with a community friend and pick at least one from the seven basic lenses and one or two in "Relate the Event's Genre(s) to Its Broader Cultural Context" (Part C). The *CLAT Companion* (www.clatmanual.com) contains indexes of more activities that could help you in this. Choose what seems most pertinent or interesting. Third, notice that many of the sparking activities we describe in Conversation 5 require research someone needs to do to complete the activity. While performing these activities, come back to Conversation 4 to do the research. Fourth, if you have an advisor or more experienced arts specialist available, work with him or her to design a research plan that includes strategically chosen activities.

Making the Process More Efficient
Sparking creativity in a genre that results in more signs of Heaven benefits greatly from knowing the features, meanings, integrations into broader culture, and grammars of a prototypical example of that genre. Applying CLAT lenses and research activities to one example of a genre will not ensure this understanding; the arts advocate would need to describe and compare multiple examples of a genre to be confident that they know what a prototypical event consists of, if they use only analytical, linear methods. This takes a long time and people often don't or won't do it.

How can we augment our understanding differently, perhaps more quickly? By reinforcing our stance as learners through relationships with people and adopting the role of children needing the help of adults. We here gather a few activities that flow particularly well from this orientation.

Research Activities
Add activities that elicit emic/insider knowledge, such as those that

- draw more directly, immediately on insights and knowledge of community experts.
- do not require abstract thinking.
- are perhaps marked as insider knowledge eliciting questions, research activities.
- use prompts to spark internal discussions between people inside the community.
- prompt people to research their own communities (see **autogenic research**).[8]

---

8 Saurman, *Singing for Survival*.

Analyze Genres and Events

You may want to learn and participate in a genre, taking note of the vocabulary of the insiders and teachers. You can also perform a feedback interview, asking questions while watching a video recording of an event that includes enactments of a genre you're interested in. How do you know when this started? Ended? Is this a good example of the genre? What makes it good? Is this the way it normally happens? What's that woman doing? That person is crying—why is he? That person is laughing—what makes it funny? Why did that person trip? Who are the best doers of [each part of the event you're watching]? What do you call what that person is doing? Include multiple community members to spark internal discussions and elicit more responses.

CONVERSATION 4A

LOOK THROUGH SEVEN BASIC LENSES

	First Pass: Look Through Seven Basic Lenses [4A]
Primary Questions	What are the basic characteristics of a particular genre enacted in an event?
Output	1. Basic Description: Begin Genre Enactment Features with elements of an enactment grouped by 7 Basic Lenses. 2. Quick Winnowing: How much is there of each lens? Focus further research on those that are especially prevalent or important. 3. Compare results of the 7 Basic Lenses: Do any of these interact? follow same underlying framework? Can we consolidate any of the lenses with any others?
Methods	Use basic existing questions, looking for patterns and meanings. • Space • Materials • Participant Organization • Shape through Time • Enactment Features • Content • Consolidation and Meanings
Genre Enactment Features will look like this (in CAP)	Features, Patterns, and Meanings categorized in 7 Basic Lenses. • How might results of this research impact Conversations 4B, 5, 6, and 7? Make a list for future reference. • Always becoming clearer and fuller.

If you are following the CLAT conversations in order, you have begun preliminary evaluations of some artistic events and genres, especially in Figure 3.2: "First-glance genre comparison chart" (Conversation 3). In Conversation 4A, we provide two tools to deepen your understanding of this artistry: "Take a First Glance at an Event" and "Look Through Seven Basic Lenses." Answering the questions in these activities through observation and conversation will begin to deepen your understanding of the artistry chosen by the community. Your primary research goal is to produce a growing Genre Enactment Features, located in the Community Arts Profile.

TAKE A FIRST GLANCE AT AN EVENT

The community has chosen a genre or genres as part of their draft plan to reach a Kingdom Goal. Their understanding will be more grounded if they reflect on a kind of event that normally enacts this genre. These simple questions help you focus on the type of artistry used in such an event. There may be more than one type of artistic genre in an event, but apply these questions to only one at a time:[1]

Name of community: _____

Location: _____

Date(s): _____

Names of Investigators: _____

- **What** artistry do people produce (e.g., name of genre, kinds of activities like painting or acting or singing or dancing)?
- **What** are some important things about this event?
- **Who** normally performs or creates it (e.g., women, men, children, caste members)? Also, gather names of prominent performers or creators.
- **Who** knows a lot about events like these?
- **Where** do people normally perform or create it (e.g., outdoors, indoors, special place)?
- **When** do people normally create or perform it (e.g., day, night, ceremony, weekly rehearsal, spontaneously for pleasure)?
- **To whom** do people normally perform or present it (e.g., potential suitors, ecstatic audience, God)?
- **Why** do people normally perform or present it (e.g., express emotions, make money, motivate to action, affirm identity, play)?
- **With what connotations** do people normally perform or present it (e.g., partying, a certain age group, spiritual, sexual)?
- **How** are new instances normally created (e.g., solitary individual, dreams, group experimentation)?

LOOK THROUGH SEVEN BASIC LENSES

In Papua New Guinea the *sing-sing* festival is an important cultural event for many language groups: it is where the songs, dances, stories, and dress convey the culture of that group from one generation to another. In one language community, Christians decided that they could not participate. An outsider began to question the Christians about what prevented them from participating. After a time, the offense to the Holy Spirit was narrowed down to one red

---
[1] See Seeger, *Why Suyá Sing*.

feather worn in the headdress. The outsider asked the Christians, "If you remove the red feather, would there be anything else in the *sing-sing* that you think would be offensive to God?" The answer came back, "No." So the Christians didn't use a red feather in their headdresses and felt free to participate in their *sing-sing*.[2]

This story is an example of how identifying the unique attributes of the form of an artistic act of communication allows you and a community to enter more accurately into its creation, improvement, integration, and celebration. Any small element of the form may evoke significant symbolic or emotive meaning. Because of the potential importance of details like these in meeting a community's goals, it's crucial that we have a way to notice them. This section provides a guide for you and the community to look at a genre enactment through specially chosen lenses.

In physical terms, a lens is a piece of glass that has been polished or otherwise changed in a way that alters any light coming through it. Depending on its maker's goal, someone who looks through a lens at an object may see that object as closer, farther, or perhaps with one color intensified. A lens, then, is a way of bringing one aspect of an object into focus. We are using this same idea metaphorically to guide our research in the arts. From this, we present a method that will guide your eyes, ears, and bodies to reveal seven categories of detail: Space, Materials, Participant Organization, Shape through Time, Enactment Features, Content, and Consolidation and Meanings.

Each lens may not reveal insights equally well in any given enactment, so if a lens does not seem to help much, choose another through which to view the artistry. Those most relevant will reveal patterns of movements, colors, sounds, and so on, which you will describe. And because these lenses describe the same thing from different perspectives, some patterns and repetitions may recur.

Discussion of each of these lenses includes the following:

- **Basic description** to help you know the kinds of things each lens is meant to bring into focus.
- **Research questions** to guide your exploration of the enactment through the lens under discussion.
- **Activities** that are particularly relevant to answering these research questions. Put the results of these activities into the description of this enactment in your Community Arts Profile.
- **Artistic Domain Features,** a discussion that highlights common connections between each lens and arts domains. Remember that artistry is stylized communication, where form often plays a larger role in determining meaning. You can follow up on these connections in Conversation 4B's research activities meant to reveal features commonly grouped in categories like music, drama, dance, oral verbal arts, and visual arts.

---

2 Chenoweth, *Sing-Sing*, 211.

For each lens, remember to relate your findings to research-discovered meanings, symbolism, and broader cultural themes.

We've designed these lenses to help you understand more about a genre enactment in an event. If it is the first enactment you have seen of its type, you won't know yet if it is a normal example or if it differs in significant ways from what usually happens. As you use the lenses to describe more enactments of this same type, you'll see both common patterns and points of divergence. The Consolidation and Meanings lens will guide you in this.

Focus your inquiries on the genre(s) the community chose in Conversation 3. Remember, however, that enactments of genres are embedded in events. You may need to look through certain lenses at other parts of the event, or even the whole event.

LENS 1: SPACE

Basic Description

Space is the location, demarcation, and physical characteristics of the area used for the enactment, which can affect its form. It can, for example, influence how participants move individually and with one another, lengthening or shortening the time it takes for participants to move through it, and other elements of the artistic enactment.

Write what you learn about how this enactment uses space in the Community Arts Profile. Include drawings, photographs, and other representations to help explain what's going on.

Research Questions

> Where did it occur? Inside, outside, or both? If inside, give type and size of building.
>
> What are some characteristics of the place where it happened (shape and size, for example)?
>
> What parts was the space separated into? Were there physical and/or conceptual markers to separate these parts?
>
> What activities were associated with each part?
>
> Who designed, controlled, or owned the space for this particular event?
>
> How did each participant's location in the space and proximity to other participants affect their contribution to the event? How did it affect other participants' experience of their contribution?
>
> From what you know of the genre of this event, did people use space in normal ways? Uncommon ways?

Activities to Help Answer the Questions

- Draw a floor diagram, including boundaries and demarcations.
- Take photographs of the place and its surroundings.
- Ask questions of participants and other cultural insiders about what happened. You may want to do this while watching a video of the event.
- Make a list of local names for the elements of space used in the event.
- What meaning(s) do people normally attach to the elements these research activities reveal? What patterns do you notice?

Artistic Domain Features

In an artistic enactment, features that interact most closely with space are often associated with drama and dance. In addition, creators of art objects manipulate space to create formal structure through features like proportion, rhythm, balance, and the like.

LENS 2: MATERIALS

Basic Description

Materials are all the tangible things associated with an event, like clothing, regalia, instruments, props, and lighting. Some objects are more important to the execution and experience of the enactment than others. They may be made by humans (as in a mask) or designated to fill a function (as an eagle feather marking regalia as royal). Objects may serve multiple purposes, conveying meaning at many levels. For example, the *Atumpan* drum (Ghana) serves both as a functional member of the musical ensemble, while indicating royalty by its shape, colors, and construction; it therefore plays both a functional and symbolic role. As another example, *kanoon* dancers in Cameroon move shakers in patterned ways that both add to the dance (experienced through visual channels) and produce sounds integral to the rhythm (experienced through auditory channels).[3] Note also that some objects in the space where an enactment takes place may be incidental to what's going on.

Write what you learn about how this enactment uses materials in the Community Arts Profile. Include drawings, photographs, and other representations to help explain what's going on.

Research Questions

> What were all the objects involved in the event?
> What is each object like physically?
> What meaning(s) do people attach to these objects?
> Were some objects treated in unusual or special ways?

---

[3] Schrag, "Bamiléké Music-Makers," 177–230.

> From what you know of the genre of this event, did people use objects in normal ways? uncommon ways?
>
> What meaning(s) do people normally attach to these elements of Materials? What patterns do you notice?

Activities to Help Answer the Questions

Make a list of objects associated with the event. Do this by observing and asking yourself and others questions like these:

> What objects were present, including structures (like buildings)?
>
> What objects did people bring expressly for the event?
>
> What did people wear?
>
> What did people hold? kick? otherwise manipulate with their bodies?
>
> Were there objects on surfaces, like walls, floors, or ceilings?
>
> Were there technologies that produced atmospheric effects and enhancements such as lighting, sound amplification, smoke, incense?
>
> Were there live objects, like animals or plants, in the event?
>
> Were there foods or drinks involved in the event?
>
> Were there human-made or natural objects that were repurposed for this event?

Describe each object by examining it and asking questions like these:

> What are the object's physical characteristics? This may include materials, design, construction, weight, and length. Kinds of source materials include fibers (from plants or animals), minerals, metals, plastics, and wood.
>
> What are local and other names for the object?
>
> Take photographs that reveal details of objects (close-ups, from various angles).

- Describe the functions and interactions of objects in the enactment through observation, interview, and other activities.
- Draw a floor diagram, showing placement of objects.
- Take photographs of the objects in their locations.
- Describe who interacted with each object, and in what ways.
- Imagine and ask how participants might have modified their actions because of the presence of objects. For example, a short microphone cord limits the range of movement of an actor. You can also ask how the presence of an object might have constrained the participants' use of space.
- List all the ways an object contributes to the execution of the event.

Learn and document how to make or use an object. Ask questions of participants and other cultural insiders about the uses and construction of objects. You may want to do this while watching a video of the event, looking at pictures of objects, or interacting with the objects themselves.

> To whom does each object belong?
>
> How old is each object? Was it created especially for this enactment or kind of event?

Artistic Domain Features

In an artistic event, objects can play significant roles in all the artistic domains. Drama uses costumes and props to show characterization and provide dramatic settings. The most common objects used to produce musical features are instruments. In dance, costumes and props may highlight motion. A storyteller might use a prop to symbolize an event in her story, and visual artists use all sorts of materials to create objects. Finally, cooks gather and process ingredients and spices to create food. Remember that each object can play roles in multiple artistic domains.

LENS 3: PARTICIPANT ORGANIZATION

Basic Description

At an artistic event, virtually everyone present participates in some way (and sometimes people who aren't even there participate by way of preparation). We focus here on the people involved in the enactment in terms of the roles they play, the ways they interact with each other through time, and how they use the space around them. Each participant in an event plays a role (given by genre and personal proclivities) that affects the form of the enactment. Roles can include creators, performers (e.g., singers, instrument players, actors, dancers, storytellers), audience (e.g., aficionados, mass, cognoscenti, hecklers), helpers (e.g., set builders, stage managers, gaffers, ticket takers, bouncers, ushers), producers, directors, and so on. Participants' histories are also relevant to the formal characteristics of an event: their skills, kin, and other relationships to each other, status and role in everyday life, and ethnic, religious, and social identities. For example, a priest may be the only one who can play certain roles in a religious ceremony.

Write what you learn about participants in this enactment in the Community Arts Profile. Include drawings, photographs, and other representations to help explain what's going on.

Research Questions

How many participants were there (include ancestors, spirits, or gods that are not physically present but believed to be there)? What were each of their roles?

How did the participants use Enactment Features to interact with each other? Were there obvious patterns (etiquette)?

How did participants interact with different sections of the event space? Were any roles associated with particular places?

Which participants exerted creative control and to what degrees?

What are the local names for the participant roles used in the event?

Who is fulfilling each role?

Why and how did each participant come to fill his/her role?

What are salient characteristics of each participant, in terms of their training, ability, reputation, and professional/caste status?

What meaning(s) do people attach to each participant role?

From what you know of its genre, were the number and roles of participants like other similar events?

Did any participants receive payment in goods, services, or money for performing their role?

What meaning(s) do people normally attach to these elements of Participant Organization? What patterns do you notice?

Activities to Help Answer the Questions

- Make audio, video, and photographic recordings of the event.
- Ask a friend involved in the enactment what role(s) you might be able to fill in this type of event. Note what background and competencies you would have to have or acquire to fill different roles. When appropriate and possible, prepare to perform a role for a future enactment of this type.
- Draw a floor diagram, showing where participants were at different times, or what roles were associated with certain places.
- Make a timeline, noting participants' actions and interactions.
- Ask questions of participants and other cultural insiders about what happened. You may want to do this while watching a video of the event.
- Make a list of local names for participant roles. Ask what privileges or obligations are associated with each named role.
- Take photographs that reveal details of participants' clothing, props, pertinent facial expressions, gestures, and the like.

Artistic Domain Features

Many roles in artistic communication are associated with the artistic domain categories we've included in the chapters below. Essentially all artistic events require an audience of some sort, someone to experience the communication. Beyond that, some typical dramatic roles include actor, spect-actor (someone who both watches and enters a drama), set designer, and director. Musical performance may have singers, instrument players, and composers. In dance, people fill roles of choreographer, soloist, and ensemble. Various oral verbal arts performances may include a teller, listener, sidekick, crafter, and affirmer. Visual arts require at least one creator, manipulator, and experiencer. Food creation roles commonly include recipe maker, chef, food manipulator, and presenter. Research these roles in more depth in the artistic domain chapters, and remember that one person could fill roles in multiple artistic domains.

LENS 4: SHAPE THROUGH TIME

Basic Description

One way to learn about a genre is by describing the shape of an event in which it occurs, splitting it into sequential segments in a hierarchical fashion. You can identify the time at which one segment ends and the next begins by noting significant changes in elements of the event as viewed through each of the other lenses. These changes are called markers. For example, markers could include pauses, sudden contrasts in features or participants, beginning and ending of participants' activities, beginning and ending of singing, and the like. The shortest segment we are interested in for this lens is the *motif*: the smallest meaningful collection of Enactment Features.

Use vocabulary from Figure 4.3 "A top-down, hierarchical description of an artistic event," to write what you learn about the shape of this event in the Community Arts Profile. Include lists, timelines, and other representations to help explain what's going on.

Research Questions

> What were the segments of the event?
>
> How did you know when one segment ended and another began? What marked these transitions?
>
> Were there parallel segments happening at the same time? How were they related?
>
> What were the important parts of each segment (onset, nucleus, coda)?
>
> What meaning(s) do people attach to these segments at each level?
>
> From what you know of its genre(s), was this event longer or shorter than normal? Did it have the same number and size of segments as normal?

Activities to Help Answer the Questions

- Make audio and video recordings of the event.
- Create a Hierarchical Segmentation Timeline. You may use one or more of the following approaches:

From a top-down perspective (in other words, macro to micro):

- While watching or listening to the recording, make a timeline of the event, highlighting its major segments by listing the transition markers with the time they occur.
- While watching each major segment, make a timeline of its subsegments, listing the transition markers with the time they occur.
- Continue dividing subsegments at finer timescales, down to the level of your research interest. This may be at the level of the motif.

From a bottom-up perspective:

- While watching or listening to the recording, make a timeline of the event, identifying the smallest meaningful chunks (sequences of Enactment Features), their beginning and ending times, and how they're assembled to create larger segments.
- See how these small segments are in turn assembled into larger ones.
- Continue assembling suprasegments at longer timescales until you've described the whole event.

From a basic level-out perspective:

- While watching or listening to the recording, make a timeline of the event, identifying the most salient activities and how they're assembled to create larger segments or divided to create smaller ones.
- Continue this process. See Figure 4.5.

Step One

Time	What Happened
13:30	Storytellers began to arrive
...	...
...	...
14:27	Everyone left the area

Step Two

Segment 1 (5 min.)	Segment 2 (12 min.)	Segment 3 (10 min.)	Segment 4 (3 min.)
...	...	...	...

Figure 4.5 Create a hierarchical segmentation timeline from a basic level outward

- Make a list of local names for the segments of the event.
- Ask questions of participants and other cultural insiders about what happened. You may want to do this while watching a video of the event.
- What meaning(s) do people normally attach to the elements these research activities reveal? What patterns do you notice?

Artistic Domain Features

Artistic domains each have traditions of splitting their enactments into smaller and smaller chunks. A genre enactment with drama features may start with a play, broken into acts, scenes, and eventually to gestures and movements. An example of music's highest hierarchical level could be an orchestral song, split into movements, verses, phrases, measures, and notes. Dances may consist of pieces, motifs, and gestures. An oral verbal art like a poem may contain stanzas and lines and beats. Visual and culinary arts may not change through time like others, though how people view objects and eat food can be split into subparts. You can explore more relationships between the Shape through Time and artistic domains in the chapters that follow, and the *CLAT Companion* (www.clatmanual.com).

LENS 5: ENACTMENT FEATURES

Basic Description

We look for patterns and meanings through all the lenses, but we need a lens that allows us to extend, detail, and deepen our understandings of patterns in artistry: Enactment Features are observable, patterned characteristics of artistry that emerge from a genre enactment's unique combination of physical and social context and participants' actions. They are the skills, processes, and conventions that the participants in an enactment must master to make it successful. In more detail, a feature is a characteristic of artistry that

- is produced by participants (e.g., singers, dancers, sculptors, storytellers, hecklers, playwrights)
- who choose embodied actions (e.g., sing, move, gather, play instrument, wear a certain color, paint a wall)
- that derive from formal systems (e.g., movement, vocal production, plot progression, color symbolism, social interaction)
- and temporal patterns (e.g., metricity, flow, timing).

The enactor(s) chooses his or her actions by considering the

- intended messages, content, and subject matter
- other participants (seen and unseen) and their responses
- location
- genre expectations: acceptable variation, source materials (e.g., written forms, orature)
- and the enactor's abilities and preferences.

Each feature

- is experienced by participants (e.g., performers, observers, audience)
- and through communication channels that encompass whole bodies (e.g., auditory, visual, tactile, spatial, olfactory).

In short, Enactment Features are things people do that can be transcribed. Transcription is reducing elements of a communication act to writing and graphics. Enactment Features are our attempt to name the elements most useful for understanding the structure of a genre's depiction; this vocabulary and process help us to begin finding out what's important, what carries meaning. Transcription can draw on existing notation systems such as Time Unit Box System (TUBS, for rhythm), staff (melody, harmony, and rhythm), Laban or Motif (movement), and writing down verbal content ethnopoetically, in a way that communicates its artistic form. It can also consist of prose descriptions of Enactment Features using specialized vocabulary. It's likely you've already written or sketched representations of patterns revealed by looking through other lenses.

Note that transcribing verbal features of an enactment requires knowing a language or working with a native speaker. This document does not teach transcription; you must learn specialized notation systems elsewhere, perhaps in the classroom with an expert. Depending on your interests, search for schools or programs accessible to you that teach notation for music, language, dance, visual arts, or drama.

Write what you learn about Enactment Features in this event in the Community Arts Profile. Include prose descriptions and notation to help explain what's going on.

Research Questions

> What do people do to send messages through communication channels?
>
> How are Enactment Features or clusters of features patterned?
>
> What meaning(s) do people attach to each Enactment Feature or cluster of features?
>
> From what you know of the genre, did participants produce Enactment Features in ways similar to other contexts in which this genre is used?
>
> What stock motifs or clichés emerge? These are memorized bundles of Enactment Features.

Research Activities and Artistic Features

Research activities

There are several ways to train yourself to attend to features of people's enactments:

- Make audio, video, and photographic recordings of the event, including genre enactments.

- Focus on the communication channels through which you perceive the features (sight, sound, smell, touch, taste).
- Focus on the common producers of features (voices, bodies, objects, and minds), and
- Focus on similarities and contrasts between clusters of Enactment Features (for example, dynamics and rhythm).

Access Enactment Features in these ways:

- Watch and listen to a video of an artistic event multiple times.
- Write a free-flowing account of your experiences of an event, noting patterns as well as unique occurrences, and
- Make educated guesses on what seems important, based on what you've learned by looking through other lenses, then check these guesses by forming research questions you can ask of insiders.

Feature perception through senses[4]

Expand your capacities to notice and relate what you perceive by focusing on each of your senses, informed by these activities:[5]

- Describe any sounds you heard. Were they, for example, muffled, melodic, piercing, or shrill?
- Describe any movements, colors, lights, and shapes that you saw. Were the colors, for example, pale, dark, glittering, bright, or vivid?
- Describe any aromas you smelled. Were they, for example, fragrant, pungent, sweet, smoky, rancid, or sweet?
- Describe any textures of objects you touched. Were they, for example, jagged, oily, rough, smooth, or bumpy?
- Describe any flavors you tasted. Were they, for example, sour, spicy, acidic, or syrupy?

Feature production

- What did participants do with their voices? Common vocal actions include singing, acting, orating, narrating, or producing sound effects.
- What did participants do with their bodies? Common bodily actions include acting, sculpting, instrument playing, and dancing.
- What did participants do with their words? Common word-related activities include poetry, singing, acting, orating, and narrating.
- What did participants do with objects? Common actions with objects include instrument playing, acting, spectacle, dancing, oratory, narrating, designing, and presenting visual artistry.

---

4 For further study on communication channels, see Finnegan, *Communicating*.

5 For extensive lists of English words to describe each sense, see the Digital Library (www.clatmanual.com).

Similarities and contrasts between clusters of Enactment Features
- How did people express intensity, weight, flow?
- How did people organize time?

Advice on knowing what features to attend to, out of an infinite number of possibilities
- Look for repeated actions.
- Look for actions that seem to provoke a strong reaction in participants.
- Note heavy contrast between bundles of features and the next set of bundled features.
- Use your own imperfect intuition to notice what might be important.
- Note where participants are focusing their attention.
- Remember what participants and other knowledgeable folks have told you is important. Look there.

Other research activities
- Listen to an audio recording of an enactment, noting patterns of things you hear.
- Stare hard and long at a photograph of the event, noting patterns of colors, shade, size and shape, balance, and lines.
- Note when certain feature combinations occur. These co-occurrences may provide clues to underlying symbolic systems that participants all refer to explicitly or implicitly during the enactment. To get at some common kinds of combinations, ask these questions:
    - ◊ How did people advance the plot through dancing or singing? See the "Dramatic Features in Enactments and Events" section (Conversation 4B).
    - ◊ How did people relate their movements to melody or rhythm or create movement motifs? See the "Dance Features in Enactments and Events" section (Conversation 4B).
    - ◊ Make a list of local names for Enactment Features or clusters of features. You can describe these using the analytical vocabulary in this chapter.
- What meaning(s) do people normally attach to the elements these research activities reveal? What patterns do you notice?

Ask questions of participants and other cultural insiders about what happened. More specifically, ask about meanings and emotions evoked by certain actions or points in the event. You may want to do this while watching a video of the event.

When appropriate and possible, learn to enact part of this kind of event. Write down what people tell you to do when teaching you, how they correct you, and insights you gain and questions that arise by attempting to produce features with your own body.

Other kinds of socially meaningful actions and their Enactment Features
Participants may produce features not associated with a particular artistic domain to express opinions and emotions. These opinions and emotions could be to affirm or reject, encourage or discourage, express pleasure or displeasure, attract or repel, assist or impede, unify or divide, goad or hinder aspects of the enactment. Examples of such features include hand clapping, stomping, cheering, ululating, heckling, "the wave," throwing rotten fruit or candy, holding up lighters or cell phones.

Participants may express basic emotions by crying, laughing, screaming, or wailing. These expressions often take on artistic form.

People may produce other bits of communication with their bodies that contribute to an event that you may not have categories for. These could include actions like snapping fingers, belching, whistling, or producing vocal overtones. Keep all your senses open to bodily communication.

Notes about Enactment Features

- Any specific artistic event will likely draw on multiple features, each of which may exist within different groupings in other traditions.

- Enactors may add unexpected features, purposefully or accidentally, and with varying degrees of skill and social license.

Artistic Domain Features

We've grouped the way Enactment Features relate to artistic domains in these categories: vocal, body movements, object manipulation, visual characteristics, rhythm, narration, and poetic devices.

Vocal Features: Participants manipulate vocal features in drama to help them act; in music to help them sing; in dance to coordinate breath with movement patterns; and in oral verbal arts to create effects by changing the pitch or timbre of their voices.

Body Movements: Participants move their bodies in ways that contribute to acting, characterization, and space organization in dramatic aspects of enactments; instrument playing in music; movement dynamics, phrasing, and body and space organization in dance; and gesturing in oral verbal arts.

Object Manipulation: In drama, people manipulate objects to help them act and produce spectacle; in music, to help them play instruments and modify their voice; in dance, to support, amplify, or facilitate movement; in oral verbal arts, to emphasize oratorical elements; and in visual arts, in making or presenting a communicative object.

Visual Characteristics: Visual features play important roles in dramatic events through costuming, makeup, puppets, and spectacle; visual elements in dance include costuming, makeup, and other elements; in visual arts, these include design and elements of composition such as line, shape, form, texture, pattern, value, and color among others.

Rhythm: Rhythmic features that contribute to musical characteristics include polyrhythm, proportional rhythm, or free rhythm. Polyrhythm consists of contrasting rhythms played simultaneously. Proportional rhythm is smaller rhythmic units that are proportions of larger units. Free rhythm is a rhythm with no clear pattern. How does external auditory rhythm affect movement in dance? What about meter used in oral verbal arts? How does the arrangement of visual elements create a sense of motion or pacing in visual arts?

Narration: Narrating features play significant roles in presenting or recounting events in drama and oral verbal arts.

Poetic Devices: Finally, participants may use poetic devices for acting in drama, song lyrics in music, and throughout oral verbal arts. You can research these and more relationships between Enactment Features and artistic domains in the sections that follow.

Each of these artistic domain categories varies according to its proportional focus on lexical meaning (that is, symbolic signs, language) vs. form qualities. Traditions that rely more on language (e.g., storytelling, song singing, drama) will normally have more features that require a greater understanding of a language to recognize and understand.

LENS 6: CONTENT

Basic Description

Content refers to the subject matter or topic of an artistic event. It is most closely tied to symbols—that is, lexical signs like words, and movements in signed languages or dances. Multiple layers of meanings may exist, and meaning may be implied or explicit. To understand content, you must connect to and inquire of people who know the language and other communication systems very well. Do love-motivated research … don't just guess.

Write what you learn about the content of this event in the Community Arts Profile. Include transcriptions of language and other content signs to help explain what's going on.

Research Questions

> How did participants communicate the subject matter at different points in the enactment?
>
> What was the enactment about? What else was it about? What was its most important point? Second most important point?
>
> What assumed background knowledge does an experiencer need to understand the subject matter?
>
> What meaning(s) do people normally attach to the elements these research activities reveal? What patterns do you notice?

Activities to Help Answer the Questions
- Record the genre enactment and the event it was part of, if likely relevant. Ask a friend to write down important words that people uttered, and meanings of any symbolic motions that occurred.
- Ask participants what they intended to communicate with their artistry.
- Ask participants what emotions or actions they hoped to elicit in other people because of the enactment.
- Ask participants what topics were angering, humorous, boring, or rousing.

Artistic Domain Features
In an enactment, features that interact most closely with content are often associated with drama, oral verbal arts, and songs in music.

LENS 7: CONSOLIDATION AND MEANINGS

Basic Description
Lens 7 analyses result primarily in a prose description of the characteristics of an enactment that qualify it as emerging from a particular genre. This depiction serves as a touchstone for evaluating various kinds and contexts of meanings you've gathered through other research and experiences.

Participants who share a history of experiencing enactments of an artistic genre develop common mental and emotional frameworks in approaching new enactments. Though variation exists in people's minds and bodies, they share many rules, expectations, grammatical structures, and motivations to decide what to do at any given moment. This is their cognitive and emotive environment, the hidden knowledge that allows composition and interpretation, informed by underlying symbolic systems.

Some systems are simple and easily discoverable. For example, the cyclic pattern of an Indonesian *gamelan* piece is quickly discernible by noting the regular interval at which the big gong in the ensemble sounds. Similarly, the metric division of a Strauss waltz into groups of three beats, with an accented first beat, does not require extensive analysis. As another example, stock characters in Thai *likay* drama are easily recognizable after a brief description of their behavior and costume conventions.

Deriving some underlying structures, however, may take intensive, methodologically rigorous analysis, interview, and participation. For example, grammatical rules governing melodic or rhythmic structure of a song, the permitted movements in a dance, or the use of space in a painting are often not immediately evident. Much of such complex scrutiny is beyond the scope of this manual. Fortunately, we've provided more rigorous tools related to Conversation 4B's brief discussions of features related to music, drama, dance, oral verbal arts, and visual arts in the *CLAT Companion* (www.clatmanual.com).

What features, patterns, and meanings need to be present to make this a good enactment of a genre in an event? You can approach such a prototypical description by a combination of the following:

1. analysis of multiple enactments of the same genre;
2. arts advocates and community representatives discussing enactments together (guided by repeatable questions); and
3. reports of community autogenic research.

Discovering Limits to Variation

One underlying system that's common to each enactment is the degree of variability its genre allows. You can research this by asking a wide variety of people questions like these:

> Which characteristics do people state must exist for an enactment to be a good example of this genre?
>
> What is acceptable but not necessary?
>
> What is not permitted?
>
> Which of these observations are contested?

Research-Discovered Meanings

Gather everything you've learned so far about meanings, symbolism, and broader cultural themes in each of the lenses. What themes, commonalities do you and community members notice?

A more scientifically thorough approach would entail analyzing and comparing multiple enactments of a single genre. This would include repeated evaluation of the output of each set of research activities: Conversation 4A's seven basic lenses; 4B's artistic domain features; and 4C's community connections, looking for

- Salient, noticeable patterns
- Salient, noticeable features
- Necessary components of a genre in an event, and
- Salient meanings attached to the features, patterns, and genre in a complete event, referencing our connotation discussion in Conversation 3.

Such analyses will allow you to describe a prototypical—or integral—enactment of a particular genre in an event.

CONVERSATION 4B

IDENTIFY ARTISTIC DOMAIN FEATURES

	Second Pass: Identify Artistic Domain Features [4B]
Primary Questions	How are shapes, colors, construction, words, melodies, aromas, touch, and so on used in each lens to add more artistry to enactments of a particular genre?
Output	1. Artistically Augmented Description: Integrate insights into Genre Enactment Features, mostly organized in (modified) Basic Lens categories. 2. Quick winnowing: How much of each artistic enhancement category does there seem to be? Focus further research on those that are especially important. 3. Research activities: Continue to explore features that reveal this as an artistic genre, still mostly tied to basic lenses, patterns, and meanings.
Methods	For the package of features produced by each Basic Lens, look through each of the five artistic lenses (or others you develop). We provide a reduced number of artistic feature research activities–prototypical, common, focused, usually productive. The *CLAT Companion* contains more comprehensive artistic research activities (see www.clatmanual.com). Some lenses that reveal additional artistic features include the following: • Music • Drama • Dance • Oral Verbal Arts (poetic, literary) • Visual Arts We have not developed these yet: • Aromas (olfactory) • Taste (gustatory) • Video • Virtual realities • Physical construction (architecture) • And many more…
Genre Enactment Features will look like this (in CAP)	Features, Patterns and Meanings with artistic details categorized in 7 Basic Lenses. • How might results of this research impact Conversations 4B, 5, 6, and 7? • Make a list for future reference.

Genres of artistic communication consist of a unique set of characteristics: how, when, why, where, with whom they happen, and their formal features. Because of this uniqueness our first goal is to describe each community's genre in its own terms. But it's also true that we humans share a great deal—bodies, cognitive structures, patterns of interaction—with the world. It's therefore not unusual to find similarities in the ways we communicate artistically, even in different cultures.

Find Basic Features of Artistic Domains

In this section we help communities benefit from insights emerging from communities of practice surrounding abstract categories of artistry often found in schools, universities, and academic disciplines. Research into these artistic categories provides more detailed knowledge that can inform cocreation processes like sparking creativity (Conversation 5) and improvement (Conversation 6). We've limited the resources in this volume to broad, elementary descriptions of five categories: music, drama, dance, oral verbal arts, and visual arts. You'll notice that we sometimes playfully use terms like *dancey* or *musicky* to emphasize that these words don't refer to universally, clearly defined categories.

You could perform similar investigations into other artistic domains with specialized features that we haven't included in this manual. Search for others exploring additional domains, like those launching the *Gastroethnomusicology Journal*.[6] Here are some possibilities, organized haphazardly by a combination of senses and common category names.

- Olfactory, or aroma: Perfumery, incense design, aromatherapy.
- Gustatory, or taste: Culinary arts, tea pouring rituals, restaurant meal preparation.
- Video stories and graphics: Cinema, video games, virtual reality, online digital media.
- Physical construction: Architecture, woodworking, civil engineering, interior design.
- Sports: Skating, fencing, racing, team competition.

As you look at an enactment through these arts-focused lenses, keep in mind what you've already learned in "Look through Seven Basic Lenses." Artistic characteristics are always intertwined with other realities in communities; you won't be able to fully understand the music, drama, dance, oral verbal arts, or visual arts features without a more complete picture. In particular, locate the enactment in its broader physical context relating to the Space lens (nationally, regionally, and locally) and its broader temporal context, connecting to the Shape lens (month, day, hour, season, and occurrence in the overall event). You should also remember that arts are complicated, and nobody can be an expert in everything; there are things you won't be able to understand about analyzing artistic production using just these sections. To make the most of some of these activities, you will need to study their specialized vocabulary.

---

[6] As of this publication, the *Gastroethnomusicology Journal* was still in the process of being launched. See https://bit.ly/4dgfXfn.

For features associated with each domain, we ask how big a role the domain seems to play in the event, discuss senses used to experience its features, give guidance on how to identify the features, and present a highly truncated list of features to look for. You'll write what you discover in the Community Arts Profile, enriching the Genre Enactment Features.

Key reminder: Your goal is not to see if a genre or event fits one of these domain categories. Rather, we want you to skim through artistic features included in each domain to see if any are present in the enactments of the genre or event you are exploring. If there are any, add them to your description of the genre or event. If not, move on to the next analysis activity.

Ways to Go Deeper

When a genre is marked with a lot of something, or it seems to play important roles, you and the community may need to learn more. Ways to do this include performing the more extensive research activities in the *CLAT Companion*, using tools in the Digital Library, consulting a specialist, and finding ways to identify emic categories for formal elements through ethnographic research.

In the *CLAT Companion*, available at www.clatmanual.com, we lead you through activities that will help you discover more artistic elements of a genre. Note that we've grouped these activities in the same way we grouped your enactment analysis above in "Look Through Seven Basic Lenses": Space, Materials, Participant Organization, Shape through Time, Enactment Features, Content, and Consolidation and Meanings. This provides continuity with what you've already found out. Note also that the deeper research tasks we suggest for each domain consist mostly of participant observation, dialogue with practitioners, written description, and transcription.

RECORDING AND COLLECTING ADVICE

Before we get to the artistic feature descriptions, here are some ideas about gathering artistry that may come in handy.

Some Purposes for Recordings

We introduced these concepts in Conversation 1, but we will now expand them for applications to analysis.

Integral enactment contexts

An integral enactment is one that is familiar to the participants and has a high number of normal social and artistic components. Here are some reasons to record arts in integral settings:

Video recording

- to discover overall flow of an enactment through time, including subdivisions
- to see how sounds are produced and by whom
- to see how movements, dynamics, phrases, and relationships are produced
- to see how artists create visual objects

Audio recording

- to transcribe melodic, rhythmic, movement, plot, and other patterns in simple performance

Analytical enactment contexts

An analytical enactment context is designed by the researcher to isolate features of artistic production. One important purpose for such recordings is to collect components of an artistic genre for analysis and comparison; these might include songs, proverbs, dances, or stories. Here are a few other reasons to design recording events in analytical settings:

Video recording

- to enable subsequent feedback (participants and others can watch and verbally annotate the video recording of an enactment with the researcher)
- to describe playing or movement or acting techniques
- to document movement in the clearest manner for future viewing
- to transcribe melodies, rhythms, and texts

Recording Lots of Songs, Proverbs, or Other Artistry

Some of the research and analysis activities we describe in the following sections will benefit from a collection of basic products of an artistic genre. Such collections will help you find patterns, contrasts, themes, and limits to variation in the genre. They will also be key in contributing to archives of the artistry for protection and sharing. Here we present guides to collecting audio recordings of songs and proverbs, but you can apply similar steps to photographs of woven bags, video recordings of dances or plays, and many other bits of artistry.

How to collect songs

Songs are a nearly universally occurring type of artistic object composed of musical and verbal characteristics.

- Discover an artistic genre that includes songs (see *Inside-out* or *Outside-in* in Conversation 1).[7]
- Ask people you know: Who are the best performers of this kind of song? Who knows the most songs (often older people)? Please introduce me to this person.
- Create an analytical recording context: meet the person, describe what you'll do, get permission to record.
- Slate the recording: at the beginning of the recording. Say, "This is *your name*, recording *so-and-so person*, at *such-and-such place*, on *such-and-such day*." Then, before each song, say, "This is song number *one*, etc."
- After each song, record someone translating the main elements of the lyrics into a language of wider communication.

---

[7] Krabill, "Hymn-Collecting."

How to collect proverbs
The vast majority of languages include condensed, specially formed bits of wisdom that we call proverbs. To truly understand a proverb, you need to learn what its words mean and other cultural information it refers to. You also need to know how it is performed in a social context: who can use it and for what purpose(s)? There is an important place for you to perform integral video or audio recordings, recording them in natural use. This is hard and usually time consuming, but possible.

There are, however, many analyses that benefit from an analytically recorded collection of proverbs. Here are a few tips to making such a collection:[8]

- Gather people together, turn on a recording device, have everyone speak in the vernacular if possible, and ask people to think of as many proverbs as possible.

- Suggest situations in which proverbs might be used. These could include what a mother might say to a daughter who is angry with a friend, or a father to a son who is misbehaving. You can also suggest topics that proverbs might address, like laziness, animals, children, or food.

- Suggest kinds of people that proverbs might mention, like debtors, merchants, old people, midwives, children, hunters, or ancestors.

- Listen to the recording with someone who knows local proverbs well and can help you translate them in a language of wider communication. When a proverb occurs in the recording, stop the device, and have your friend(s) help you write and translate it.

EXAMPLES OF ARTISTIC DOMAIN FEATURES

Musical Features in Enactments and Events
Musical features have to do with patterned, stylized sounds in an artistic enactment. Actions that produce sounds most frequently include singing and other vocal production, and participants' interaction with instruments, their own bodies (e.g., in clapping), or other parts of their environment (e.g., in stomping the ground).

How much?
From what you've already experienced, how much musicky stuff seems evident in this event or enactment?

Senses used
Musical things are primarily experienced through auditory channels, though visual channels play important roles in helping the experiencer understand auditory information. Isolating the part of a single drum in a percussion ensemble, for example, may require visual attention to the drummer's playing.

---

8 Moon, *African Proverbs*; Unseth, "How to Collect," "Comparing Methods," "Using Local Proverbs," and "Collecting, Using, and Enjoying Proverbs"; Walters, "Nuosu Proverbs."

Watching a person play an instrument may also be the only way to understand playing technique, as in a rattle rhythm produced by complex, multidirectional movement.

Identifying musical features

Research activities most helpful in understanding musical aspects of enactment include audiovisual recording, ethnographic interview, and participant observation.

Some common features

Read the short list of features below, then listen to the sounds people make during an event with them in mind. Describe anything you hear that relates to these terms in the Genre Enactment Features (in the CAP). Note how any of what you've learned about musical features might increase meaning or effects of the artistry.

- **Notes**: Sounds with pitches.
- **Melody**: A succession of musical notes.
- **Beat**: A single unit of time, whether sounded or not.
- **Rhythm**: The whole feeling of sounds moving through time, or the pattern of long and short notes occurring in a song.
- **Timbre**: The quality of a tone produced by a voice or instrument. Initial descriptions might include rough, smooth, raspy, breathy, nasal, or creaky.
- **Instruments**: Objects emitting patterned sounds, usually through a person acting on the object somehow.
- **Tempo**: The speed at which beats occur.
- **Dynamics**: The volume and changes of volume in a piece or song.
- **Song**: A composition consisting minimally of rhythm, melody, and text. Note that *text* refers to words, which are not strictly a musical feature.
- **Form**: The organization of musical materials.

Dramatic Features in Enactments and Events

Dramatic features have mostly to do with how participants recreate actions, or create a world of possible actions, in a story event. Acting—taking on someone's persona for a role—is central to events with dramatic features.

How much?

From what you've already experienced, how much drama stuff seems evident in this event?

Senses used

Drama features are usually experienced through listening to and watching an event. What would you miss if you covered your ears or closed your eyes?

Identifying dramatic features

We learn about dramatic features of a tradition by observing rehearsals and enactments, by participating in the activities of drama groups, and by analyzing scripts, transcripts, audio recordings, or video recordings of events.

Some common features

Read the short list of features below, then watch and listen during an event with them in mind. Describe anything that relates to these terms in the Genre Enactment Features (in the CAP). Note how any of what you've learned about dramatic features might increase meaning or effects of the artistry.

- **Performance space**: Where the event happens and its characteristics.
- **Actor**: A person who portrays a character.
- **Character**: A make-believe person represented by an actor.
- **Dramatic setting**: The imagined location of a story.
- **Costumes**: The clothes performers wear.
- **Props**: The movable objects actors interact with.
- **Scenery**: Background objects that represent a location.
- **Plot**: The organized pattern of events that make up a story.
- **Audience's relationship to performed reality**: Whether the experiencers are meant to interact with the performers, or merely observe.

Dance Features in Enactments and Events

Dance features have to do with patterned, stylized movements in an event. Observers normally see performers use their bodies in the space surrounding them (their kinesphere), the environment in which they move, interactions with others, and sometimes objects that accentuate or otherwise alter the results of their actions.

How much?

From what you've already experienced, how much dancey stuff seems evident in this event?

Senses used

Dancey things are primarily experienced through visual channels, though they often intertwine almost inextricably with an event's musicky features like rhythm and meter. A performer also feels his or her own body moving in its personal surroundings and the environment, hears the atmosphere (e.g., music, clapping, vocalizations, breathing, impact of feet on floor, etc.), and responds to it.

Identifying dance features

Research activities most helpful in understanding the dance aspects of enactments include audiovisual recording, ethnographic and embodied interviews, participant observation, and written and drawn descriptions.

Some common features

Read the short list of features below, then watch people during an event with them in mind. Describe anything you hear that relates to these terms in the Genre Enactment Features (in the CAP). Note how any of what you've learned about dance features might increase meaning or effects of the artistry.

- **Floor plan**: boundaries of the space, permanent objects, and "snapshots" of dancers beginning and ending a movement pattern and their pathway to get from point A to point B.
- **Total dance form**: The highest structural level; the summation of all the integrated structural units.
- **Kinesphere**: How participants use their bodies in the space surrounding them.
- **Body parts and how they relate to each other**: The head, the tail, the two arms, and the two legs all connected to the core of the torso.
- **Phrasing**: Movement energy or intensity, with such contrasts as even or changing levels, accented spurts, elasticity, or buoyancy.
- **Effort**: How a performer senses and moves through Space and Time, and their relationship to gravity (Weight).
- **Dynamics**: Movement quality denoting whether performers employ Effort in ways that resist or give in to gravity or momentum.

Oral Verbal Arts Features in Enactments and Events

Oral Verbal Arts features are normally ways people modify words and combinations of words to make them, for example, memorable, motivating, or aesthetically pleasing. Verbal elements are usually expressed aloud, with vocal modifications and gestures. We have defined this category ourselves, extremely loosely, to account for the innumerable ways people emit words, including through signed language. Examples include genre categories like stories, proverbs, parables, puns, tongue twisters, song lyrics, riddles, heckling, odes, lullabies, and thousands more—each usually connected to other genres and events.[9] To limit this complexity and respond to many users' contexts, the *CLAT Companion* (www.clatmanual.com) gives special attention to song texts, stories, proverbs, and oratory.

How much?

From what you've already experienced, how much do participants employ poetically modified words in this event?

Senses used

Oral verbal features are centrally experienced through auditory channels, but almost always integrate or exist alongside elements requiring other senses, especially visual cues.

---

[9] An open-access journal dedicated to oral verbal art forms can be found at https://oraltradition.org.

Identify Artistic Domain Features

Identifying oral verbal features

We find out about verbal features of a tradition by observing events with words, transcribing texts live or from audio or video recordings, and learning to enact examples of such genres. Essential to almost all analyses are three-line interlinear translations:

1. Writing down or typing the full text in its original form and language.
2. A line with a word-for-word literal translation in a language everyone knows.
3. A line or lines containing a free, natural translation of a whole segment.

Some common features

Read the shortened list of features below, then watch and listen during an event with them in mind. Describe anything that relates to these terms in the Genre Enactment Features (in the CAP). Note how any of what you learn about verbal features might increase meaning or effects of the artistry.

Overall characteristics

- **Verbal play**: A highly creative act that overlaps with other features. It is often found in storytelling by means of various semantic devices, including metaphor, allegory, metonymy, puns, humor, and so on.
- **Rhythm or pulse**: This often is structured by syllables that come together in a certain number of beats or patterns.
- **Text density**: Number of lines per verse, number of verses per poem or song, number of syllables per line, or number of notes per syllable (in song).

Poetic devices related to words themselves

- **Lexical repetition**: Use of the same word in more than one context.
- **Homonyms**: Two or more words that share the same pronunciation and spelling but with different meanings.
- **Archaic language**: Words, phrases, or grammatical structures no longer used in normal speech.
- **Borrowed words**: Words adopted from another language.

Poetic devices related to sound

- **Assonance**: Rhyme referring to the same or similar vowel sounds in neighboring words.
- **Rhyme**: The same or similar vowel sounds at the end, beginning, or middle of lines.
- **Vocable**: Word or syllable without referential meaning, whose sound when produced is in focus.
- **Ideophones**: Words that sound like the thing they refer to.
- **Consonance**: Close correspondence of sounds.
- **Alliteration**: Repetition of the same or similar sounds at the beginning of words.
- **Rhythmic speech**: Pattern of emphasis through time.

Poetic devices related to meaning

- **Semantic categories**: Examples include similes, metonymy (where a word or expression stands for another one, e.g., sweat = hard work), synecdoche (when part of something refers to the whole; e.g., set of wheels = car), personification, hyperbole, euphemism (describing something socially unpleasant in indirect terms), and symbols.
- **Rhetorical questions**: Meant to persuade rather than elicit information.
- **Metaphors**: Figures of speech in which a word or phrase corresponds to an object or action that is not literally applicable.

Visual Features in Enactments and Events

Visual communication, like any other kind of communication, uses signs to convey or create meaning. As we've discussed, each culture agrees upon relationships between its lexical, iconic, and indexical signs and their meanings. The study of visual symbolism is the attempt to find the meaning behind visible signifiers, through research. These culturally defined meanings are often contained in shapes or colors. Meanings can also be combined in specific ways through a visual grammar (patterns that are governed by rules).

Creators of artistic objects choose materials that will allow them to produce the visual features they desire. Characteristics of materials that can inform these choices include strength, plasticity, smoothness, texture, color, shape, and the like.

Artistic objects generally retain their form through time and are often integrated into enactments of performance genres and events. An object, then, is not an event itself. Experiencing the process of its creation, however, is an event, as is someone scrutinizing a painting hanging in a museum. The length of time that an object exists varies from hours to centuries (e.g., compare a sandcastle below a beach's tide line to a stone cathedral).

To limit this complexity and respond to many Manual users' contexts, the *CLAT Companion* (www.clatmanual.com) includes more research activities relating to visual features than we have in this section.

How much?

From what you've already experienced, how much do participants employ visual features in this object or event? Most art forms have a visual component—paintings and sculptures, the movements of the body or hands in dance, the colors and costumes in drama, the visual composition of musical instruments, and so on.

Senses used

Visual features are primarily experienced through the eyes, often initially at a subconscious level. Note that some visual features may also be experienced through touch: people can feel textures and shapes. This may be especially important for visually impaired experiencers or other participants involved in an event where there is little or no light.

Identifying visual features

We discover visual facets of enactments primarily through direct observation (including handling or other types of interactions with objects), creating and examining photo- and videographic recordings, ethnographic interviews, learning to make an example of a genre, and participant observation.

Some common features

Though visual artistry is not always performed by participants in real time, its features are the building blocks of visual communication. Read the shortened list below, then examine an object, recording, or enactment with them in mind. Describe anything that relates to these terms in the Genre Enactment Features (in the CAP). Note how any of what you learn about visual features might increase meaning or effects of the artistry.

- **Line**: "The path made by a pointed instrument: a pen, a pencil, a crayon, a stick. A line implies action because work was required to make it."[10]
- **Shape**: A two-dimensional, flat area enclosed by lines, textures, or colors, limited to height and width. Form is a three-dimensional defined space that has depth and encloses volume.
- **Value**: The lightness or darkness of a part of an image compared to other parts of the image. Value can be based on a gray scale, from black to white, or in tints and shades of colors.
- **Color**: The visual response to the wavelengths of light reflected from something, identified as red, blue, green, etc. Communities may assign meanings to certain colors. For example, in a graduation ceremony, the colors of the gowns and hoods have a meaning known by those who understand such things. The color of the front of the hood identifies the discipline in which the degree was earned, while the colors of the trim and back represent the school colors of the granting institution. Related to color are the following:
    - **Hue**: The prototypical color definition in a culture.
    - **Shades**: Darker variants of a color formed by adding varying amounts of black to the hue.
    - **Tints**: Lighter variants of a color formed by adding varying amounts of white to the hue.
- **Texture**: The literal or implied sense of feeling that a visual message evokes, such as roughness or softness—the message creator substitutes an imagined sense of touch by a visual representation.

A Challenge to Explore More Kinds of Artistry

Remember that these five kinds of artistry represent a limited number of possible domains. Please continue the work by exploring others, such as perfumery, culinary arts, cinema, architecture, sports, and so on.

---

10 Feldman, *Varieties of Visual Experience*, 207.

CONVERSATION 4C

DISCOVER DEEPER COMMUNITY CONNECTIONS

	Third Pass: Discover Deeper Community Connections [4C]
Primary Questions	How do the forms and features revealed in First- and Second-pass research connect to broader community patterns and dynamics?
Output	1. Cultural Category Descriptions: Integrate insights into Genre Enactment Features. 2. Quick winnowing: How relevant does each cultural category–its meanings, patterns, and dynamics–seem to be? Extend your research on those that are especially significant.
Methods	For package of features produced by First- and Second-pass research: • Connect to each community connection category and questions. • Continue attention to how features, patterns, meanings contribute to cultural connections.
Genre Enactment Features will look like this (in CAP)	Features, Patterns, and Meanings with artistic details integrated into sociocultural characteristics of the genre enactments. • How might results of this research impact Conversations 4B, 5, 6, and 7? Make a list for future reference. • Aim for organic, holistic, socioartistic insights.

Nothing you encounter in a community exists in isolation. Words, clothes, houses, food, movements, facial expressions, family—everything is interwoven, like threads in fabric. Likewise, events with artistic communication exist in relationship to other parts of a society and interact with local, regional, national, and global realities. These complexities sometimes result in artistic and/or social fusions and may fuel change. Understanding how an enactment connects to its broader context allows you to enter more fruitfully into its creation, evaluation, integration, and celebration.

Through relationships and analyses in previous Conversations, you've already developed valuable insights into this community's inner and outer workings. Conversation 4C offers a framework that should produce fresh and deeper insights. We've chosen several categories of cultural investigation that have proved especially illuminating when applied to artistic activity.[11] Each topic consists of the central question or questions that should guide your investigation, aspects of the topic that have proven relevant for others, and research activities to get you started. The CAP's Genre Enactment Features section contains a section for your discoveries.

---

[11] You may want to consult Ember and Ember's "Basic Guide to Cross-Cultural Research," especially their HRAF database on World Cultures to suggest more research questions and topics common to many cultures.

Note also that you can't be sure of the reality of broader cultural themes unless you have had a detailed familiarity with actual artistic communication. Facts without themes are trivial. Themes without facts are vapors. So keep investigating genres in events, guided by activities in this conversation.

For each topic ask:
1. How does this relate to what you've already learned about the enactment (lenses in 4A) and artistic features (domains in 4B) and their meanings?
2. How might results of researching each category connect to various signs of Heaven (Conversation 2)?

We've defined *meaning* as "ideas and emotions a community or individual attaches to elements of their internal or external experiences." This Conversation focuses on meanings shared or contested at a community level, always discovered through research.

Pray throughout all your activities and relating to people.

ARTISTS

People are at the core of artistic communication. They learn, perform, and pass on the skills and knowledge that make such communication effective. They add their individual skills, interests, and goals to existing traditions. They are the keepers of artistic treasures. Though everyone creates, some people have exceptional knowledge and skills in particular genres and events. So, any plan a community makes to draw on its arts for Kingdom Goals must include informed understanding of and interaction with artists at its core.

As you've discovered in Conversation 4A's Lens 3, "Participant Organization," we value relationships with other people who often play important roles in enactments of genres and events. And then there are those who encourage or limit acceptance of certain types of artistic communication in a community. But God calls us to learn from, welcome, and encourage artists; without them, plans will never succeed.

The exploratory activities that will help you answer the questions in this section have to do with getting to know people: interviews, participation, and observation. In addition to the tasks below, you may decide to study formally or informally with a skilled artist. Join artists in their personal and artistic worlds. Learn how local composers create. Ask to watch an artist teach someone else. Share your own life and artistic gifts with him or her. These are our people.

Who Are Artists Related to This Kind of Genre?

Everyone in a community is likely to be involved in artistic communication in some way—by listening, watching, singing, sculpting, writing, dancing, composing, admiring, critiquing, etc. Some people, however, have more knowledge and skills related to creation, enactment, and transmission; our focus now is on these people. Every community categorizes people with gifts of artistry in different ways, and few use broad categories like *musician* or *artist*. More often, an artist is given a role and identity in his or her language of singer, player of a particular instrument, mask maker, or other such designation. Note also that artistic genres themselves may require composers and enactors to be of a single gender, family of origin, age, caste, or other feature.

To find artists involved in a type of enactment you've experienced, perform activities like these:

- Through interviews, list the roles of participants in an event. Revisiting "Participant Organization" in Conversation 4A will help you in this.
- Choose one of these roles and ask friends and other community members who some of the most respected fillers of that role are. Repeat this for other roles.
- Over time, ask, listen, watch, and confirm the skills and reputations of artists you get to know. Everyone will have different combinations of skills and attributes, and so will play different roles in Kingdom activities. You may find, for example, an older man who knows the most stories in a genre but is not the best teller. The community may decide to have the older man lead the choice of which stories to record on an audio product they create for wide distribution but have someone else perform.

How Do Artists Relate to Their Communities?

A community may ascribe high, neutral, or low status to an artist associated with a particular genre. Though the status level may be determined by the individual character of an artist, respect or disrespect is often associated with a particular artistic role. People who play drums associated with royalty, for example, may enjoy high levels of respect and honor. Artists who enact genres for activities a society deems less respectable—for example, lewd dramatic entertainment in a brothel—may be merely tolerated. We need to be aware of community attitudes when encouraging artists to create for Kingdom purposes, because these feelings will have a strong effect on how deeply Christians embrace their activities.

Some communities have established roles for those who create arts for other people. In West Africa, especially in areas influenced by Islam, there may be a local form of *griot* (praise singer). There are examples from Nigeria, Benin, and Ghana where such a Muslim praise singer agreed to work with a biblical text and compose and record a Scripture song.[12] Investigate whether an established form of composing for patrons is already in place. Note that such professional composers are used to working for some form of compensation. *Composers-for-hire* also appear in some Asian cultures, including parts of Nepal and the Philippines. In Daasanech society on the Kenya/Ethiopia border, a man pays a woman *gaaro* specialist to compose songs relating important events of his life. On the other hand, most Daasanech mothers compose songs for their babies but are not paid. Investigate how a community compensates an artist, either monetarily or through some other means.

---

12 Neeley, "Reflections of a Gatekeeper"; Wedekind, "The Praise Singers."

To find out how artists involved in a type of event you've experienced relate to their society, perform activities like these:

- Through discreet and sensitive interviews, ask people their opinions of people who fill each role in an artistic event.
- As you get to know an artist, ask how they are treated by different segments of society, and if and how they get paid for their work.

How Do People Become Artists in This Genre or Event?

Becoming an artist in a particular genre may be largely determined by societal patterns, achieved by individual effort and skill, or—most often—through a combination of the two. In parts of West Africa, for example, members of certain castes are expected to work as professional singers and storytellers. Because of this societal expectation, children in these castes are taught musical skills and enactment practices from a young age. In other cultures, people are encouraged primarily to follow individual interests and skills.

To find out how artists become involved in a particular genre, perform activities like these:

- Do a biographical study of an artist's life, using common journalists' questions: Where have you lived? How did you learn the skills associated with this role? Who has influenced you in your art? Why did you follow this path? Describe some important events in your life that impacted your artistry.
- Similarly, ask people knowledgeable in a genre to describe its history: Where did it originate? Who were important figures in its development? When did important steps in the genre's development take place?

CREATIVITY

We define artistic creativity as occurring when one or more people draw on their personal competencies and their community(ies)' social and symbolic systems to produce an enactment—event or work—of heightened communication that has not previously existed in its exact form.[13] To find out how creativity works in the community you're working with, you'll need to get inside what is a very dynamic process. You can do this through asking questions, participating in creative acts, and commissioning new works. As you participate in a community's process, you can discover how new works are created and who creates them.

Who Are the Creators of New Works?

Creation can be performed by an individual specialist—someone who is recognized for their abilities, or a casual "one-shot" composer who writes for

---

[13] See also concepts of person, symbolic domain, and field in Csikszentmihalyi, *Creativity*, 23–31, and a more comprehensive discussion of creativity in Schrag and Van Buren, *Make Arts*, 12–16.

a particular occasion—or a collaboration of several individuals. Building on what you've discovered in Conversations 4A, and 4B, find out who the creators of the artistic elements of an event are by watching a live or video recording of an enactment, or looking at an object with artistic features with a friend and ask questions like these:

- Who made this, and when?
- Who made each element of this event, and when? Examples of elements might include a dance move, a song, a play, a poem, a structure, or a woven cloth.

How Do New Examples of This Form Come into Being?

Composition can take place through deliberate and conscious effort or be received through dreams or visions. If through conscious effort, an individual may make it happen, a group may work on it together, or it could be a combined effort (several composers working on different parts or at different times).

Techniques for composition include the following: conscious generation of an element of a genre, like a song, poem, dance, or mask; taking parts of old works and putting them together in new ways; improvisation; communal re-creation; creating out of emotional stress after a particularly meaningful or traumatic situation; and composition-in-performance. To find out how people generate new works, perform activities like these:

- Watch a live or video recording of an enactment, or look at an artistic object with a friend and ask questions like these: What did people do to make this? Who was involved?
- Commission a new work in the genre, then ask the creator(s) what steps they will follow. You can also ask if you could document the process by written notes, photographs, and/or video.

What Does "New" Mean in This Art Form?

Creativity is about making something new. But each community values and defines newness in different ways. If a group esteems continuity more than innovation, then they may discourage changes in a tradition. If they have the opposite view, they may reward creators who depart significantly from tradition, including fusions, transformations, repurposing, and other modifications.

To find out how people involved in the creation of this art form think about newness, perform activities like these:

- Interact with a creator while he or she is making something. Ask what aspects of the new enactment differ from existing creations, and which are the same. Ask if they can list any principles, wisdom, or proverbs that guide their creativity.
- Ask a group of people if they can remember an example of a work that jarred them because it was too new. Ask if they can isolate an element that displeased them.

Where Do the Components of Creativity for This Genre Lie?

Each community performs arts that draw on a unique combination of its components of creativity—creators, language and other symbolic systems, and audience and gatekeepers. Each component, in turn, can vary in its nearness to the community, measured geographically, conceptually, and in communal identity. According to this rubric, a community may have creators and enactors that draw on symbolic systems residing in local traditions, in traditions from other communities, in regional or national artistic genres, or in the artistic traditions of a distant culture.

Creators: Where are the creators, the individuals and groups who compose and perform each element of this enactment? This may refer to singers, instrument players, lyricists, composers, playwrights, sculptors, and others.

Language and other symbolic systems: In what communities do the systems and skills underlying their artistic production reside? This speaks to systems of language, melody, scale, rhythm, timbre, poetic devices, dramatic characterization, movement, repertoire, and the like. Also included are competencies such as instrument building and means of learning enactment skills, such as formal and informal educational structures.

Audiences and gatekeepers: Where are the individuals and groups who influence artistic production most in this context? This comprises knowledgeable audiences; highly and widely regarded enactors; commercial, social, religious, or aesthetic gatekeepers; and others.

Figure 4.6 provides an example of this kind of analysis, a model you and a community can follow with an artistic genre they know.[14]

Location		Creativity Components		
		Creators	Language and Other Symbolic Systems	Audience and Gatekeepers
Distant–Near	Community	enactors		song choices in enactment
	Region or Nation		language(s) of lyrics	songbook publishers
	World	composers	musical, rhythmic, conceptual systems	

Figure 4.6 Creativity components of young Congolese churches

As a rule of thumb, the nearer a kind of artistry's creativity components are to the community, the more likely it is to thrive and engender relationships with more types of people (e.g., in a church's connections to its neighbors).

---

14 Schrag, "Music in the Newer Churches," 359–67.

TRANSMISSION AND CHANGE

Participants in an artistic enactment learned its associated skills and knowledge somehow. This transmission may have happened in a socially structured way, through schools, lessons, or formal apprenticeships. It could also have been transmitted informally, through learning by watching, or individual exploration. Methods of transmission could include aural activities like repetition of an expert's singing, playing, or acting. The process could also include written helps, like music notation or a dance score. This human-to-human transfer always includes some change: teaching and learning processes are not purely mechanical, people remember inaccurately or forget completely, or the type of artistry may *require* its enactors to break traditions or produce as utterly never-heard-or-seen-before expressions as possible (as, for example, in free jazz). Each individual has different interests and levels of skills that also affect what they learn.

How Are Competencies Passed on to Others?

To find out how people learn this type of genre, perform activities like these:

- Ask participants in the enactment to tell how they learned to do what they did, and if you can participate in or watch that process sometime. As you watch, note the interactions between people, how more knowledgeable people are treated, and what objects are part of the process.

- If these genre enactments are part of a long tradition, ask an older person how and when people used to learn it. Then ask if they still learn it this way, and if not, what has changed to make the difference.

How Has This Form Changed Historically?

To find out how this type of enactment has changed over time, perform activities like this:

- Find older and newer recordings or examples of an art form. Watch, examine, or listen to them with a knowledgeable person and ask how the two differ. Ask what might have caused differences.

- Ask people familiar with the form how it might have changed over time. You may find that forms have changed very little, especially in rituals.

LANGUAGE(S)

The language(s) and types of language used in an artistic enactment can reveal much about its relationship to the broader culture. Song lyrics in a regional or national language support regional or national identity. A tapestry woven with a minority language's unique alphabet may accentuate identification with a minority community. It's also common in artistic communication to use archaic forms not used in everyday speech, or more ceremonial or intimate (that is, different registers). This may reflect a sense of mystery or fear associated with a genre, or it may simply have been frozen in an ancient form for other reasons.

Remember that in addition to the symbolic meanings normally associated with a language, its use can index experiences (e.g., like those in a refugee camp or church) or approximate sounds or shapes in the external world (e.g., onomatopoetic rooster crows or letters arranged to together form a flower). Refer especially to what you learned by looking through Conversation 4A's Content Lens and Conversation 4B's Oral Verbal Arts category.

Finally, some genre enactments may include words or other elements from a neighboring language community. If so, explore subjects like these: What are the attitudes of each one to the other? How do the languages compare in levels of prestige or status? How close are the languages to each other linguistically (e.g., degree of inter-comprehension)? Do they share a broader culture identity, or kinds of artistry?

What Language(s), Dialect(s), and Register(s) are Appropriate for This Form?

Watch or listen to a recording of an event or look at an object with someone who knows a lot about it. List every component containing language in any form—spoken, written, signed, drawn, and so on—and write down answers to questions like these:

> What language(s) or dialect(s) is this in? What communities speak each language, and where are they geographically?
>
> Can you imagine someone saying this in normal speech, or is it a special kind of language? Do you understand what it means?

What Status and Identity are Associated with Each Language?

With the same list of language types used, ask questions like these:

> When you hear or speak this type of language, who does it make you think of? Do you feel positive, negative, angry, neutral, etc. toward this language or its communities? Do you identify the language as *yours*?
>
> Why do you think the creator(s) used this type of language?

SUBJECT MATTER

The verbal content of songs, proverbs, plays, tapestries, and other arts flows from the minds, experiences, and histories of the participating individuals and communities. Sometimes artistic communication reveals information about subjects that is nearly inaccessible otherwise, such as spiritual actors or historical events. At other times, it communicates the values of the community in memorable form; proverbs are a strong example of this. The references of textual content may be metaphorical or cryptic, so your first understanding may not be the only one, or the deepest.

As with Language(s) you learned engaging with Conversation 4A's Content Lens and Conversation 4B's Oral Verbal Arts category may suggest further questions and research activities.

To explore patterns in the subject matter addressed by artistic communication, perform activities like these:

- Make a list of the elements in an event that have verbal content, like songs, proverbs, or stories. Ask an expert to describe the messages in each. Ask: What is this about? What are they trying to communicate? Is there a lesson? If so, who is the lesson for?
- As you watch a recording or read a transcription of an event, ask a small group of participants to list all the references to people, objects, places, events, or spiritual beings. Ask them to describe each. Record or write down their answers.

CULTURAL DYNAMISM

Healthy communities maintain a mix of continuity and change. Artistic genres can feed into community vitality through interactions between their stable and malleable elements. Stable elements tend to resist change; they occur regularly in time and place and are tightly organized. More malleable elements are less predictable (perhaps marked by improvisation) and more loosely organized. Cultural dynamism happens when artists masterfully use the most malleable elements of their arts to invigorate the most stable. I've started calling these interacting elements *artistic dynamos*.[15]

The figures below identify dynamos associated with artistry in Ngiembɔɔn communities, West Cameroon.[16] Figures 4.7 and 4.8 refer to enactments of the *kànɔɔn* genre, marked by sung call and response form and prominent rhythm producing instruments. Figure 4.9 highlights the intentionally didactic content of calls in the closely related *leneŋe mboŋ* genre.

Song Form	Infrastructures	Contributions to Dynamic Interplay	Tangible Energy Produced
Malleable	Call	Interest, connection to enactment location	Songs have energy, draw interest
Stable	Response	Time to prepare	

Figure 4.7 Artistic dynamo: Song form in the *kànɔɔn* genre

---

15 See Schrag, *Artistic Dynamos*, 144–51 (ArtisticDynamos.com). People are exploring community flourishing energized by interactions between stable|malleable pairs in more and more contexts, including multicultural worship (Kim, "Diaspora Musicians"), food (Nelson, "Straight from the Pot"), Scripture engagement (Petersen, "Arts Development"), songwriting (Connor, "Creativity"), and more.

16 Schrag, *Artistic Dynamos*, 148–49.

Rhythm	Infrastructures	Contributions to Dynamic Interplay	Tangible Energy Produced
Malleable	Big drum patterns	Interest	Songs have energy, draw interest
Stable	Shaker patterns	Reference pulse for predictable performance frame	

Figure 4.8 Artistic dynamo: Rhythm in the *kànɔɔn* genre

Community Values	Infrastructures	Contributions to Dynamic Interplay	Tangible Energy Produced
Malleable	Sung proverbs and names	Teaching, reminding	Common moral and narrative frame promoting solidarity
Stable	Proverb and persona repertoire	Authoritative moral and ideal reference	

Figure 4.9 Artistic dynamo: Community values in the *leneŋe mboŋ* genre

Without creative, malleable structures to infuse new energy into the stable structures, the stable structures will decay and dissipate. And without stable undergirdings, the creators in malleable forms will have no dependable reference points to anchor their creativity.

Discuss these questions with artists to begin to understand the interplay between stable and malleable elements:

- **To identify stable artistic elements:** Which art forms or aspects of art forms occur most regularly, with the least amount of variability and tight organization?
- **To identify malleable artistic elements:** Which art forms or aspects of art forms occur with less predictability and are more loosely organized?
- **To identify interactions between stable and malleable elements:** Look for any artistic elements in the domains of rhythm, enactment organization, or shape through time that interact in pairs. For example, does the rhythmic structure of an enactment have some parts that never change, allowing a master percussionist to improvise?

IDENTITY AND POWER

We express who we are or who we want to be by choosing what, how, and where to communicate artistically. This means that every dance step, song, story, proverb, hairstyle, piece of jewelry, and woven cloth is an act of identity affirmation. These affirmations relate to social power structures in different ways, which can cause controversy. It is important, then, to know how an art form fits into its local and wider communities, so they can make informed decisions in expanding the Kingdom of Heaven. Be cautious and humble in addressing issues of power.

Arts for a Better Future (ABF) participants choose Identity more than any other Kingdom Goal (see Conversation 2). In particular, people from minority communities yearn to affirm and integrate their traditional lifeways and arts deeply into the ways they follow Jesus. Often this is in the face of more powerful populations or systems denigrating their communities, especially in churches; other subgroups experience similar exclusion.[17] Higher status groups may or may not be aware that this is happening. Reflect with the community as much as possible about the mechanisms and dynamics of this injustice so communities can design wise arts-fueled activities that will effect change (see Conversations 4D and 5).

Who Identifies with This Form and How?

To explore participants' identification with this type of event, perform activities like these:

- Make a list of elements associated with the event: language, dress, colors, instruments, and so on. Ask a friend which group each of these is associated with.
- Interview participants in the event to find out demographic information: age, gender, education, occupation, geographic origin, ethnic self-identification, language(s) spoken, and religion. Avoid discussing categories that may cause contention or invite danger.
- Ask participants why they are involved in this event.

How Does This Form Relate to Social Stratification, Gender, or Other Distinctions?

Artistic communication can affirm power structures, as with national anthems or royal pageantry. People can also use artistic forms to oppose power, as in early African American rap and Rastafarian reggae. Art forms can be expressed publicly or in hidden ways. Examples of public expressions affirming power include national anthems and West African praise songs. Less direct and visible comments on power occurred when enslaved people in the United States embedded antislavery messages in spirituals. To research this type of event's relationship to power, perform activities like these:

- Transcribe any texts associated with this enactment, like song lyrics or story content. Examine them to see if there are overt messages affirming or opposing a person, institution, or other entity. Discreet discussion with a friend may help you find out if there are any hidden messages.
- Observe an enactment. Did people communicate messages that challenged authority, something you haven't seen them do elsewhere? Artistic action can provide a safe place for contestation or resolving conflict.

---

17 For one historical and theological explanation of this situation in the church, see Schrag and Swijghuisen Reigersberg, "Ethnodoxology."

AESTHETICS AND EVALUATION

People find pleasure in their experience of artistic communication for many reasons: the group solidarity it may engender, the association of the experience with an enjoyable memory, or satisfaction in the attributes of an art form. This last possibility has to do with aesthetics, the study of the criteria people use to judge an artifact with respect to attributes perceived to be intrinsic to it. Though there may be overlap between different communities, every society has a unique set of criteria they use to judge the inherent value of works of art they experience. In other words, there is no formal characteristic of artistic communication that is intrinsically pleasing, beautiful, or good.[18]

Humans can also experience artistry with *dis*pleasure. They quickly judge others' arts negatively by their own aesthetic standards. We must avoid such assessments in ourselves at all costs, and help others search the reasons for their own evaluations. Here are a few activities you can perform to find out how the community you're working with approaches correction and evaluation in general. Ask a friend questions like these:

> Would you correct someone older or younger, or in roles of higher or lower status than you? If so, how? The community might value direct correction in some contexts or require indirection.
>
> How would these same kinds of people correct you?

Here are ways to explore evaluation of an artistic object's form:

- Ask people what makes a component of an art form good or bad.
- Observe experts teaching an art form to someone else—perhaps you—and write down what advice they give or mistakes they correct. These may point to an ideal.
- Notice items that are put in a place of prominence, spoken of with reverence, or that take special expertise and time to create. These are likely to have ideal characteristics. Ask people what makes them good or pleasing.
- Gather a small group of people to watch and listen to a recording of an enactment or look at an artistic object. Ask them to say what's good or bad about it.

TIME

Artistic communication intersects with time in two important ways. First, because most arts provide some sort of rhythmic structure, people often experience time during enactments differently than they do in other parts of life. Goodridge describes movement rhythm in artistic expression as "a patterned energy flow of action, marked in the body by varied stress and

---

18 See Margolis, *Language of Art*, 44; Fitzgerald and Schrag, "But Is It Any Good?"

directional change; also marked by changes in level of intensity, speed and duration."[19] People often think about and experience time in particular ways in an event. Participants may feel time flowing more quickly, more slowly, or in unpredictably complex ways. In addition, the structure, flow, and timing of an enactment may intersect with broader cultural temporal patterns. In many communities, certain events only occur at specific moments in agricultural, religious, or other calendrical cycles.

To find out more about the intersection of artistic and community time, perform activities like these:

- Soon after an event, ask participants questions like these: How did you know when to do certain things? How did you experience time? Was it linear, cyclical, or flowing in waves? Did it feel sacred? When else do you experience time this way?
- Ask a small group of people to list all the times an event of this type occurred in the last two years. Do you notice any temporal patterns? Ask why they happened when they did.
- Ask experts in a genre to describe the passage of time during their participation in the artistry. Do they explicitly connect this description to broader calendrical cycles?

EMOTIONS

Capacity to express and evoke emotion is one of the most celebrated characteristics of artistic communication. The arts have a way of connecting a sound, sight, movement, scent, or taste directly to potent, emotionally charged memories. They also often provide a socially acceptable release for intense feelings, as lamentations and wailing do for grief. In addition, artistic communication can envelop a person's whole being, allowing gifted performers to magnify emotions in others by playing with their expectations of the art form. Finally, the arts are often associated with trance, ecstasy, and other states of overwhelming emotion.

To research an event's connections to emotion, perform activities like these:

- Watch a recording of an event and write down what emotions that participants—including audience members—appear to express. Afterward, discuss your interpretations with someone who was there, noting differences and ways to learn more about what happened.
- Watch a video recording of an artistic event with people who were there. Watch the observers, and when they exhibit any emotion—joy, surprise, sadness, anger, disdain, etc.—stop the recording and ask about what they're responding to. Make a list of the words they use to describe their emotions and what was going on in the enactment that sparked them. Record their comments.

---

19 Goodridge, *Rhythm and Timing*, 43.

- Ask friends if they remember an artistic event that evoked very strong emotion in them. Have them describe the event and their reactions.
- Participate in an enactment of a genre, reflecting on your own emotions. Proceed with caution if people in the event seek trance states. Advice and prayer with a Christ-follower familiar with the genre are especially important here.

COMMUNITY VALUES

Artistic communication often provides community members a place to challenge authorities. However, how artists organize and perform the communication may also reveal important aspects of a community's values and social structures. Reflecting on the physical and social organization of participants may provide insight into broader community values. To research relationships between an artistic event and broader community values, observe an event and afterwards ask questions of participants like these:

- How do participants interact with representatives of authority within the event? How does this differ from such interactions in other contexts?
- Does the physical organization of participants show a hierarchical structure, as in the first, second, and third seats of performers in a symphony orchestra? Or are participants organized on the same physical level? Answers to these questions may reflect values of hierarchical vs. egalitarian social structures elsewhere in the community.
- In what ways, if any, are participants encouraged to express themselves individually? What signs of free vs. rigid atmosphere are there? Answers to these questions may reflect values of conformity vs. nonconformity elsewhere in the community.

DECISION-MAKING

How communities tend to make decisions touches the core of the CLAT process. Each Conversation entails people choosing among various options to varying degrees, and communities differ in *how* they make choices. We touched on this in Conversation 2's "Methods for Specifying Kingdom Goals" and will rely heavily on related insights in Conversation 5; activities meant to spark creativity require judgments regarding innovations.

Approaches to making decisions are inherently intertwined with other Conversation 4C topics, including Community Values, Transmission and Change, Aesthetics and Evaluation, and Creativity. From a cursory scan, for example, communities organized hierarchically may only allow people at certain social levels to make specific types of decisions. More egalitarian groups may favor meetings or processes with ideals of including everyone's voice.

Yates and de Oliveira's "10 Cardinal Decision Issues," which I list below, provide a more thorough framework.[20] The interrelated topics lend themselves to ethnographic interviews, small group discussions, and observation.

1. **Need**: "Does a decision need to be made?" People may view their situations as positive or negative, and thus be more likely to see change as opportunities or threats.
2. **Mode**: "Who (what) decides, and how?" Does a group place value on individuals making decisions or including more people, maybe asking advice or opinions? And are they more likely to appeal to intuition or logical procedures?
3. **Investment**: "What will it cost to make this decision?" How much mental energy, time, or money does the group normally expend in the decision-making process. Indecisiveness requires extra time, allowing for more people to be involved.
4. **Options**: "What are the alternatives?" How capable are people of thinking creatively, suggesting multiple possible futures? Studies have shown that "only people who adopted an 'integration' acculturation strategy—identifying with both their host and heritage cultures—were more creative."[21]
5. **Possibilities**: "What could happen if that action were taken?" Collectivist communities are likely to gather more information than individualistic, often resulting in better founded decisions.
6. **Judgment**: "What *would* happen if that action were pursued"? A lack of overconfidence, and a tendency to value situation-specific explanations of events versus causal—for example, someone must have used sorcery to kill a man—may result in more accurate judgments.
7. **Value**: "What will particular people like and dislike, and how much?" How much importance do people put on one person's opinion versus communal viewpoints? Also relevant, how much do people tolerate loss? Communal groups with low loss aversion are more likely to take risks.
8. **Tradeoffs**: "Every alternative has at least one flaw, so what now?" How does a community evaluate inevitable strengths and weaknesses of different choices?
9. **Acceptability**: "How can we get others to agree with our decision?" Must such a process emphasize direct or indirect communication? Are any participatory approaches appropriate? Do any of the factors touch on sacred—that is, normally uncompromisable—values? If so, research suggests that symbolic gestures like asking for people's involvement, permission, or forgiveness can lead to compromise and understanding.

---

20 Yates and de Oliveira, "Culture and Decision Making"; Yates and Potorowski, "Evidence-Based Decision Management."

21 Yates and de Oliveira, 111.

10. **Implementation**: "How can we implement this decision?" Concrete, actionable plans like those in Conversation 5 make implementation more likely.

COMMUNAL INVESTMENT

The amount of energy a community invests in different kinds of artistic activity varies widely. A grandfather speaking a proverb to his granddaughter involves only two people, requires no preparation, costs no money, and lasts for only a few seconds. A funeral for a king in West Cameroon, on the other hand, may last a month, include hundreds of people, and require significant finances to pay for food, transportation, and gifts. An assessment of the social, material, financial, and spiritual resources a community invests in an event provides important clues to its importance and influence.

To research a community's investment in an event, observe, ask, and write down information about the following parameters:

- length of time of the enactment
- status of scheduled time and location: high status, low status
- amount of preparation
- cost of the enactment
- enactment space: status, size, expense, exclusivity
- participants: number, status, exclusivity, level of skill or professionalism
- complexity: number of relevant features

CONVERSATION 4D

ENCOURAGE CHURCHES TO INTEGRATE ARTISTRY MORE HOLISTICALLY

This book is about the Kingdom of Heaven, always with the future New Creation in mind. As we outlined in the Introduction, God's primary expression of his Kingdom on Earth is to be the church: The New Testament refers to the body of Christ-followers (*ekklesia*), and Paul describes us collectively as Jesus's bride (Eph 5:25–33). Jesus laid the groundwork for the church by demonstrating and telling what living in the Kingdom entails, and making salvation possible through his death, resurrection, and ascension. The Kingdom of God figured prominently in Jesus's last teachings and exhortation to be his witnesses "in Jerusalem, and in all Judea and Samaria, and to the ends of the earth" (Acts 1:3–8).

I have sometimes despaired of the church because of the ugliness and deep sin that frequently marks it, both historically and now. Happily, while revising this manual, God graciously transformed my heart, renewing my hope and love for his gathered followers. We get to join God as he makes the church more beautiful, pure, vibrant, healthy, and expanding—a boon to our faith and witness to the world.

Part of this beautifying has to do with arts in the church: most congregations have not yet adopted an incarnational, local arts approach like CLAT. We often encounter resistance, especially from church leaders. We wrote Conversation 4D in part with this common reality in mind, providing context and tools to help Christ followers change their hearts and minds. These tools will be even more effective in churches where there is no resistance.

On one hand, we can treat a local church in a community like any other context where artistic communication happens—it uses artistic genres with unique forms and meanings and is guided by particular social norms and patterns. This means that you can help churches explore their arts using the guides we've already presented in Conversations 1, 2, 3, and the rest of Conversation 4. They will also likely want to incorporate some of these ideas and tools into Conversation 5's activities.

On the other hand, we care very deeply that God's people integrate arts into their gathered lives with Scripture as a standard. They likely include brothers, sisters, mothers, fathers, and children in Christ: we engage as members of a family. This may lead us to act with more agency as convincers and advocates.

Conversation 4D consists of these sections:

- What Are Churches Like?
- Overcoming Theological and Worldview Objections
- Biblical and Theological Foundations
- Tools to Help Churches Integrate Arts More Fully, Faithfully, and Fruitfully
- Where There Is No Church

WHAT ARE CHURCHES LIKE?

Christian congregations take multiple forms. Paul, John, and other New Testament writers planted, visited, and counseled a prototype: local gatherings of Christ-followers. These are congregations of Christ-followers in a place, meant to be known by their love, organized as Christ's body with complementary gifts, extending the Kingdom, like nodes in a network that interact with each other, can consist of very few to large numbers of people (see Matt 18:15–20) and exhibit varying types and degrees of sin and Christlikeness. The seven churches addressed by John the Revelator (Rev 2–3) reveal unnerving spiritual and social complexity. In addition, churches exist in contexts that can differ starkly in how free they are to express themselves, sometimes experiencing oppression and violence.

Though every local church exists in a particular geographical location, each also connects to broader Christian communities—denominations, networks, Catholic or Orthodox orders, etc. These historical and relational ties influence a church's arts in many ways and may change over time. The second Vatican Council's *Constitution on Liturgy*, for example, has resulted in artistic experimentation, including the composition of indigenous masses.[22]

However, Christianity's spread in the last few hundred years was fed by evangelical fervor and facilitated by European colonial expansion. Many missionary organizations adopted the prevailing evolutionary view of the world's cultures, which placed European artistry at the apex of Christian civilization.[23] As a result, many churches around the world were taught and embraced Euro-American artistic genres. Often, local churches have stronger ties to distant denominational church practices rather than building bridges to their surrounding communities (see 4C's discussion of where loci of creativity lie). More recently, globalization, urbanization, forced and unforced migrations, internationally marketed worship song industries, and nearly ubiquitous access to the internet have led to more multicultural churches and unpredictable complexity.

God understands all of this, of course, and has invited us to help extend his Kingdom. Frequent discussions with God, individually and with as many people as possible, asking for love and discernment, play particularly important roles in this work.

OVERCOMING THEOLOGICAL AND WORLDVIEW OBJECTIONS

The principles for addressing theological objections to unfamiliar uses of arts in Christian communities are the same as those guiding this entire manual. In short, dialogue with objectors in ways that encourage their input, show respect for and knowledge of their beliefs and practices, treat them as complete

---

22 Vatican, "Sacrosanctum Concilium," no. 37–38.
23 Schrag and Swijghuisen Reigersberg, "Ethnodoxology."

human beings, and paint a biblically based vision of a better future. We provide advice and tools here that can help you address common problems and misunderstandings.[24]

Strategies and Tips for Lasting Change

We want to help change the theological landscape in the global church. Here are a few categories of actions that individuals have used successfully—some with immediate effects, others with longer time horizons. The more commonplace Scripture-based approaches to artistic communication become, the fewer objections will need to be overcome. For each of the principles below that came out of my life experience, Roch Ntankeh provides examples and illustrations of how it has worked in his context.[25]

Use invitations to preach and teach to share biblical texts about arts and church life

Several times in my life I wearied of promoting the use of local arts: people often responded with indifference, belittlement, impatience, or an inability to understand. But each time, I prayed and God brought to mind friends with artistic gifts whose churches had ignored or rejected. I had no choice but to continue, making the most of every opportunity that arose.

> **Roch**: Biblical understanding of the use of local elements is often crucial. Since these leaders are generally open to biblical teaching, it's more effective to convince them by sharing what biblical texts say. I remember preaching on Psalm 150 in a church in Bukavu in the Democratic Republic of Congo (DRC), and after my preaching, the leaders of this church decided to create a choir that would use the *lulaga*, a local string instrument from the Shi community, which had never been used in the church and had many negative connotations. Thus, raising awareness through Scripture is the essential first step.

Help Christ-followers experience new ways to use artistry

I wish everyone would find or develop a portable bit of artistry that they can use to give a glimpse of the new reality we yearn for. Countless times all over the world I've told the story of the *Chorale Ayo*, illustrated by playing on a *kundí* that Punayima Kanyama crafted, singing *gbagurus* he composed.[26] In many contexts, people had "Aha!" moments that changed the way they thought and acted. Even playing an audio or video recording of doing something old in a new

---

24 See additional theological resources in the Digital Library at www.clatmanual.com and in these sites: Calvin Institute for Christian Worship (https://worship.calvin.edu/), Worship Resources International (https://worship-resources.org/, with resources in various languages), and GEN's "Theology and Arts in Ministry" initiative at https://worldofworship.org/theology..

25 Personal communication that I translated from French and edited. See also, Ntankeh, "Local Arts Training for Pastors."

26 See "La Chorale Ayo: The Love Choir" in four languages at GEN's YouTube site: https://youtube.com/user/ethnodoxology/videos.

way has opened doors. God gave us sensing bodies so we could hear, see, feel, smell, touch, taste, weep, laugh while experiencing an artistic expression. Actual artistry touches our hearts, minds and wills in a way that talking seldom does.

Roch: Although raising awareness through Scripture can be convincing, the concrete example is always more powerful than the lesson. At a meeting in Togo where I was to present a reflection aimed at encouraging leaders to explore and use local arts, I played a traditional instrument (*sanza*) from my home region in Cameroon and sang in my native language (*Medumba*). I could not have predicted the impact. After my presentation, I was asked several times to come and perform worship with my instrument, because it showed that it could be done. People sometimes need to see to believe.

Song creation workshops can have both a direct and indirect impact. Direct impact occurs when workshop participants are transformed by the creative activities during the sessions. Indirect impact occurs when the creations are presented at the workshop's closing ceremony. Guests, sometimes indifferent to local arts, change their opinion when they hear and see what is presented, thus becoming advocates themselves to a wider audience. I'll illustrate this with a story from Bukavu in the DRC. The Dean of Theology, Peace and Development at the Université Évangélique en Afrique was among the guests at the closing ceremony of a composition workshop organized by the Seed Company. Afterward, he expressed a wish for us to come and teach at his institution, which mainly trains pastors and future pastors.

Integrate ethnodoxological content wherever people teach theology

Michael Ortiz, international director of the International Council for Evangelical Theological Education (ICETE), believes that a profound shift toward rigorous, globally available theological education is crucial to the scripturally grounded growth of the church.[27] He also maintains that "the future of theological education will become more promising as it embodies and elevates the ethnodoxology voice."[28] More people in more places need to develop and teach more theology related to ethnodoxology.

Roch: Seminaries, Bible schools, and theological education by extension are strategic places where those who will become tomorrow's church leaders are trained. So I thought it would be strategic to reach them with a university course entitled *Ethnodoxology* aimed at second- and third-year students. The main aim of this course is to help future church leaders transform their

---

[27] Ortiz, "Theological Education." See also Whittaker, "Ethnodoxology."

[28] Plenary address at the Global Ethnodoxology Network's 20th Anniversary celebration in Dallas, Texas (10 September 2023).

perception not only of the use of local arts, but also to provide them with the tools they need to play an active role in the field when it comes to the use of local arts.

Gain credentials, knowledge, and relationships that make your voice more credible
Roch demonstrated this in response to specific ministry needs. With goals to influence and help heal relationships between worship leaders and pastors in Cameroon, Roch became both worship leader and pastor. He also received his PhD in Theology and Intercultural Studies, with a concentration in ethnomusicology at the Cameroon University of Evangelical Theology, where he serves as Assistant Director of the master's Program. Roch has taken his growth as a scholar seriously, publishing in both Christian and secular contexts.[29] This has allowed Roch the authority and qualifications to develop and teach courses and workshops in ethnodoxology, mission theology, and local arts for development in different regions in Africa and beyond.[30]

Do workshops and other activities described in Conversation 5
Communities can hold workshops—including Arts for a Better Future (ABF)—that include much of the content and many of the strategies we discuss in this section.

BIBLICAL AND THEOLOGICAL FOUNDATIONS

Vital to all engagement is the belief that *every* community has intrinsic value. Lamin Sanneh observes that beginning with Jesus, Paul, Peter, and others,

> the characteristic pattern of Christianity's engagement with the languages and cultures of the world has God at the center of the universe of cultures, implying equality among cultures and the … relative status of cultures vis-à-vis the truth of God. No culture is so advanced or so superior that it can claim exclusive access … to the truth of God, and none so marginal … that it can be excluded. All have merit, none is indispensable.[31]

Jesus adopts, transforms, puts aside, and attaches new meaning to elements of every community, each in a unique way.

Theologians, missionaries, pastors, and others have reflected much on *how* this Jesus-shaping happens and what it looks like. We touch on many related dialogues in this manual, but deeper familiarity may help you engage with church leaders and structures in some contexts. Here are a few

---

29 See, for example, Ntankeh, "Arts: A Powerful Communicator," and Ntankeh "Le Mangabeu et la modernité."

30 A rapidly growing number of institutions around the world are teaching and granting degrees in ethnodoxology related fields. See the "Coalescence" section of Schrag and Swijghuisen Reigersberg, "Ethnodoxology."

31 Sanneh, *Disciples of All Nations*, 25.

salient, interrelated conversations and references: polycentric mission,[32] local theologizing,[33] incarnational ministry,[34] and problematizing terms like contextualization, enculturation, and positive hybridization.[35]

Scripture Authorizes Local Artistry in the Church

From the opening verses of the biblical story, we are presented with the activity of an Artisan God who forms humans from dust and ribs and endows them with the capacity to create as a reflection of God's image and as acts of worship. Not surprisingly, this sense of participation in the divine creative process unleashed a flurry of artistic expression throughout the biblical narrative. God's people in the Old Testament were perpetually busy designing, building, equipping, and maintaining stone altars, arks, cities of refuge, royal palaces, and places of worship artistically adorned with furnishings, garments, and musical instruments under the watchful eye and care of officiants responsible for rituals, annual feasts, song composition and liturgies. For the construction of the Tabernacle, Yahweh specifically chose a group of artists and filled them with his Spirit—a rare expression in the Old Testament—to make divinely-commissioned works of gold, silver, bronze, stone and wood for the Lord's dwelling place (Exod 31:1–5).

But Jesus turned all of this on its head. He told a woman from a minority, scorned community,

> You will worship the Father neither on this mountain nor in Jerusalem. You Samaritans worship what you do not know; we worship what we do know, for salvation is from the Jews. Yet a time is coming and has now come when the true worshipers will worship the Father in the Spirit and in truth, for they are the kind of worshipers the Father seeks. God is spirit, and his worshipers must worship in the Spirit and in truth. (John 4:21–24)

The New Testament begins against the Old Testament backdrop of feverish construction and artistic production. Jesus is even presented as the son of a carpenter—maybe a stone mason. But with the announcement of his public ministry, the selection of the disciple band, and the eventual birth of the early church, physical building and production seem to cease. There are no church constructions for the first three centuries of the new movement. No standard hymnbook—oral or written—is mentioned as a complement to the Hebrew Psalms. No instructions are given regarding specific clothing designed for worship, of religious objects, smells, and bells for liturgical usage,

---

32 Yeh, *Polycentric Missiology*; Yeh, "What Is Polycentric Mission?"; Wild-Wood, "Modern African Missionaries"; Mātenga, "Reimagining Missions"; and Handley, *Polycentric Mission Leadership*.

33 Amoateng, "Engaging Theology"; Chu, "Analysis of Stanley Hauerwas' Theology"; Chow, *Chinese Public Theology*; Kenmogne, "Theologizing in Context."

34 Rah, "Incarnational Ministry."

35 For articles and books on contextualization, see the footnotes in the Tool for "Careful Contextualization."

of choir formations or rehearsals, or of universally required décor, seating arrangements, candles, altars, or pulpits for worship spaces. These "omissions" are not an oversight, but rather the natural implication of newly formed faith communities wherever two or three were gathered in Jesus's name. Singing no doubt happened through "psalms, hymns and spiritual songs" (Eph 5:18–19), but local agency in each community was free to shape and implement worship patterns, times, spaces, and places appropriate and meaningful to local cultures and settings.[36]

In Samaria, Jesus prophetically announced this radical departure from past practice, unleashing another outpouring of creativity resulting in the vast diversity of arts in churches around the world. True adoration and worship happen not in this place or that, through these arts or those, but locally, where Christ-followers gather in the Spirit and in truth. This is a foretaste, a glimpse of Jesus's irresistible draw to his throne in Heaven.

Don't Copy Artistic Forms Mentioned in the Bible

In our approach, the artistic life of each Christian community need not be restricted to the artistic genres mentioned and used in the Bible. From Jesus's incarnational example of becoming a human being in a particular human culture (Phil 2), to the early spread of Christianity throughout the Roman Empire and the translation of Scripture into thousands of languages, Christianity is all about being born anew in every tribe and nation and language. The psalmist's charge to praise God "with timbrel and dancing" (Ps 150:4) doesn't mean we need to figure out and copy exactly what a timbrel is, its tuning, and the kinds of musical features associated with it. Rather, Psalm 150 encourages us to use every art form at our disposal to praise God.

Interpret Scripture Well

Before integrating Scripture into artistic creations, artists should understand the Scripture well. The key principle of biblical interpretation is to interpret Scripture according to the author's intent. Biblical scholars Duvall and Hays imagine an "Interpretive Journey" between the "biblical village" and "our village[s] today" that shows how to interpret Scripture according to authorial intent.[37] This five-step voyage can help Christian artists share Scripture more accurately, understandably, and influentially with their communities.

1. **Understand** the biblical text "in the biblical town," the way the original audience would have understood the text in their context. Additional biblical background knowledge may be needed to discern how the original audience understood the message. Many helps can be found in Bible study guides, books, and through internet searches.

2. **Measure** the width of the river to cross. What are the differences of culture, language, time, and situation between the biblical audience

---

36 Stallsmith, "Languages of Worship."

37 Duvall and Hays, *Grasping God's Word* (ch. 2). For a clear Catholic perspective with links to other resources, see Just, "Biblical Exegesis."

and the intended audience? The river between the original audience and today's audience may be narrow when many cultural aspects link the audience with them, or wide when the passage seems difficult to understand or apply.

3. **Build** a "principle bridge" over the river. What are the key theological principles in this text? The principle(s) should be relevant to both the biblical audience and to us today. They should be true for all people for all time. (The way we apply these truths may look different in different cultures when we get to Conversation 5.)

4. **Look** at the biblical map. Consider other passages that may help us understand this passage. Scripture interprets Scripture: different passages may address different aspects of the same problem or topic. We can be unbalanced by looking at only one side of an issue, or balanced by considering all the Scripture that deals with a topic. Well-rounded Bible knowledge is needed to make good applications of Scripture to our lives today.

5. **Grasp** the text in our town. Observe how the principle in the text can be applied to life today in our forms of expression. For example, we could discover a parallel situation in the local culture today. Make your applications specific. Many applications may be drawn from the same principle. The way the application is realized may be different in different cultures, but the principle will be the same.

Christ-followers, including artists, need to interpret Scripture founded on the principle of authorial intent, being wary of the receptor's intent undermining our understandings. If we interpret Scripture as the author meant—as much as we are able—we are on solid ground. If we interpret what we want it to mean, we are on shaky ground.[38]

Artists are a little bit like teachers. They need to compare the audience's point of view with Scripture's point of view on a topic and discern what pieces of information are missing for their audience to understand the applications of Scripture. By understanding Scripture well, they can make their enactment answer the types of questions their listeners are likely to ask.

Scripture-infused creativity normally relies on the knowledge and skills of more than one person. This may include experts in a genre, pastors, translators, professors, people in a community who experience artistry, and others. But people who God has given artistic gifts own their own faith more fully when they walk through this journey for themselves and understand each part of it, rather than having someone else tell them how to interpret Scripture. We seek to follow the example of the Apostle Paul who wrote, "But that does not mean we want to dominate you by telling you how to put your faith into practice. We want to work together with you so you will be full of joy, for it is by your own faith that you stand firm" (2 Cor 1:24 NLT).

---

38 Duvall and Hays, *Grasping God's Word* (ch. 10).

What kinds of background information does a person need to interpret Scripture accurately? Knowledge about the original recipients' culture and historical situation and how those differ from their own; an overarching knowledge of the metanarrative of Scripture (the big picture) to know where any given Scripture portion fits; the context of a given passage; the genre in which the passage is written; and typical questions the audience is likely to ask, to be able to answer them in the enactment or recording.

Make the presentation of the message specific to the people based on their assumptions. Some local assumptions may need to be affirmed as true and good, and others may need to be challenged and corrected by Scripture. Bible translator Harriet Hill found that among the Adjukru people of Côte d'Ivoire, contextual helps, whether provided orally or in writing, improved comprehension by an average of 39.2 percent.[39]

Let's look at an example. Romans 16:16 says, "Greet one another with a holy kiss." In the "biblical village" this is a common way to greet someone warmly. The "river of difference" for some cultures today is that kissing signifies a relationship reserved for husband and wife, or kissing does not exist at all in their experience. The "principle bridge" is that we should greet one another warmly, as a family member. When we "grasp the text in our town," the way to express an appropriate greeting differs from culture to culture. Some would bow and others would hug, but the essential is the principle of greeting each other warmly. We could even make a song for newcomers to our church to make them feel welcome and accepted.

Some Biblical References to Artistic Communication

You can use these statements[40] and Scripture references for discussion with church leaders:

God created humans in his own image.
Creativity and imagination are part of the reflection of God's image in every human being (Gen 1:27). God created *ex nihilo* (out of nothing; Gen 1), while humans create *ex creatio* (out of what God already created; Ps 96:1).

Aesthetic pleasure comes from God.
"God made ... trees that were pleasing to the eye and good for food" (Gen 2:9). We are free to value and celebrate pleasure that comes from artistic form.

Humans are culture shapers.
God put Adam in the garden to cultivate it and keep it (Gen 2:15) and has told us that we will reign with him at the end of time (Matt 24:45–47; 25:31–34; Rev 22:5). God wants humans to shape and make culture, to steward beauty.

God calls people to artistic communication.
God gave Bezalel his Spirit, understanding, knowledge, craftsmanship, and teaching abilities to make artistic designs for the building of his tabernacle

---

39 Hill, *Communicating Context*, 363.

40 For more, see Lausanne Movement, "Redeeming the Arts."

(Exod 31:1–6). He will certainly give us skill, too, as we are also working to build his church, which is the body (Eph 4:11–13). We should develop our own artistic gifts and encourage others to develop theirs.

God uses diverse forms of arts for multiple purposes.
He used visual art to bring repentance (Num 21:1–8), drama to prophesy (Ezek 4), many different arts to worship, lament, instill fear, rejoice, repent, teach, celebrate, fight battles, and other purposes.

Diverse expressions please God.
The psalmist in Psalm 150 encouraged his listeners to include as wide a range of artistic forms to worship God as possible: harp, lyre, tambourine, dancing, strings, flutes, and cymbals. We should do the same.

Most of Scripture consists of artistic forms of communication.
The Bible contains proverbs, songs, stories, poetry, drama, descriptions of visual imagery and dance, and other artistic forms of communication; only a small proportion is propositional and didactic.[41] Jesus's primary method of communication was parables (Matt 13:13).

Heart and allegiance are more important than the form of artistic communication.
God said, "Away with the noise of your songs!" (Amos 5:23–24) because his people were unrighteous and unjust. He also said that "those who trust in idols, who say to images, 'You are our gods,' will be turned back in utter shame" (Isa 42:17).

No one should be forced to change good parts of their culture to worship God.
In Acts 15 the early church decided that Gentiles did not need to become Jews to be followers of Christ.

God has opened up worship from a single earthly place to an unlimited number of places.
Jesus says that true worshipers "worship the Father in the Spirit and truth," not in a particular place (John 4:19–24). This feeds into the reality of people from every nation and language coming to gather around God's throne in Heaven, worshiping in the ways they have learned (Rev 7:9–10).

One culture's music and other arts do not communicate universally to someone from a different culture.
This is a fact. Like spoken language, artistic forms communicate meaning that is assigned within a culture. In other words, artistic meaning must be learned within a community in the same way that a language is learned. And outsiders must perform research to learn these meanings.[42]

---

41 Frost, "Why Consider Local Genres."
42 Negrão, "Not a Universal Language."

TOOLS TO HELP CHURCHES INTEGRATE ARTS MORE FULLY, FAITHFULLY, AND FRUITFULLY

The tools in this section help you learn how Christian communities function artistically in all their social contexts, with Scripture as a guide. Some address similar content with varying approaches and levels of rigor. Choose and modify the tools that best fit your context. Note also that you will likely draw on other sections in Conversation 4D.

Tool: Comparative Chart of Musical Instruments Mentioned in the Old Testament

Sometimes Christian communities have developed strong negative associations with particular artistic objects (e.g., instruments) or genres. Figure 4.10 helps show how objects have no inherent moral value: it is the heart of the person using an object that determines whether God is pleased with that object.

Participants
Identify those in a church or school who influence, control, and/or implement artistry—that is, gatekeepers.

Tasks
Help a group discover this truth for themselves by starting with an empty chart and following these steps:

1. Write the Scripture references along the top of a chalkboard or whiteboard.
2. Ask someone to read each passage aloud, then ask the group to say each instrument that was mentioned. Write the names of the instruments under the passage.
3. Ask the group to note instruments that occur in more than one column. Circle those.
4. Ask the group to describe the purpose of each event. Write this purpose under each passage.
5. Ask the group if they can find a correlation between certain instruments and certain purposes.
6. Ask what principles they can derive from this exercise. Then discuss how they can apply these principles to the use of arts in their Christian community.

Daniel 3:5 king's court (false worship)	Isaiah 5:12 drunken party (secular)	Psalm 150 praising God (true worship)	2 Samuel 6:5 1 Chronicles 15:16-29 religious procession (true worship)
flute (end-blown)		flute (end-blown)	
animal horn trumpet		shofar trumpet	shofar trumpet silver trumpets
reed pipe	reed pipe		
lyre	lyre	lyre	lyre
larger lyre	larger lyre	larger lyre	larger lyre
bow harp all kinds of instruments		string and woodwind instruments	
	frame drum	frame drum	frame drum
		cymbals	cymbals
		loud cymbals	
			rattle
	dance		dance

Figure 4.10 Same instruments used for both godly and ungodly purposes

Tool: Interview Gatekeepers

Engaging with influential and passionate people in a personal, informal context helps build relationships, and may open doors for sparking activities.

Participants

Identify a small group of those in a church or school who influence, control, and/or implement artistry—that is, gatekeepers. In one of my own church contexts, I interviewed a group consisting of the lead pastor, the pastor of community life and evangelism, an arts advocate, and an elder also part of the worship arts team. The interview helped shape a one-day workshop we later led, including who was invited.

Tasks

Ask questions like these in an informal context, recording the conversation if they agree:

1. What types of people are engaged in church activities?
2. How are arts used presently?
3. How has this changed in the history of the church?
4. What would you each like to see happening with music and other arts?
5. What evangelistic outreaches is the church currently involved in?
6. Are there any kinds of arts that you or others would deem inappropriate?
7. What will it take to keep this conversation going?
8. Who else might be able to contribute?

Tool: Find and Evaluate How We Use Arts in Our Church

Churches and other Christian communities have not usually reflected deeply on their use of music and other arts. This tool leads people through a thorough process to rectify such situations.

Participants

These activities could be part of a workshop, small group meetings, or in mentoring or discipling relationships.

Tasks

Start with an empty chart on paper, a white board, or other discussion aids to answer the three broad questions below.

1. What are our arts?

The approach to identifying a church's artistic life is like that which we described for the broader community in "Take a First Glance at a Community's Arts" (Conversation 1) and "First Glance Genre Comparison Chart" (Conversation 3). Put whatever you discover into the Community Arts Profile. Gather leaders and participants in various aspects of church life, and lead them through activities like these:

- List all the contexts in which people act as part of this Christian community. These contexts could include—but are not limited to—the following: Bible studies; home groups; Sunday school; adult education; corporate worship services; spiritual mentorships; Mass; Vacation Bible School; children's ministries; food pantry; visits to people who are sick; rites like baptism, weddings, and funerals; healing services; holiday celebrations; social outings; retreats and camps; outreach activities; festivals; concerts; prayer vigils; individual or family devotions.

- For each context the group has listed, write down if people use any forms of artistic communication. If so, write what those forms are. Common kinds of arts in Christian communities include singing, preaching, drama, storytelling, sculpting, carving, designing space, incense, dancing, making banners, drawing, reading or reciting poetry. Note also that rituals are common in Christian communities; they may be artistic events in themselves (e.g., as forms of drama or pageantry), and they often include artistic elements.

- List all the people who have significant artistic gifts, whether they use them in the church or not. For each person in the Christian community with artistic training and gifts, list the kind(s) of arts they have skills in, and their competencies (e.g., composing, performing, drawing). Church leadership may be unaware of many of the gifts that its members have. In this case, you may want to help them perform a more thorough investigation through a simple questionnaire or oral investigation.

2. How do our arts compare with those of our surrounding communities?

These steps will help churches decide how to better connect to the people in their geographical context. See especially "Church Life" and "Personal Spiritual Life" in Conversation 2. Remember that this is part of a broader process in which churches critically evaluate different artistic genres for potential use.

a. Consult the list you made above of all the kinds of arts that the Christian community uses in everything it does.

b. Consult the list of artistic genres used in the church's surrounding community you created in Conversation 1.

c. Mark each genre of artistic communication that exists both in the church and in its surrounding community.

d. For each genre that exists in both, discuss and write down ways in which their enactment and purpose differ in each context.

e. Make a list of all the genres in the surrounding community that are not used in the church. Discuss reasons why these are not being used and explore their potential for use.

3. Are we using our arts in ways that reach our goals?
In Conversation 2, we highlighted a few reasons that a Christian community might act to extend the Kingdom of Heaven: to deepen corporate worship, improve spiritual formation, extend its witness, etc. A brief survey of how people used the arts in the Bible reveals a longer list: celebrate victory (Exod 15), accompany processions (2 Sam 6), adoration (2 Chr 5), cultural festivals (2 Chr 35:15), repentance (Ps 51), dancing (1 Chr 15), funerals (Matt 9:23), strengthen church (1 Cor 14:26), express happiness (Jas 5:13), express sadness (Ps 6), spiritual warfare (2 Chr 20:21–23), healing (1 Sam 16), and more. It's important to remember that not every use of the arts shown in Scripture serves as a positive example—Aaron crafted a golden calf as an idol (Exod 32), but we should not imitate him.

In addition, the Bible points to even more purposes of the church, including confession, witness, prayer, teaching, thanksgiving, discipleship, lamentation, evangelism, encouragement, exhortation, mind renewal, reconciliation, forgiveness, correction, commemoration, building solidarity, creating contextual equivalents, and testimony. Though we can't create an exhaustive list of all potential purposes, it is essential that each church identify the reasons they do things, so they can evaluate whether the arts they use help bring them about. This process may also reveal additional biblical aims that the community realizes they should adopt. The following steps can help the community do this:

a. Consult the list of all the contexts in which people act as part of their Christian community, church.

b. Choose at least one context in which artistic communication exists and list its purposes. Refer to the paragraphs above for ideas.

c. List ways in which the form(s) of artistic communication used in each context support or detract from its purposes. You may need to go deeper into the features of these arts, beginning with Conversation 4, Part A's "Look Through Seven Basic Lenses."

d. Use what you've discovered for sparking activities in Conversation 5.

Tool: Apply a Heart Arts Questionnaire to a Christian Community

In this activity, the aim is to find out the artistic genres that most touch people's hearts in wider society and in any existing Christian congregations. The responses will provide strong indicators of artistic genres that could be used for Kingdom purposes (1 Sam 16:23; 2 Kgs 3:15; Ps 81:1–3) and help the community answer questions like these:

- What forms of expression in the surrounding community could be most appropriate to express joy and reverence in corporate worship? What would be the reaction of believers and nonbelievers to those? What artistic genres could you choose? How can you draw on the characteristics of this genre—the people involved, where it happens, the form of the event, the objects involved, the languages used—to deepen worship in a community?
- How could church planters and congregations evaluate the forms and symbolic meanings of the artistic genres that could be used in worship times?
- If your worship community is multicultural, how could you celebrate diversity in unity? How could each ethnic group feel equally involved, at the same time as drawing people together?
- In what ways do people communicate truth with each other in your society? How could these methods be used in penetrating ways (e.g., for preaching, evangelizing, liturgy, teaching)?
- How could you use some of these ideas when you interact with other communities (e.g., for outreach, missions, church planting, interfaith dialogue)?

Participants

Church leaders, corporate worship musicians, and someone good with forms and numbers.

Tasks

1. Define the community or community subgroup (e.g., ethnic or language groups, church) to be surveyed.
2. Based on the findings in your Community Arts Profile, draw up a list of common genres of artistic communication that are used in your church and its surroundings, along with the associated uses and meanings for each category. This may include local, national, regional, and global styles. It will also probably include a range of styles from traditional to modern and secular to religious. If this is a long list, combine similar styles and reduce it to a manageable number (ten to twenty maximum) for people you will interview.
3. Decide how large a representative interview group should be.
4. Decide who will conduct the interviews and how you will structure them (individually or in groups, orally or in written form). If two people conduct the interviews in person, you will be able to answer questions; one person can ask the questions and another person record the answers.

5. Devise the questionnaire:
    a. Provide interviewees with the list of common forms of arts used in your society.
    b. Ask questions about age, ethnicity, mother tongue, and reading languages.
    c. Ask what types of arts generate instant and powerful positive emotions in people's hearts, such as exceptional joy, energy, peace, or comfort.
    d. Make a way for people to rate their top four or five artistic genres, e.g., scoring them from one to five (if done orally, maybe using the fingers of one hand). This can give a clearer result.
    e. Make a space to indicate if interviewees are believers. This will help you to compare and contrast the results more easily.
6. Conduct the survey and focus in equal measure on every relevant social group and decade (aged 0–10, 11–20, etc.).
7. Collect and analyze the responses; list those with high scores in order. Take special note of the artistic preferences of minority groups.
8. Compare the results and identify differences with your current use of arts in gatherings.
9. Carefully assess each high-scoring genre in terms of its associations and its potential in worship, discipleship, evangelism, etc.
10. Make plans to further investigate each of these high-scoring genres, asking questions like: Who is gifted to develop these for Kingdom purposes? What might be the response of different sectors of society? How can they be introduced?

Tool: Study 1 Corinthians 13–15[43]

We have seen Christians from hundreds of indigenous groups in Asia freed to start creating their own local art forms by simply studying 1 Corinthians 14:7–19 and answering the questions of what these verses say about language, what they say about singing and musical instruments, and how they might respond to what they understood (while also having them explore their culture through the senses). So often we have heard people say something in response like, "We need to be using our own music!" It is our understanding that an important shift takes place in worldview after this basic exercise (and much prayer).

In short, a common animistic worldview element that often carries over into "Christian" thinking is this: persuading supernatural beings to comply with our wishes requires specific outward acts. This can lead to thinking that God requires us to sing, dance, or dress in specific ways. The 1 Corinthians

---
[43] Adapted from Todd Saurman, Mary Saurman, and Matt Menger, personal communication, July 2022.

verses clearly state how important accurate communication of God's message is whether we are speaking, praying, or singing. When people start to evaluate what they have been communicating with their songs and other non-verbal expressions (dress, dance, architecture, etc.) it often becomes clear that they have been communicating that God is foreign to their local communities. We have seen this clear up one of the biggest roadblocks to people finding their own way to creating local arts together as a Christian community.

A well-prepared facilitator can also then draw out whether there is understanding of the biblical context. Chapter 13 in 1 Corinthians is about the purposes of love. Chapter 15 contains much of the message that God wants us to communicate. And all other examples of songs and instruments in the Bible imply that they are songs and instrument tunes that communicate within the local culture (in case anybody has further questions or doubts).

Tool: Careful Contextualization—How to Avoid Both Syncretism and Irrelevance

One of the most common concerns that people have about integrating new art forms into their Christian community's life is that it will lead to syncretism. In other words, how can we know when the use of a particular artistic genre or musical instrument is syncretism—an inappropriate mixing of Christianity with another religion, or when it is simply an expression of good biblical contextualization (wisely engaging culture and local context in expressing biblical Christian faith and practice)? [44]

When a certain element of a community encounters Christ (e.g., artistic forms or rituals), the following situations may ensue, depending on the Christians' approach (see Figure 4.11).[45]

---

[44] Departing from Hiebert, "Critical Contextualization," I believe the adjective *careful* now expresses our approach more clearly and fully than *critical*. For further discussion on contextualization, see the following articles: Barber, "Globalization, Contextualization, and Indigeneity"; Brown, "Contextualization without Syncretism"; Ekpenyong and Okoi, "Africanization of Christianity"; Goheen, *Introducing Christian Mission Today*; Guirguis, "History of Contextualization"; Harris, "Contextualization"; Hiebert, "Critical Contextualization"; Hesselgrave, "Contextualization"; Labeth, "Struggling to be Creole"; Shaw, "Contextualizing"; and Whiteman, "Contextualization."

[45] Adapted from Shetler, "Communicating the New Information"; West, "Equipping Urban Believers"; and Hiebert, *Anthropological Insights for Missionaries*.

Christians' approach to their local artistic forms and rituals	Immediate effect	Ultimate effect
Total rejection	Local art form goes underground	Dualism–people act as Christians in some contexts, relying on other beliefs in other contexts
	Christian community seen as foreign	Rest of community rejects Christ
Careful Contextualization	Christian community follows a process that leads to acceptance, rejection, transformation of the art form, or creating something completely new	Community encouraged to integrate Christian (biblical) truth and actions into their lives through appropriately contextualized forms
Total acceptance	Christian community maintains all local traditions in spite of its contradictions with Scripture. "They worshiped and served created things rather than the Creator" (Rom 1:25).	Syncretism–people inappropriately mix their Christian faith with another belief system

Figure 4.11 Results of Christians' approaches to artistic forms

The only ultimate effect that we want to work towards is that resulting from transformation. In many ways, the process we describe below is a condensation of the whole Creating Local Arts Together process.

This brief overview of a process the community and arts advocate can follow should help skeptics see a trustworthy way forward. Make sure the community makes the decisions for each step.

Gather Information
Uncover the reasons that an existing form or ritual is done by

- identifying (using name if it exists) the existing form or ritual people want to examine.
- describing in detail the forms or ritual.
- verbalizing the reasons for and consequences—benefits—of enacting it.
- listing beliefs that underlie its enactment.
- describing the consequences—misfortune or harm—of not enacting it.

Study Biblical Teachings
Together, relate Scriptures to the reasons and consequences motivating people to perform the form or ritual, always making those reasons and consequences overt. These observations could be in the form of

- what we always thought (cultural beliefs underlying the reasons and consequences, yet clash with Scripture)

- but what we didn't know (beliefs that present a scriptural answer to the reasons and consequences, thus aligning with Scripture).

Evaluate Forms and Meanings

It's especially important for communities to lead this evaluation process.

- Note where the form resonates with Scripture.
- Note where there is conflict between the form or ritual and Christian truths.
- Encourage exploration of and modifications possible that would make scriptural truths clear.

Encourage Wisdom in Moving Forward

- Based on the evaluation, encourage the believers to craft a modified or new ritual or art form (genre enactment) that fulfills the purpose for which it was included in the community's life yet remains biblically accurate.
- Encourage the Christian leaders to present the transformed ritual or art form to Christ-followers, explaining how and why they suggest adopting these choices. Also, check any modifications with non-believers to see what they understand the changed practice to mean. This can be an opportunity for believers to explain their reasons for the change, asking for input, and witnessing to Christ's truth.
- Encourage Christian leaders to create a plan to integrate this transformed art form or ritual into the life of the Christian community.

Plan to address other points of worldview conflict through the same process. See Figure 4.12 for another way to envision implications of contextualization choices.

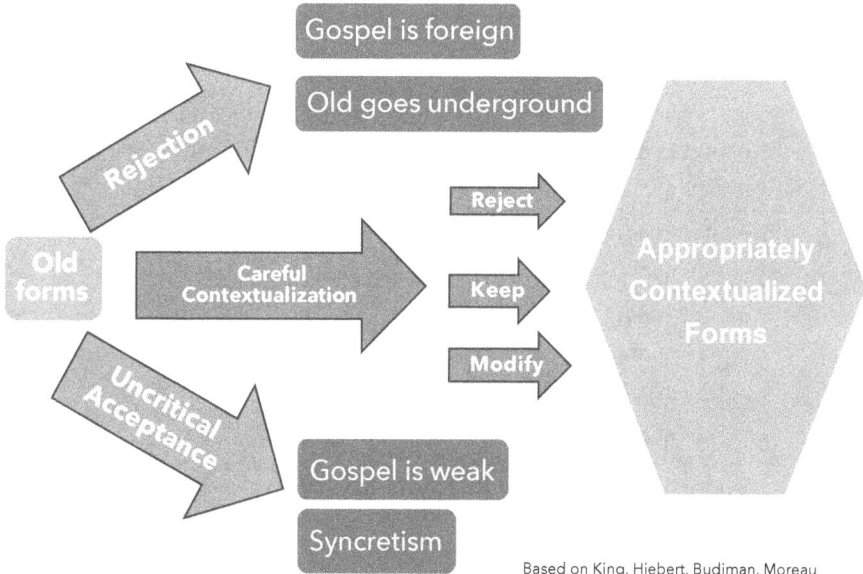

Based on King, Hiebert, Budiman, Moreau

Figure 4.12 Graphic presentation of contextualization process

Tool: Evaluate Worship Meetings Using Biblical Principles

What do you need to do to prepare yourself to encounter more of God's presence? First, there are spiritual factors, but second, we more easily draw near to God when we use the languages and cultural forms that are most familiar to us. For example, some believers sense God's presence in quiet reverence, structure, and formality. Others experience the Holy Spirit in exuberance, spontaneity, and informality. Most need a bit of both! But what forms are they? How should they be used?

This activity is a twofold study. It could be conducted in one or more workshops, or it could be spread out over several weeks. The aim is to ask questions about the whole breadth of a local congregation's communal worship experience. The purpose is to assess the appropriateness of each worship activity in the light of both Scripture and culture.

Participants
Church leaders, a representative group of believers, an ethnoarts facilitator.

Tasks

1. Define the ethnic and language groups under consideration. Then list the ways society normally expresses itself in communal life outside of church. Focus especially on values and practices common to biblical worship:

    a. When and how do people normally gather in groups?

    b. In group life, how do people show joy, contrition, respect, thankfulness, sorrow, etc. (e.g., with a dance, a song, prostration, abstinence from food, gift giving)?

    c. How do people instruct others, tell stories, rebuke others, share personal needs and griefs, give to the needy, etc.?

    d. What are the most common practices of celebration and meal sharing?

    e. What place do music or other art forms have in these activities?

2. Over several sessions, conduct a joint biblical study on the forms used in corporate and personal worship of God. Consider these passages together:

    a. worship as a daily offering of our whole lives (Luke 9:23; Rom 12:1)

    b. wholehearted and heartfelt adoration (Deut 6:5; John 4:24)

    c. the use of the voice and body in worship (e.g., 2 Sam 6:14–15; 2 Chr 5:12–13; Pss 47:1, 5–6; 95:6; 134:2; 150; Luke 5:8; 1 Tim 2:8; Rev 5:8–14; 19:4)

    d. worship as a communal activity (1 Cor 14:26; Col 3:12–16)

    e. spontaneity, order, spiritual gifts, and leadership in corporate worship (1 Cor 12–14)

    f. intercessory prayer in corporate worship (1 Tim 2:1–8)

    g. Bible reading and instruction in worship (1 Tim 4:13; 2 Tim 3:14–4:5)

Encourage Churches to Integrate Artistry More Holistically

      h. baptism, communion, healing, offerings, etc., in meetings of worship

      i. the use of space, movement, music, poetry, creeds, and set texts in worship (Eph 5:18–20; Rev 7:9–12)

3. Compare each aspect of biblical worship with patterns of life you have identified in the surrounding community:

    a. In corporate worship, what community art forms might best express biblical praise, prayer, learning, and devotion? What musical instruments might be used?

    b. What physical postures are both biblically and culturally appropriate?

    c. What is a suitable physical layout of the meeting space?

    d. Who should lead corporate adoration (e.g., the preacher, priest, church leader, singer)? Should they stand, sit, or kneel?

    e. In giving instruction, what is the place of Bible reading, exposition, storytelling, parables, catchphrases, memorization, group repetition, poetry, proverbs, movement, gesture, acting, chant, music, song, visual illustration, and questions from the audience?

    f. What is the most culturally fitting way to do Bible reading? Should the Bible be placed on a special or dedicated desk?

    g. What cultural factors are important for Communion, baptism, offerings, notices, healing prayer, etc.?

    h. What will help worshipers from this community to express biblical spontaneity in expressions like prayer, song, dance, and prostration?

    i. Are community members more liberated by formality or informality? Should meetings follow a regular structure? What are the roles of silence and order? Should set texts or responses be used (e.g., the Lord's Prayer, creeds, prayer formulas)?

    j. Considering your answers to all of the previous questions, what helps worshipers to most easily find freedom to praise, listen, and draw near to the living God?

    k. In what ways do these culturally appropriate ways of communing with God compare to the traditions of the church? How can both respect the authority and traditions of the church and promote freedom?

> "Everything must be done so that the church may be built up." (1 Cor 14:26)
>
> "Where the Spirit of the Lord is, there is freedom." (2 Cor 3:17)

Tool: Evaluate a Christian Community Using the Worship Wheel

Romans 12:1–2 shows that worship is something that flows from our whole bodies and should mark every aspect of our lives. Sometimes, however, a church's view of worship is limited to corporate gatherings with music.

The Worship Wheel exercise[46] helps churches see a broad range of worshipful activities in their lives that can be animated by integrating their local arts. The Saurmans have divided these activities into four categories: Arts for the Lomrd; Arts for self; Arts for others; and Arts for celebrations and ceremonies. Note that the Holy Spirit needs to animate every action, and that we have provided some examples in each category.

Figure 4.13 Worship wheel

Participants
Church leaders, musicians and other artists, a representative group of believers, an ethnoarts facilitator.

Tasks
Pray for God to lead you as you use the Worship Wheel tool.
Do a group Bible study, using John 4:18–26; Romans 11:33–12:3; and Ephesians 5:14–21. Explore together what the Bible says about true worship:

> Do these texts give commands about the time, place, or order of service in meetings for New Testament worship?
>
> Are there any poetic texts in this passage? What does this say about the use of art forms in church life?

---

46 Adapted from Saurman, "The Worship Wheel," 168.

> If the Holy Spirit gives new believers new artistic messages to communicate, whose artistic styles will be used? (See 1 Cor 14:15; Eph 5:18–19.)
>
> Who should believers sing to (e.g., God, oneself, other believers, the community)?
>
> When the Bible says that we should "worship in … truth" and "speak to one another with … songs," what biblical truths are the topic of the songs?

Staying with these Bible texts, focus now on culture:

> How do these passages affirm what you are already doing?
>
> Can you see any gaps in your church arts practice in the following areas?
>
> —the range of arts
>
> —the range of artistic styles
>
> —the range of Scripture truths in song
>
> —arts created by believers in their own styles
>
> —arts that address God, oneself, other believers, or people in the community

Turning to the Worship Wheel, make a list of your regular songs or other art forms that

> Speak to God—what topics?
>
> Speak to oneself—what functions?
>
> Celebrate special occasions—what occasions?
>
> Speak to others—what functions?

Evaluate and act on what we've discovered.

> Where are the gaps in your arts repertoire? What do you consider most important for the needs in your society or congregation(s)?
>
> If you are holding an arts creation workshop, who can create the arts you would like to develop?
>
> Can you act on these ideas now? If not, plan by asking these and similar questions: Which gaps can we fill? What is the best way to fill the gaps? Who can help us to do this? When could we start?

Tool: Assess a Multicultural Christian Community's Arts

In multiethnic churches, the church's diversity is not always reflected in its artistic expressions. The majority group often dominates artistically, to the disadvantage of others. If church leaders want their members to interact better between cultural groups and to worship as true equals, they will usually need to take intentional steps to help people cross cultural divides. This activity is designed to chart a way forward. It could be done as a workshop or as a whole church study over several weeks. An ever-growing number of organizations and written resources can help you to learn more about this topic.[47]

Participants

Church leaders, artistically gifted believers, an ethnoarts facilitator.

Tasks

Conduct a Bible study on the cultural diversity of the church of God. Explore these passages together:

- Genesis 1:26–27 (all are equal and made in God's image)
- Genesis 12:3 (God's desire is to bless all peoples)
- Psalm 67 (all the nations are to praise God)
- Isaiah 19:23–25 (former rival nations worship together)
- Acts 2:11 (all nations hear the Bible's message in their own languages)
- Romans 15:5–11; Colossians 3:11–16 (diversity and unity in love and worship)
- Revelation 21:26–27 (cultural diversity in the age to come)

Assess your current multicultural strategies in these areas:

- **Leadership:** How can the leadership become multicultural?
- **Fellowship:** How can the church help believers interact well across cultures?
- **Pastoral care:** What issues may be different for members of different cultures?
- **Outreach:** What are the natural social networks of different cultural groups?

Assess the current arts strategy of your meetings. For example, do you

- welcome visitors warmly but continue with your previous arts?
- separate believers into congregations based on language, culture, and/or age?
- invite members of different groups to use their own songs and other arts from time to time?
- rotate the arts leadership between different cultures?
- mix up members of different cultures in the musical or other arts team(s)?
- regularly and gladly sing songs all together from the cultures represented?
- create new art forms which blend elements from various of the members' cultures?

---

47 The Digital Library (www.clatmanual.com) will document the growing list of resources for multiethnic worship, but some organizations and resources available at the time of publication include these: Proskuneo Ministries, https://proskuneo.org; The Ethnos Project, http://ethnos.us/resources/the-ethnos-project/; Songs to Serve, https://songs2serve.eu/; Davis and Lerner, *Worship Together*; Harris, "Review: Disharmony"; Kim, *Diaspora Musicians*; Lim, "Right Kind of Worship"; McKay, "Worship Arts Ministry"; Padiath, "Reconciled in Christ"; Roberts, "Diversity in Worship"; and Van Opstal, *Next Worship*. A number of chapters in the *Ethnodoxology Handbook* (11, 14, 77, and 132–136) are helpful as well, such as Collinge, "Intercultural Worship."

Conduct the Heart Arts Questionnaire for your congregation (if you have not already), including one or two preliminary questions about heart language, place of birth, education, age group (0–10, 11–20, etc.), and gender. Then ask a few deeper questions:

> What arts are we missing if we are to be genuinely multicultural?
>
> How can we embrace different styles more?
>
> What should we make a priority?
>
> When would be a good time to introduce these ideas?

Tool: Attend or Hold an Arts For a Better Future (ABF) Workshop

The week-long ABF workshop provides a structure that church leaders and other Christ-followers can use to evaluate and plan for change in how they use arts in more Scripture-based ways. The ABF website at www.artsforabetterfuture.org and the Digital Library (www.clatmanual.com) contain more detailed descriptions and rationale, teaching materials, processes necessary to play different roles (including attending and hosting), and other resources related to ABF.

Participants

Administrators, mission leaders, field practitioners, artists, worship leaders, and minority community members have all learned from ABF. Even though it is great to take as an individual, it is even better with a team so you can explore and plan together. In fact, we divide into working groups for the last phase, so you will leave with plans for communities you care about.

To be especially clear: participants do *not* have to identify as artists or artistically gifted. Everyone can create and encourage others to create. One of ABF's key admonitions is to *embrace imperfection.*

Tasks

We want the Kingdom impacts of ABF to spread quickly and widely, without diluting the unique elements that make it so effective. So we have tried to craft a dynamo—that is, a generator, an energy producer—relating stable organizational, conceptual, and methodological infrastructure to the more malleable features of geography, urban and rural contexts, artistic forms, etc. Roles needed to put on an ABF workshop reflect the largely stable structures: Host Organizer(s); Two Lead Instructors; Associate Instructor(s); Phase 2 Community Representative (CR); Phase 3 Facilitators; Mentees; Arts with God Facilitators; and Documenters.

Figure 4.14 represents a sample schedule for ABF, which leads participants through the CLAT methodology three times.

	Sunday	Monday	Tuesday	Wednesday	Thursday	Friday
7:15-8:00		Breakfast	Breakfast	Breakfast	Breakfast	Breakfast
8:15-9:00		Arts with God	Arts with God	Arts with God	Arts with God	Arts with God
9:00-10:15		**Phase 1 Begins** Setting the Scene: Creating Local Arts Together (CLAT)	Select Local Arts to Reach Kingdom Goals (3)	Spark Creativity for The Sakha (5)	**Phase 3 Begins** Tools for Kingdom Creativity in a Community You Know	Plan in Groups
10:15-10:45		break	break	break	break	break
10:45-12:00		**Phase 2 Begins** Meet the Community: The Sakha of Siberia (1a)	Analyze: Learning about an Artistic Event (4a)	Spark Creativity for The Sakha	Plan for Kingdom Creativity in a Community You Know	Plan in Groups
12:00-2:00		Lunch, free time	Lunch, free time	Lunch, free time	Lunch, free time	Lunch, free time
2:00-3:15		Exploring the Arts Among the Sakha (1b)	Analyze: Identifying Arts Within an Enactment (4b)	Improve and Celebrate your Creativity (6/7)	Plan in groups	Excite Us! Share Your Plans
3:15-3:45		break	break	break	break	Farewells
3:45-5:00	5:30 Registration & 6 PM Dinner	Discover and Specify Kingdom Goals for The Sakha (2)	Analyze: Connecting the Event to its Cultural Context (4c)	Arts and the Kingdom of Heaven	Plan in groups	God sends you out with courage!
5:00-6:00		Dinner	Dinner	Dinner	Dinner	Finished by 5 pm
Evening	7-8 pm Get to know each other, course overview			Social night: share your "heart arts"		

Figure 4.14 Sample schedule for Arts for a Better Future

Tool: Do "Arts with God" Devotional

Arts with God devotional times are designed to provide a space for a group or individual to interact with God through Scripture in diverse artistic forms.

See the Digital Library (www.clatmanual.com) for modules and more detailed guidance.

Participants

Participants may be attending ABF, a church retreat, small group meetings, other group event, or integrate these activities into their individual times with God.

Tasks

To open up new, fresh forms of prayer and worship, Arts with God sessions must (1) embed Scriptures deeply; (2) integrate arts from as many artistic domains as possible throughout an event (dance, drama, visual arts, poetry, singing, storytelling, etc.); (3) and draw on skills and experiences of instructors, participants, and local communities whenever possible, guiding them to lead Arts with God sessions in participatory, worshipful ways.

The Digital Library (www.clatmanual.com) includes detailed guides for existing modules, or people can design their own. Here are summaries of three commonly used examples:

- **Blackout Poetry.** Read Psalm 139:23–24 together. Participants think how they might select words from a page of a book to create their own message, possibly unconnected from the original text.
- **Worship through The Pen.** Read Psalm 62 together, with everyone responding to the imagery of God as our strong rock through any form of poetry, word art, written prayers, or prose.
- **Worship through Dramatic Tableaux.** Groups prepare "frozen pictures" for key moments during the reading of Scripture passages, having the audience open their eyes just for those moments.

Whenever possible, debrief participants afterward with questions like, "What did God show you about yourself or himself? "What parts of this experience were difficult for you—did you learn anything from those?" "In what new ways did you encounter God's Word?"

Impact

Participants have produced amazing bits of artistic communication that have challenged, encouraged, and touched everyone. One person reflected: "Since my gifts have never been in the realm of music, I felt that I could never adequately worship God with something I created myself. Arts with God changed that!" Arts with God has also helped overcome insecurities ("I couldn't do that ... I'm not a painter!"), resulted in more people being equipped for service (Eph 4:11ff), and knowing more Scripture with more imagination and lasting impact.

WHERE THERE IS NO CHURCH

CLAT-like methodologies are often appropriate in places with other majority and minority religions, where Christianity has become a superficial identity marker, and in other communities indifferent or hostile to Christians. Many ABF-inspired projects, for example, have been designed to engage with such communities. And I hope more people will use the religiously neutral *Make Arts for a Better Life* volume.[48] Further discussion of such approaches remains beyond the scope of this book.

---

48 Schrag and Van Buren, *Make Arts for a Better Life*.

Conversation 5

Spark Creativity

We've finally reached a climactic moment in our cocreation process. If you and a community have been following a CLAT linear approach, in Conversations 1–4, you might think of it as the point in a pregnancy when the baby is born. Preparation and nurture have accompanied the miraculous invisible growth of the infant in the mother's womb. In our metaphor, new artistry is about to enter the world, and you and community members are the midwives.

Conversation 5 will guide communities in designing and implementing plans connecting their artistry to Kingdom goals. To provide a concrete starting point, refer to the draft statement produced in Conversation 3 (see Figure 3.1, reproduced here as Figure 5.1). Since capturing those first thoughts, the community will have broadened and deepened their understandings of many CLAT elements through genre and event research in Conversations 4A, 4B, 4C, and 4D.[1] The passage of time may also have included return to analyses in other CLAT conversations, further significant reflection, changes in social or physical contexts, prominent events, the involvement of new influential participants, and other unpredictable developments—each potentially contributing to Real Life CLAT reformulations.

Before diving into Conversation 5, then, it may be helpful to draft another plan informed by current realities. By the end of this conversation, the community will be able to take fruitful, well-grounded steps toward more signs of the Kingdom.

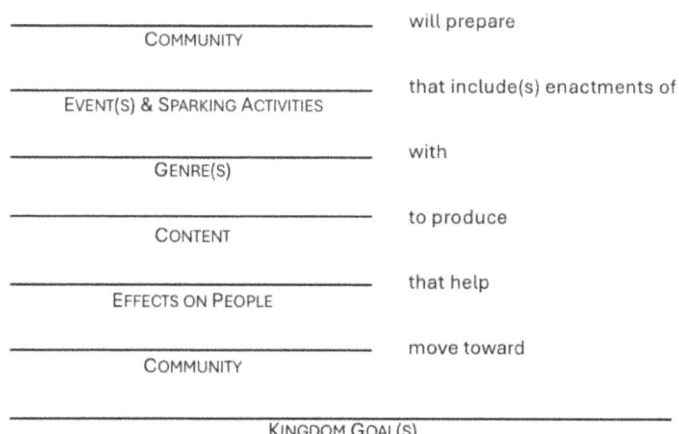

Figure 5.1 Drafting another plan connecting events to Kingdom Goals

We now show how to design an Activity that gets down to the nitty-gritty of creating new artistry, mostly a fleshing out of the Events element.

---

1 Conversations 6 and 7 will address how these new creations will grow in quality and influence.

In *Real Life CLAT*, communities will return to other Conversations repeatedly, modify or replace elements, or will already have embarked on a sparking activity. As always, remain both focused and flexible.

A community can follow this process to craft a sparking activity:

- What is a sparking activity?
- Review Creativity and Artists.
- Identify opportunities to maximize and barriers to overcome.
- Decide on a type of activity.
- Design a new activity or modify an existing activity.
- Perform the activity.

Note that some activities might build on one another. You'll also see that many activities we describe contribute to multiple Kingdom effects. For example, you may commission an artist to create a new Scripture-infused work in a traditional genre for a celebration. From this, people in the community will learn more about God, which feeds into "Witness" in our Church Life Kingdom Goal category. But the social status of the genre will also increase, which ties into the appropriate affirmation of God's creativity we discuss in Identity and Sustainability. This is good—the more Heaven, the better.

WHAT IS A SPARKING ACTIVITY?

A sparking activity is anything anybody does that results in the creation of new, modified, or repurposed artistry. In different places, acts of creativity will require different amounts of community investment, from low to high. For example, the act could be as casual as suggesting to a friend that she respond with painting during an oration at a meeting that afternoon, or it could entail the enormous complexity of planning a festival involving scores of artists and government officials.

A sparking activity may also lead to immediate fruit or provide a structure where future creativity can happen. In the Mono example, Punayima's apprentices didn't compose new *gbaguru* songs right away, but they each learned to make, tune, and play a *kundi*; this developed their capacity to compose in the future. Finally, such sparking activities may fold in many or all seven Creating Local Arts Together (CLAT) conversations or focus on just one. As we'll see, workshops often include times to identify Kingdom Goals, perform initial analysis of genres, and create and improve works. Other kinds of activities may focus solely on the act of creating.

A **sparking activity** can be as brief as a word or as immense as a multiyear project with global partners. In any case, the community needs to see the sparking activity in the context of the whole cocreation process.

With this backdrop, here are components you and the community need to describe in the Community Arts Profile when designing a sparking activity:

> **Title and summary:** A brief overview of the activity and its main purposes. Include its overall type—commissioning, workshop, showcase event, mentoring, apprenticeship, publication, creators' club, or something you make up (not more than a paragraph).
>
> **Participants:** All the types of people who ideally need to be involved for the activity to succeed. This may include creators and gatekeepers of various kinds. Identify actual people when possible.
>
> **Kinds of things needed from the Community Arts Profile:** Information someone needs to learn about the community or genre(s) for the activity to succeed. Note which information is already in the Community Arts Profile, and that which still needs exploration. Much missing information will be revealed in research activities in Conversation 4.
>
> **Resources needed:** Financial, technical, logistical, permissions, communication media, and other requirements to make the activity happen.
>
> **Tasks:** The items that someone needs to perform to carry out the activity. You may make these as detailed or broad as you like, depending on your context. The sample activities we provide below are somewhere in the middle.
>
> **Big Picture analysis:** To identify which of the seven conversations are present in this activity, make three lists:
>
> 1. CLAT conversations included in the activity;
> 2. CLAT conversations done outside the activity, such as analysis of an event that someone else already did; and
> 3. plans to address any missing conversations in the future.
>
> At least some of this information should already be in the CAP.

Figure 5.2 Steps to designing a sparking activity

REVIEW CREATIVITY AND ARTISTS

Refer to research associated with "Creativity" and "Artists" in Conversation 4C, then consider the following:

Creativity

Communities usually follow patterns to make artistry, and to act artistically. Ideally, you and the community will be able to integrate some of these dynamics into the sparking activity; the familiarity will smooth the creation process and likely increase the quality of its products. On the other hand, all people are primed to create because they carry God's image, and so are usually agile in adopting new methods; individuals or subgroups may follow their own idiosyncratic processes. The activity you and the community design will likely include both familiar and new kinds of invention. Never stop asking and observing.

In the Mono case, I asked Punayima to compose a new example of *gbaguru* based on one of Jesus's parables. Punayima asked questions, thought awhile, started playing a repeated pattern on his *kundi*, then said he needed to be by himself to compose the song. Others may compose in a pair or group, with pencil and paper, in dreams or visions, on paid commission, with spontaneous improvisation, or use any number of methods.

Artists

Think carefully about the meristems. A meristem is the region in a plant in which new cells are created—the growth point. Likewise, the growth point in artistic production usually consists of one or a few key people from whose mind and body the art emerges, the artists. We want to love, protect, and encourage these people. Like every other human, they reflect God's image and so are inherently valuable. But in our sparking activities, they are also the crux of creativity. The hub. The nub. The people we cannot do without. Their skill and reputation may also exert the most influence on how others respond to their new artistry. It's important, then, to include people who will create the best artistry and have the social respect that helps it spread in the community.

So, when a community chooses the composers (we include everyone who makes something, such as painters, weavers, game designers, architects, playwrights, and the like), they should look for people who are already recognized as having experience and skill in creating within a genre and its events. There may be many such qualified people to choose from, or only a few.

If you are working in a Christian community, finding someone who is both a Christian and an experienced composer may be difficult. In this case, the community may consider commissioning the work from a non-Christian. Questions to ask in this case: Are they interested, skilled and knowledgeable, respected by their community? If their name is made known, will that be a help or hindrance to acceptance of the work? What do local Christians think of the idea?

Commissioning Scripture-based artistry from non-Christian composers sometimes works well. For example, the most respected and popular musician among the Akyode of Ghana was not a Christian. However, he had a good reputation within the society, his name would help the composition's acceptance, he was interested, and the local church saw nothing wrong in approaching him.[2] In Ghana's Nkonya culture, however, the most famous composer was viewed as a drunkard, and the local church decided against approaching him.

Local crafters of CLAT activities will be able to make lists of potential experienced composers, deciding how closely they want to adhere to historical genre constraints and other dynamics.

---

2 Neeley, "A Case Study," 118–29.

IDENTIFY OPPORTUNITIES TO MAXIMIZE AND BARRIERS TO OVERCOME

Identify potential barriers and opportunities in the community associated with creativity in the genre. Review the discussions of strengths and hopes in Conversation 2—"A Tool to Help People Choose Kingdom Goals" or some other method they used. Discoveries in Conversation 4D may also help. Here are a few common examples of opportunities and barriers:

Opportunities

- talented artists eager to use their gifts in new contexts
- government interest in promoting local art forms
- growing recognition of the value of local arts and fear for their loss in the wider community
- a respected champion of local arts in the community who can lead innovation

Barriers

- negative attitudes toward use of local language and art forms in some domains
- lack of knowledge and skills associated with a genre (this was the barrier that Punayima's apprenticeship program was designed to overcome)
- apathy toward change or the community
- declining interest in local cultural forms due to urbanization and globalization

After discussing these examples with community members, ask questions like:

> What might help us spark a rich flowering of new works in this genre(s) or event(s)? How could we draw on these opportunities when designing a sparking activity?
>
> What might stop us from achieving this creativity? How could we overcome these barriers when designing a sparking activity?

Put the results of this conversation in the Community Arts Profile.

DECIDE ON A TYPE OF ACTIVITY

In this section, we present overviews and helps for several common types of activities that spark creativity—a small sample of many possibilities. We also point you to more resources when available.

FOSTER RELATIONSHIPS

In the CLAT process, we approach everyone we encounter with respect and humility, expecting warm relationships to emerge. Sometimes, however, conditions suggest that nurturing gentle, long-term friendships *itself* results in fertile soil from which creativity can emerge. When communities see themselves as less valuable than others, or when political or religious factors don't allow for noticeable, public events, we may think of personal discussions with individuals or small groups as a sparking activity. Such interactions focus on building trust, asking good questions, and listening. This may entail multiple engagements over a long time. As relationships deepen and knowledge increases, arts advocates may make suggestions that include creativity with new purposes. Participatory methods of engagement like those listed in Conversation 2 may also serve as activities over longer periods.

I cultivated personal and professional bonds with two men who have become particularly influential in advocating for local arts in Cameroon and beyond. Ferdinand Doumtsop continues to research for and help organize cultural festivals for Ngiemboon communities, and Roch Ntankeh teaches seminarians and pastors principles of ethnodoxology.

COMMISSIONING

We define **commission** as follows: *to charge an artist or group of artists with the task of creating a new instance of an artistic genre for an agreed-upon purpose.* Consider commissioning in almost all circumstances. It's often the most direct way to spark creativity because it requires as few as two people in dialogue. Commissioning commonly consists of these steps:

1. With the community, identify
   - the event for which the item will be created
   - the purpose(s) for the created item (e.g., literacy, church worship, or community development)
   - the genre(s) of creation (e.g., *haiku, olonkho,* or musical theater)
   - the content
   - the creator(s)
   - the gatekeepers who should be included in the process

2. Then
   - work with the maker(s) in the creative process, including evaluation and revision of the work(s)
   - prepare the rest of the community and the event organizers for a public presentation
   - explore other distribution means, including recordings
   - explore ways that this work, and others like it, can enter other domains of the community's life

Respect and trust in your relationship with the creators and gatekeepers—people who can close or open doors to a new work's acceptance—are crucial to the commissioning process. Ask confidants what sort of compensation is appropriate for the artist, genre, and event. Compensation may be in the form of money, services, goods, social capital, or goodwill borne of friendship.

Think through the commissioner's roles during the composition process. Who will decide what's good and what needs to be changed? How much freedom will the artist have to innovate? As much as possible, the commissioner and artist should agree on these things before the composition process begins.

One other curious case arises: Can you commission yourself to create something? Spark yourself? Certainly, people decide to compose new things on their own. We encourage this but insist that you should always act in relationship to a community. Too often individual artists make something new without any conversation with the community it's meant for and present it to them timidly or defiantly for acceptance. It's much better to include gatekeepers early in the making of new things so everyone has a stake in its success.

WORKSHOPS

Workshops are short events—typically one or two weeks—that gather people to make progress together on a particular task. Consider a workshop when there is an organization in a community that can provide logistics and goals that will motivate participants to set aside the rest of their lives for a while; examples of such organizations include cultural associations, churches, and nongovernmental organizations. Workshops produce a ferment of productivity when participants interact with each other in a concentrated way.

There are many potential goals for workshops that draw on artistic communication: produce excellent translations of certain biblical Psalms, compose songs for church worship, create and record works with dramatic content to be distributed through radio or other media, weave cloths communicating health messages—the possibilities are endless.

> In one case in Indonesia, local partners requested a songwriting workshop. A group of musicians was inspired to write songs before coming, and afterward, they decided to continue creating together. They had a strong desire to record their songs and make music videos. An arts worker's offer of technical help with audio and video recording was the spark they needed to produce three albums and over thirty videos. At first, they were excited to create and record, but over time they began to find specific purposes for their songs in line with Kingdom Goals. They have now expanded to work with two children's arts groups and explore local dance styles. Several people are now learning to facilitate the CLAT process independently in their own and neighboring communities.[3]

---

3 Connor and Menger, "Strengthening Christian Identity."

SHOWCASE EVENTS

You may help a community plan or run a festival or competition that highlights creativity in local artistic genres.[4] Festivals are events designed to showcase a community's cultural identity and creative output. Many ethnic or religious groups already have celebratory gatherings that may be open to including new works of art produced by Christians. It may also be possible to start a new festival tradition fueled by Christians' celebration of their God-given artistic gifts. Prizes for the best new works add the energy and excitement that events like these produce. Festivals also provide great opportunities for cooperation between different Christian, cultural, religious, and other groups within a community.

Showcase events normally emerge from a five-phase process:

1. **Imagining and planning.** How will we get from here to there? The larger the event, the more planning it requires. Some communities excel in creating detailed schedules and goals. Other communities excel in pulling together fabulous celebrations through organic social dynamics. Contribute ideas, but don't impose a system.

2. **Promotion and networking.** How can we ensure the participation of key artists and a wide public? Festivals sometimes incorporate contests or prizes to motivate artists. Make sure to clearly communicate the kinds of arts that will be rewarded and how they will be evaluated.

3. **Composition and preparation.** Will artists have time and resources to create and practice their performance or prepare an exhibition?

4. **Running the event.** Try to create a sense of common purpose, flexibility, and joy as the event unfolds. Also, try to get as many people as possible to play roles in making the event happen.

5. **Evaluation and planning.** A big event requires a dedicated time afterward to graciously evaluate with key people how it went. It's also a great moment to see how the event relates to all the seven CLAT conversations and discuss the possibility of similar future events.

MENTORING

Sometimes because of your age, education, or social position you may enter a long-term relationship that benefits an individual artist or group of artists. This relationship usually develops over time from personal rapport and common goals. Mentors may help influence a mentee's professional, spiritual, and character growth, opening doors to new opportunities and sharing instructive stories from their own lives. Mentorship includes reciprocal learning as well; especially if the relationship crosses cultures, the mentee will teach the mentor skills and cultural insights. Over time, this bond often grows increasingly deep and satisfying.

---

4 See, for example, *kwaya* contests in Tanzania, described in Barz, *Performing Religion*.

APPRENTICESHIP

Apprenticeship consists of providing a structure consistent with existing cultural forms where artistic experts can transfer their skills and knowledge to other members of their community. Structured apprenticeship makes sense when experts in the genre exist, contexts for transfer of competencies in the genre are declining, and when community members value the genre.

A community may institute such a program in this way:

- Choose a genre to be taught.
- Choose a master of the genre.
- Choose the apprentices.
- Design a training context that: (a) draws on familiar educational forms; (b) includes a place, time, and frequency that the expert and apprentices can commit to; (c) covers the knowledge, skills, and attitudes crucial to the genre; and (d) lasts long enough for apprentices to reach a sustainable level of competency.
- Implement the program.
- During the program, explore how participants can continue to develop their skills and enact their artistry in various contexts.

PUBLICATIONS

Almost any activity will have more long-term success if it turns thoughts and artistic production into recorded media. Paper, recordings, and electronic data of all kinds allow ideas and artistry to live beyond a single moment and reach people beyond a single place. Periodicals and websites make it possible to disseminate information and inspire discussion on a wide range of topics. Audio and video products can be used to provide content for training programs and entertainment. Publications become repositories of history and biography when people begin to forget what came before them.

General aspects to planning a publication include the following:

- Determine the intended audience(s).
- Identify editors, advisors, and contributors.
- Solicit, select, and prepare the materials to be published.
- Determine a scheme for the distribution of the publication.
- Determine a schedule for ongoing publication.
- Carry out the publication and distribution.
- Develop and use feedback tools (e.g., online comments, letters to the editor, surveys, etc.) to help determine past effectiveness and plan for future developments.

> In the 1990s, I and Sumatran colleagues (Indonesia) came to an understanding of issues surrounding the incorporation of Batak traditional music into the worship of the Batak church. To provide a forum for discussion of these issues, we formed an advisory panel and created a quarterly church news and information periodical, Nada Dasar. In the Batak language, nada dasar is the central tone around which melody and harmony revolve and to which they ultimately resolve—analogous to the place held by Jesus Christ in the life of the Christian. It has allowed readers and leaders to address questions related to choral festival criteria, choir rehearsal technique, vocal technique, music theory, the function of music in the liturgy, and the like. —*Rob Hodges*[5]

> In West Cameroon, Ferdinand Doumtsop, Hubert Sob Lontsi, and several other university-aged people wanted to counteract the loss of traditional knowledge precipitated by widespread migration from Ngiemboon kingdoms to cities. They published a paper journal called *Mûɔ lá'*—"child of our village" in the Ngiemboon language—with "articles describing Ngiemboon traditions, proverbs, specialty foods, interviews with older tradition-bearers, charts connecting calendars based on the traditional eight-day Ngiemboon week with those representing the international seven-day week, descriptions of musical instruments and carved masks, articles in both French and Ngiemboon, news of cultural events, and many other topics."[6] —*Brian Schrag*

CREATORS' CLUBS

Artists often form associations, clubs, and fellowships to encourage each other, critique each other's work, share resources and ideas, perform, and collaborate on products. Groups like these meet regularly in certain places and times, have expectations—however modest—of each other, and often center on a particular art form and purpose. In Western Cameroon, scores of Ngiemboon associations meet each week to practice and improve songs in one of a dozen traditional dance genres. Roberta King has coined the phrase *new song fellowship* to describe a group that meets to compose new Scripture songs in sub-Saharan Africa.[7]

When starting or reshaping a group, consider the following:

- A meeting place and time that accommodates the members and allows for artistic activity.

---

5 For further information, see Hodges, "Church Music News," 25–27.

6 For more details, see Schrag and Van Buren, *Make Arts*, 230–31. The journal is now online at www.mouola.com, an integral component of a cultural revival that includes a nationally publicized and successful arts festival, MANEKOU'O 2024.

7 King, *A Time to Sing*, 5.

- A discussion of the goals for the group and expectations of its members. This could vary from fluid and informal to strict and explicit, depending on the group's wishes.
- If the group forms part of a church or wants to create things for Christian communities, then it's essential to integrate spiritual formation into its activities. Artists act like God in their creativity (except that he does it out of nothing) and sometimes get drawn into unhealthy applications of the power they yield. Prayer, Bible study, accountability, and other disciplines need to provide a spiritual anchor for all artists' creative directions and enactments.

DESIGN SPARKING ACTIVITIES

In this section, we describe several sparking activities that you can use as models, organized according to the Kingdom Goals in Conversation 2. Many of them integrate the activity categories above (Commissioning, Workshops, etc.); others represent additional types. They are all distilled from actual experience but leave most of the details for communities and you to complete for their contexts; in particular, we seldom include resources you need, since they are so often dependent on local context. You may also choose to design a new activity, making sure to address each of the components we describe: title and summary, participants, kinds of things you'll need from the Community Arts Profile, resources needed, tasks, and big picture analysis. Note that multiple sparking activities may benefit from integrating some of the same research activities or tools. For example, Arts with God modules (Conversation 4D) may inject spiritual breath into events involving gatherings. Or you might skip all this and do what seems right. It might work.

IDENTITY AND SUSTAINABILITY

Communities can promote positive cultural identity through local arts by organizing cultural celebrations (such as concerts, festivals, contests, etc.), documenting (through written descriptions, audio recordings, photography, and video), and publishing (on locally distributable media, websites, etc.). These activities should always be done with the leading and input of key community members and artists, and always in ways that will be appreciated by the community itself.

Meet a Community and Its Arts Again

Your activities in gathering information about a community's arts that we describe in Conversation 1 may in themselves increase a positive sense of identity. Go back and fill in some gaps.

Help Organize a Festival Celebrating Community Art Forms

The purpose of this activity is to encourage and invigorate the use of local arts in a community. A festival can raise the status of the local arts, aid in their preservation, encourage innovation, and bring about positive changes.

Participants

Invite individuals from as many different social, age, and economic groups as possible, including community leaders, church leaders, skilled artists, members of older generations, and younger people with a passion for their culture. By including all these groups, the festival will be more likely to bring about lasting artistic change, particularly if younger people are engaged. Note that a church's involvement in the organization and implementation of the festival could result in deepened relationships and witness.

Kinds of things you'll need from the Community Arts Profile

A list of artistic genres ("Take a First Glance at a Community's Arts," Conversation 1), an initial comparison ("First Glance Genre Comparison Chart," Conversation 3), and event descriptions ("Take a First Glance at an Event," Conversation 4, Part A) that include as many genres as possible.

Resources needed

Dependent on the local context.

Tasks

1. **Initial community meeting.** Meet with community representatives to discuss the list of artistic genres, ask and offer reasons why they are valuable, and explain the benefits a festival celebrating these arts could provide.

2. **Logistics.** After initial commitment to a festival, discuss goals and plans through questions like these:

   a. Who will organize the festival? Work toward broad inclusion and unity.

   b. What items need to be in the budget and how much will it be? Who will underwrite the budget?

   c. Which arts will be promoted? Who are the influential and respected artists that should be included? Who oversees inviting them?

   d. Shall the festival include competitions for new works in traditional forms?

   e. When should the festival take place? Should it be included as part of another regular cultural event, ritual, or festival?

   f. How do we want to use audio and video recordings? The organizing group should plan to obtain any necessary government or local permissions from authorities, and permissions from artists for the future use of recordings (see "Sample Permission Form," Conversation 1).

3. **Implement the plans.**

4. **Evaluate and plan for continuity.** After the festival, meet with the organizers or a larger community forum.

a. Evaluate community involvement, quality of the artistic works, and overall successful and unsuccessful aspects of the event. What parts of the festival are the community excited about? Did anything catch their attention?
b. Decide whether the festival should become a regular event.
c. Explore how the community can draw on the excitement and new works for other purposes. Did new purposes for traditional arts emerge? For example, it might be more possible after the festival to promote local arts for use in Christians' spiritual lives or in health education. Plan for more activities that feed into signs of Heaven.
d. Plan to create products from recordings of aspects of the festival and their distribution, such as recordings, a website, storybook, collection of poetry, or song books. There also might be interest in developing a Community Arts Archive housed locally or in a government or educational organization. (See the activity "Help Develop Multimedia Collections of Local Arts" below.)

Your roles as an arts advocate will vary according to the skills and needs of the community. You may be able to contribute through making and organizing audio and video recordings, obtaining authorizations for use, and in providing international perspective on the value of their arts. You could also publish an article about the festival, an artist, or a particular tradition. If you are an outsider to an artistic tradition, you might lend prestige by learning to enact one of the showcased genres. Approach this humbly, though, to ensure that your efforts to learn and enact are viewed positively.

Commission a New Work in an Older Genre for an Existing Showcase Event

Older artistic traditions lose value in communities in part because social changes make them less common, so less visible. One way to counteract this is by commissioning new works that are shown or performed in contexts like festivals, church services, radio and TV programs, or concerts. It's important to ensure that the new work is of high quality, and that people can connect practically and emotionally with it.

Participants
Expert(s) in an older artistic genre, and organizers of a community event.

Kinds of things you'll need from the Community Arts Profile
Description of an event in the commissioning genre using "Take a First Glance at an Event" (Conversation 4, Part A). You can follow other research paths that seem relevant in "Look Through Seven Basic Lenses" (Conversation 4, Part A) and "Identify Artistic Domain Features" (Conversation 4, Part B). You will also want to explore a few subjects like Artists, Creativity, Aesthetics and Evaluation, Emotions, and Community Values shown in "Discover Deeper Community Connections" (Conversation 4, Part C).

Resources needed
Dependent on the local context.

Tasks

1. With friends and colleagues, identify an influential community event that would provide a natural setting for new kinds of arts. Then explore what artistic genre and artist(s) would be most likely to result in positive emotions and excitement.
2. Conversely, you might know an artist well and decide to look for an event where a work in his or her genre could be showcased.
3. Work with the artist(s) in the creation of a prototype of something new.
4. Communicate with the event organizer(s) in locally appropriate ways. Explain that you and others hope to increase the profile and positive identity associated with the community's heritage. Bring an audio, video, or photographic recording of what the artist created. Invite the organizer(s) to help shape the content or form to better meet community goals.
5. Follow procedures associated with the event in preparations, rehearsal, payment, and other logistics.

Evaluate and Plan for Continuity
After the event, meet with the artist(s) and organizer(s). Review how everything went and discuss whether this type of commissioning could become integrated into future events.

Help Develop Multimedia Collections of Local Arts

This activity is intended to raise the status and visibility of a community's arts by showcasing them in a multimedia collection. This collection will allow the community access to past events, help them teach new artists, innovate for the future, and encourage the continued use of their arts.[8]

Participants
Recordists, secretarial help, artists, and people with technical expertise and access to technical resources.

Kinds of things you'll need from the Community Arts Profile
A list of artistic genres ("Take a First Glance at a Community's Arts," Conversation 1), an initial comparison ("First Glance Genre Comparison Chart," Conversation 3), event descriptions ("Take a First Glance at an Event," Conversation 4, Part A) that include as many genres as possible, and a list of key artists associated with each genre.

Resources needed
Multimedia collections are often expensive and require technical skills and equipment. Before beginning a project like this, consider whether there is

---

8 See also Seeger and Chaudhuri, *Archives for the Future*; ARSC, "Education and Training in Audiovisual"; and SIL, "Language and Culture Documentation."

1. an individual or organization with the needed skills that could provide partnership, or else someone will need to be trained in how to create and maintain the collection.
2. equipment available, such as computers, speakers, projectors, smartphones, apps and recording devices.
3. ongoing funding and availability of personnel for maintaining and developing the collection.

You will also need to consider where the collection will be kept: is there an existing building or organization in the area or will a building and/or infrastructure need to be created?

These items are essential to plan for because this is not a cheap or easy project to create and maintain; many critical archives have disintegrated due to lack of continued funding and training resources. However, this activity can be incredibly beneficial to a community; even a very limited collection is better than no collection at all.

Tasks

1. **Identify the purpose(s).** Before beginning, the collection needs to have a purpose. Is this going to be a collection of local genres of stories, songs, stools, or rite of passage dances created by community members? Is this an archive for audio and video recordings of ceremonies? If we are going to include physical items such as clothing or sculptures or musical instruments, do we need a large space to store and/or display them? Are the items in the collection loanable or shareable?

    The community's felt needs and desires are very important to the creation of a multimedia collection. They may, for example, want digital audio files to put on their mobile devices. Or they may be interested in having a place where groups of people could come watch videos of ceremonies being performed by experts. It could be a paper-based library, with photographs and local-language books, stories, folktales, and poetry.

    They may want a place to store and display important items while they are not being used—instead of the community's special attire and ceremonial musical instruments sitting packed away in between uses, why not have them on display?

    This is a very important item because if the final product (collection) does not meet their desires and needs, the community won't have much use for it. The community must see value in this project for it to be anything more than an unused, dusty, or unused web-based archive.

2. **Identify the users.** If this collection is to benefit the community, it needs to be easily accessible and usable. The audience needs to be identified.

3. **Identify who will maintain the collection.** Multimedia devices and formats are constantly changing, and the collection will always need someone who is informed about technology and can keep the files

available in the latest formats. The collection will quickly become useless to the community otherwise. Before beginning, either a person or an organization (government, library, NGO, etc.) needs to be identified that will become a partner in keeping this collection running and up to date.

4. **Identify a location for the collection.** Even in the digital age, a physical location is still needed. Housing an entire collection on a website may require lots of funding and expertise. In addition, a web-only collection may not be very accessible to a community in a country with limited internet access. The location could be something as simple as a laptop in a room.

5. **Identify the media.** What devices do people use to share and access audio and video files. Do they own computers? Do they know how to use a computer? Do they have mobile devices that can play audio and video files? Do they have their own phones, flash drives, or CD/DVD players, or do they need to be available so people can watch and listen right there? Would it be better to have a projector set up so that lots of people can watch a video at the same time, or is a computer monitor enough? Once the media is known, it is possible to set up the collection in the most accessible way possible.

6. **Acquire artistry.** Plan for and record or collect the artistry of key artists in the community.

Constantly provide the community with products of your research (audio and video recordings, photographs, articles, etc.). If you have the technical skills needed, providing the community with tangible fruit throughout your work can really help them understand how a central collection could be a great benefit to them. For instance, as you make field recordings, share them with those you've recorded digitally or in physical formats like CDs or DVDs. If you record a formal event or ceremony, share it with community leaders as a gift. Sometimes these sorts of gifts can create a powerful motivation from within the community itself.

Publish Recordings and Research in Various Forms and Contexts

Publishing helps people identify and promote what they value to local, regional, national, and international communities. Though here we discuss presentations through booklets, websites, and academic articles, media could also include books, flash drives, DVDs, concerts, social media, art exhibitions, etc. This activity dovetails well with the "Help Develop Multimedia Collections of Local Arts" activity above. When presented as one equal voice among thousands of the world's artistic expressions, the community learns that each voice has something unique and special to contribute.

Participants

Depending on the publishing format, you may need to include a web designer, recordist, photographer, printer, editor, exhibition designer, or others. Involve community leaders and artists.

Kinds of things you'll need from the Community Arts Profile

A list of artistic genres ("Take a First Glance at a Community's Arts," Conversation 1), an initial comparison ("First Glance Genre Comparison Chart," Conversation 3), event descriptions ("Take a First Glance at an Event," Conversation 4, Part A) that include as many genres as possible, and a list of key artists associated with each genre.

Resources needed

Dependent on the local context.

Tasks

Website. With artists and community leaders:

1. Create a prototype site with these sections: Meet *[Name]* Communities; Contexts for *[Name]* Artistic Communication; Cultural and Spiritual Initiatives Using *[Name]* Arts; Conversations about *[Name]* Arts; Other Resources Related to *[Name]* Arts.

2. Discuss the site and its social context with community stakeholders. Show prototype to a small group of primary stakeholders, discussing issues like these:

    a. Should the community's arts be shown to a wider group through a website like this? If so, who are the intended audiences and what are the purposes?

    b. Who should control the website's content? Process of publishing? Management of the site? Technical implementation?

    c. What personal and legal permissions are needed to publish the website?

    d. How should the presentation change?

3. Create a plan in which the community takes control of the website.

Booklet. With artists and community leaders:

1. List the art forms that they would most like to share with others.

2. Choose overall booklet design, visual representations of each art form (e.g., sketch or photograph), writers of text explaining each art form.

3. Identify publisher, funding, number to print, and distribution plan.

Academic Article.

1. Identify audience as regional, national, or international.

2. Identify several organizations likely to publish information about the community's arts.

3. Identify one or two people who can write an article satisfying the standards of the organization's publication. If no one within the community has these skills, a trusted outside researcher may fill this role. It may be appropriate to cowrite the article with a community expert.

4. Write the article, modifying it according to the suggestions of important community stakeholders.
5. Submit the article according to the organization and publication's requirements.

Identify and Mend Ruptures in Arts Transmission

Participants
Include people from as many segments of the community as possible, including older and younger, urban and rural, leaders, local artists of many kinds, and teachers.

Kinds of things you'll need from the Community Arts Profile
A list of artistic genres ("Take a First Glance at a Community's Arts," Conversation 1), an initial comparison ("First Glance Genre Comparison Chart," Conversation 3), and an understanding of transmission (see "Transmission and Change," Conversation 4, Part C).

Resources needed
Dependent on the local context.

Tasks[9]

1. Using participatory methods, mediate a discussion of topics like these (see "Steps to Specifying Kingdom Goals" in Conversation 2):
   - What kinds of local wisdom and arts do you have in your communities?
   - What is still strong? Why?
   - What is being lost? Why?
   - What do you want to protect from being lost?
   - How have wisdom and arts been passed on in the past? What caused the process to stop?

2. With this discussion as background, explore actions the community might take to help pass this information on to the youth and children of the community. These could include modifying older education systems (such as initiation schools) or tying into newer community channels (like government schools). They may also establish new systems like community groups or public opportunities where older adults teach younger adults and children about playing instruments, storytelling styles, dances, poetry creation, sculpting, painting, etc.

3. Make an action plan and discuss who will take responsibility for carrying it out.

---

[9] For further discussion of this kind of task, see Saurman and Saurman, "Applied Ethnomusicology"; and Saurman, *Hmong Songs in Education*, especially 100–34, "The Workshop Plans and Process."

HEALING

Among many other ways, artistry can play pivotal roles in physical, emotional, spiritual, relational, and ecological restoration (creation care). Here are some activities that can help.

Organize an Arts and Trauma Healing (ATH) Workshop

Trauma is often a barrier between people and their ability to hear and interact with God. The arts are a powerful way for people to engage with both their pain and God as they process their trauma. Due to both the need to have specialized training in working with people in trauma and the power of the arts, it is important that you either gain education in arts and trauma healing (ATH, see options below) or locate someone who already is trained who can come in and lead a workshop.

Participants

Working with an ATH facilitator, assist in locating participants for healing groups. Include church leaders, Bible translators, or victims of any kind of trauma. Be sure to consider power dynamics and other barriers to safety for each participant.

Kinds of things you'll need from the Community Arts Profile

A list of artistic genres ("Take a First Glance at a Community's Arts," Conversation 1), an initial comparison ("First Glance Genre Comparison Chart," Conversation 3), and an understanding of emotional connections to artistry (see "Emotions," Conversation 4, Part C). Explore in more depth how people in the community mourn, express strong emotions through various arts, and use rituals to pass through difficult times.

Resources needed

For training, contact the Arts and Trauma Healing (ATH) program coordinator at Dallas International University (ATH@diu.edu) to explore options for training in your context.

Options might include:

1. Identifying someone from your group/ministry to receive training to hold the workshop yourself. Education options include a single course with follow-up mentoring, or a graduate certificate in Arts and Trauma Healing.

2. Arranging a training workshop in your context to train a group of people to be able to lead healing groups in order to reach more people.

3. For more resources on Arts and Trauma Healing, see the Digital Library (www.clatmanual.com).

Tasks

These are broad kinds of tasks. Use *Healing the Wounds of Trauma*[10] for concrete directions.

1. Gather people traumatized by war, disease, fears, or anything else.
2. Lead participants through Bible studies addressing suffering, forgiveness, God's power, and other relevant topics.
3. Lead participants through arts-based healing exercises.
4. Help Christian leaders translate lessons into their community's language, if necessary.
5. Train community members to facilitate trauma healing workshops for others.

Commission Local Artists to Address Community Health Problems

Participants

When possible, partner with existing nongovernmental organizations and local groups and artists already addressing serious health needs in their communities. Include expert creators of the artistic genres chosen and experts in the health information they wish to communicate.[11]

Kinds of things you'll need from the Community Arts Profile

Refer to a list of artistic genres ("Take a First Glance at a Community's Arts," Conversation 1), an initial comparison ("First Glance Genre Comparison Chart," Conversation 3), and how people create in the chosen genre ("Creativity," Conversation 4, Part C). Explore in more depth how people in the community use art forms to pass on trustworthy and important information and types of content associated with a genre ("Subject Matter," Conversation 4, Part C).

Resources needed

Dependent on the local context.

Tasks

1. Gather artists, community leaders, and health experts who are concerned about the health problem.
2. Decide together who should create the new artistry, what the content should be, and how it should be disseminated.
3. Have the creator(s) make a prototype of the new thing in a comfortable setting and time frame and present it to the advocacy group. Evaluate and improve the artistry according to helps in Conversation 6.
4. Implement the events in which the artistry will be expressed.
5. Plan for continued methods of creating arts to address physical and social needs.

---

10 Hill, Bagge, Miersma, and Hill, *Healing the Wounds of Trauma*.

11 See also, Van Buren, "Applied Ethnomusicology and HIV"; Barz, Koen, and Brunnel-Smith, "Introduction: Confluence of Consciousness"; Schrag, Harris, and Van Buren, "Make Arts for a Better Life."

Organize a Special Event to Play Traditional Games
Though the focus of this activity is on play and recreation, games and sporting events also feed into increasing a community's sense of identity and value; developing solidarity; and transmitting language, values, and history to more people.

Participants
Include experts in the game genre, children, parents, community leaders, and good organizers.

Kinds of things you'll need from the Community Arts Profile
The community has chosen an artistic genre that includes competition or communal play. Analyze a whole event to identify its artistry. This may exist in the form itself, in costumes or equipment, or special artistic communication that participants and others perform before, during, or after an event. Also ask friends about how they view play, leisure, and competition.

Resources needed
Dependent on the local context.

Tasks
1. Gather a small group to organize the special event.
2. Decide the date, time, location, order of events, celebration of those who excel (if appropriate).
3. Decide who to invite and how to spread the word. If this is a new kind of event, start with a smaller group. If it catches on, such events could become bigger.
4. If many people who attend are unfamiliar with the game, explain its history and rules.

Hold an "Alternatives to Violence Workshop"
A key element of avoiding violence where there is hurt is preemptive conflict resolution. The aim is to creatively transform unhealthy relationships through sharing, caring, improved communication skills, and sometimes even surprise and humor.

Participants
Focus on people who live in communities where conflict is strong, but who want to avoid violence. A trained Alternatives to Violence facilitator could organize such a workshop.

Kinds of things you'll need from the Community Arts Profile
Information on genres containing storytelling and dramatic elements.

Resources needed
Alternatives to Violence Project is a network of volunteers who run workshops to teach people how to keep conflict from turning into violence.[12]

---

12 See https://avpusa.org and https://avp.international or search online for a chapter in your area. See also Africa Sings (https://africasings.com/), a project founded by GEN Global Advisory Council member Daniel Dama, which aims at building peace in West Africa through arts and music via seminars, workshops, events, and training.

Tasks

Role playing and other forms of drama allow participants to explore possible approaches to different forms of conflict. Important insights are gained through the role plays, which are flexibly adapted and debriefed as they run, helping those involved to assess and digest whatever is learned.

Organize an Environment-Themed Art Show

When faced with the sublime beauty of the natural world, humans cannot help but react in awe. Often, the reaction is artistic: a poem written in praise of the honeybees, a dance created to imitate birds' courting dances, paintings of powerful waterfalls or delicate lilies, a drum circle echoing the rhythms of thunder. Through an art show, participants can highlight the positive aspects of creation or draw attention to negative consequences of human activity. The organizers can choose to invite professional or skilled artists to show off their work for all, or the community may choose to showcase their own creations.

Participants

Work with the local community to determine who to invite to participate in the art show or performance. Encourage gatekeepers to include novice artists or decide as a community that you will show your own arts. If you anticipate too many submissions, work with local leaders in the arts to assemble a panel of judges or determine another culturally acceptable way of limiting the number of submissions.

Kinds of things you'll need from the Community Arts Profile

A list of artistic genres ("Take a First Glance at a Community's Arts," Conversation 1) and an initial comparison ("First Glance Genre Comparison Chart," Conversation 3). Try to specify a narrower goal than just "environment." Does the community need clean water? Are they suffering from slash and burn farming techniques? Are they delighting in the abundance of natural fruits and vegetables available for food? Is this event a celebration of what the community has or a call to action?

Resources needed

If organizing a more formal art show with a panel of judges and professional art submissions, consider first developing a database of all artists to invite. This should be done through conversations with local artists already involved in the "scene." For a professional-looking show, some of these materials will be needed:

- Frames and hanging fixtures
- Walls to hang items on, weather-protected venue

For an artistic event outside the realm of visual arts, you may need:

- A space / venue for playing instruments or dancing
- A sound system (if a large group)
- Costumes
- Program

Tasks
These are broad kinds of tasks:
- Gather people creating artworks or those enjoying interacting with them.
- Create the organizational team for the event.
- Determine the focus/purpose of the art event (i.e., educational? celebratory?).
- Promote event, talk with artists, possibly set a date to jury submissions.
- Hang show (if visual) or rehearse (if dance/music).
- Set opening date.
- Have the show! Celebrate!

JUSTICE

Used thoughtfully, artistic communication can result in fairer social systems, help turn eyes and hearts to marginalized people, support individuals' acquisition of skills and knowledge that raise their social status, among many other examples of increasing justice. Here are a few examples of how this can happen.

Several of the activities related to justice include literacy components. These may benefit from a software app called Bloom.[13] Bloom is a simply and elegantly designed resource for minority language communities. It offers a rapidly growing library of literature addressing both local and widely relevant topics. It also provides an uncomplicated app that communities can use to create paper, talking, comic, sign language, and interactive books in multiple formats.

Hold Workshops that Magnify Marginalized Voices

Questioning power relationships can be dangerous. This activity should be carried out with much patience and as widespread community involvement as possible.[14]

Participants
Work with a group of people in a community who suffer from being outside social power structures. Common categories include women, members of minority ethnic groups, children, handicapped, or poor people.

Kinds of things you'll need from the Community Arts Profile
A list of artistic genres ("Take a First Glance at a Community's Arts," Conversation 1), an initial comparison ("First Glance Genre Comparison Chart," Conversation 3), a general understanding of power relationships between different community subgroups, and a specific understanding of how certain artistic genres are used to promote or circumvent power relationships ("Identity and Power," Conversation 4, Part C).

---

13 See https://bloomlibrary.org, noting both the "read" and "resources" tabs.
14 See also Mlama, "Reinforcing Existing Indigenous Communication."

Resources needed
Dependent on the local context.

Tasks

1. Talk individually to people who represent marginalized groups in the community, exploring how they are treated by others. If they have already organized themselves, offer your services in helping integrate arts into their activities. Decide together how, when, and where to meet for a workshop.
2. Review the artistic genres that exist in the wider community and within their own subcommunity.
3. Evaluate each genre in terms of its potential to safely communicate grievances to those in power. During church services, women in the African Apostolic Church in southern Africa are allowed to admonish men for abusing them, without fear of retaliation.[15] If such forms exist, discuss what messages the group wants to communicate, and when they could communicate it. Then commission someone in the group to compose it.
4. Evaluate each genre in terms of its potential to provide a sense of solidarity among people in the group. Local genres with song, dance, drama, or visual messages could provide appropriate fodder.
5. Plan for continued creativity and community-building activities.

Commission an Alphabet Song

Songs help people remember new information. This activity shows you how to help a local composer create a new song in a familiar style that lists the building blocks of literacy skills—letters.

Participants
Work with one or several teachers, songwriters, and/or poets who know a local style appropriate for teaching. At least one of these people needs to know how to write the language well, to write the composition down for others to learn.

Kinds of things you'll need from the Community Arts Profile
Look at artistic genres of song that can have lots of repetition. Also consider the kinds of songs, riddles, or poems people use to teach children or adults.

Resources needed
You will need a recorder and means to distribute copies in the format you choose to help people learn the new song.

Tasks

1. Decide who your intended audience is. You may choose to make one alphabet song for everyone, or one for adults and another for children.
2. List all the symbols in the alphabet on a sheet of paper. Choose words that begin with each of these sounds.

---

15 Jules-Rosette, "Ecstatic Singing."

Spark Creativity

3. Discuss what kind of a song would best help people learn these symbols. If there is a call-and-response form, you may want to imitate that to ask questions and give answers that teach the letters with words or sentences. You could associate a word with each sound, or a sentence with each sound.
4. Ask someone talented in the song genre to make a song that matches the words or sentences with a melody. The tune must be an appropriate kind of song for teaching your intended audience.
5. Test the new song with a few literacy students and literacy program leaders to make sure it is easy to remember, fun, and accepted. Encourage revisions in response to feedback.
6. Plan how to teach teachers the new song so they in turn can teach it to their students. Ask students to teach it to friends or family.

> In the Waodoni language of Peru, for example, animals make vowel sounds, so the Waodani made a call-and-response song to teach the vowels. The song gives questions and answers like, "What does the wild pig say? The wild pig says 'æ.'" You might want to ask if birds make consonant sounds. Other people, like the Quechua Ambo-Pasco, taught each letter of the alphabet with a word that begins with that letter. Their song says, "What are we going to learn today? We're going to learn our letters today. With A we say algu [dog]. With B we say bandera [flag]. With C we say cuchi [pig]." After every four letters, they repeat the question, "What are we going to learn today?" Others, like the Sango in Central Africa, created an alliterative poem associating each letter with a sentence that uses that letter many times. Each line of the poem repeats a new letter many times. The poem became the words to "The Sango Alphabet Song."   —Pat Kelley and Michelle Petersen

Commission Local Visual Art for Books and Literacy Materials

Participants
Work with local visual artists, book makers, literacy specialists, people from the community to check the illustrations with, and respected leaders.

Kinds of things you'll need from the Community Arts Profile
Since each culture follows unique visual rules, perform the activity "Analyze the Message of an Image" in the *CLAT Companion* (www.clatmanual.com). For example, in some cultures, *big* means *near* and *small* means *far*, but in other cultures *big* means *important* and *small* means *less important*. The more you can learn about local visual rules and how people show stories, the better. Do people portray one event per image, or do they portray many events in the same image? Maybe people find a key moment to illustrate instead of a series of events like a comic strip, or maybe they put many events all in one picture.

How does their art reflect how they depict events in life? That helps decide content in literacy materials and illustrations.

Resources needed

Have available the texts you want illustrated, perhaps sample illustrations from other works.

Tasks

1. Gather a group of literacy specialists, visual artists, and respected leaders. Decide the goals of what you would like to illustrate. Illustrations may be needed for local language calendars, wall hangings, educational materials, Scripture portions, and Bible studies.

2. Find local artists. Agree to pay normal local wages as appropriate for similar work.

3. Tell the local artist the story you would like illustrated. He or she needs to understand it well enough to tell it back to you before he or she can draw it well. Talk together about the main characters, actions, emotion, and main point of each illustration before the artist begins to draw. You may want to ask the artist to put a member of the intended audience somewhere in the picture to help with audience identification so the audience will learn well from the illustration. Women tend to identify with women, men with men, and children with children. Agree about characters to be illustrated, their actions, and their emotions.

4. Ask the artist to create three or four rough drafts. Ask him or her not to put too much time into rough drafts; these are just to give ideas.

5. Look at the rough drafts together. For each illustration ask questions like, "Why is the jaguar so big and the man so little?" The artist may tell you that the jaguar is more important to the story, or more dangerous, so you should not impose your rule that relative size indicates relative distance. Make sure all the people or animals and objects needed to understand the story well are in the picture and no key people are left out. Make sure that the correct action is shown happening, and that characters' emotions are what the story calls for. If you find changes are needed so that complete information is communicated, then ask the artist to revise the rough draft. Be aware that the local culture may portray things in ways you do not expect, and emotion may be shown differently than you expect. Rather than telling the artist to change something, there may be times when you want to wait and see what people say in the next step.

6. Together, decide which of the drafts the artist should develop further.

7. Ask three or more members of the intended audience to look at the next rough draft illustration(s). Ask what they see, what they think the artist is trying to say, what they like, what they don't like, and if anything offends them. Find out if the illustration communicates the story's action, intent, and emotion accurately to them or not. Tell their ideas to the artist to help the artist make a good final illustration.

8. Check with community leaders before finalizing the illustrations(s). If the illustration is of a historical event, the choice to contextualize or not (whether to make participants more local or more historical) should be made and checked with local community leaders. If another revision is needed, make changes.

Promote Literacy through Local Arts Presentations

People will be more likely to integrate literacy into their lives if they connect it to other domains of their lives. This activity describes how to commission literacy-promoting visual, musical, dramatic, or other artistic expressions associated with normal community events like dances or celebrations.[16]

Participants
Work with literacy experts, artists in genres chosen for activities, and community leaders.

Kinds of things you'll need from the Community Arts Profile
The artistic genre chosen to carry the message needs to be in use already in the community for carrying similar types of messages. You need to know what kinds of messages carry what kinds of meaning, and make the form match the content.

Resources needed
Dependent on the local context.

Tasks

1. Choose a community event that would provide a good forum for promoting literacy. These could be festivals, church gatherings, sporting events, or other contexts.

2. Together, list possible problems for someone who doesn't know how to read. For example, the person (1) can't read instructions on medicine; (2) misses a bus because he or she couldn't read the schedule; (3) needs legal government paperwork done; or (4) needs to know something written but there's no one around who can read it to them, so they don't know what to do and go home without accomplishing what they needed to do. Choose one of these problems as the story idea.

3. Discuss the different artistic genres of communication that exist in the community. Imagine benefits and drawbacks of using each to communicate the story. Choose one or more genres.

4. Have experts in the chosen genre(s) lead the process of creating a new work, which may include drama, poetry, song, illustration, comic, or picture to connect with people. When they have told what happens without knowing how to read, add a verse or another act to the skit or another picture showing an alternate case where someone has learned to read and the situation plays differently. The person's self-esteem comes up because they can do paperwork at the government office, give the medicine correctly, take the right bus, or otherwise not be dependent on someone else.

---

16 See also Foerster and Saurman, *Culturally Relevant Language Development*.

5. Discuss the possibility of presenting the promotional art to the leaders of the community.
6. Show the work to a few people from your intended audience and ask for their feedback on how to make it better before you show it to many people.
7. Present the artistry.
8. In addition to enacting works to directly show the value of reading, artistic expressions that have another goal—such as presenting Scripture or health information—also provide motivation for reading since they require reading indirectly as a skill to make them. Among the Supyire of Mali, the possibility of being chosen to act in radio dramas was a major motivation to attend literacy classes, to be able to read scripts. Also, many people want to learn how to read so they will be able to read song books and participate more fully in choirs.

Integrate Local Arts into Methods to Teach Reading

Arts can help people move from the known (e.g., orally communicated words in local songs or proverbs) to the unknown (visual representations of those same words). This activity shows you how to work with people involved in teaching literacy in a community to show the best ways to use local arts in their work.

Participants
Include community leaders, literacy experts, and gifted and creative teachers and artists.

Kinds of things you'll need from the Community Arts Profile
Focus on genres that have verbal (see the Oral Verbal Arts section in Conversation 4, Part B) and visual (see the Visual Arts section in Conversation 4, Part B) components. Every culture has some kinds of art forms that can lead toward literacy by helping them make conceptual associations between visual arts and letter shapes or movements used in making the letters. Woodburning and carving on gourds can tell a story in pictures in the Huanca Quechua area of Peru. Symbols woven or printed on cloth, scarves, or rugs carry meaning in the Middle East. Henna designs on hands carry meaning in India.

Resources needed
Dependent on the local context.

Tasks
Literacy leaders and other community leaders meet to list artistic resources that may help them teach more people to read. Following are a few possible ways to connect known arts to reading and writing:

1. Use movements people know to teach them how to write similar movements. Help people make the conceptual jump from three-dimensional, concrete objects and movements to two-dimensional symbols by relating the two-dimensional symbols to similar three-dimensional objects and known movements. For example, if you are teaching an Arabic letter that looks like a hand cupping three stones, have students make this motion and say the letter name.

Spark Creativity

2. Use the lyrics of songs, proverbs, stories, riddles, or other verbal arts as texts to learn to read. If using a genre with song, put the lyrics to a song on a wall in a classroom and have students sing as they follow the words. Some people learn to read by following along with songs as they are sung in church.

3. Performance provides content for teaching reading. If participants act out something that's happened, such as, "Show us how old Weepy went out and speared the wild pig," the teacher can ask what words Weepy used, such as "Let's spear! Wild pig!" Then the teacher can use the vocabulary that comes out of the performance to teach reading. Teachers can write these statements on a board and ask people to read them back. This teaches well how reading has meaning.

4. Ask local artists to illustrate a picture book or posters of community activities such as planting, growing, harvesting a crop, visiting a friend, knitting, or making a meal. Ask literacy students to tell you the steps needed to complete the activity, or the recipe for the food. Ask them to read the board back to you together. This connects literacy with life.

5. Ask students to draw pictures of community activities and write a simple sentence about the picture.

6. Ask students to write a song to go with pictures, events, or stories. Ask the students to read the song's words while you all sing the new song together.

Turn Orature into Literature

People need literature in their local language on a wide range of topics to motivate them to become literate. This activity shows you how to transcribe the texts of oral arts like songs, stories, or riddles to provide motivation for reading and to broaden the range of available reading materials in the local language.

Participants
Work with literacy specialists, experts in genres with high verbal content, and visual artists.

Kinds of things you'll need from the Community Arts Profile
Familiarity with genres containing significant elements of oral verbal arts.

Resources needed
Dependent on the local context.

Tasks

1. To make the easiest reading materials, transcribe local folktales, songs, and proverbs people already know. It is important to record our cultural heritage so that the next generation does not forget our wisdom.

2. Make a second level of literacy materials by recording personal stories and writing them down, or else train local authors to write their own experience stories. We can learn from one another's experiences.

A calendar showing an important event that takes place each month would be a good communal experience story (e.g., in March the rains come [or whatever happens in that month], so we ... [whatever we do in that month]). A song could be created to go with this too.

3. Make a third level of literacy materials by asking local authors to teach new content in local terms, and by training creative authors to imagine stories that have not happened. People want to know many kinds of things and imagine many kinds of stories, so different types of materials need to be created to interest as wide an audience as possible. We can learn by imagining how things can change, and by learning new information from outside our culture, expressed by local authors in our culture's ways. We can also create new songs and dramas and write them down for presentations. What community events need new songs and dramas whose words we can write down and teach?

4. Make a fourth level of reading materials by asking local translators to translate important works such as Scripture or health information that comes from another culture.

5. Ask a local artist to illustrate all these kinds of materials, using visual rules of the community.

6. Test all materials with a small audience of at least three people before teaching them to a larger audience. Make sure literacy materials are clear, accurate, natural, acceptable, and interesting. After testing, revise the material before presenting it to a larger audience.

7. Distribute the finished materials to literacy programs and community leaders. Make sure important people know where the materials are available for purchase. Advertise materials via public enactments or media.

Integrate Local Arts into Educational Curricula

Participants
Work with mother-tongue teachers, local arts experts, and school directors.[17]

Kinds of things you'll need from the Community Arts Profile
A list of artistic genres ("Take a First Glance at a Community's Arts," Conversation 1) and initial comparison ("First Glance Genre Comparison Chart," Conversation 3).

Resources needed
Dependent on the local context.

Tasks

1. Look together at the school's curriculum.
2. Look together at the local art forms that carry meaning within various cultural contexts. Discuss and plan ways to integrate cultural knowledge and materials into specific parts of the curriculum.

---

17 See M. B. Saurman, "Culturally Relevant Songs" and *Hmong Songs in Education*.

Here are some examples of integrating a local genre that uses stitching into existing school classes:

- **Cultural studies:** traditional stitching patterns and their meaning.
- **Reading:** a story about a mother stitching a traditional outfit for her daughter to wear for New Year's Day.
- **Writing:** have a community expert come into class and talk about the traditional dress and stitching patterns; then have students write a creative story about this experience.
- **Science:** take the students to collect leaves and berries, then demonstrate how to color cotton through traditional dyeing techniques.
- **Math:** cut various lengths of dyed string used for stitching and have children measure the lengths.

3. Evaluate the success of these methods with teachers and other school personnel.

SCRIPTURE

Local artistic forms of communication feed into Bible translation in many ways.[18] Literature, discussions, and presentations providing conceptual frameworks and guidance in using local arts in the process of Bible translation are bourgeoning.[19] This growing interest derives in part from a spreading, deepening recognition that many (if not most) biblical source texts have strong characteristics of artistic genres, such as those related to songs, stories, poems, parables, histories, and proverbs. Attending to these artistic genres during the translation process can help make the final written translation communicate more like the original did. Also contributing is the development of methods and tools to produce oral translations that communicate more effectively where non-written forms are necessary.

A growing body of literature describes methods to connect biblical genres with local genres during translation.[20] Some organizations are also integrating

---

18 Frost has drafted a guide to applying each of the CLAT Conversations to Bible translation processes, which has been used by Arts for a Better Future participants and organizers. Available in the Digital Library (www.clatmanual.com).

19 Frost provides a compelling rationale for engaging local arts as part of translation projects in her article "Why Consider Local Genres in Translation?"

20 Examples include Beil, "Genre Analysis and Translation"; De Vries, "The Notion of Genre"; Dickie "Community Translation and Oral Performance" and "Translating Psalms for Performance"; Green, "An Orality Strategy"; Salisbury, "Translating the Psalms"; Unseth, "Analyzing and Using Receptor Language" and "Receptor Language Proverb Forms"; Wendland, "An Overview," *Studies in the Psalms, LiFE-Style Translating, Translating the Literature of Scripture*; and Zogbo & Wendland, *Hebrew Poetry in the Bible*.

and supporting ethnoarts-informed approaches for Bible translation.[21] A critical gap in current resources is a comprehensive analysis of each passage of Scripture through a genre lens. The need is urgent. In the meantime, however, some genre-related helps for translators exist.[22]

Because Scripture is a bedrock of our faith, we must apply especially rigorous standards and bring in translation consultants and other experts when necessary. In this manual, make sure to draw on "Interpret Scripture Well" and "Address Theological Objections" in Conversation 4, Part D, and all of Conversation 6—Improve Results.

Hold a Scripture Translation Workshop

The purpose of this workshop is to produce high-quality translations of selected Bible portions by drawing on characteristics of local art forms. Such a workshop is helpful when a community is ready to translate Scripture that has significant artistic characteristics in the original languages, such as songs (e.g., Psalms, Mary's song, Moses's and Miriam's songs), parables, and proverbs. The community gathers participants for one to two weeks to (1) evaluate their song and poetry genres as potential guides for target poetic forms of translations, and (2) render certain passages with characteristics of these local genres.

Participants
Include Bible translators, experts in song and poetic artistic genres, and spiritual leaders.

Kinds of things you'll need from the Community Arts Profile
You can prepare to integrate the arts into a Scripture Translation Workshop by performing the research described in the Oral Verbal Arts section in Conversation 4, Part B.

Resources needed
Dependent on the local context.

Tasks
You will contribute to both the planning and execution of such a workshop.
Planning. During the planning phase, you will help

1. identify artistic features of the biblical source text(s). A good place to start is by noting how biblical languages mark parallel lines—parts of a text related to each other by similarity, building one on the other, or contrast.

---

21 Among others, these currently include organizations such as these: Psalms: Layer by Layer (https://psalms.scriptura.world/w/Welcome); SIL Ethnoarts (https://ethnoarts.sil.org); Translation Toward Transformation (https://translationtowardtransformation.org); and Wycliffe South Africa (https://wycliffe.org.za/what-we-do/bible-storytelling) are just a few organizations that may provide practical help.

22 These include viewing the whole canon as literature. See, for example, Alter and Kermode, *Literary Guide to the Bible*; Fokkelman, *Reading Biblical Poetry*; Frost and Harper, "Processing Pain through Artistry"; Ouahaibi, *Psalms of Passion for God*; Pluger, "Translating Proverb-like Sayings"; and Van der Lugt, *Cantos and Strophes*.

Spark Creativity

2. evaluate local artistic genres that exist in the target language for significant overlap of connotations, functions, and content with the biblical source genres.
3. find artists who have skills in the local genres with the most potential to inform translation. In simplified terms, poets should be part of the team that translates poetic sections of Scripture, storytellers for stories, and skilled users of proverbs for translating proverbs. It's important for leaders to invite these artists so they can provide skilled, knowledgeable input.

Execution. During the workshop, you

1. will study and describe the features of the target artistic genres. Co-occurring boundaries between text and tune are the most common poetic features in the world. So the first thing to do is find functional equivalents of the line between biblical and target poetic features. Meter is very common.
2. will lead a process by which participants decide how these features should best inform target forms of the written Bible translation.
3. may also work with the artists to commission new works based on the translated Scripture that they can integrate into their communities' lives.

Like all workshops, leaders should plan for activities that enhance group unity, and provide theological grounding and chances for spiritual transformation. You may enter any of these other aspects of the workshop according to your gifts and the leaders' needs.

Note that you can also apply these same principles in contributing to a translation team in their daily work. So when a team begins to translate orally based passages like Psalms or Proverbs, you can serve as a resource. You can help them look at the poetic features of the biblical language, examine poetic features of local art forms, and help them figure out how to connect the two. Often the best method of connecting the two is to record, listen, and re-record as improvements are suggested. Once a good oral draft is made, it can be written down.

An additional benefit to making full use of artistic features in Bible translation is this: if translators create written translations of the Scripture that have characteristics of local artistic genres, the steps to creating additional Scripture products will be shorter and clearer. Composers with the task of creating Scripture songs will bless you.

Commission an Oral Narrative Enactment of Scripture

Participants

Include trusted Christian leaders and Bible expositors and experts in the oral narrative genre you choose.

Kinds of things you'll need from the Community Arts Profile
You will want to know as much as you can about genres that include significant verbal content. Refer to "Oral Verbal Arts Features in Enactments and Events" (Conversation 4, Part B).

Resources needed
Dependent on the local context.

Tasks

1. Choose a biblical story.
2. Choose a local oral narrative genre.
3. Identify a local oral narrative genre expert.
4. Describe features of the genre, guided by "Look Through Seven Basic Lenses" (Conversation 4, Part A), and "Oral Verbal Arts Features in Enactments and Events" (Conversation 4, Part B).
5. Commission an expert to create a new story. Discuss the biblical text with the composer in detail and ask him or her to communicate that same story in the local oral narrative genre you've identified.
6. Critique and improve the new work, especially in terms of aesthetic quality, clarity, and accuracy of the message.
7. Integrate into existing enactment venues.

CHURCH LIFE

Among many additional benefits, arts can help the body of Christ worship God with their whole lives, engage with Scripture together, contextualize God-honoring rituals, introduce people to Jesus, and mature as Christ's beautiful bride. Here are a few ways this can happen.

To frame your thoughts, remember that local churches usually relate to people in their geographical surroundings and to larger, historically connected Christian movements. It's therefore crucial to gain an understanding of the art forms used to communicate in both contexts. With this background understanding, the church can decide which forms they should use to work toward various Kingdom Goals. "Encourage Churches to Integrate Artistry More Holistically" (Conversation 4, Part D) outlines these kinds of explorations.

In a vibrant Christian community in Cameroon, distrust had developed between pastors and worship leaders. Neither group believed the other understood or respected the importance of its ministry. Pastor and musician Roch Ntankeh, a man respected by both groups, orchestrated a service of crying out to God, repentance, forgiveness, and reconciliation. Pastors and worship leaders kneeled and cried in front of their brothers and sisters, granting forgiveness and restoring relationships.

Hold a Corporate Worship Workshop

In this activity, artists and leaders in a local congregation or group of congregations meet to figure out how to worship better together. This could happen during a week-long gathering, a series of weekly meetings, or other time frame that meets the community's needs. In the case of multiple congregations, the workshop includes sessions when everyone is gathered, and times when delegations meet separately to discuss issues, create, and plan for their unique contexts.

Mindsets

To increase the likelihood of positive outcomes, as far as possible, leaders should plan activities that support

- **Group cohesion.** We want to create a context of hospitality, mutual aid and support, common vision and mission, in accordance with local social norms.

- **Theological or ideological grounding.** When appropriate to the workshop, we want participants to know biblical foundations for use of the arts and be able to communicate these to others in compelling ways when needed. If the community does not recognize the Bible as authoritative, you may use other books or ideas to provide conceptual foundations.

- **Spiritual transformation.** When done in a Christian context, we want to help participants and instructors understand this work as ministry, to be open to God's conviction and anointing, and to leave with a new or renewed sense of their gifts and roles in the expansion of God's Kingdom.

These elements can be crucial. For example, workshops marked by participants who don't get along have ended in failure if interpersonal conflicts are not addressed. God often uses Arts with God activities to infuse love and peace into workshops—consult the Tool in 4D and our Digital Library (www.clatmanual.com) for many examples and guides.

Participants

Make sure you include experts in local artistic genres, respected church leaders, representatives of as many age and ethnic groups in the community as possible, and others with spiritual and organizational influence in the church.

Kinds of things you'll need from the Community Arts Profile

These activities will have you drawing on and adding to the list and descriptions of genres in the church, as well as those used in the surrounding community. A good goal would be to record answers to the questions in "Take a First Glance at an Event" (Conversation 4, Part A) for each genre, make preliminary comparisons ("First Glance Genre Comparison Chart," Conversation 3), and "Discover a Christian Community's Arts" for the church (Conversation 4, Part D). The more of this information you have before the workshop, the less time you'll need to devote to basic data gathering while it's happening.

Resources needed

Dependent on the local context.

Tasks

1. **Plan the event.** A team that includes church leaders, artists, and an arts advocate (someone like you) should plan the event. Use Figure 5.3 (on next page) to guide your planning. This team will choose the people best suited to perform each task. The rest of these steps occur during the workshop.

2. **Orient the participants.** With the participants, discuss logistics, finances, transport, schedule, and the workshop's purposes, outcomes, products, and guidelines for evaluation and improvement (Conversation 6).

3. **Explore biblical foundations.**[23] Describe biblical and conceptual foundations of arts in the Kingdom of Heaven, choosing from the following and/or developing your own:
   a. "All the Arts, From All the World, For All of God's Kingdom" (from the "Prepare Yourself" chapter at the beginning of this manual).
   b. "Interpret Scripture Well" and "Address Theological Objections" (Conversation 4, Part D).

4. **Address any disruptive community problems.** There may be a history of miscommunication and misunderstanding between artists, missionaries, pastors, or others in this community. If so, pray, confess to each other, and forgive one another.

5. **Identify the church's arts.** Make a list of each Christian community's arts using "Discover a Christian Community's Arts" (Conversation 4, Part D).

6. **Identify the surrounding community's arts.** Consult a list of artistic genres in the surrounding community or create it using "Take a First Glance at a Community's Arts" (Conversation 1).

7. **Evaluate the church's arts.** Follow the guide, "Evaluate How a Christian Community's Arts Currently Fulfill Its Purposes" (Conversation 4, Part D). Also, examine each art according to the origins of its elements, using Figure 4.6 in "Creativity" (Conversation 4, Part C). Focus on questions like these: How could the church's purposes in corporate gatherings be improved through better use of its arts? Does the meeting communicate clearly to each group within the community? Are people's hearts, souls, minds, and bodies deeply engaged and moved in corporate adoration?

8. **Choose a purpose.** Choose one or more of these purposes to focus on for the rest of the workshop. You may want to use "A Tool to Help People Choose Kingdom Goals" we outline in Conversation 2.

9. **Choose an art form.** Refer to Conversation 3 to help decide whether some artistic forms could be added, removed, or modified to better meet the purposes of your gatherings. Choose one or more of these for further development.

10. **Create.** Have groups of artists and spiritual leaders create or adapt works in these forms to accomplish the purposes identified earlier.

---

[23] See also Krabill et al., eds., *Ethnodoxology Handbook* (especially the Foundations and Stories sections).

11. **Celebrate and integrate.** Discuss local and wider community authority structures and decide the best ways to integrate these innovations into church life. These plans should include specific media and dates and locations for enactment and distribution. Conversation 7 will be helpful in this process. If possible, introduce the new works at a larger community event at the end of the workshop. Implement the plans for further integration and celebration, underlining the importance of humility.

Sample Corporate Worship Workshop Schedule[24]

Figure 5.3 outlines a week-long workshop schedule that has been used successfully for promoting local artistic genres' use in church worship.[25] Conversation 4D contains resources that can be integrated into church-based workshops.

	Sunday	Monday	Tuesday	Wednesday	Thursday	Friday	Saturday
08:00		Arts with God	Arts with God	Arts with God	Arts with God	Arts with God	Arts with God
08:30		01 Intro to the workshop	05 Biblical teaching about worship	09 Methods of creating new works	12 Using instruments ———— Fusions	15 Plan for integration	18 Final recording, workshop evaluations
10:00		Break	Break	Break	Break	Break	
10:30		02 Artistic genres	06 Diversity of gifts Bible study	10 Worship Wheel ———— Choose a theme and Scripture verses for a composition	13 Improve our creations ———— Poetic form, critiquing songs	16 Groups select new works and prepare for recording	Collect evaluations, distribute travel money (per diem)
12:30		Meal	Meal	Meal	Meal	Meal	
14:30	Opening Ceremony	03 Formal characteristics of a genre	07 Intro to composition	11 Groups compose & record	14 Groups critique & improve their creations; record	17 Final recording/ evaluation	Closing ceremony
15:30		04 Evaluation of artistic genres for use in church worship	11 Groups compose & record				
16:30	Meal	Meal	Meal	Meal	Meal	Meal	

Figure 5.3 Sample corporate worship workshop schedule

---

24 Many people use *Community Arts for God's Purposes*—a condensation of this manual—as a text for arts workshops in a growing number of languages.

25 Adapted from Mary Beth and Todd Saurman, "Principles for Leading Ethnomusicology Workshops."

Help Preachers and Teachers Incorporate More Local Arts

In this activity, trainers and motivators in a Christian community gather. They explore how they can integrate more of their community's arts into their preaching and teaching.

Participants
Experts in local artistic genres, pastors, preachers, teachers, and larger community gatekeepers.

Kinds of things you'll need from the Community Arts Profile
You will want to know as much as you can about genres that include significant verbal content. Refer to "Oral Verbal Arts Features in Enactments and Events" (Conversation 4, Part B).

Resources needed
Dependent on the local context.

Tasks

1. Gather everyone in a Christian community involved in teaching and preaching at any level. This could be an informal meeting confined to a local congregation.

2. Show the list of local artistic genres you prepared in Conversation 1. Add any previously forgotten ones to the Community Arts Profile. Note especially those with strong verbal content, such as genres that tell stories, enact dramas, or present oratory or proverbs.

3. Have each participant tell which, if any, of these genres they have integrated into their preaching or teaching. How did it work?

4. Discuss which of the genres seem to be most promising in communicating scriptural truths in memorable, penetrating ways.

5. Together, help each other plan to incorporate one new genre into their preaching or teaching within a reasonable time frame.

6. Gather after participants have had a chance to try their innovation, and discuss difficulties, successes, and ideas for further use.

7. Plan to discuss the use of local genres in training the church at regular community meetings.

Hold an Artistic Genre Workshop

In this activity, Christian leaders choose a particular artistic genre they want to help develop for Kingdom purposes. They then gather creators and performers in this genre to produce new, Scripture-infused examples of the genre and explore potential purposes for them. In some ways, this activity ignores the Conversation 1, Conversation 2, … Conversation 7 approaches and leads you to just start making stuff and see where it goes. Arts can spread in ways you never imagine.

Participants

Include experts in the artistic genre, respected church leaders, representatives from a church congregation, and facilitators of the workshop.

Kinds of things you'll need from the Community Arts Profile

It would be great to have a Corporate Worship Workshop (above) before this workshop for a community. In the Corporate Worship Workshop, participants identify the artistic genres that are currently used in the church and list the arts of the community. They also evaluate the church's arts and decide together which artistic genres they want to develop more for the corporate worship of the church. To identify potential purposes of the arts, there needs to be preliminary research to find what purposes the current arts in the church are fulfilling and what purposes are not being fulfilled by arts.

Resources needed

Dependent on the local context.

Tasks

1. **Preparation meeting:** Church leaders and facilitators meet to choose one or more artistic genres they want to develop based on the evaluation of the church's arts and discuss potential purposes for new arts that will be created in the workshop.
2. **Plan the workshop:** Facilitators of the workshop set the dates and place that key leaders and artists can come for the workshop and communicate the purpose of the workshop to those who are invited in advance.
3. **Orient the participants:** With the participants, discuss logistics, finances, transport, schedule, the workshop's purposes, outcomes, products, and guidelines for evaluation.
4. **Explore potential purposes of this artistic genre:** In small groups or open discussions, (a) discuss what purposes this art form has been used for in the church, (b) evaluate the present use of the art form, and (c) discuss what kind of new materials the participants need to develop or what other purposes can be fulfilled through this art form.
5. **Choose purposes:** Decide one purpose or more depending on the number of participants. If there is a big number of participants, divide the group into small groups to work for various purposes of this art form.
6. **Create together:** Artists can bring their unfinished works if they already have an idea or have started to create before the workshop, and they can work together with other artists to cocreate new materials. They can consult church leaders and congregation representatives on deciding Scripture verses that are the basis for the creation.
7. **Presentation and evaluation:** If it is a big group, each small group can present what they created and invite evaluation and feedback. If it is a small group, they can present it to the church leaders and congregation

representatives and get feedback from them. Evaluate together if the new materials will fulfill the purposes they decided together. Revise the works based on the feedback.

8. **Plan for integration and celebration:** Discuss how these new arts can best be integrated in church services. Discuss what kind of church events can be a good channel to introduce the new materials and share them with the rest of the congregation. Decide when, where, and how they will perform the new creations.

Hold an Arts Creation Workshop on Worldview Themes

The purpose of this activity is to employ artistic communication to address difficult issues at the intersection of Christian truths and local community beliefs and practices. We're using genres containing songs as an example. However, genres containing other elements like proverbs, storytelling, drama, and visual communication could speak to such problems just as well.

Participants
Include composers, pastors, and denominational leaders.

Kinds of things you'll need from the Community Arts Profile

1. Choose genres containing song from the Community Arts Profile.

2. Through observation and discussions with various levels of the community, ask the question, "In our community, what areas are the most difficult to live out as a follower of Christ?" We have chosen four areas for this example. In light of these, ask, "What do community members believe about birth, death, how to make a living, and male and female relationships?" Record answers.

Resources needed
Dependent on the local context.

Tasks

1. Discuss with church leaders that the purpose of the workshop is to compose Scripture-based songs in traditional and church styles that address non-Christian worldview issues. Ask for their authorization and for their ideas concerning location and dates to hold the workshop.

2. With these church leaders, identify song genres participants will be composing in, and form a team of local artists gifted in those genres.

3. Form a planning team to prepare for promotion, costs, travel information, the formation of a local organization team, and other logistics.

4. Write up a flyer explaining about the workshop and distribute it.

5. Send a letter to central church leaders with a schedule for travel and the workshop.

6. One month before the workshop, contact the central church leader for a list of names of those attending.

7. Make travel arrangements, prepare materials, and practice lessons with team teachers.
8. One week before the workshop, contact the local organizing director to make sure all is in order (lodging, food arrangements, teaching area, blackboard, etc.).
9. Travel with the team to workshop destination, arriving the Sunday before the workshop is scheduled to begin.
10. Present the goals of the workshop in the Sunday morning worship service to elicit prayer and encourage participation.
11. Sunday afternoon before the workshop, hold a time of prayer with local church leaders for the workshop, discuss the schedule and general plans for the workshop, and adjust as needed after receiving local input.
12. Present workshop overview (six days plus Sunday morning presentation):
    a. Remind participants that God uses Scripture to affirm some parts of every culture and challenge others. This workshop is about beliefs and practices in our community that need to be addressed scripturally and through prayer.
    b. Discuss local community worldview on issues of birth, death, making a living, and male and female relationships.
    c. Follow the "Careful Contextualization" tool in Conversation 4, Part D.
    d. Divide the entire group into four groups and compose one song on each of the four categories each day (alternate categories each day among the groups).
    e. Each evening, include a time of critique (self, community) around the fire as songs are sung and taught.
    f. Perform a consultant critique before recording songs on Saturday afternoon.
    g. Sunday morning in church, present the new songs and celebrate them!

Organize an All Arts Celebration

Plan a concert, festival, or other big event that showcases all the artistic gifts represented by members of a Christian community.

Participants

Include Christian artists, pastors, organizers, and the Christian community.

Kinds of things you'll need from the Community Arts Profile

In addition to the list of artistic genres, arts appropriate for communication in the church should be identified. Also identify who in the church can participate in these arts.

Resources needed
Dependent on the local context.

Tasks

1. Church community members work together to discover what artistic genres and styles are known within the church.
2. Local pastors, Christian artists, and organizers meet to discuss and plan the event: location, time, day, and who will be involved.
3. Artistic works may be commissioned specifically for this event.
4. If culturally appropriate, some arts could involve the whole community (i.e., improvised dramas with spect-actors, sing-alongs, dancing, dress).
5. Make the event a celebration of God's creativity and the gifts he's given this community.

Study the Bible in More than One Form as a Group

We remember Scripture better when we study the message in more than one format. This activity describes how to lead a Bible study that includes multiple formats, including print Scripture; song, poetry, drama, and other types of Scripture-infused enactments; and audio or visual recordings of Scripture.[26]

Participants
Choose a wise, respected leader with Bible knowledge. Also include people gifted in local art forms and people who want to study Scripture.

Kinds of things you'll need from the Community Arts Profile
This activity requires a list of genres of artistic communication to evaluate for use in a Bible study. Explore "Arts With God" in the Digital Library.

Resources needed
Dependent on the local context.

Tasks

1. Decide how often, when, and where the group will meet. This activity assumes a weekly meeting, but this could vary widely.
2. Introduce how this type of group Bible study functions socially.[27] Leading a Bible study group is much different than preaching a sermon. Being part of a Bible study is more like playing together on a soccer team. The leader is like a coach who helps people train regularly without exhausting or injuring themselves. He works to strengthen his team's muscles. A Bible study leader works to strengthen the group's spiritual muscles by helping them remember Scripture and think about how to apply it to their own lives.

---

26 See also Hill and Hill, *Translating the Bible into Action*.

27 For discussions of related study groups, see Kohls and Brussow, *Training Know-How*; and Reagan, *Non-Western Educational Traditions*.

3. The leader gathers existing resources on the Scripture passage the group will study. These could be printed versions in local or regional languages, concordances, songs that contain the Scripture, etc. Here is a sample of the first weeks of a multi-form Bible study:

   - **Week 1:** Study the passage with available resources.

   - **Week 2:** List the artistic genres that exist in the church and surrounding community, using "Take a First Glance at a Community's Arts" (Conversation 1). Evaluate each of these genres for possible use in the study using "Take a First Glance at an Event" and "First Glance Comparison Chart" (Conversation 3). Choose one genre that could relate the Scripture passage, and commission one or more people within the group to create such a new work. The genre could be one that includes musical, dramatic, visual, oral verbal (e.g., storytelling), or dance elements.

   - **Week 3:** Participants share their creations, teach them to the others when possible, and tell how the process has impacted them. Discuss ways that they could be improved (see Conversation 6).

   - **Other weeks:** Choose genres with different kinds of artistic features in them, especially dramatic, storytelling, and visual. Again, participants create new works inspired by the Scripture, share them the following week, teach them to the others when possible, and tell how the process has impacted them.

   - **Explore occasions for enactment or presentation** of the new works together. Who else may benefit from the new works? Discuss together different ways that everyone can share what they have created with their neighbors, a school, or the wider church community.

4. If the Bible study continues, remember to ask these kinds of questions:

   - What Scripture means a lot to us, and what purpose does it have in our community? How can our (wider) community learn what we've learned?

   - Who is our audience for this performance or object? How much do they already know about our message? Is our presentation of Scripture clear, accurate, and natural for them? We don't want to change the meaning (lexical, iconic, or indexical) of Scripture. We may need to change elements of how we communicate Scripture so people will understand it better or feel more keenly attuned to the importance of God's message.

   - What forms fit our purpose well? Remember, people will retain more if they experience the message in more than one way.

   - What is the main idea we hope people understand? Is this the main idea emphasized by the enactment?

Improve a Current Church Ceremony, Ritual, or Practice

This activity was developed with a particular Central African church community's baptism practice in mind. You may adapt it to other church activities such as weddings, communion, funerals, and others.

Participants

Include church leaders, those desiring to receive baptism, parents and family members, and church members. Depending on the cultural context, consider working with church leaders before including others.

Kinds of things you'll need from the Community Arts Profile

Analyze current practices of baptism as larger events containing subevents, performing the research in Shape through Time (Conversation 4, Part A). Explore catechism training (who teaches, how they teach, what materials are available for teaching and for the students to use to learn, physical labor and gifts required of the candidates, the role of the arts, other activities done during their training), any exam at the end of training, preparations for the celebration, the actual baptismal service, and any other services.

List the genres of local arts used during the current baptism practices (song, marching and dancing, musical instruments, clothing, etc.). Explore the ritual nature of the event: importance of carefully following particular actions, the place of the baptism, the march to the water source and the return, who participates and how.

Resources needed

Dependent on the local context.

Tasks

1. With a small group of various levels of church leaders and qualified lay people (both men and women), specify the Kingdom Goals that the event really is supposed to represent. Ask questions like these: What strengths are there in the present ceremony? What weaknesses? Examine traditional circumcision practices as well as traditional birth and burial celebrations to see if any parallels can be made to the baptism experience. Discuss the current teaching program to determine what results it produces.

2. At regional church leaders' meetings, discuss the pros and cons of the present baptism practice using the results of the small group discussions as a springboard.

3. Select a commission to study the issue; include at least one senior pastor, one trained theologian, one Bible school teacher, a leader of a women's group, and pastors from both rural and town churches.

4. Ask questions like these of the commission (refer to "Evaluate How a Christian Community's Arts Currently Fulfill Its Purposes," Conversation 4, Part D):

5. What Kingdom Goal is reached through a baptism service?
    a. How well is the present practice meeting that goal?
    b. How effective is the material being taught?
    c. How effective is the teaching method?
    d. What percentage of the newly baptized are still active in the church after one year? After two years? Why do those who are no longer active fall away?
    e. What are the most important biblical principles that need to be taught to the new converts?
    f. What recommendations does the commission have for changes in the program?
    g. How could artistic forms of communication (e.g., local types of song, dance, storytelling, and proverbs) be used to make the process of learning the catechism and celebrating baptism more effective and the message better understood?
6. At the next regional church leaders' meetings, present the commission's findings. Delegate the responsibility to this commission to revise the baptism rite in the following ways:
    a. Develop a catechism program based on Bible teaching lessons through local storytelling:[28] candidates memorize Bible stories, proverbs, and verses for each main lesson in the current catechism; candidates compose new Scripture-based songs for each main lesson; some candidates learn to embroider a key word for each main lesson onto a scarf; other candidates learn how to wood burn a key word for each main lesson into a mortar or chair or plaque.
    b. Seek approval for the new program from leaders at all levels of church hierarchy.
    c. Produce a catechism guide in languages used in the community and wider church community, briefly detailing each point of each main lesson. Use sketches, pictures, and diagrams to supplement and clarify the text.
    d. Plan workshops for pastors, catechists, deacons, and women's group leaders to teach them the new material in a way that they will be able to repeat in their home churches.
    e. Pray for and find funding to assist with food at workshops and for printing new catechism guides.
    f. At workshops, determine which local art forms will help exemplify the true meanings of baptism at the actual ceremony and how that can be done well (drama, instrumental music, vocal music, marching to the water and back again, clothing the candidates wear, the receiving line when they come out of the water, etc.).

---
28 Walters, "Tell Me a Story" (Parts 1 and 2).

g. Help the pastors and catechists draw up plans as to when and how they are going to begin to incorporate these new teachings into their catechism program and to teach it to their church members.

h. At the end of the workshop, include a time of commissioning/dedicating those who will be teaching the new program.

7. With the commission members, determine evaluation procedures.
8. Pray that it will all come together to bring about a change in the spiritual life of the church!

Hold a Contest for New Ways to Memorize Scripture

Institute a competition for the best new work communicating a given Scripture passage in a local artistic genre.[29] The process will include explorations on how to create, to what degree texts can be modified to fit the form, and other issues relevant to the creative process.

Participants

In the planning phase, include Christian leaders and competent performers of several local artistic genres, including the young people. The competition phase could be opened to the entire community. The judges will include spiritual and artistic leaders.

Kinds of things you'll need from the Community Arts Profile

The survey of artistic genres produced in Conversation 1, and "Creativity" (Conversation 4, Part C).

Resources needed

Dependent on the local context.

Tasks

1. With a planning team:
   a. List the artistic genres known to be available in the community.
   b. Discuss the importance of integrating Scripture into all aspects of people's lives, studying the biblical texts in "Studying and Remembering Scripture" (Conversation 2).
   c. Design the competition according to community approaches to critique, based on research you've performed in "Aesthetics and Evaluation" (4c) and on authority structures. Choose judges prayerfully and carefully, making sure to include people who are acknowledged experts in Scripture and local artistic genres. Choose prizes and figure out finances.
2. Communicate through available media (posters, radio, texts, local artistic genres, Internet, etc.):
   a. Purposes of the event (including to find new ways to remember Scripture, and to raise awareness of God's artistic gifts to the community).

---

29 See Barz, *Performing Religion*, and Hill & Hill, *Translating the Bible into Action*.

Spark Creativity

   b. Participants' tasks: Choose a need or dream that the community has now, Scripture in the community's language that addresses that need or dream, and a kind of traditional art form (at least their grandparents' generation created in it). Make something new in the genre with the Scripture as its content.
   c. Date, time, and other logistics.
   d. Determine judging criteria:
      i. Is the content and importance of the Scripture maintained? Some incidental words may be changed to fit the form of the genre, but not the core message.
      ii. How well does the chosen Scripture speak to a need, problem, or dream of the community?
      iii. Has the genre existed in the community for at least two generations? (If you are not focusing on deeply rooted genres, you can omit this stipulation.)
      iv. Is the creative output an excellent example of the genre?
3. Execute the plan. This will need to coincide with community norms and calendrical cycles.

Commission Arts for Community Events

The goal of this activity is to commission an excellent example of a local artistic genre that (1) carries scriptural content that speaks to community needs, and (2) can be performed at a familiar community event.

Participants
Choose wise Christians, expert composers, and performers.

Kinds of things you'll need from the Community Arts Profile
This activity requires having a list of artistic genres within a community, and knowing how people create new works within them; see Figure 3.2.

Resources needed
Dependent on the local context.

Tasks

1. With a group of Christ-followers and people experienced in local artistic traditions, evaluate existing artistic genres according to their potential for communicating scriptural truth. Guided by the list of artistic genres in the Community Arts Profile, start asking questions like these about each genre: Does it have spiritual, social, or sexual connotations? What kind of content does it communicate? How many people know how to create new examples in this genre?
2. List and discuss upcoming events according to their potential for connecting with many and/or influential people, and possibilities for entering their planning and execution.

3. Reflect on biblical truths and stories most likely to connect with community concerns. Decide on a concern and a Scripture passage that speaks to that concern.
4. Decide on an artistic genre that could carry this message well.
5. Explore how new works are created within this genre, based on research you've performed in "Creativity" (Conversation 4, Part C).
6. Identify an expert or experts in the genre. Meet and ask him or her to create a new example of the genre. Observe or enter into their normal processes of creation.
7. Through live enactment or audio or video recording, present the new work to spiritual leaders and experts in the genre for critique and improvement. Evaluate according to biblical fidelity, communicational clarity, and meeting standards of the genre derived through the seven basic lenses (Conversation 4, Part A).
8. Work with the creator to improve any shortcomings.
9. Perform or display the work at the event.

PERSONAL SPIRITUAL LIFE

Among many additional benefits, arts can help people energize and deepen their communication with God, adopt disciplines leading to long-term spiritual growth, understand and apply Scripture better, and flourish as Christ-followers. Here are a few ways this can happen.

Encourage People to Commune with God through Multiple Arts

Many Christians tend to communicate with God primarily by sitting and reading Scripture. Others are unsure how to incorporate times of reflection and communication with God into their lives at all. This activity introduces people to other forms of communication at a prayer retreat, and helps participants plan to integrate arts into their times with God.

Participants
Gather members of a Christian congregation, pastors, and church leaders.

Kinds of things you'll need from the Community Arts Profile
Perform "Discover a Christian Community's Arts" (Conversation 4, Part D).

Resources needed
Dependent on the local context.

Tasks
1. Have pastors and church leaders choose a theme for the prayer retreat that will encourage the church in relevant ways.
2. Plan logistics of the retreat: location, time, etc.

3. Consult artistic church members to create activities or prayer stations where the attendees can pray and meditate using arts that are familiar and meaningful to the culture. These could include art forms with special vocal features, dance, poetry, storytelling, acting, song, and others.

4. Invite church members to come to the retreat.

5. As a final activity, have participants plan one way they will enliven their communion with God with some form of artistry.

Mentor Someone in More Arts-Infused Spiritual Disciplines

Participants
Bring together someone who is mature and still eager to learn, and someone younger in the faith. Encourage mentoring relationships between people only after much prayer and discussion.

Kinds of things you'll need from the Community Arts Profile
Investigate community patterns of mentoring relationships.

Resources needed
Dependent on the local context.

Tasks
As part of the mentoring relationship, explore some of the following practices together, adapting them to fit local art forms. Calhoun's *Spiritual Disciplines Handbook* provides excellent, practical introductions to these and more.[30] Also, St. Mary's Press has published a series called *Companions for the Journey* with practices from many noted Christians.

Here are some examples:

1. Follow liturgical calendars. Many larger church communities have developed yearly patterns of readings, poetry, and prayer. *The Book of Common Prayer* is one example.

2. Integrate singing into fixed-hour prayers. Some traditions identify certain times of the day as appropriate for certain kinds of prayer and meditation. *The Divine Hours*, by Phyllis Tickle, has made this accessible to many people.[31] Create your own chants or melodies for the psalms and hymns.

3. Use imaginative contemplation in Bible study. Often influenced by the life and writings of Ignatius of Loyola (1491–1556), some Christians integrate their imaginations into the study of Scripture. They read a story about Jesus and then imagine themselves in the scene, seeing, smelling, tasting, hearing the actions, and waiting for what Jesus might say to them.

4. Encourage the mentee to experiment with other forms of artistry while communing with God, including those that contain dance, journaling, story writing, drawing, singing, painting, and anything else that the individual can use to express himself or herself to God.

---

30 Calhoun, *Spiritual Disciplines Handbook*.
31 Tickle, *The Divine Hours*.

Commission a Verbal Art Form of Resolve that Will Help People Apply Scriptural Truths to Their Lives

Artistic forms of communication help us remember truth, but they can also help people move us to act on that truth. "I Am Determined to Walk with Jesus" is a song in African American churches that fills this role.

Participants
Include both artists and spiritual leaders.

Kinds of things you'll need from the Community Arts Profile
Refer to a list of genres that exist in the community.

Tasks

1. Examine each genre for how well it can communicate resolve, fortitude, determination, and similar emotions. Choose one.
2. Commission an excellent composer in that genre to create a new work that encourages people to love and obey Jesus no matter what.
3. Have the composer present his or her creation to a small group of spiritual and artistic leaders in the community for affirmation and improvement (see Conversation 6).
4. Introduce and teach the new composition to the wider community, asking God to bring it to people's minds when they are losing their focus on Jesus.

PERFORM THE ACTIVITY AND DESCRIBE THE RESULTS

Do what you and the community planned. Hold your plans lightly. Listen to God. Learn from mistakes. Enjoy the process. Describe what happens in the Community Arts Profile. Enough said.

CONVERSATION 6

IMPROVE RESULTS

We want communities to integrate creativity into their lives in such a way that their Kingdom Goals are met, maybe even exceeded. Conversations 2, 3, and 5 should have awakened everyone in the CLAT process to Heaven-sourced transformations. Evaluating according to criteria agreed upon by the community helps them make their imperfect artistic communication more effective. Remember that the goal of evaluating is construction, not destruction, building up, not tearing down (Eph 4:29). Reflection for improvement. Note, too, that communities can greatly reduce the need for critique by including the right people from the beginning of the cocreative process: gatekeepers like social, government, and religious leaders, expert creators and enactors, genre experts, and content experts.

Results of Conversation 4's research and analysis may prove invaluable to improvement. The more we understand and can talk about an art form, the more we can identify elements that hinder positive effects from happening. Each of the processes below should include frequent reference to the Community Arts Profile (or its contents, stored in people's minds). Tools in Conversation 4D may also prove helpful.

In Conversation 6 we present the following reminders and approaches:

- Communities decide what's good and bad
- Follow comforting guidelines
- Consider three evaluation tools

COMMUNITIES DECIDE WHAT'S GOOD AND BAD

How do you decide what's good or bad?[1] When, for example, someone says, "I never liked the Beatles' music," do they mean they didn't like their tunes, they didn't like their lyrics, or they didn't like their long hair? People are seldom able to articulate what exactly they like or don't like about an artwork. This is not surprising, because artistic communication works through all the kinds of signs we discussed in Conversation 3: Lexical (words), iconic (similarity), and indexical (associations). This leads to the production and reception of a staggering number of possible signs and their associated meanings.

---

1 Much of the following is derived from Fitzgerald and Schrag, "But is it any good?"

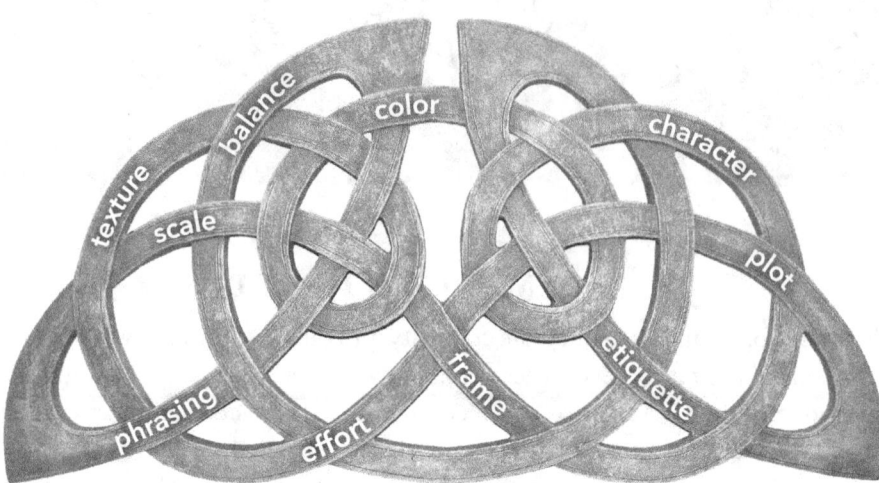

Figure 6.1 Sample intertwined artistic features in an enactment

If you glance through all of the research activities in Conversation 4—especially in the fuller version of Conversation 4B in the *CLAT Companion*—you'll see that people could be evaluating arts according to any of these kinds of signs: line; syntax; enjambment; rhyme; assonance; alliteration; metaphor; simile; verses; stanzas; refrains; pulse; tempo; meter; accents; figures; motifs; phrases; tonal center; keys; intervals; modes; scales; range; tessitura; themes; contours; cadences; parallel, chordal, or polyphonic relationships between concurrent pitches; formulas; progressions; tonality; strophes; iterations; through-composition; theme variation; solo; duo; trio; choir; unison; vibrato; accompaniment; use of space; characterization; number and location of participants; blocking; plot structure; idea; dramatic premise; frames; improvisation; movements; gestures; movement phrasing; dynamics; efforts; spatial relationships; visual unity; balance; rhythm; proportion; line; shape; value; color; hue; shade; tint; texture. And so on. And so on. See Figure 6.1 for a sample of some of these intertwined artistic features.

But there's more. Not only are the kinds of signs seemingly endless, but each group and individual may have diverse associations with any given sign. One person may smile whenever he hears Latin percussion because he met the woman who would become his wife at a party where they danced the samba. Another person may detest samba because her fiancé broke up with her at a similar event. There could be countless signs multiplied by countless associations at an artistic event, any one of which could make it fail.

And unbelievably, our predicament seems even more dire. Not only does productive research and evaluation require us to perceive an infinite number of signs, their combinations, and their meanings. Community members involved in the CLAT process also need to be aware of personal relationships, social dynamics, and other elements emerging from this manual's Framing the Seven Conversations, and Conversations 1, 2, 3, 4, and 5. An epic poet might perform brilliantly, but if an influential audience member is holding a grudge against him, the community might ultimately dismiss the artist's skill.

FOLLOW COMFORTING ADVICE

Take a deep breath. The complexity of artistic communication should keep us humble, but there are several factors that make identifying criteria for improvement possible. We here present these factors as guidelines for designing evaluation and improvement exercises.

Trust Local Systems

Groups usually share a sense of when an artwork is good or not and have ways of communicating what needs to be fixed. Perform the research in "Aesthetics and Evaluation" and "Decision-Making" (Conversation 4, Part C) to find out how correction normally works in the community. In some situations, they may get rid of inferior products by blocking them from future presentation and letting them die.[2]

Evaluate according to Effects

In Conversation 3 the community identified the effects that new artistry should have on people to move them toward Kingdom Goals. Refer to these in the Community Arts Profile and summary statements. To evaluate whether a new work had the desired effect, observe and ask about experiencers' responses to the new bits of artistry. Did it have the effects the community wanted? If an orator's enactment is meant to motivate people to join a parade celebrating their ethnic identity, but participants watch distractedly and then disperse to their homes, then the oration failed.

Relax, but Keep Learning

No one can study all possible signs, so do this with community members: watch people's reactions to an enactment, listen to what they say, and dip into the research activities in Conversation 4 related to the genres you're working with regularly—maybe one activity a week or month. For example, if you're getting to know people who carve fruit, schedule these research activities, detailed in the *CLAT Companion*: "Describe Spatial Relationships between an Object's Visual Features," "Document the Creation of an Object," and "Identify the Role(s) in Visual Art Creation." Then start learning to carve the fruit yourself. This education will sensitize you to factors that may prove important in the improvement of new artistry.

> In the initial process of setting Scripture portions to local Baka song forms in Cameroon, I collaborated with two Baka men—Tombombo, who normally helped me with translation, and Mai, a well-known musician and composer. Together we worked daily to translate and versify certain selected verses according to prototypical Baka song-text features. One day the two men set off

---

[2] Fitzgerald and Schrag's article "But is it any good?" offers a valuable, semiotic approach to identifying and analyzing signs related to songs. This is a great resource if you want to go deeper in expressive form analysis.

to compose a Scripture song based on a text from Exodus 15—"The Song of Moses." A couple of days later, the duo returned with harp and voices, ready to perform their new composition. However, while they performed, on the outside I beamed with approval, but on the inside, I sighed with disappointment. Many things about the song obviously "worked," but certain other features did not; revisions would need to be made.

Because of my music research and long experience living among the Baka, I was able to critically examine—even as a cultural outsider—a new Baka song composition. I gradually noticed that one sequence of the melodic intervals in one phrase of the melody of the song intuitively sounded "unnatural." As it turns out, in the Baka music tradition, there are certain sequences of melodic intervals that have never occurred in any of the hundreds of songs that I had recorded. My preliminary melodic analysis was also suggesting that there were certain grammatical restrictions on which interval types may follow others and for how long.

To illustrate, it is not, for example, uncommon for a melodic phrase in the modern Western music tradition to descend stepwise five to seven steps in succession before reversing melodic direction (for example, "Joy to the World" or "Twinkle Twinkle Little Star"). Most people with wide exposure to popular Western music can comfortably sing melodic sequences like these. An average Baka, on the other hand, cannot (with ease) sing such a prolonged succession of stepwise intervals; it exceeds the traditionally and subconsciously accepted limit of successive steps (that is, major or minor seconds) allowed in typical Baka intervallic syntax. So, just as certain grammatical patterns must be respected to facilitate effective speech, so it is with patterns of musical tones.

Left unrevised, the original melody, as composed by Tombombo, was never heard sung by anyone other than him. Since the song was composed with the specific purpose of being sung by any assembly of Baka Christians, it would need to be changed. Therefore, the melody was tactfully criticized—with all the culturally appropriate attending strategies of politeness—and then revised to employ only those melodic features truly characteristic of the Baka song tradition. In this way the melody posed no problem in effecting its purpose, given that now any Baka person would be able to naturally participate in singing the song.   —Dan Fitzgerald

CONSIDER THESE EVALUATION TOOLS

If previous conversations have produced charts, lists or other kinds of data, bring them out as reference for Conversation 6. Hopefully, most of this is in the Community Arts Profile.

Artistic activity can benefit from evaluation at multiple points in the cocreative process. For example, reflection for improvement should take place during the initial act of creation, and after composers have presented their work to the community. Keep these bits of advice in mind as the community decides when and how to improve artistry produced by the sparking activities in Conversation 5.[3]

What follows are three successfully implemented tools for you to consider using in the evaluation process. People have developed many other approaches, including additional methods to check Scripture orally.[4] One possible element of oral drafting and checking is connecting characteristics of a particular Scripture passage's genre with a local genre that can communicate the content and connotations of the passage faithfully, memorably, and familiarly. See the Digital Library at www.clatmanual.com for more.

Tool: Design a Straightforward Process

We need to check art forms to know if the intended audience attaches accurate and natural meanings to the product. So, for example, if we draw a picture for children, we need to know if the symbols and colors in the picture are meaningful, if the overall message of the picture is clear, if the image(s) are natural for them to both understand and imitate (as best they can), if they can easily absorb and restate the meanings of the visual image, and if the image clearly comes from their cultural context, etc. We also want to check with some experts in the community to know if the art forms relate meaningfully to the whole community.

Here are some ideas for checking an art form, but the approach should be designed appropriately for each cultural context.[5]

Who should help with the checking?

- four or five intended audience members
- at least two older experts in the community

Use all the following tests with each of these people

It is important to write down anything you learn about the art form so that improvements can be made. Checking with each person can take anywhere from five minutes to about twenty minutes. It is important to take time and learn as much as you can about what needs to be improved.

---

3 A further resource is this classic manual on pretesting with many examples: Haaland, *Pretesting Communication Materials*.

4 See Dickie, "Community Translation and Oral Performance," and Dickie, "Translating Psalms for Performance."

5 Adapted from Saurman and Saurman, "Song Checking."

Test for meaning
Show or demonstrate the artwork.

- Ask a representative of the intended audience to tell you what the artwork communicates to them.
- Listen to them and see if they seem to understand the propositional, indexical, and iconic meanings. If the work includes biblical texts, make sure that people understand it accurately.
- If not, show them the artwork again and ask them to describe what they understand.
- Write down their responses, noting what parts of the artwork are clear and what parts are unclear (this could be words, phrases, themes, colors, patterns, actions, etc.).

Test for naturalness
Show or demonstrate the artwork.

- Ask a member of the intended audience if they can reproduce some portion of the artwork back to you. Let them do this on their own and see what they can remember.
- If they are having some difficulty remembering, show or demonstrate the artwork again.
- Ask them again to reproduce some portion of the artwork.
- If they are having some difficulty, you can prompt them a little, but it is wise to not prompt much.
- Write down parts that are difficult to replicate.

Test for ownership and accuracy
Does the genre parallel that used by the intended audience?

- Ask a representative of the intended audience how they feel about the artwork.
- Would they use it? How would they use it? Would they enjoy hearing, seeing, or experiencing the artwork? When?
- What do they not like? What would they change? What would make the art better or more meaningful for them?
- Does it feel to them as though it's their own? Does it feel as though it belongs to their community?
- Is this form consistent with the listener's learning or education level? local teaching methods? the appropriate language and symbols or sounds?

Correct the artwork
Take the results from the arts checking to the artwork creator or meet with the creation committee and change or adjust its unclear portions.

Test for effectiveness
Test again to see if you communicated effectively to the intended audience.

Tool: Design with Analytical Rigor

Here is a process you can follow that will increase the likelihood of useful evaluation results:

Local Social Structures. Identify and work through local social structures and help everyone involved provide correction in locally appropriate ways (using standards of politeness, respect, indirection, roles within a social hierarchy, etc.).

Criteria. Define together the criteria for deciding how good a work is and how it could be improved. We have found this standard helpful: a created work is good insofar as its features work together to effect the purposes demanded by the context of its enactment and experience. These purposes could include the work's theological correctness, accuracy of information communicated, ability to communicate, ability to touch people through its aesthetic quality, ability to motivate to action, etc.

Elements. Identify the elements of an artistic communication event (see "Take a First Glance at an Event," Conversation 4, Part A). These should include how the work utilizes space, materials, participants, shape through time, enactment features, feeling, content, themes, and community values.

Purposes. Identify the purpose(s) of the artistic communication event. These could include to educate, motivate to action, etc.

People. Identify people to include in the process of evaluation. These people need to have the knowledge, skills, and respect necessary to critique various elements.

Objects. Identify objects that can provide a focal point and reference for discussion, so that you don't have to rely exclusively on memory for critique. These could include song texts, drama scripts, musical notation, masks, dance moves, and video and audio recordings.

Affirm and Encourage. Together affirm the aspects of the creation that work well and encourage the creators to do something even better based on the evaluation.

Figure 6.2 lists examples of evaluation in several creative contexts.

Kinds of Elements to Evaluate	Examples of Such Elements	Qualified Evaluators	Example Methods of Evaluation
Space/location, time, participants, etc.	Storytelling around a fire at night, with all ages	Genre experts, traditional leaders	With written summary of the event description: Discuss relationship to genre.
Enactment Features (music, drama, dance, oral verbal arts, and visual arts)	Proverb choice, movement characteristics, melody shape	Expert enactors	With audio and video recordings: Review for aesthetic/technical successes, weaknesses of enactment. Transcribe melody, lyrics, movements, poetic features, colors, etc., for analysis.
Message(s)	Theological content	Church leaders	With transcriptions of texts: Analyze texts of songs, dramas, stories (with back-translation if critiquer doesn't know language) according to clarity, truth. Comprehension testing: ask experiencers what they understood.
	Medical content	Health worker	
Purpose(s)	Church use: education, worship, evangelism, AIDS Education	Agenda setters for the communication event	With a summary of all aspects of the event, discuss degrees that the event fulfilled its intended purposes and other purposes, and how the event could be improved; may use a focus group or exit interviews

Figure 6.2 Examples of evaluation components

Tool: Design with Scriptural Fidelity Focus

There are three kinds of checks to help make Scripture-infused arts better. For all three, ask open-ended questions that lend themselves to exploratory answers, not yes-no short answers. In all these discussions, explore whether the artistry produced is in a genre that carries the Scripture passage's message, import, and emotions faithfully.

1. Self-check

Ask the artist to think of ways to make the work communicate more clearly to the desired audience. Encourage the artist to think about the work from the audience's point of view, taking into consideration the prevalent background knowledge and worldview assumptions of the local area. What could we change that would make the work clearer? To what extent is the most important thing the artist wants to communicate the most important thing the audience is likely to grasp from this enactment?

2. Consultant check

When the text of an artistic work is based closely on Scripture, the need for evaluation and improvement is especially important. In these cases, experts in Scripture and the arts should be consulted. When consultants don't speak the local language, they need a translation into a language they know well.

Two types of translation are important for evaluation. First, a *word-for-word translation* reveals poetic and discourse features of the text. Although slight adjustments of word order may be made, it follows the original text almost exactly. Second, a *free translation* attempts to convey the original meaning naturally in the target language. This helps the consultant understand the overall importance of the text. Translations will be better if they result from following these guidelines: the translator should be a mother-tongue speaker of the source language; the translator should not already be familiar with the text; the translation could be oral and audio recorded, or written; if the translator doesn't understand what the artist meant, they should discuss it together; if there are unintended misunderstandings, the artist should strongly consider changing the text.

With these translations in hand, check whether the material has these characteristics:

- relates Scripture meaningfully to aspects of local worldviews
- the rate of information flow is neither too fast nor too slow
- meaning, form, style, and emotion go together
- not insulting to any group
- non-offensive portrayal of sensitive issues, like violence
- believable portrayal of interesting characters
- balance of character development and actions
- biblical background knowledge is either already generally known or provided
- follows the discourse rules of similar materials in the genre
- the way the material opens and closes (greetings and leave-takings, for example) is culturally appropriate
- time frame is clear

3. Community check

The third check tests the material with a small section of the intended audience before the material is presented to a larger audience. In general, the same person who made a translation and the artist should *not* check the work with the community.

Record the work, play it back for the focus group, and ask questions like these:

- What was it about? What else was it about? *For an illustration or visual artwork*: What do you see? What else do you see? *After a dance*: What did you see? What else did you see? *After a song*: What did you hear? What else did you hear? *After a drama*: What happened? And then what happened? And then what happened? Do not tell people the answers.
- What do you think the author/artist/storyteller/actors/dancers wanted to communicate? What did you learn? Do not explain the intended meaning to them; if you do, you will not get a valid impression of their comprehension.
- What did you like? What did you appreciate?
- What did you not like? Did anything offend you? What might others be offended by?

Testers should talk with the creator(s) and work together to revise the work accordingly.

CONVERSATION 7

CELEBRATE AND INTEGRATE FOR CONTINUITY

Everything that we can sense or think about cycles through birth, growth, decay, and death. People, ideologies, songs, flowers, buildings, waves, customs, vehicles, wildebeests, cakes, hats, galaxies ... they all come and go. Of course, the length of each cycle and stage varies widely, and sometimes the intermediate steps get skipped altogether. And occasionally part of something that has died gets resurrected, as when the forgotten works of a sixteenth-century painter are found and inspire artists centuries later. So why don't we just join the ebb and flow, the wax and wane of history? Why do we try to make some things last longer and others not? How do we know when to integrate and celebrate for continuity, and when to fold our hands and rest?

In Conversation 7 we'll provide a few ideas that will help you and the community wrestle with these daunting questions in your cocreative context. Specifically, we'll give some pointers on how to

- choose what to integrate and celebrate
- act to keep good things going
- understand more about how continuity works
- know when to let go[1]

CHOOSE WHAT TO CELEBRATE AND INTEGRATE

Your first choice here is simple: integrate and celebrate the arts that you have been engaging with in Conversations 2–6. You've walked with a community as they've identified goals consistent with the Kingdom of Heaven, decided on certain kinds of artistry that can move the community closer to these goals, implemented actions that resulted in new bits of this artistry and then improved them. And all along the way you and community members have been listening to God, trying to discern what he's up to. This process has ensured as much as possible that the creative processes and people you've been engaging with are the ones that should take root and flourish.

But all situations change all the time. This invigorating fact (or frustrating, depending on your personality) means that communities need to regularly reassess their present and think about the future. The constituency of a community will alter, new modes of communication will enter, government policies will evolve—so the kinds of artistic communication best suited for growth toward a better future will change. Here are some suggestions for initiatives in the months and years ahead.

---

1 See Schrag's chapters in the *Ethnodoxology Handbook*, "Planning an Arts Showcase Event" (481–84) and "Evaluating and Improving Local Arts" (485–91).

Encourage a Community to Make Intentional Creativity a Habit
Go through the cocreative cycle in this manual again: Conversations 1–7. The more a community does this, the more it will become a familiar, regular process that flows naturally and efficiently through members' lives.

Encourage Continuity in Minority Arts
Globalization, urbanization, missionary activity, wars, political extremism, ecological crises, and other factors often (though certainly not always) lead to the devaluation of, declining interest in, and increased vulnerability of minority communities and their art forms. The end of Revelation 21 suggests that elements of every culture will last into Heaven. When we all sing, dance, act, paint, and tell truth in similar ways, we impoverish the global church on Earth and maybe even in the New Creation (at least at the beginning). So don't assume that global trends are necessarily God's plans. Every bit of God-created diversity we can experience helps us know God better.

Encourage Multicultural Expressions
This value on uniqueness extends to multicultural communities, especially churches. No two churches embracing more than one community is like another. This means that each church that is profoundly multicultural has the chance to craft utterly distinctive combinations of artistry.

A bourgeoning movement reflecting on multicultural worship has emerged. You can find a growing number of published resources, organizations, workshops, conferences, blogs, bands, and so on. People are producing theologies, methodologies, consultancies, and case studies. Refer to the "Assess a Multicultural Christian Community's Arts" tool in Conversation 4D and the Digital Library (www.clatmanual.com) for more resources.

Encourage Continuity in Arts that Are Most Fragile
Diversity and fragility are closely connected. The *Ethnologue* counts over 3,000 of the 7,000-plus languages used in the world today as endangered.[2] Other aspects of these communities—including artistic forms of communication—normally experience similar fragility. We should take special note of the artists and their art forms in the world's margins. God's image is there.

Encourage Continuity in Arts that Are Most Likely to Flourish
We want new artistry to make positive differences in a community, so innovations that spread like wildfire can be and do great things.

As you reflect on these guidelines, you'll realize that they sometimes work counter to each other. Well, that's the way life is. If the community listens to God and grows in wisdom, they'll do fine.

---

2 See *Ethnologue*, "How Many Language Are Endangered?" (https://www.ethnologue.com/insights/how-many-languages-endangered).

ACT TO KEEP GOOD THINGS GOING

Your first task here is also simple: if you've followed the cocreation cycle with a community, you've already done what's most important for sustainability. The most important way to keep something good going is to start it in the right way. We've encouraged you to make relationships, encourage others to create, get to know and value artists, include all the important artists and decision makers in sparking activities, and help make artistic products and their presentations better. These activities make it more likely that a critical mass of key community members will champion this new thing, resulting in persistent momentum into the future.

However, you might still need to plan activities that inject energy into strategic points. Following are a few ideas.

Integrate

Integrating has to do with making artistic practice part of normal patterns of community life. A good place to start is to reflect with the community on the ways that they teach each other things like new songs, dances, and carving skills. If possible, their plans should include these means of transmission. To keep creativity going, the community may decide to repeat sparking activities like workshops or commissioning. Existing social groups like dance associations or literacy clubs may also be motivated to keep creating. Or communities might decide to form new groups that meet regularly to help members create for Kingdom purposes, like the creators' clubs we described in Conversation 5. Each of these ideas feeds into repeated parts of community life, so the engines of creativity keep running.

Celebrate

Good things happen when you celebrate the intrinsic value of artistic expression and share it with the wider community and the outside world. Celebrating the positive and redemptive aspects of local art thus serves to strengthen the cultural esteem of a community and protect an invaluable cultural heritage. By affirming local arts, you serve as an advocate for a community's unique expressions and foster conditions for further artistic flowering. You also help others hear and understand their unique stories, perceptions of the world, and values.

Ways to celebrate new and older art forms include

- presenting them to community officials and leaders
- disseminating recordings
- performing at festive social events
- entering contests

The "Identity and Sustainability" goals and activities (Conversations 2, 5) offer more detailed suggestions for celebration.

Evaluate

Every so often, look at the community's cocreative activities and see what the results are. Try to develop an environment in which everyone recognizes that everything can be improved, and everything has a life cycle. This will help in planning.

UNDERSTAND HOW CONTINUITY WORKS

Though this section isn't essential to a community's cocreative success, reflecting on the underlying dynamics of sustainability will help everyone make wiser choices. Here are a few principles.

Good Creativity Spawns More Creativity

The more something satisfying happens, the more it's likely to happen again. Good begets good. So do lots of good things.

Recurring Events Help

It's hard to break a habit. So keep working until enough people have the habit of creating and enjoying new arts that it would take more energy to stop it. These habits become the stable infrastructure on which people can lean when improvising. See "Cultural Dynamism" (Conversation 4, Part C) for more.

Artistry Needs to Fill Four Conditions to Be Sustainable

Underneath our cocreative cycle lie four strong social dynamics, each of which is necessary for the ongoing life of an art form.[3]

- **Function**: concerns solidifying or creating social uses for artistic activity. The more positive uses an art form has, the higher status it enjoys. Without status, no one will want to make or experience an art form.

- **Acquisition**: consists of the ways that the skills, competencies, and knowledge associated with an art form are passed on to others. Without acquisition, no one new will ever learn to create in the form, and it will die.

- **Motivation**: determines why people choose to use certain arts for social functions.

- **Environment**: affects how the surrounding society supports the use of an art form or not.

  > I am an ethnomusicologist who lived among and performed research with speakers of the Alamblak language in Papua New Guinea from 2003 through 2006. One of the instruments I documented was the *nrwit* (*garamut* in Tok Pisin), a hollowed length of tree trunk, between four and six feet long, and between two and four feet tall, with a long, thin opening in the top. The *nrwit* player holds a beater stick, three to four feet long, and strikes

---

3 Adapted for artistic language from Lewis and Simons, *Sustaining Language Use*; and Lewis and Simons "Assessing Endangerment."

a nodule at the edge of the slit with the blunt end of the beater. The deep, resonant sound from the *nrwit* carries over a great distance and can be used to send messages within or beyond the village. An individual nuclear family might own one *nrwit*, which rests on the ground just outside the family home, sheltered from the weather by the overhanging eaves of the roof. Alamblak people stated that previous generations used the *nrwit* to say anything that people could say, although the signaling system is not sonically imitative of the spoken language. By the time of my fieldwork, the system had fallen into disuse, and only a few older men were able to play the signals. Other people said that they could understand some signals when they heard them but could not themselves produce *nrwit* communication. Today the primary use of the *nrwit* is announcing the death of a village resident.

Signaling on the *nrwit* has been reduced to an identity reminder for the Alamblak ethnic community. No one has more than symbolic proficiency. Recordings and documentation exist, but people are not using the signal system. Kondak, the acknowledged expert who taught me the *nrwit* patterns, died in 2010. People could, if they choose, re-learn the *nrwit* patterns, likely in an adapted form rather than the exact traditional system; at this point, it seems unlikely. As mobile phones become a larger part of communication in Papua New Guinea, people will have the option to send text messages, similar to the *nrwit* signals. But when I asked an Alamblak friend about this, he pointed out an important difference: the *nrwit* sends one message to entire villages at once, but text messages go only to one individual. Community involvement is a Melanesian ideal that is not well-suited to mobile phone communication.

The *nrwit* tradition is on the verge of extinction, which affects me personally: I have concern for my Alamblak friends and have hopes for the very best for their lives. They've lost something of great value.　　　　　　　　—Neil Coulter

Artistic Sustainability on a Hopeful to Hopeless Scale

Linguists have tried to understand the rapid rate of language death in the world today, thereby developing models that can be applied to artistic communication. The following list describes eight possible states of an artistic genre's vitality:[4]

1. **International:** An art form reaches this level when an international "community of practice" forms around it.
2. **National or regional:** The art's reputation grows beyond the home community. Community members may receive financial or other support from the regional or national level.

---

4 Slightly revised text from Coulter, "Assessing Music Shift." See also Harris, *Storytelling in Siberia*, and Grant, *Music Endangerment*.

3. **Vigorous:** This is the pivotal level for artistic vitality. In this level, oral transmission and largely traditional contexts of education are intact and functioning. People have sufficient opportunities for enactment, and young people are learning by observation, participation, and appropriate educational contexts. An art can exist comfortably at this level without needing to move higher.

4. **Threatened:** The first level that hints at downward movement, toward endangerment. An art is still performed/produced, but changes are becoming noticeable: diminishing enactment contexts, more time given to more recent introductions, more rural-urban movement.

5. **Locked:** The art is known by more people than just the grandparent generation, but its enactment is restricted to tourist shows or other contexts that are not integrated into the everyday life of the community. The repertoire is fixed and nothing new is being added to it. Participation and creative energy decline noticeably.

6. **Shifting:** The grandparent generation is proficient in this art, but fewer contexts exist for passing it on to younger people. Possibly the younger people do not express interest (or are perceived that way by their parents and grandparents). The art is not dead or endangered at this level, and can be revitalized, but signs point to downward movement and likely endangerment.

7. **Dormant:** Functional contexts for enactment are gone, but recordings and other ethnographic description exist. A community could reacquaint itself with the art, but its rebirth would likely be something different than what it was.

8. **Extinct:** No one in the community can create or enact in this art. Probably no enactment has occurred in the lifetime of anyone currently living. No documentation exists. This is rarer, as most arts grow into other styles, or stylistic elements are perpetuated in related styles.

If you can identify the state of vitality of the art in which the community is interested, then you can plan cocreative activities more wisely. The closer it is to state eight (extinct), the more energy it would require to spark creativity.

ALWAYS LOOK AHEAD

> "He who was seated on the throne said, 'I am making everything new!' Then he said, 'Write this down, for these words are trustworthy and true.'" (Rev 21:5)

Our future is a remade cosmos. There's no need to worry that something good will be lost—the Signs of Heaven Jesus wants to flow into the New Creation will be there. What a community doesn't fix or finish on this *now and not-yet* Earth will be available in our certain future.

Celebrate and Integrate for Continuity

I believe that the precarious situation of many artists in the world requires us to seriously consider becoming their advocates. But each of us needs to know whom God is calling us to serve, and act accordingly. If you know who these people are, then stubbornly act on their behalf—even when it's not easy.

Here's part of a poem I wrote for my father, imagining him first waking in the New Creation:[5]

Memories

Each memory you tried to keep from slipping out of reach is now standing—
> solid.
> Available.
> Concrete.

Re-experiencable in all its fullness of people, shapes, smells, story, tangibility, graspability. School friends, motor scooters, combines, crunching snow, aunts and uncles and cousins and parishioners and parents and grandparents—voices, accents, clothes, machines, smells, mountaintops … every scene and character and era of your story sits ready for you to relive and share.

It's not going anywhere, surviving only by the connection of a twisted, tearing, tottering twine to—
> flitting memories
> decaying objects
> fading photographs

All this is barely a beginning.
You'll know beyond any doubt that
> God loves no one more than you
> You reflect God's image no less than anyone else
> There's no social ladder compelling you to climb

God says, "You're alright. Enjoy!"

Ultimately all we do is about God, not what he created. So take Sabbath rests. Let things go when they no longer make sense. You're not running the universe.

---
5 Schrag, "Memories," www.firstmomentsinheaven.org.

CLOSING 1

QUICK REFERENCE

A Better Future: More Signs of the Kingdom

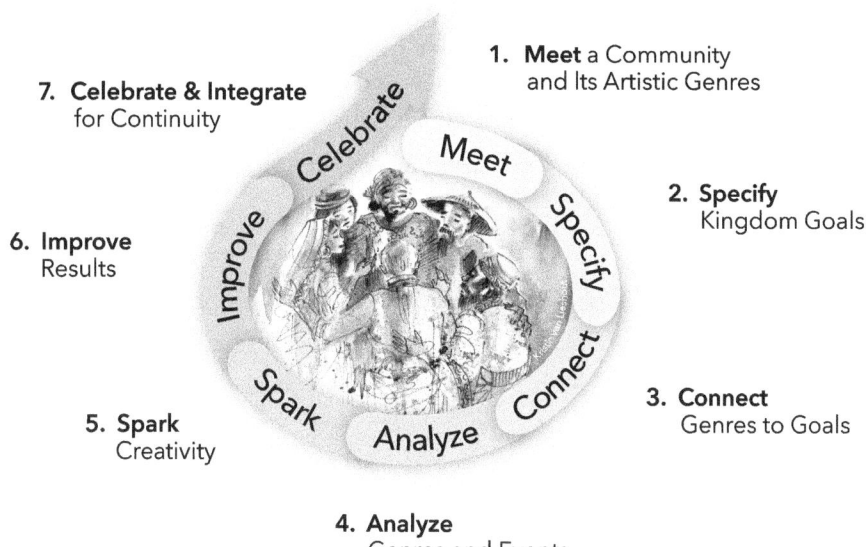

Figure 7.1 Creating Local Arts Together idealized model

1. **Meet a Community and Its Arts.** Explore artistic and social resources that exist in the community. Performing Conversation 1 allows you to build relationships, to participate with and understand the people, and to discover the hidden treasures of the community.

2. **Specify Kingdom Goals.** Discover the Kingdom Goals that the community wants to work toward. Performing Conversation 2 ensures that you are helping the community work toward aims that they have agreed on together.

3. **Connect Genres to Goals.** The community chooses an artistic genre that can help them meet their goals, and activities that can result in purposeful creativity in this genre. Performing Conversation 3 reveals the mechanisms that relate certain kinds of artistic activity to its effects, so that the activities performed have a high chance of succeeding.

4. **Analyze Genres and Events.** Describe the events and their artistic forms as a whole. Describe the forms in relationship to broader cultural context. Performing Conversation 4 results in detailed knowledge of the art forms that is crucial to sparking creativity, improving what is produced, and integrating it into the community.

5. **Spark Creativity.** The community implements activities they have selected to spark creativity within the genres and events they have chosen. Performing Conversation 5 actually produces new artistic works for events.

6. **Improve Results.** The community evaluates the results of the sparking activities and makes them better. Performing Conversation 6 makes sure that the new artistry exhibits the aesthetic qualities, produces the impacts, and communicates the intended messages at a level of quality appropriate to its purposes.

7. **Celebrate and Integrate for Continuity.** The community plans and implements ways that this new kind of creativity can continue. Identify more contexts where the new and old arts can be displayed and performed. Performing Conversation 7 makes it more likely that a community will keep making its arts in ways that produce good effects long into the future.

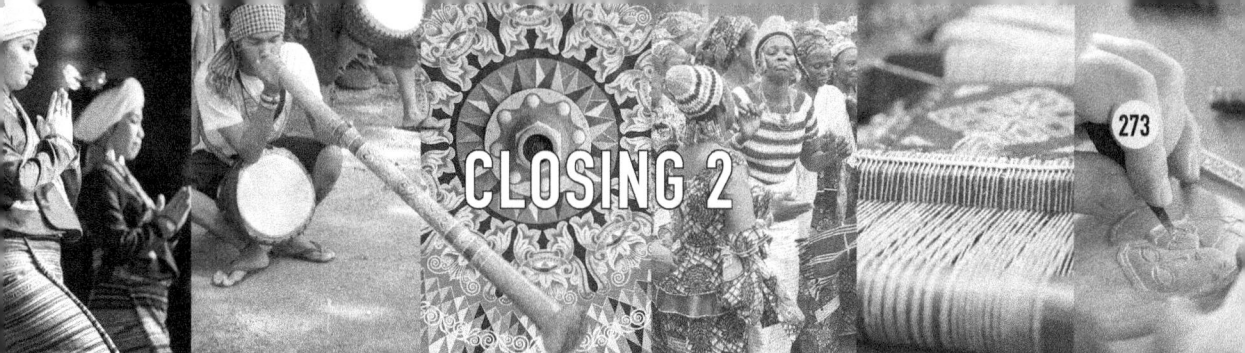

SAMPLE COMMUNITY ARTS PROFILE (CAP) OUTLINE

We've created a file that provides spaces to describe and capture the results of activities you and a community do related to this manual. Essentially, it restates many of this book's sections, so you know where to include results of activities you perform. In the file, you will replace the capitalized words with words appropriate to your context. For example, COMMUNITY NAME would be substituted with the name of the community you're working with, such as Sakha, the Bach clan, or *l'Eglise Catholique de Tchinga*. You are free to modify the structure, categories, and content of your CAP however you'd like. What follows is an example of the table of contents of a CAP yet to be filled in. For an editable version of this CAP, go to the Digital Library at www.clatmanual.com.

[COMMUNITY NAME]
Name of arts advocate(s):
Dates of work represented by this document:

SUMMARIZE PLANS, ACTIVITIES, RESULTS

"Creating Local Arts Together" Cycles Completed (to any degree)
List of Events and Genres Researched (to any degree)

CREATING LOCAL ARTS TOGETHER CYCLE

Conversation 1: Meet a Community and Its Arts
Take a first glance at a community
Take a first glance at a community's arts
Start exploring a community's social and conceptual life
Prepare to use research methods to learn more
Celebrate a community's arts from the start
Summarize results and challenges of this conversation

Conversation 2: Specify Kingdom Goals
Gather voices to imagine signs of Heaven
Explore strengths and hopes
Explore difficulties and challenges
Choose a goal or goals to focus on now
Summarize results and challenges of this conversation

Conversation 3: Connect Genres to Goals
> Describe the process of identifying Effects, Content, Genre, Events, and Sparking Activities
> List the Effects, Content, Genre, Event, and Sparking Activities chosen
> Summarize results and challenges of this conversation

Conversation 4: Analyze Genres and Events
> Decide what research you will perform
> Perform research, entering results in "Genre Enactment Features"
> Summarize results and challenges of this conversation

Conversation 5: Spark Creativity
> Describe community views on creativity and artists
> Identify opportunities to maximize and barriers to overcome
> Decide on the type of activity
> Design a new or modify an existing activity
> Perform the activity
> Summarize results and challenges of this conversation

Conversation 6: Improve Results
> Choose and modify an evaluation tool
> Perform the tools for evaluation and improvement
> Summarize results and challenges of this conversation

Conversation 7: Celebrate and Integrate for Continuity
> Choose what to integrate and celebrate
> Plan actions to keep good things going
> Summarize results and challenges of this conversation

GENRE ENACTMENT FEATURES [GENRE NAME]

A: Event Analysis: EVENT NAME
> Brief description
> First glance at the event
> Enactment lenses on an event

B: Artistic Aspects of an Event
> Musical features
> Dramatic features
> Dance features
> Oral verbal arts features
> Visual features
> Interrelationships between formal elements of the event

C: Broader Cultural Context of an Event
- Artists
- Creativity
- Transmission and Change
- Language(s)
- Subject Matter
- Cultural dynamism
- Identity and power
- Aesthetics and Evaluation
- Time
- Emotions
- Community values
- Decision-Making
- Communal investment

D: Encourage Churches to Integrate Artistry More Holistically: CHURCH NAME
- Discuss biblical and theological foundations for arts
- Choose tools to help churches integrate arts more fully, faithfully, and fruitfully
- Describe the outcomes of using the tools

Global Ethnodoxology Network's Core Values

GEN'S CENTRAL COMMITMENT

GEN seeks to remain faithful to a biblical vision of the future by encouraging communities of Jesus followers in every culture to engage with God and the world through their own artistic expressions. GEN offers networking, training, and resources to support the growing movement furthering these goals. Sound theology undergirds each of the values summarized in this document.[1]

SEVEN CORE VALUES THAT GUIDE GEN

1. Christian Worship
GEN celebrates the stunning variety of Christian worship patterns in the global church.
Ethnodoxology's central focus is worship. Worship is the act of adoring and praising God, ascribing worth to Father|Son|Spirit as the one who deserves homage, allegiance, and faithful service. From individual to corporate devotion, worship denotes a lifestyle of being in love with God. The global church exhibits an astounding array of worship patterns, demonstrating the enormity of God's creativity and the diversity of the Body of Christ.

2. Potent Arts
GEN recognizes arts as indispensable to human thriving.
The arts are integral to personal and individual expression, and in initiating, transmitting and reinforcing interpersonal and group communication. They permeate communities, marking messages as important, embedded in, and separate from everyday activities, drawing not only on cognitive, but also experiential, bodily, multimodal, and emotional ways of knowing. Arts instill solidarity, reinforce identity and serve as a memory aid. They inspire people to action, provide socially acceptable frameworks for expressing difficult or new ideas, and open spaces for people to imagine and dream.

3. Historical Awareness
GEN situates its goals and activities within global, regional, and local histories and in their sociocultural dynamics.
We recognize the complex and constantly changing nature of every individual's and community's artistry and worship practices, including our own. Because Euro-American art forms have largely accompanied the spread of Christianity in recent centuries, local artistic traditions—especially those of ethnolinguistic minorities—often remain outside the

---

[1] A PDF version of GEN's Core Values can be found at https://worldofworship.org/core-values. In addition, see illustrative stories on this topic in the Sep/Oct 2023 issue of *Mission Frontiers:* https://bit.ly/4dNw6cx.

church. Ethnodoxology seeks to redress this imbalance by retaining a robust engagement with representatives of local, older, often rural artistic histories. We also celebrate urban multicultural, multiartistic identities and creativity that mark more and more Christian communities, developing resources to help them craft unique worship practices.

4. Human Agency

GEN respects the right and capacity of every individual and all communities to shape their own artistic realities.

Artistic products are made, appreciated and given value by people. We endeavour to encourage the diversity of human artistic ingenuity locally and wheresoever these arts are exported. We acknowledge, honor, celebrate and value the unique artistic creations and contributions of individuals and communities. Therefore, we cultivate these gifts both in our own communities and in those we endeavor to encourage and collaborate with so that they can continue to explore their unique identities and giftings—the dynamic arts that are the heart of the people as individuals and in community.

5. Locally-Grounded Methods

GEN favors methods that amplify local agency and creativity.

We encourage the development of a wide variety of arts in the life and worship of the church, acknowledging the importance of local decision-making in the choice of art forms. Given our emphasis on individual and community agency, we choose participatory methods like appreciative inquiry in ethnographic research and sparking creativity. We esteem local categories and practices of artistry as primary, rooting our analyses in the practitioners' worldview. This affirms the communicative, motivational, identity-strengthening power of locally created expressive arts. In short, we embrace a "Find It—Encourage It" model of arts engagement rather than a "Bring It—Teach It" model.

6. Academic Rigor

GEN carefully integrates insights and methods from the many disciplines that contribute to accomplishing its goals.

We value and develop resources that provide holistic views and positions from a variety of disciplines. Among others, these include performance studies; folkloristics; creativity studies; musicology; orality; anthropologies of arts—music, poetics, choreography, dance, theater, visual arts; along with missiology, worship studies, and other theological disciplines. In our research, writing, and practice we endeavour to maintain high academic standards as well as performances and products that best emulate the creative and representative attributes of the works generated by individuals and communities. Ethnodoxologists need not be professional academics, but they must plan, and act informed by rigorous, nuanced, analytical ideas.

7. Confident Hope
GEN embraces holistic visions of better futures that all communities can work toward.

Ethnodoxologists nurture spaces that are life-enhancing and where people can imagine and plan for better lives. Kinds of "better" include having more justice, health, artistic diversity, love, well-being, creativity, vibrant churches, vital spiritual formation, and awe-inspiring, transformational adoration of God.

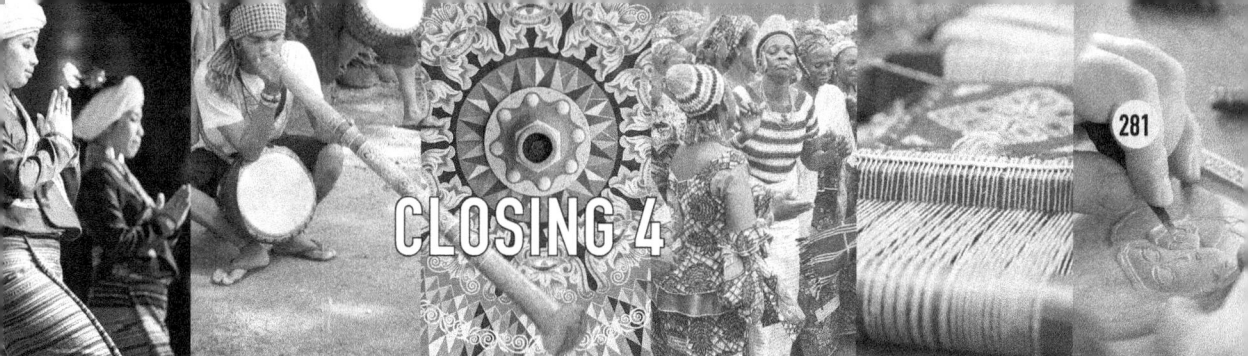

CLOSING 4

INDEX OF ARTISTIC DOMAIN RESEARCH ACTIVITIES

These research activities are described in more detail in the *CLAT Companion* (available for free download at www.clatmanual.com).

MUSICAL FEATURES IN ENACTMENTS AND EVENTS

Explore how participants change their musical behavior in response to their physical space
Explore how participants design or use space to affect musical sounds
Determine the form of a song or piece
Identify the roles of musical production
List musical instruments
Describe each musical instrument in several ways
Describe instrumental and vocal timbres
Determine the number of notes per speech syllable in a song
Determine and describe the texture(s) of a piece or song
Determine and describe the rhythm(s) of a piece or song
Determine and describe the tempo(s) of a piece or song
Determine and describe the dynamic(s) of a piece or song
Determine and describe the notes of a piece or song
Explore relationships between melody, rhythm, and other features of sung text
Identify and briefly describe speech surrogates

DRAMATIC FEATURES IN ENACTMENTS AND EVENTS

Describe how participants design space
Describe the enactment space configuration and directionality
Explore how participants use materials to evoke an imagined story
Summarize how costumes, props, set pieces, and lighting combine to show dramatic setting
Audio and/or video record a dramatic enactment in preparation for structure analysis
Using a play script or enactment transcription, write a French scene analysis
From your French scene analysis, create a plot summary
From your French scene analysis, write a dramatic intensity curve
Observe or participate in a rehearsal of an enactment

Discover who is responsible for the creation and execution of different aspects of the enactment
Describe the members of the enactment group and what part each plays
Describe the audience's relationship to performed reality
Describe how participants use their enactment space
Describe to what extent actors prepare their enactments in advance and to what extent they improvise
Describe the acting in a given enactment as realistic, Brechtian, or codified
Prepare for vocal feature analysis
Ask if characters' ways of speaking indicate their region(s)
Describe general sections of speech
Perform a line and get feedback on emotion and intent
Identify paralinguistic features of expressing emotion
Describe how actors modify their appearance to convey character
Describe the event's blocking
Determine the idea, theme, or dramatic premise
Describe an event's plot structure
Describe an event's temporal structure
Identify and describe a play's plot elements
Describe the degree of plot malleability
Identify who holds creative control in determining the play's structure and main point
Describe each character's type
Determine what characters want
Determine broad roles of the character
Describe the actor's relationship to his or her character
Determine whether characterization is direct or indirect
Determine the frame of the play
Explore the type of the event further
Determine the ways musical elements interact with dramatic elements

DANCE FEATURES IN ENACTMENTS AND EVENTS

Draw a floor plan of part of the dance
Identify all movement-related objects and their functions
Determine the form of a dance
Describe the basic organization of dancers
Describe how dancers relate to each other
Identify parts of the body involved in patterned movement
Describe broad characteristics of patterned movement
Identify characteristic types of movement phrasing
Identify characteristic types of movement dynamics or efforts
Identify effects of different content on movement
Perform embodied interviews

ORAL VERBAL ARTS FEATURES IN ENACTMENTS AND EVENTS

Isolate verbal elements of an audiovisual recording of an event
Transcribe the verbal texts of a recorded event
Locate each recorded verbal element nationally, regionally, macrolocally, and microlocally
Explore how participants modify their verbal actions in response to their physical space
Explore associations between the temporal occurrence of a recorded oral verbal element and broader cultural factors
Identify and describe the length of each verbal element in the event
Determine the temporal form of the artistic verbal enactment (narrative, poetry, narrative poetry, proverbs, oratory)
Identify the roles of participants producing verbal content (narratives, oratory, proverbs, poetry, songs)
List objects and describe how participants use them to emphasize or otherwise modify verbal content
Identify the poetic features of verbal content
Identify how participants use physical gestures to modify their verbal production
Identify how participants modify their voices in their verbal production
Identify the range of content expected in a verbal enactment
Identify basic elements of a story's plot
Analyze an oral (monologue) narrative
Make a preliminary musico-poetic analysis of a song
Compare the rhythmic devices of three or more songs

VISUAL FEATURES IN ENACTMENTS AND EVENTS

Describe spatial relationships between an object's visual features
Identify and describe the materials used in an object
Document the creation of an object
Compare two visual snapshots of an event
Write the history of an object
Identify the role(s) in visual art creation
Describe how people manipulate art objects
Describe how people experience objects with stylized visual features
Describe the visual features of a static object
Elicit a visual symbol's story
Analyze the message of an image
Identify the frame of a biblical story image

CLOSING 5

Index of Sample Sparking Activities

IDENTITY AND SUSTAINABILITY

Meet a community and its arts, again
Help organize a festival celebrating community art forms
Commission a new work in an older genre for an existing showcase event
Help develop multimedia collections of local arts
Publish recordings and research in various forms and contexts
Identify and mend ruptures in arts transmission

HEALING

Organize an arts and trauma healing (ATH) workshop
Commission local artists to address community health problems
Organize a special event to play traditional games
Hold an Alternatives to Violence workshop
Organize an environment-themed art show

JUSTICE

Hold workshops that magnify marginalized voices
Commission an alphabet song
Commission local visual art for books and literacy materials
Promote literacy through local arts presentations
Integrate local arts into methods to teach reading
Turn orature into literature
Integrate local arts into educational curricula

SCRIPTURE

Hold a Scripture translation workshop
Commission an oral narrative enactment of Scripture

CHURCH LIFE

Hold a corporate worship workshop
Help preachers and teachers incorporate more local arts
Hold an artistic genre workshop

Hold an arts creation workshop on worldview themes
Organize an all arts celebration
Study the Bible in more than one form as a group
Improve a current church ceremony, ritual, or practice
Hold a contest for new ways to memorize Scripture
Commission arts for community events

PERSONAL SPIRITUAL LIFE

Encourage people to commune with God through multiple arts
Mentor someone in more arts-infused spiritual disciplines
Commission a verbal art form of resolve that will help people apply scriptural truths to their lives

Glossary

Some of our definitions may surprise you. This results in large part from an emphasis on elements that cohere with our overall conceptual frameworks. Please adopt these meanings while engaging with this manual, reshaping them as you wish in your own scholarship. See www.ethnoarts.sil.org/faq/terminology for a closely related lexicon of terms particularly germane to language and community development.

agency: The ability of a group or an individual to exert power, usually in terms of making decisions.

analytical enactment: Instantiation of all or part of a genre designed by a researcher to isolate features of artistic production.

artist: Someone with exceptional knowledge and skills associated with some aspect of a community's artistry, such as composition or enactments of artistic communication genres.

artistic communication: An act of conveying messages marked by heightened attention to form and visceral and emotional impact. A system of signs—intricately entwined with language—intentionally altered from normal conventions to evoke particular stylized frames. Artistry.

artistic creativity: When one or more people draw on personal competencies and their community(ies)' social and symbolic systems to produce an enactment—event or work—of heightened communication that has not previously existed in its exact form.

artistic domain: A high level, abstract, imprecise category of artistic communication. In this manual, this term refers to features associated with Euro-American categories, including music, dance, drama, oratory, architecture, culinary and visual arts. Other societies organize their thoughts and words about arts differently.

artistic event: See *event, enactment*.

artistic genre: See *genre*.

artistic genre enactment: See *enactment*.

artistry: See *artistic communication, enactment*.

arts: A general term that refers to forms of communication marked by patterns that differ from a community's everyday communication. See *artistic communication*.

arts advocate: Anyone who advocates the use of local arts for a community's benefit. Also sometimes referred to as an ethnoarts advocate.

arts consultant, Christian: A specialist who researches and encourages Scripture-infused creativity in local artistic forms of communities around the world. Sometimes referred to as an ethnoarts consultant, ethnoarts specialist, or ethnoarts worker.

autogenic research: Investigation performed and often initiated by community members on their own communities. Related terms include auto-ethnographic research, community-based ethnography, self-research, and research with auto-actionary outcomes.

catalyst: Someone or something that starts an action that keeps going on its own. Metaphorical use of a particular kind of chemical reaction.

church: A community of Christ-followers, existing locally (church) and universally (Church). The body of Christ.

CLAT: The acronym for the Creating Local Arts Together process.

cocreation: A way of thinking about the Creating Local Arts Together (CLAT) process. It emphasizes Father|Son|Spirit's intimate involvement and the multiple roles people play in purposeful artistic production. Communities retain primary agency in such creativity.

commission: To ask an artist or group of artists to create a new instance of an artistic genre for an agreed-upon purpose. Though frequently a collaborative process, artists retain primary agency.

communication, artistic: See *artistic communication*.

community: A social group of any size whose members share a story, identity, and ongoing patterns of interaction. Communities are internally complex and constantly changing.

composition: A discrete example of a genre. See *enactment*.

contextualization: Wisely engaging culture and local context in expressing biblical Christian faith and practice.

creativity: See *artistic creativity*.

cultural domain: A broad category of cultural meanings or phenomena that includes smaller categories. Examples include emotions and aesthetics.

cultural theme: Any principle that recurs in several cultural domains and defines relationships among sets of cultural meanings.

effects, of artistry: Changes in a person or group tied to meaning(s) they attribute to creating, enacting, experiencing, participating in, remembering, or otherwise engaging with types of artistry. These changes could include the way people feel, act, understand, remember, pray, talk, think, relate to others, and so on.

emic: A viewpoint from inside a community being studied.

enactment: A full or partial instantiation of a genre marked by artistry. A particular category of communication, a set of ideas made concrete and experienceable during an event. We sometimes refer to enactments as artistry, or bits of artistry.

ethnoarts: Study of the artistic communication of a community and its applications to their betterment. Often focuses on minority—especially ethnolinguistic—groups. An emerging discipline.

ethnocentrism: An attitude in which people evaluate aspects of a different culture based on values and assumptions from their own.

ethnodoxology: The interdisciplinary study of how Christians in every culture engage with God and the world through their own artistic expressions. See other definitions at the GEN site here: https://bit.ly/3UWN8O5.

ethnography: The investigation and description of communities through direct, purposeful interaction with people. A performance or enactment ethnography relates how sounds, movements, dramatizations, and other artistic products are conceived, made, appreciated and influence individuals, groups, and social and artistic processes.[1]

ethnomusicology: The study of music *in* and *as* culture.

etic: A viewpoint from outside a community being studied.

event: Something that occurs in a particular place and time containing the enactment of at least one artistic genre. It is experienced through sensory pathways, divisible into shorter time segments, and related to larger sociocultural patterns of a community. The scope of an event can vary widely depending how broad or narrow your focus is.

gatekeeper: A person who exerts significant influence on whether a community accepts an innovation or not, who has a personal or social stake in its success or failure.

genre: A community's shared category of communication marked by artistry and characterized by a unique set of formal characteristics, enactment practices, and social meanings. Genre is an abstraction held by multiple community members as patterns and meanings in their minds and bodies.

integral enactment context: Enactment of a genre in an environment that has many social and artistic components that are familiar to the participants.

---

[1] Inspired by Seeger, "Ethnography of Music."

Kingdom goals: Objectives that are consistent with the Kingdom of Heaven as described primarily in the New Testament. They are incomplete manifestations of Heaven on Earth.

Labanotation: A system for transcribing dance movements.

language (or language-based) development: The series of ongoing, planned actions that a language community takes to ensure that their language continues to serve their changing social, cultural, political, economic, and spiritual needs and goals.

local artistic genre: A type of artistic language that a community knows well enough to create, enact, teach, and understand from within, including its forms, meanings, language(s), and social context(s). Local artistic genres can include those with long traditions in a community, or can be adopted or fused with other genres. Communities usually identify them as their own. We sometimes refer to these as *local genres* or *local arts*.

local arts: See *local artistic genre*.

meaning: Ideas and emotions a community or individual attaches to elements of their internal or external experiences.

meristem: The region in a plant in which new cells are created; the growth point.

multicultural: Any event, process, community, or artistic enactment that includes elements or people from more than one ethnic, national or other foundational social grouping.

music: Humanly organized and heightened sound.

object: A type of genre enactment that is material, marked by artistry, and perceived through sensory pathways. Objects generally retain their form through time and are often integrated into enactments of performance genres, events, and other objects.

orality: A preference for and reliance on oral communication; a learned framework for expressing mind and heart through all five senses.[2]

orature: A body of works communicated orally, such as stories, myths, and folklore.

organology: The study of musical instruments.[3]

participant observation: An investigative practice used in ethnographic research in which the researcher engages in life activities with the participants of the study.

performance: A type of genre enactment marked by participants producing artistry that progresses through time. See *object* for contrast.

phenomenology: A philosophical approach to the structures and meanings of our experiences of events. See *meaning*.

polysemy: The ability of one form or symbol to hold multiple meanings.

qualitative research: An approach in which the researcher collects open-ended, emerging, and evolving data with the primary intent of developing themes from the data. The results tend to focus on meanings and experiences.

quantitative research: An approach that focuses on specific variables and the testing of specific hypotheses, that employs strategies such as experiments and surveys, and that yields statistical data. The results tend to focus on numbers and frequencies.

reflexivity: The acknowledgment that representations of reality are constructions of a person and informed by their own choices and viewpoints. Especially important for those performing ethnographic research.

revitalization / cultural revitalization: Strengthening the vitality of a dead or dying tradition through research, creation, and use of indigenous resources.

rule of thirds: In photography, a frame can be divided into three vertical and three horizontal sections. Many people believe that an object becomes more prominent if it is not in the center of the frame, but rather along those lines and especially at their intersections.

Scripture engagement: A process where Scripture translated in the language of the users is intentionally integrated in their individual and community life.

---

[2] Our thanks to Chuck Madinger for help in defining this term. For more information on orality, see the Institutes for Orality Strategies at https://i-os.org.

[3] For an amusing exploration of the origins and obscurity of this term, see https://bit.ly/3QQ35Ty.

semiotics: Semiotics is the study of signs and symbols and how they are used to communicate meaning. It examines the ways we bring our background and experience to the creation and interpretation of signs (whether spoken or written language, images, sounds, or objects) and how we individually and communally perceive these signs in different contexts and cultures to produce common understandings.

sign types (in the theory of semiotics):

    Lexical (or propositional). A conventional *symbolic* sign relates a sign and an object *through language*—propositional, conventional, referential language.

    Iconic. Relates a sign and an object *through resemblance*: the sign looks or sounds or feels in some way like the object it points to.

    Indexical. Relates a sign to its object *through co-occurrence in actual experience* (i.e., by association). Sometimes called "connotation."

sparking activity: anything anybody does that results in the creation of new artistry. See *catalyst*.

stable|malleable dynamo: Consists of two socially constructed elements interacting in ways that produce energy. One element is marked by a significant level of temporospatial predictability, the other exhibits more variability.

sustainability: Usually used for development projects, a desired characteristic where what is initiated in a community will be continued or further developed.

syncretism: Combining Christian beliefs with those of another religion or worldview that leads people away from the truth.

tacit knowledge: Information held by culture-bearers (community insiders) that is not easily expressed.

taxonomy: A set of categories organized on the basis of a single semantic relationship which shows the relationships of all the terms in a domain.

transcription: Graphic representation of aspects of artistic communication.

Bibliography

Achebe, Chinua. *Things Fall Apart*. Penguin Classics, 2006.

Adolphs, Ralph. "Cognitive Neuroscience of Human Social Behavior." *Nature Reviews Neuroscience* 4 (2003): 165–78.

Alcorn, Randy. *Heaven: A Comprehensive Guide to Everything the Bible Says about Our Eternal Home*. Tyndale Momentum, 2004.

Alcorn, Randy. *We Shall See God: Charles Spurgeon's Classic Devotional Thoughts on Heaven*. Tyndale House Publishers, 2011.

Alter, Robert, and Frank Kermode, eds. *The Literary Guide to the Bible*. Belknap Press, 1987.

Amoateng, Kofi. "Engaging Theology and Theological Education in the Majority World: Recognizing Visual and Symbolic Theology from the Akan People's Illustrations." *Global Forum on Arts and Christian Faith* 6 (November 2, 2018): A27–42. https://artsandchristianfaith.org/index.php/journal/article/view/53.

Anderson, Janna, Lee Rainie, and Emily Vogels. "Experts Say the 'New Normal' in 2025 Will Be Far More Tech-Driven, Presenting More Big Challenges." *Pew Research Center*, February 18, 2021. https://www.pewresearch.org/internet/2021/02/18/experts-say-the-new-normal-in-2025-will-be-far-more-tech-driven-presenting-more-big-challenges.

Anthony, Douglas R. "A Beautiful, Wonderful Gospel." *Alliance Life* 159, no. 3 (May/June 2024). https://issuu.com/cmalliance/docs/24_05may-06jun_alliance-life_lo-res.

Apel, Willi. *Harvard Dictionary of Music*. Harvard University Press, 2003.

Aronis, Alex B. *Developing Intimacy with God: An Eight-Week Prayer Guide Based on Ignatius' "Spiritual Exercises."* AuthorHouse, 2003.

ARSC. "Education and Training in Audiovisual Archiving and Preservation." Accessed May 4, 2024. https://arsc-audio.org/education-training.

"Arts with God." Global Ethnodoxology Network. Accessed May 23, 2024. https://tinyurl.com/ABF-artswithGod.

Ball, Philip. *The Music Instinct: How Music Works and Why We Can't Do Without It*. Oxford University Press, 2012.

Ball, William. *A Sense of Direction: Some Observations on the Art of Directing*. Drama Publishers, 1984.

Barber, Karin, John Collins, and Alain Ricard. *West African Popular Theatre*. Indiana University Press, 1997.

Barber, Ron. "Globalization, Contextualization, and Indigeneity: Local Approaches to Indigenous Christianity." *Missiology* 48, no. 4 (2020): 376–91. https://doi.org/10.1177/0091829620916918.

Barton, Ruth Haley. *Sacred Rhythms: Arranging Our Lives for Spiritual Transformation*. InterVarsity Press, 2006.

Barz, Gregory. *Performing Religion: Negotiating Past and Present in Kwaya Music of Tanzania*. Amsterdam: Rodopi, 2003.

Barz, Gregory. *Singing for Life: HIV/AIDS and Music in Uganda*. Routledge, 2006.

Barz, Gregory, Benjamin Koen, and Kenneth Brunnel-Smith. "Introduction: Confluence of Consciousness in Music, Medicine, and Culture." In *The Oxford Handbook of Medical Ethnomusicology*, edited by Benjamin Koen et al., 3–17. Oxford University Press, 2008.

Bauman, Richard, ed. *Folklore, Cultural Performances, and Popular Entertainments*. Oxford University Press, 1992.

Berry, Wendell. *What Are People For?: Essays*, 2nd edition. Counterpoint, 2010.

Betuel, Emma. "Art Therapy Is Finally Being Taken Seriously as a Tool for Boosting Health." Inverse, November 12, 2019. https://www.inverse.com/article/60833-art-therapy-world-health-organization.

Biel, Łucja. "Genre Analysis and Translation." In *The Routledge Handbook of Translation Studies and Linguistics*, edited by Kirsten Malmkjær, 151–64. Routledge, 2017.

Biswas, Ranjita. "Dancing Away the Pain." *Guardian Weekly*. October 12, 2010. http://www.guardian.co.uk/world/2010/oct/12/kolkata-women-trafficking-dance-therapy.

Blaising, Craig A. "A Critique of Gentry and Wellum's, *Kingdom Through Covenant: A Hermeneutical-Theological Response*," *Master's Seminary Journal* 26, no. 1 (Spring 2015): 122.

Boal, Augusto. *The Rainbow of Desire: The Boal Method of Theatre and Therapy*. Routledge, 1995.

Bonhoeffer, Dietrich. *Creation and Fall: A Theological Interpretation of Genesis 1–3*. Macmillan, 1959.

Brown, Rick. "Contextualization without Syncretism." *International Journal of Frontier Missions* 23, no. 3 (2006): 127–33. http://www.ijfm.org/PDFs_IJFM/23_3_PDFs/brown%20c45.pdf.

Buchanan, Mark. *The Rest of God: Restoring Your Soul by Restoring Sabbath*. Thomas Nelson, 2007.

Burk, Denny, John G. Stackhouse Jr., Robin A. Parry, Jerry L. Walls. *Four Views on Hell*. 2nd ed, edited by Preston Sprinkle. Zondervan, 2016.

Calhoun, Adele Ahlberg. *Spiritual Disciplines Handbook: Practices That Transform Us*. InterVarsity Press, 2005.

Camlin, David A., Helena Daffern, and Katherine Zeserson. "Group Singing as a Resource for the Development of a Healthy Public: A Study of Adult Group Singing." *Humanities and Social Sciences Communications* 7, no. 60 (2020). https://doi.org/10.1057/s41599-020-00549-0.

Campbell, Karen. "God Looks Back on Us." In *All the World Is Singing: Glorifying God through the Worship Music of the Nations*, edited by Frank Fortunato, with Paul Neeley and Carol Brinneman, 110–15. Authentic, 2006.

Chaiklin, Sharon, and Hilda Wengrower, eds. *The Art and Science of Dance/Movement Therapy | Life Is Dance*. 2nd ed. Routledge Taylor and Francis Group, 2016. https://uat.taylorfrancis.com/books/edit/10.4324/9781315693477/art-science-dance-movement-therapy-sharon-chaiklin-hilda-wengrower.

Chang, Heewon, Faith Ngunjiri, and Kathy-Ann Hernandez. *Collaborative Autoethnography*. Routledge, 2013.

Chenoweth, Vida. *Melodic Perception and Analysis*. Ukarumpa, Papua New Guinea: Summer Institute of Linguistics, 1972.

Chenoweth, Vida. *Sing-Sing: Communal Singing and Dancing in Papua New Guinea*. Christchurch, New Zealand: University of Canterbury, 2020. https://vidachenoweth.com/wp-content/uploads/2020/12/sing-sing.pdf.

Chow, Alexander 曹榮錦. *Chinese Public Theology: Generational Shifts and Confucian Imagination in Chinese Christianity*. Oxford: Oxford University Press, 2018.

Chu, Gillian. "Analysis of Stanley Hauerwas' Theology in Post-Umbrella Movement Hong Kong." *Journal of the Regent College Student Association: Academic Symposium*: 14–22, 2018.

Coggins, David. "Response to 'What Are Some Historical Examples of Technological Advancements Disrupting Creative Industries, and How Did Those Industries Adapt?'" *Quora*, June 22, 2023. https://www.quora.com/What-are-some-historical-examples-of-technological-advancements-disrupting-creative-industries-and-how-did-those-industries-adapt.

Colgate, Jack. "Relational Bible Storying and Scripture Use in Oral Muslim Contexts." *International Journal of Frontier Missions* 25(3): 135–42. http://www.ijfm.org/PDFs_IJFM/25_3_PDFs/colgate.pdf.

Collinge, Ian. "Intercultural Worship: A Contemporary Understanding of Church and Worship in the Global Age." In *Arts across Cultures: Reimagining the Christian Faith in Asia*, edited by Warren R. Beattie and Anne M. Y. Soh, 119–40. Regnum Books International, 2022. https://bit.ly/4bcapB7.

Collins, Samuel Gerald, et al. 2017. "Ethnographic Apps/Apps as Ethnography." *Anthropology Now* 9, no. 1: 102–18. https://doi.org/10.1080/19428200.2017.1291054.

Connor, Matt. "Creativity, Liminality, and Metaphor in Songwriting." *Ethnodoxology: Global Forum on Arts and Christian Faith* 10 (2022): A61–76.

Connor, Matt, and Matt Menger. "Strengthening Christian Identity through Scripture Songwriting in Indonesia." *Religions* 12, no. 10 (2021): 873. https://doi.org/10.3390/rel12100873.

Corbitt, Seve, and Brian Fikkert. *When Helping Hurts: How to Alleviate Poverty Without Hurting the Poor … and Yourself*. Moody Publishers, 2014.

Coulter, Neil. "Assessing Music Shift: Adapting EGIDS for a Papua New Guinea Community." *Language Documentation and Description* 10 (2011): 61–81.

Crouch, Andy. *Playing God: Redeeming the Gift of Power*. InterVarsity Press, 2013.

Csikszentmihalyi, Mihalyi. *Creativity: Flow and the Psychology of Discovery and Invention*. HarperCollins, 1996.

Cuthbert, Anne Shirley. 2023. "Church-Based Curriculum Integrating Literacy and Spiritual Development among a Local Language Community." *Journal of Language Culture and Religion* 4 (2): 7–47. https://www.diu.edu/jlcr/volume-4-number-2/.

Darko, Daniel. *First the Kingdom of God: Global Voices on Global Mission*, edited by Beth Snodderly. William Carey International University Press, 2014.

da Silva, Lauren, curator. *On Earth as in Heaven: An Anthology*. Flourish Hub Media Company, 2022.

Davis, Josh, and Nikki Lerner. *Worship Together in Your Church as in Heaven*. Abingdon Press, 2015.

Davis, Matthew. "Health through Song: Outreach Workers in Benin and Guatemala Use Lyrics to Promote Health." *Harvard Medical Alumni Bulletin* 73 (1999): 36–41.

Delton, A. W., and A. Sell. "The Co-evolution of Concepts and Motivation." *Current Directions in Psychological Science* 23, no. 2 (2014): 115–20.

De Sousa, Avinash. "Client-Centered Therapy." *Indian Journal of Applied Research* 4, no. 2 (2014): 10–13.

De Vries, Lourens. "The Notion of Genre and the Nature of Bible Translations." *Notes on Translation* 13, no. 2 (1999): 26–42.

Dickie, June F. "Community Translation and Oral Performance of Some Praise Psalms within the Zulu Community." *The Bible Translator* 68, no. 3 (2017): 253–68. https://doi.org/10.1177/2051677017728564.

Dickie, June F. "Translating Psalms for Performance and Their Use in Various Ministries within the Church: Examples from South Africa." *The Bible Translator* 73, no. 1 (2022): 6–25. https://doi.org/10.1177/20516770211066935.

Doğuş Varli, Özlem. "Towards to Gastroethnomusiciology-I." (in Turkish) *Ethnomusicology Journal* 5, no. 1 (2022): 97–139.

Dooley, Robert A., and Stephen H. Levinsohn. *Analyzing Discourse: A Manual of Basic Concepts*. SIL International, 2000.

Dossa, Parin, and Jelena Golubovic. "Community Based Ethnography." *The International Encyclopedia of Anthropology*, edited by Hilary Callan, 1–7. John Wiley & Sons, 2018. http://doi.org/10.1002/9781118924396.wbiea2267.

Dutton, Denis. *The Art Instinct: Beauty, Pleasure, and Human Evolution.* Bloomsbury Press, 2009.

Duvall, J. Scott, and J. Daniel Hays. *Grasping God's Word,* 4th ed. Zondervan, 2020.

Earley, Justin Whitmel. *The Common Rule: Habits of Purpose for an Age of Distraction.* IVP Books, 2019.

Ekpenyong, Obo Ekpenyong, and Ibiang Obono Okoi. "Africanization of Christianity: Henry Venn's Indigenization of Christianity." *International Journal of Humanities and Innovation* 4, no. 2 (2021): 82–85. DOI: https://doi.org/10.33750/ijhi.v4i2.134.

Eldredge, John. *All Things New: Heaven, Earth, and the Restoration of Everything You Love.* Thomas Nelson, 2017.

Ember, Carol R., and Melvin Ember. "Basic Guide to Cross-Cultural Research." Accessed September 28, 2023. http://hraf.yale.edu/cross-cultural-research/basic-guide-to-cross-cultural-research.

Engelland, Chad. *Phenomenology.* The MIT Press, 2020.

Ethnologue. "How Many Languages Are Endangered?" Accessed May 5, 2024. https://www.ethnologue.com/insights/how-many-languages-endangered/.

Ezhevskaya, Anna. "Russian Bards in America." PhD Diss, Dallas International University, 2023.

Fargion, Janet Topp, ed. *A Manual for Documentation, Fieldwork, and Preservation for Ethnomusicologists,* 2nd ed. Society for Ethnomusicology, 2001.

Feldman, Edmund B. *Varieties of Visual Experience,* 4th ed. New York: Adams, 1992.

Ferguson, Tom. "Music, Drama, and Storying: Exciting Foundations for Church Planting." In *All the World Is Singing: Glorifying God through the Worship Music of the Nations,* edited by Frank Fortunato, with Paul Neeley and Carol Brinneman, 199–204. Authentic, 2006.

Ferraro, Gary, and Susan Andreatta. *Cultural Anthropology: An Applied Perspective,* 9th ed. Wadsworth, 2011.

Ferro, Lígia, and David Poveda, editors. *Arts and Ethnography in a Contemporary World: From Learning to Social Participation.* Tuffnel Press, 2019.

Fiebrink, Rebecca. "Will AI Kill the Future of the Creative Arts?" Open to Debate podcast, 2023. https://podcasts.apple.com/us/podcast/will-ai-kill-the-future-of-the-creative-arts/id216713308?i=1000637919701.

Finnegan, Ruth. *Communicating: The Multiple Modes of Human Interconnection.* Routledge, 2002.

Fitzgerald, Dan, and Brian Schrag. "But is it any good? The role of criticism in Christian song composition and performance." *Ethnodoxology: Global Forum on Arts and Christian Faith* 2, no. 1 (2014): A2–A19. https://artsandchristianfaith.org/index.php/journal/article/view/7.

Foerster, Liz, and Mary Beth Saurman. *Producing Culturally Relevant Language Development Teaching Materials.* SIL International, 2021.

Fokkelman, J. P. *Reading Biblical Poetry: An Introductory Guide.* 1st ed. Westminster John Knox Press, 2001.

Fortunato, Frank, Paul Neeley, and Carol Brinneman, eds. *All the World Is Singing: Glorifying God through the Worship Music of the Nations.* Authentic, 2006.

Frakes, Jack. *Acting for Life: A Textbook on Acting.* Meriwether, 2005.

Franklin, Karl J. *Loosen Your Tongue: An Introduction to Storytelling.* Graduate Institute of Applied Linguistics, 2009.

Frost, Katie Hoogerheide. "Why Consider Local Genres in Translation?" *Journal of Translation* 20, no. 1 (2024): 91–117. https://doi.org/10.54395/JOT-KHFLG.

Frost, Katie Hoogerheide, and Joshua L. Harper. "Processing Pain through Artistry: Old Testament Poetry of Exile and Ezekiel 19." *Journal of Language Culture and Religion* 3, no. 2 (2022): 17–30. https://www.diu.edu/jlcr/volume-3-number-2/.

Fujimura, Makoto. *Art and Faith: A Theology of Making.* Yale University Press, 2021.

Fung, Patrick. "Cooperation in a Polycentric World." Plenary presentation, WEA Mission Commission Global Consultation, Panama City, Panama, October 3–7, 2016.

GEMeDOT. "Soul Connection," 2018. Smartphone app. Accessed September 16, 2022. https://gemedot.com/soul-connection/.

Giurchescu, Anca, and Eva Kröschlová. "Theory and Method of Dance Form Analysis." In *Dance Structures: Perspectives on the Analysis of Human Movement*, edited by Adrienne Kaeppler and Elsi Evancich Dunin, 21–52. Budapest: Akadémiai Kiadó, 2007. http://db.zti.hu/neptanc_tudastar/pdf/biblio/l00162.pdf.

Global Environments Network. "Art as Environmental Justice: Social and Creative Interventions for Planetary Healing." Accessed September 12, 2022. https://globalenvironments.org/art-as-environmental-justice-social-and-creative-interventions-for-planetary-healing.

Goheen, Michael. *Introducing Christian Mission Today: Scripture, History, and Issues.* IVP Academic, 2014.

Goldbard, Arlene. *Art Became the Oxygen: An Artistic Response Guide.* US Department of Arts and Culture. https://usdac.us/artisticresponse.

Goodridge, Janet. *Rhythm and Timing of Movement in Performance: Drama, Dance and Ceremony.* Kingsley, 1999.

Goopy, Suzanne, and Anusha Kassan. "Arts-Based Engagement Ethnography: An Approach for Making Research Engaging and Knowledge Transferable When Working with Harder-to-Reach Communities." *International Journal of Qualitative Methods* 18 (2019). https://doi.org/10.1177/1609406918820424.

Gowey, Bill. "Walking Out the Gospel among the People." *Mission Frontiers* (Sept–Oct 2010): 19–20.

Grant, Catherine. *Music Endangerment: How Language Maintenance Can Help.* Oxford University Press, 2014.

Grant, Stuart, Jodie McNeilly-Renaudie, and Matthew Wagner, eds. *Performance Phenomenology: To the Thing Itself.* Palgrave Macmillan, 2019.

Gray, Tony. "Destroyed Forever: An Examination of the Debates Concerning Annihilation and Conditional Immortality." *Themelios* 21, no. 2 (1996): 14–17.

Green, Robin. "An Orality Strategy: Translating the Bible for Oral Communicators." MA Thesis, Graduate Institute of Applied Linguistics, 2007. https://www.diu.edu/documents/theses/Green_Robin-thesis.pdf.

Greenwald, Michael L., Roger Schulz, and Roberto Dario Pomo. *The Longman Anthology of Drama and Theater: A Global Perspective.* Longman, 2001.

Griffin, Em, Andrew Ledbetter, and Glenn Sparks. *Looseleaf for First Look at Communication Theory.* 11th ed. McGraw Hill, 2022.

Grimes, Joseph E. *The Thread of Discourse: Janua Linguarum.* Mouton, 1975.

Guirguis, Youssry. "History of Contextualization." *Journal of Adventist Mission Studies* 15, no. 2 (2020): 165–84. DOI: https://dx.doi.org/10.32597/jams/vol15/iss2/11/.

Haaland, Ane. *Pretesting Communication Materials: With Special Emphasis on Child Health and Nutrition Education: A Manual for Trainers and Supervisors.* Rangoon: UNICEF, 1984.

Hackney, Peggy. *Making Connections: Total Body Integration through Bartenieff Fundamentals.* Routledge, 2000.

Handley, Joseph W. *Polycentric Mission Leadership: Toward A New Theoretical Model for Global Leadership*. Regnum Books, 2022.

Harris, Holly Reynolds. "To Serve Life, Not Death: An Exploration of the Artistry and Philosophies of Horizon Zero Dawn." MA thesis, Dallas International University, 2021.

Harris, Robin. "Contextualization: Understanding the Intersections of Form and Meaning." *EM News* 3, no. 4 (2007): 14–17. https://www.worldofworship.org/wp-content/uploads/2023/12/Syncretism-Form-Meaning-E-Dox-version.pdf.

Harris, Robin. "The Future of Ethnodoxology in Arts and Mission." *Mission Frontiers* 45, no. 5 (Sept/Oct 2023): 32–35. https://rdwrc.wciu.edu/2024/11/arts-worship-and-mission-in-todays-church.

Harris, Robin. Review of Kersten Priest's "Disharmony in the 11:00 a.m. Worship Hour." *EM News* 8, no. 3, 1999 (2000): 13–14. https://www.worldofworship.org/library/harris-reviewing-kersten-priest-disharmony-in-the-1100-hour/.

Harris, Robin P. *Storytelling in Siberia: The Olonkho Epic in a Changing World*. University of Illinois Press, 2017.

Harris, Robin, and Brian Schrag. "A Practical Approach to Arts and Mission Courses: Reflections on 'Arts for a Better Future.'" In *Arts Across Cultures: Reimagining the Christian Faith in Asia*, edited by Warren R. Beattie and Anne M. Y. Soh, 165–82. Fortress Press, 2023. https://www.worldofworship.org/library/reflections-on-arts-for-a-better-future.

Harris, Robin, Héber Negrão, and Roch Ntankeh. 2024. "Visual Affect as Validation of Truth." In Lausanne's *State of the Great Commission Report*, ed. Matthew Niermann. Accessed May 18, 2024. https://lausanne.org/report/trust/visual-affect-as-validation-of-truth.

Harrison, Klisala. "Value Alignment in Applied and Community-Based Music Research." *MUSIIKKI* 50, no. 1–2 (2020): 69–87. http://musiikki.journal.fi/article/view/95488/53932.

Hasselbring, Sue. "Steps for Nine Participatory Tools for Language Programs." GEN Virtual Library. Accessed May 16, 2024. https://www.worldofworship.org/library/nine-participatory-tools.

Hatcher, Jeffrey. *The Art and Craft of Playwriting*. Story Press, 1996.

Hatton, Howard A., and David J. Clark. "From the Harp to the Sitar." *Bible Translator* 26, no. 1 (1975): 132–38.

Herman, Judith. *Trauma and Recovery: The Aftermath of Violence—From Domestic Abuse to Political Terror*. Harper, 2015.

Hernandez Mathis, Cindy. "The Vocation of the Catholic Artist." *First Things* (October 23, 2023). https://www.firstthings.com/web-exclusives/2023/10/the-vocation-of-the-catholic-artist.

Heschel, Abraham Joshua. *The Sabbath*. Farrar, Straus, & Giroux, 2005.

Hesselgrave, David J. "Contextualization That Is Authentic and Relevant." *International Journal of Frontier Missiology* 12, no. 3 (1995): 115–19. http://www.ijfm.org/PDFs_IJFM/12_3_PDFs/01_Hesselgrave.pdf.

Hiebert, Paul G. *Anthropological Insights for Missionaries*. Baker Book House, 1985.

Hiebert, Paul G. "Critical Contextualization." *Missiology* 12, no. 3 (1984): 287–96. https://doi.org/10.1177/009182968401200303.

Hill, Harriet Swannie. *Communicating Context in Bible Translation among the Adioukrou of Côte d'Ivoire*. Ann Arbor, MI: UMI, 2003.

Hill, Harriet, Richard Bagge, Pat Miersma, and Margaret Hill. *Healing the Wounds of Trauma*. American Bible Society, 2015.

Hill, Harriet, and Margaret Hill. *Translating the Bible into Action*. 2nd ed. Langham Global Library, 2022.

Hogan, Christine. *Practical Facilitation: A Toolkit of Techniques*. Kogan Page Limited, 2003.

Hood, Mantle. "The Challenge of Bi-Musicality." *Ethnomusicology* 4 (1960): 55–59.

Hoogerheide, Katie, and Robin Harris. "Engaging the Arts in God's Mission." In *Spirituality in Mission: Embracing the Lifelong Journey*, edited by J. Amalraj, G. W. Hahn, and W. D. Taylor, 167–76. William Carey Library, 2016.

Hopper, Elizabeth. "An Introduction to Rogerian Therapy." ThoughtCo, August 1, 2021. https://www.thoughtco.com/rogerian-therapy-4171932.

Hughes-Freeland, Felicia. "Dance on Film: Strategy and Serendipity." In *Dance in the Field: Theory, Methods and Issues in Dance Ethnography*, edited by Theresa J. Buckland, 111–21. St. Martin's Press, 1999.

"Human Relations Area Files—Cultural Information for Education and Research." HRAF. Accessed April 23, 2024. https://hraf.yale.edu/.

Hutchinson Guest, Ann. *Labanotation: The System of Analyzing and Recording Movement*. Routledge, 2005.

Hutchinson Guest, Ann, and Tina Curran. *Your Move: The Language of Dance Approach to the Study of Movement and Dance*. Taylor & Francis, 2008.

"Inside 'the Most Diverse Square Mile in America.'" 2022. *Yahoo News*. CBS News. https://news.yahoo.com/inside-most-diverse-square-mile-140538150.html.

Isasi-Diaz, Ada Maria. "Kin-dom of God: A Mujerista Proposal." In *In Our Own Voices: Latino/a Renditions of Theology*, edited by Benjamín Valentín, 171–90. Orbis Books, 2010. Accessed April 9, 2024. http://hdl.handle.net/2027/heb.31279.0001.001.

James, Steven L. "Recent New Creation Conceptions and the Christian Mission." *Canadian Theological Review* 4, no. 1 (2015): 24–35. Accessed March 5, 2024. https://jrichardmiddleton.files.wordpress.com/2020/05/ctreview-2015-v4.1-james.pdf.

Johnson, Julene, and Jeff Chapline. "The National Endowment for the Arts Guide to Community-Engaged Research in the Arts and Health," 2016. https://www.arts.gov/impact/research/publications/national-endowment-arts-guide-community-engaged-research-arts-and-health.

Johnston, Clay, and Carol Orwig. "Your Learning Style and Language Learning." In *LinguaLinks Library, Logos Edition*. SIL International, 2016. https://www.sil.org/resources/publications/entry/67412.

Jones, Arun W. "Hybridity and Christian Identity." *Missiology* 50, no. 1 (2022): 7–16.

Jules-Rosette, Bennetta. "Ecstatic Singing: Music and Social Integration in an African Church." In *More than Drumming: Essays on African and Afro-Latin American Music and Musicians*, edited by Irene V. Jackson, 119–44. Greenwood, 1985.

Just, Felix. "Biblical Exegesis: Methods of Interpretation." Accessed May 11, 2024. https://catholic-resources.org/Bible/Exegesis.htm.

Kaner, Sam. *Facilitator's Guide to Participatory Decision-Making*, 3rd ed. Jossey-Bass, 2014.

Keller, Susan. "Deciding and Planning Together: Engaging Oral-Preference Communicators Using a Participatory Approach." *Orality Journal* 4, no. 2 (2015): 9–40. https://www.worldofworship.org/library/keller-deciding-and-planning-together-a-participatory-approach.

Kenmogne, Michel. "Theologizing in Context: An Example from the Study of a Ghomala' Christian Hymn." *Global Forum on Arts and Christian Faith* 6 (Feb 23, 2018): A14–26. https://artsandchristianfaith.org/index.php/journal/article/view/48.

Kim, Joy Hyunsook. "Diaspora Musicians and Creative Collaboration in a Multicultural Community: A Case Study in Ethnodoxology." MA thesis. Dallas International University, 2018. https://www.diu.edu/documents/theses/Kim_Joy-thesis.pdf.

King, Roberta. *A Time to Sing: A Manual for the African Church*. Nairobi: Evangel Publishing House, 1999.

King, Roberta, and William Dyrness, eds. *The Arts as Witness in Multifaith Contexts*. IVP Academic, 2019.

Kirby, Michael. "On Acting and Not-Acting." In *Acting (Re)Considered*, 2nd ed. Routledge, 2002.

Klem, Herbert V. *Oral Communication of the Scripture: Insights from African Oral Art*. William Carey Library, 1982.

Koch, Sabine C., Roxana F. F. Riege, Katharina Tisborn, Jacelyn Biondo, Lily Martin, and Andreas Beelmann. "Effects of Dance Movement Therapy and Dance on Health-Related Psychological Outcomes. A Meta-Analysis Update." *Frontiers in Psychology* 10, 1806 (2019). https://pubmed.ncbi.nlm.nih.gov/31481910.

Kohls, Robert L., and Herbert L. Brussow. *Training Know-How for Cross-Cultural and Diversity Trainers*. Duncanville, TX: Adult Learning Systems, 1995.

Krabill, James R. "Hymn-Collecting among the Dida Harrists." *Global Forum on Arts and Christian Faith* 2, no. 1 (2014): A20–36.

Krabill, James R. "Why Arts and Mission Belong Together." *Mission Frontiers* 45, no. 5 (Sept/Oct 2023): 8–10. https://rdwrc.wciu.edu/2024/11/arts-worship-and-mission-in-todays-church.

Krabill, James R., general ed., Frank Fortunato, Robin P. Harris, and Brian Schrag, eds. *Worship and Mission for the Global Church: An Ethnodoxology Handbook*. William Carey Library, 2013.

Krüger, Simone. *Ethnography in the Performing Arts: A Student Guide*. PALATINE, Higher Education Academy, 2008. https://researchonline.ljmu.ac.uk/id/eprint/543.

Labeth, Ruth. "Struggling to Be Creole: A Case Study of Musical Contextualization in the French Caribbean Evangelical Churches." *Global Forum on Arts and Christian Faith* 9 (2021): A54–70. https://artsandchristianfaith.org/index.php/journal/article/view/141.

Ladd, D. Robert, and James Kirby. "Tone—Melody Matching in Tone-Language Singing," in *The Oxford Handbook of Language Prosody*, edited by Carlos Gussenhhoven and Aoju Chen, 676–88. Oxford University Press, 2020.

Langberg, Diane. *Suffering and the Heart of God: How Trauma Destroys and Christ Restores*. New Growth Press, 2015.

Lassiter, Luke Eric. *The Chicago Guide to Collaborative Ethnography*. University of Chicago Press, 2005.

Laurie, Greg. *As It Is in Heaven: How Eternity Brings Focus to What Really Matters*. NavPress, 2014.

Lausanne Movement. "Redeeming the Arts." Accessed May 2, 2024. https://lausanne.org/wp-content/uploads/2007/06/LOP46_IG17.pdf.

Lester, P. M. *Visual Communication: Images with Messages*, 4th ed. Thomson-Wadsworth Publishing, 2003.

Lewis, C. S. *The Business of Heaven: Daily Readings*. Reissue edition. HarperOne, 2017.

Lewis, C. S. *The Great Divorce*. ValdeBooks, 2024.

Lewis, C. S. *The Last Battle*. Reprint edition. HarperCollins, 2002.

Lewis, C. S. *Mere Christianity*. Revised & Enlarged ed. Harper San Francisco, 2001.

Lewis, Paul, and Gary Simons. "Assessing Endangerment: Expanding Fishman's GIDS." *Revue Roumaine de Linguistique* 55, no. 2 (2010): 103–20.

Lewis, Paul, and Gary Simons. *Sustaining Language Use: Perspectives on Community-Based Language Development*. Leanpub, 2017.

Liew, Tat-siong Benny, Fernando Segovia, et al. *Colonialism and the Bible: Contemporary Reflections from the Global South*. Lexington Books, 2020.

Lim, Swee Hong. "What Is the Right Kind of Worship ... If You Want North American Congregations to Sing Global Songs?" *Global Forum on Arts and Christian Faith* 5 (Oct 27, 2017): A48–57. https://artsandchristianfaith.org/index.php/journal/article/view/43.

Lipoński, Wojciech. *World Sports Encyclopedia*. St. Paul, MN: MBI, 2003.

Longacre, Robert E. "Discourse Structure, Verb Forms, and Archaism in Psalm 18." *Journal of Translation* 2, no. 1 (2006): 17–30.

Longacre, Robert E. *The Grammar of Discourse*, 2nd ed. Plenum, 1996.

Longacre, Robert E., and Shin Ja J. Hwang. *Holistic Discourse Analysis*. SIL International, 2012.

Longacre, Robert E., and Stephen H. Levinsohn. "Field Analysis of Discourse." In *Current Trends in Textlinguistics*, edited by Wolfgang U. Dressler, 103–22. Walter de Gruyter, 1978.

Lord, Maria. "Talmou Songs of the Pouye of Papua New Guinea: Stable and Malleable Properties of a Single-Melody Genre." MA thesis, Dallas International University, 2019. https://www.diu.edu/documents/theses/Lord_Maria-thesis.pdf.

Lupton, Robert. *Toxic Charity: How Churches and Charities Hurt Those They Help, and How to Reverse It*. HarperOne, 2012.

Macchia, Stephen. *Crafting a Rule of Life: An Invitation to the Well-Ordered Way*. IVP Books, 2012.

Maletic, Vera. *Dance Dynamics: Effort and Phrasing Workbook*. Grade A Notes, 2004.

Malkemus, Samuel Arthur. "Toward a General Theory of Enaction: Biological, Transpersonal, and Phenomenological Dimensions." *Journal of Transpersonal Psychology* 44, no. 2 (2012): 201–23.

Manaher, Shawn. "Create vs Craft: Do These Mean the Same? How to Use Them." The Content Authority. Accessed February 7, 2024. https://thecontentauthority.com/blog/create-vs-craft.

Margolin, Leslie. "Rogerian Psychotherapy and the Problem of Power: A Foucauldian Interpretation." *Journal of Humanistic Psychology* 60, no. 1 (2020): 130–43.

Margolis, Joseph. *The Language of Art and Art Criticism: Analytic Questions in Aesthetics*. Wayne State University Press, 1965.

Marsen, Sky. "The Role of Meaning in Human Thinking." *Journal of Evolution and Technology* 17, no. 1 (2008): 45–58. https://jetpress.org/v17/marsen.htm.

Martin, Ralph P. *A Hymn of Christ: Philippians 2:5–11 in Recent Interpretation & in the Setting of Early Christian Worship*. InterVarsity Press, 1997.

Mātenga, Jay. "Reimagining Missions: Everyone to Everywhere." *WEA Mission Commission* (blog), October 10, 2024. https://weamc.global/everyoneverywhere.

McKay, Sherrie L. "Worship Arts Ministry: Transitioning from Monocultural Worship to a Multiethnic Worshiping Community." DMin Diss., Nazarene Theological Seminary, 2022. https://www.worldofworship.org/library/multicultural-worship-arts-ministry-transitioning-from-monocultural-worship-to-a-multiethnic-worshiping-community.

McKee, Robert. *Story: Substance, Structure, Style, and the Principles of Screenwriting*. HarperCollins, 1997.

McKinney, Carol. *Globetrotting in Sandals: Field Guide to Cultural Research*. SIL International, 2000. https://archive.org/details/globetrottingins0000mcki.

McLaughlin, Buzz. *The Playwright's Process: Learning the Craft from Today's Leading Dramatists*. Back Stage Books, 1997.

McManus, Erwin Raphael. *The Artisan Soul: Crafting Your Life into a Work of Art*. HarperOne, 2015.

Middleton, J. Richard. *A New Heaven and a New Earth: Reclaiming Biblical Eschatology*. Baker Academic, 2014.

Mlama, Penina. "Reinforcing Existing Indigenous Communication Skills: The Use of Dance in Tanzania." In *Women in Grassroots Communication*, edited by Pilar Riaño, 51–64. Sage, 1994.

Mollica, Richard F. *Healing Invisible Wounds: Paths to Hope and Recovery in a Violent World.* Vanderbilt University Publishers, 2008.

Moon, W. Jay. *African Proverbs Reveal Christianity in Culture: A Narrative Portrayal of Builsa Proverbs Contextualizing Christianity in Ghana.* American Society of Missiology Monograph Series, vol. 5. Pickwick, 2009.

Myers, Bryant L. *Walking with the Poor: Principles and Practices of Transformational Development.* Orbis, 1999.

Myers, Helen. "Fieldwork." In *Ethnomusicology: An Introduction*, edited by Helen Myers, 21–49. Norton, 1992.

Neeley, Paul. "A Case Study: Commissioning Scripture Songs among the Akyode of Ghana." *Research Review* (Legon, Ghana), supplementary issue no. 10 (1997): 118–29.

Neeley, Paul. "Reflections of a Gatekeeper." *EM News* 6, no. 1 (1997).

Negrão, Héber. "The Arts Are Not a Universal Language." *Lausanne Global Analysis*, September 14, 2022. https://lausanne.org/content/lga/2022-09/the-arts-are-not-a-universal-language.

Nelson, Hannah. "Straight from the Pot: Cuisine and Power in West Africa and in the Epic of Sunjata." MA thesis. Dallas International University, 2018. https://www.diu.edu/documents/theses/Nelson_Hannah-thesis.pdf.

Nichols, Michael P. *The Lost Art of Listening.* Guilford Press, 2009.

Ntankeh, Nana Lie Roch. "Local Arts Training for Pastors in Cameroon and DRC." *Mission Frontiers* 45, no. 5 (2023): 26–27.

Ntankeh, Roch. "The Arts: A Powerful Communicator." *AFRIGO: Encouraging the African Church in World Mission* 9, no. 1 (2024): 7.

Ntankeh, Roch. "Le Mangabeu et la modernité: une analyse ethnomusicologique."
In *Culture et modernité au Cameroun: l'art au service du développement*, edited by A. C. Pangop Kameni and H. Fotso, 178–215. Douala: Gracas, 2022.

Ortiz, Michael. "Theological Education Can't Catch Up to Global Church Growth." *ChristianityToday.com*, June 2, 2023. https://www.christianitytoday.com/ct/2023/may-web-only/theological-education-global-church-growth-icete.html.

Ouheibi, Moncef. *Psalms of Passion for God.* (Arabic) Second Edition. Al Kalima, 2018.

Pacheco-Vega, Raul, and Kate Parizeau. "Doubly Engaged Ethnography: Opportunities and Challenges When Working with Vulnerable Communities." *International Journal of Qualitative Methods* 17 (2018): 1–13.

Padiath, Christopher Silas. "Reconciled in Christ: An Intertextual Biblical Model for Ethnodoxology Practice in Local Church Ministry." Doctor of Educational Ministry Diss., Southern Baptist Theological Seminary, 2018. https://www.worldofworship.org/library/reconciled-in-christ-an-intertextual-biblical-model-for-ethnodoxology-practice-in-local-church-ministry.

Padilla DeBorst, Ruth. "Living Well Together in the Creation Community." Accessed May 11, 2024. https://open.spotify.com/episode/6O3KZgnvzOIdxDBNPBZXTJ.

"Participatory Methods: Resources." Accessed April 26, 2024. https://www.participatorymethods.org/resources.

Pauwels, Luc, and Dawn Mannay, eds. *The SAGE Handbook of Visual Research Methods*, 2nd ed. SAGE Publications, 2020.

Pentak, Stephen, and David A. Lauer. *Design Basics*. 9th ed. Cengage Learning, 2015.

Petersen, Michelle. "Scripture Relevance Dramas." *Ethnodoxology: Global Forum on Arts and Christian Faith* 4, no. 4 (2010): 22–31.

Petersen, Michelle. "Arts Development for Scripture Engagement." *Ethnodoxology: Global Forum on Arts and Christian Faith* 5, no. 1 (2017). https://artsandchristianfaith.org/index.php/journal/article/view/31.

Pinker, Stephen. *The Language Instinct: How the Mind Creates Language*. William Morrow, 1994.

Pluger, Chris. "Translating New Testament Proverb-Like Sayings in the Style of Local Proverbs." *The Bible Translator* 66, no. 3 (2015): 324–45.

Popjes, Jack. "Now We Can Speak to God—in Song." In *Worship and Mission for the Global Church: An Ethnodoxology Handbook*, James R. Krabill, general ed.; Frank Fortunato, Robin P. Harris, and Brian Schrag, eds., 262–63. William Carey Library, 2013.

Portugal, Elsen. *Authenticity in Fusion Music: A Case Study among Indigenous Churches in Brazil*. Wipf & Stock, 2024.

Rah, Soong-Chan. "Incarnational Ministry in the Urban Context." *Missio Dei: A Journal of Missional Theology and Praxis* 3, no. 2 (August 2012). http://missiodeijournal.com/issues/md-3-2/authors/md-3-2-rah.

Reagan, Timothy. *Non-Western Educational Traditions: Alternative Approaches to Educational Thought and Theory*. Lawrence Erlbaum Associates, 1996.

Renkema, Jan. *Discourse Studies: An Introductory Textbook*. Amsterdam: Benjamins, 1993.

Richards, Paul. "A Quantitative Analysis of the Relationship between Language Tone and Melody in a Hausa Song." *African Language Studies* 13 (1972): 137–61.

Ricoeur, Paul. *Time and Narrative*, vol. 1. University of Chicago Press, 1984.

Roberts, Laura. "Diversity in Worship: Applying a Process for Artistic Multicultural Practices in Emerging Multiethnic Church Plants." *Ethnodoxology: A Global Forum on Arts and Christian Faith* 12 (2024): A75–89. https://artsandchristianfaith.org/index.php/journal/article/view/223.

Robertson, Becky. "Seven Core Values that Guide GEN." *Mission Frontiers* 45, no. 5 (Sept/Oct 2023): 11–31. https://rdwrc.wciu.edu/2024/11/arts-worship-and-mission-in-todays-church.

Rogers, Carl Ransom, and Richard E. Farson. *Active Listening*. 2nd ed. Mansfield Centre, CT: Martino, 2015.

Rohr, Richard. *Falling Upward: A Spirituality for the Two Halves of Life*. Jossey-Bass, 2011.

Roser, Max. "The Future Is Vast—What Does This Mean for Our Own Life?" Accessed April 16, 2024. https://ourworldindata.org/the-future-is-vast.

Rubin, Judith Aron, ed. *Approaches to Art Therapy: Theory and Technique*. 3rd ed. Routledge, 2016. https://doi.org/10.4324/9781315716015.

Salisbury, Murray. "Translating the Psalms by Singing Them: Promoting Heart Engagement and Poetic Power." Bible Translation Conference. Dallas, Texas, 2015.

Sanders, Charles. "Embracing the Winds of Change: Recommendations for SIL in Further Moving through Missional Paradigms." DMin Diss, Gordon-Conwell Theological Seminary, 2020. Accessed May 6, 2022. www.sil.org/resources/archives/84417.

Sanneh, Lamin. *Disciples of All Nations: Pillars of World Christianity*. Oxford, 2008.

Saurman, Mary Beth. "Culturally Relevant Songs: Teaching Tools in Education Programs." Paper presented at the joint conference of the Sixth Symposium of the International Council for Traditional Music Study Group on Music and Minorities and the Second Symposium of the International Council for Traditional Music Study Group on Applied Ethnomusicology, Hanoi, Vietnam, July 19–30, 2010.

Saurman, Mary Beth. "The Effect of Music on Blood Pressure and Heart Rate." *EM News* 4, no. 3 (1995): 2.

Saurman, Mary Beth. *Hmong Songs in Education Through a Therapeutic Lens: An Innovative Approach in Northern Thailand*. Bangkok, Thailand: White Lotus, 2021.

Saurman, Mary Beth, and Todd Saurman. "Applied Ethnomusicology: The Benefits of Approaching Music as a Heart Language." *Journal of Language and Culture* 23, no. 2 (2004): 15–29.

Saurman, Mary Beth, and Todd Saurman. "Some Principles for Leading Ethnomusicology Workshops: Encouraging the Development of New Songs in the Lives of Believers." Paper presented at the *Global Consultation on Music and Missions*, St. Paul, MN, 2006.

Saurman, Mary Beth, and Todd Saurman. "Song Checking." In *All the World Will Worship: Helps for Developing Indigenous Hymns*, 3rd ed., edited by Brian Schrag and Paul Neeley, 179–85. EthnoDoxology/ACT, 2005.

Saurman, Todd. "Singing for Survival in the Highlands of Cambodia: Revitalization of Music as Mediation and Cultural Reflexivity." PhD diss., Chiang Mai University, Chiang Mai, Thailand, 2013.

Saville-Troike, Muriel. *The Ethnography of Communication: An Introduction*. Blackwell, 2002.

Schechner, Richard. *Performance Studies: An Introduction*. 4th ed. Routledge, 2020.

Schellenberg, Murray. "Does Language Determine Music in Tone Languages?" *Ethnomusicology* 56, no. 2 (2012): 266–78.

Schiffrin, Deborah, Deborah Tannen, and Heidi E. Hamilton, eds. *The Handbook of Discourse Analysis*. Blackwell, 2001.

Schippers, Huib, and Catherine Grant. *Sustainable Futures for Music Cultures: An Ecological Perspective*. Oxford University Press, 2016.

Schrag, Brian. *Artistic Dynamos: An Ethnography on Music in African Kingdoms*. Routledge, 2022. http://ArtisticDynamos.com.

Schrag, Brian. *Creating Local Arts Together: A Manual to Help Communities Reach Their Kingdom Goals*. Pasadena, CA: William Carey Library, 2013.

Schrag, Brian. "First Moments in Heaven." Accessed May 5, 2024. https://www.firstmomentsinheaven.org.

Schrag, Brian. "How Bamiléké Music-Makers Create Culture in Cameroon." PhD diss., University of California, Los Angeles, 2005.

Schrag, Brian. "Motivations and Methods for Encouraging Artists in Longer Traditions." In *Decolonization, Heritage, and Advocacy: An Oxford Handbook of Applied Ethnomusicology*, vol. 2, edited by Jeff Todd Titon and Svanibor Pettan, 187–219. Oxford University Press, 2019.

Schrag, Brian. "Music in the Newer Churches." In *The Wiley-Blackwell Companion to World Christianity*, edited by Lamin Sanneh and Michael McClymond, 359–67. Wiley Blackwell, 2016.

Schrag, Brian, and Julisa Rowe. *Community Arts for God's Purposes: How to Create Local Artistry Together*. William Carey Publishers, 2020.

Schrag, Brian, and Muriel Swijghuisen Reigersberg. "Ethnodoxology." In *The Oxford Handbook of Music and Christian Theology*, edited by Steve Guthrie and Bennett Zon. Oxford University Press, forthcoming.

Schrag, Brian, and Kathleen Van Buren. *Make Arts for a Better Life: A Guide for Working with Communities*. Oxford University Press, 2018.

Schrag, Brian, and Paul Neeley, eds. *All the World Will Worship: Helps for Developing Indigenous Hymns*, 3rd ed. EthnoDoxology Publications, 2005.

Schrag, Brian, Robin Harris, and Kathleen Van Buren. "Make Arts for a Better Life: How to Develop Artistic Creations to Meet Community Needs and Aspirations." Workshop presented at the Mayo Clinic Humanities in Medicine Symposium, *Engaging Across Disciplines: Toward a Practice of Transdisciplinarity*. October 9, 2021.

Seeger, Anthony. "Ethnography of Music." In *Ethnomusicology: An Introduction*, edited by Helen Myers, 88–109. Norton, 1992.

Seeger, Anthony. *Why Suyá Sing: A Musical Anthropology of an Amazonian People*. University of Illinois Press, 2004.

Seeger, Anthony, and Shubha Chaudhuri, eds. *Archives for the Future: Global Perspectives on Audiovisual Archives in the 21st Century*. Calcutta: Seagull Books, 2004.

Shaw, R. Daniel. "Contextualizing the Power and the Glory." *International Journal of Frontier Missiology* 12, no. 3 (1995): 155–60. http://www.ijfm.org/PDFs_IJFM/12_3_PDFs/08_Shaw.pdf.

Shaw, R. Daniel, and William R. Burrows. *Traditional Ritual as Christian Worship: Dangerous Syncretism or Necessary Hybridity?* Orbis Books, 2018.

Shawyer, Richard. "Indigenous Worship." *Evangelical Missions Quarterly* 38, no. 3 (2002): 326–34.

Shelemay, Kay Kauffman. *Soundscapes: Exploring Music in a Changing World*. Norton, 2001.

Shetler, Joanne. "Communicating the New Information of Scripture When It Clashes with Traditional Assumptions." Paper presented at the Evangelical Missiological Society Southeast Regional Meeting, Conyers, GA, 2011.

SIL International. "Language & Culture Documentation and Description." Accessed May 13, 2019. https://www.sil.org/resources/publications/lcdd.

Smith, David Woodruff. "Phenomenology." In *The Stanford Encyclopedia of Philosophy* (Summer 2018 Edition), edited by Edward N. Zalta. https://plato.stanford.edu/archives/sum2018/entries/phenomenology/.

Spradley, James. *The Ethnographic Interview*, Reissue Edition. Waveland Press, 2016.

Spradley, James. *Participant Observation*. Reissue edition. Waveland Press, 2016.

Stallsmith, Glenn. "Languages of Worship." *Global Forum on Arts and Christian Faith* 12 (Mar 6, 2024): A1–12. https://artsandchristianfaith.org/index.php/journal/article/view/209.

Stone, Ruth. "Communication and Interaction Processes in Music Events among the Kpelle of Liberia." PhD diss., Indiana University, 1979.

Sutterfield, Ragan. *Cultivating Reality: How the Soil Might Save Us*. Wipf & Stock, 2013.

Tanoto, Anderson. "Tomorrow's Climate Leaders Will Come from Emerging Economies. Here's Why." *World Economic Forum*, 2021. https://weforum.org/agenda/2021/01/tomorrows-climate-leaders-emerging-economies.

Tapia, Andrés T. "Musicianaries." *Christianity Today* 40 (1996): 52–53. https://www.christianitytoday.com/ct/1996/october7/6tb052.html.

Taylor, Matthew R. "Allusive Walls: Disclosing Identity through Brownsville's Murals." MA thesis, Dallas International University, 2023. https://www.diu.edu/documents/theses/Taylor_Matthew-thesis.pdf.

"The Kingdom of God Is Near!" n.d. *Theology of Work* (blog). Accessed April 20, 2024. https://www.theologyofwork.org/the-high-calling/kingdom-god-near.

Thompson, Evan. *Mind in Life: Biology, Phenomenology, and the Sciences of Mind*. Harvard University Press, 2010.

Tickle, Phyllis. *The Divine Hours*, pocket ed. Oxford University Press, 2007.

Tillis, Steve. *Rethinking Folk Drama*. Greenwood Press, 1999.

Troutman, Chris. "Crying Ukhai: Engaging the Mongolian Church with the Folk Rock Genre." *Ethnodoxology: Global Forum on Arts and Christian Faith* 9 (2022): A31–A53.

Two Bears. "Seeing the Whole." In *The Greening of Faith: God, the Environment, and the Good Life*, edited by John E. Carroll, Paul Brockelman, Mary Westfall, and Bill McKibben. University of New Hampshire Press, 2016. http://muse.jhu.edu/book/46481.

UNESCO. *Atlas of the World's Languages in Danger*, 3rd ed. Edited by Christopher Moseley. UNESCO Publishing, 2010. www.unesco.org/culture/languages-atlas/.

UNESCO. "Indonesian Angklung." Accessed April 27, 2024. https://ich.unesco.org/en/RL/indonesian-*angklung*-00393.

University of Pennsylvania Libraries. "Ethnography: Doing Ethnography." Accessed April 23, 2024. https://guides.library.upenn.edu/ethnography/DoingEthnography.

Unseth, Peter. "Analyzing and Using Receptor Language Proverb Forms in Translation, Part 1: Analysis." *The Bible Translator* 57, no. 2 (2006): 79–85.

Unseth, Peter. "Collecting, Using, and Enjoying Proverbs." *SIL Forum for Language Fieldwork* 2008-002, September 2008. https://sil.org/system/files/reapdata/11/86/88/118688255437507137631691704459331007426/SILForum2008_002.pdf.

Unseth, Peter. "Comparing Methods of Collecting Proverbs: Learning to Value Working with a Community." *GIALens* 8, no. 3 (2014). http://diu.edu/documents/gialens/Vol8-3/Unseth_collecting_proverbs.pdf.

Unseth, Peter. "How to Collect 1,000 Proverbs: Field Methods for Eliciting and Collecting Proverbs." *Proverbium* 25 (2008): 399–418.

Unseth, Peter. "Receptor Language Proverb Forms in Translation, Part 2: Application." *The Bible Translator* 57, no. 4 (2006): 161–70.

Unseth, Peter. "Using Local Proverbs in Ministry." *Evangelical Missions Quarterly* 49, no. 1 (2013): 16–25.

Van Buren, Kathleen J. "Applied Ethnomusicology and HIV and AIDS: Responsibility, Ability, and Action." *Ethnomusicology* 54, no. 2 (2010): 202–23.

Van der Lugt, P. *Cantos and Strophes in Biblical Hebrew Poetry: With Special Reference to the First Book of the Psalter*. Brill, 2005.

Vatican. "Sacrosanctum Concilium." Accessed May 1, 2024. https://www.vatican.va/archive/hist_councils/ii_vatican_council/documents/vat-ii_const_19631204_sacrosanctum-concilium_en.html.

Vlach, Michal J. *The New Creation Model: A Paradigm for Discovering God's Restoration Purposes from Creation to New Creation*. Theological Studies Press, 2023.

Walls, Jerry L. *Heaven, Hell, and Purgatory: Rethinking the Things that Matter Most*. Brazos Press, 2015.

Walters, Susan Gary. "Nuosu Proverbs: Aesthetics and Artistry in Form." *Proverbium: Yearbook of International Proverb Scholarship* 39, no. 1 (2022): 325–53. https://doi.org/10.29162/pv.39.1.65.

Walters, Susan Gary. "Tell Me a Story (Part 1): Characteristics of the Art of Narrative." *Ethnodoxology: Global Forum on Arts and Christian Faith* 11, no. 1 (2023): A25–41. https://artsandchristianfaith.org/index.php/journal/article/view/205.

Walters, Susan Gary. "Tell Me a Story (Part 2): The Power of Stories for Diffusing Innovations." *Ethnodoxology: A Global Forum on Arts and Christian Faith* 11, no. 1 (2023): A43–59. https://artsandchristianfaith.org/index.php/journal/article/view/207.

Wedekind, Klaus. "The Praise Singers." *Bible Translator* 26, no. 2 (1975): 245–47.

Wendland, Ernst R. *LiFE-Style Translating: A Workbook for Bible Translators*, 2nd ed. SIL International Publications in Translation and Textlinguistics 2. SIL International, 2011.

Wendland, Ernst R. "An Overview of 'Literary Functional Equivalence' (LiFE) Translation." Revised, February 2024. Accessed May 11, 2024. www.academia.edu/3168198/_Literary_Functional_Equivalence_LiFE_Translation–A_Brief_Description.

Wendland, Ernst R. *Studies in the Psalms: Literary-Structural Analysis with Application to Translation*. SIL International, 2017.

Wendland, Ernst R. *Translating the Literature of Scripture*. Illustrated edition. SIL International, 2004.

West, Amy. "Equipping Urban Believers to Meet Traditional Pressures." Paper presented at the Evangelical Missiological Society Southeast Regional Meeting, Conyers, GA, 2011.

Whiteman, D. L. "Contextualization: The Theory, the Gap, the Challenge." *International Bulletin of Missionary Research* 21, no. 1 (1997): 2–7. https://doi.org/10.1177/239693939702100101.

Whittaker, Sue. "Ethnodoxology: What It Means and Why It's Essential for Church Planting," 2016. International Mission Board. Accessed May 1, 2024. www.academia.edu/48925932/Ethnodoxology_What_it_Means_and_Why_its_Essential_for_Church_Planting.

Whittaker, Sue. *Music and Liturgy, Identity and Formation: A Study of Inculturation in Turkey*. Pickwick Publications, 2021.

Wild-Wood, Emma. "Modern African Missionaries. A Reassessment of Their Impact in Uganda 1890s–1920s." *Exchange: Journal of Contemporary Christianities in Context* 50, nos. 3–4 (2021): 270–88. https://doi.org/10.1163/1572543X-12341602.

Woodley, Randy S. *Shalom and the Community of Creation: An Indigenous Vision*. Eerdmans, 2012.

Wright, N. T. "How Can the Bible Be Authoritative?" *Vox Evangelica* 21 (1991): 7–32. Accessed March 5, 2024. Excerpt: https://ntwrightpage.com/2016/07/12/how-can-the-bible-be-authoritative.

Wright, N. T. *N.T. Wright on the Future of the World*. Vol. 74, no. 4. Fuller Curated, 2014. Accessed February 8, 2023. https://fullercurated.libsyn.com/nt-wright-curated-4.

Wright, N. T. *Simply Jesus: A New Vision of Who He Was, What He Did and Why It Matters*. HarperCollins, 2011.

Wright, N. T. *Surprised by Hope: Rethinking Heaven, the Resurrection, and the Mission of the Church*. HarperOne, 2008.

Wright, N. T. "What Is God's Future for the World?" *Occasio* (blog), May 3, 2014. https://timneufeld.blogs.com/occasio/2014/05/nt-wright-at-fuller-4-what-is-gods-future-for-the-world.html.

Yates, Frank, and G. A. Potorowski. "Evidence-Based Decision Management." In *The Oxford Handbook of Evidence-Based Management*, edited by D. Rosseau, 198–222. Oxford University Press, 2012.

Yates, J. Frank, and Stephanie de Oliveira. "Culture and Decision Making." *Organizational Behavior and Human Decision Processes* 136 (Sept 1, 2016): 106–18. https://doi.org/10.1016/j.obhdp.2016.05.003.

Yeh, Allen. *Polycentric Missiology: 21st-Century Mission from Everyone to Everywhere*. IVP Academic, 2016.

Yeh, Allen. "What Is Polycentric Mission?" *Evangelical Missions Quarterly* 60, no. 1 (2024). Accessed May 11, 2024. https://missionexus.org/what-is-polycentric-mission.

Yoder, Carolyn. *The Little Book of Trauma Healing: When Violence Strikes and Community Security Is Threatened*. Good Books, 2020.

Zogbo, Lynell, and Ernst R. Wendland. *Hebrew Poetry in the Bible: A Guide for Understanding and for Translating*. 2nd ed. UBS Helps for Translators. United Bible Societies, 2020.

Scripture Index

Genesis
1   83
1:26–27   198
1:27   17, 68, 183
2:2   75
2:9   183
2:15   83, 183
2:19–20   102
12:3   198
12:10   76

Exodus
15   188
23:10–12   76
31:1–5   180
31:1–6   184
32   188

Leviticus
23:22   76
26:34   75

Numbers
21:1–8   184

Deuteronomy
6:5   194
10:18   78
15:7–8   78
25:4   76

1 Samuel
16   188
16:23   191

2 Samuel
6   188
6:5   186
6:14–15   194

1 Kings
19:4   72

2 Kings
2:21–22   76
3:15   189

1 Chronicles
15   188
15:16–29   186

2 Chronicles
5   188
5:12–13   194
7:14   76
20:21–23   188
35:15   188

Psalms
6   188
9:18   78
12:5   78
35:10   78
47:1, 5–6   194
51   188
67   198
72:12–14   78
81:1–3   191
95:6   86, 194
96:1   183
96:9   86
100:2   86
139:23–24   201
146:7   78
150   184, 186
150:4   181

Proverbs
11:24–25   78
14:31   78
18:9   83
22:22–23   78
31:8–9   78

Nehemiah
9:15   78

Isaiah
5:12   186
10:1–3   78
19:23–25   198
40:28   113
42:17   184
58:6–11   78
58:12–14   75

Ezekiel
4   184
36:35   64

Daniel
3:5   186
4:31–32   72

Amos
5:23–24   184

Matthew
4:23   13, 72
4:24   72
5:5–8   8
5:14–16   6
6:10   1, 66
8:28   72
9:23   188
11:28   75
11:28–29   72
13:13   184
16:2–3   102
18:15–20   176
19:28   3
19:28–30   8
22:29   88
24:45–47   1835
25:31–34   183
25:34–40   78

Mark
1:15   1
2:27   75
12:24   88
12:29–30   86
12:29–31   2

Luke
1:46–55   78
4:18   78
4:21   88
4:43   5
6:20   78
6:20–26   78
6:46–49   85
9:23   194
10:1–18   65
10:9   72
21:7   102
24:45   88

John
4:18–26   196
4:19–24   184
4:21–24   86, 180
4:24   194
10:10   67
13:34–35   6
13:35   74–75
14:27   67

Acts
1:3–8   175
1:11   8
2:11   198
2:42   86
8:35   88
17:2, 11   88
17:10–12   92
17:24–28   17

Romans
1:25   192
8:18–21   76
8:21   64
8:22–24   72
11:33–12:3   196
12:1   194
12:1–2   86, 195
13   78
15:4   88
15:5–11   198
16:16   183

1 Corinthians
8:18–30   1
8:12–14   194
14:6–19   86
14:7–19   190
14:15   197
14:26   188, 194–95
15:35, 51–53   64
15:35–55   67

2 Corinthians
1:24   182
3:17   195
3:18   72
5:17   6
5:18–20   6
9:6–13   78

Galatians
3:28   69, 74
5:22–23   72

Ephesians
3:10   6
4:11–13   184
4:29   253
5:14–21   196
5:18–19   181, 197
5:18–20   86, 195
5:25–33   175

Philippians
2:3b–8   12

Colossians
1:15–17   17
1:15–20   5, 76
3:11   74
3:11–16   198
3:12–16   194
3:23   83

2 Thessalonians
3:10   83

1 Timothy
2:1–8   194
4:13   88, 194
5:18   83

2 Timothy
3:14–4:5   194
4:16   88

Hebrews
4:1–11   75
10:24–25   86

James
1:27   78
2:5   74
2:15–17   78
5:13   188

2 Peter
3:13   4, 64

Revelation
7:9   68
7:9–10   67, 184
7:9–12   195
19:10   86
21:1   64
21:4   72
21:5   6, 64, 268
21:24, 26   67
21:26–27   198
22:5   183

Subject Index

A

agency
  community   xii, 16
  local   28–29, 31, 181, 278
anthropology   37, 49, 52
apprenticeship(s)   53, 165, 211
aroma(s)   141, 148
artificial intelligence (AI)   10
artistic communication   2–4, 32, 45, 53, 93, 105, 137, 147, 160, 166, 171, 225, 255
artistic element(s)
  malleable   169, 170
  stable   167–68
artists   160–62, 180
arts advocate(s)   xiii, 7, 28, 66, 215
Arts and Trauma Healing (ATH)   221
Arts Creation Workshop   242
Arts for a Better Future (ABF)   ix, 26, 28, 30, 33–34, 169, 179, 199
Arts with God devotional   200
autogenic research   31

B

Bible
  artistic forms   84
  stories   85, 90, 94
bi-musicality   52
blessing songs   121
Bloom, software app   225
body movements   79, 143

C

Christian rites   89
church   8, 14, 175, 180, 184
  deaf   113
  global   177
  growth   178
  history   13
  leadership   187
  local   95, 175–76
  multicultural   41, 264
  multiethnic   197
  purposes   188
  traditions   195
church-planting   29
cocreative context   263
colonialist ideologies   31
commission   208, 215
communication, artistic   37
community   28, 39
  collectivist   173
  definition   27
  multicultural   24
  values   172
Community Arts Archive   215
Community Arts Profile (CAP)   41, 43, 205, 213
community development   36, 104
compensation   161, 209
contextualization   191–93
creation care   76–77
culinary arts   139, 148
cultural enactments   48
cultural identity   213
cultural performances   48

D

dance   3, 34–35, 58, 73, 79, 81, 135, 137, 143, 148
  circle   25
  khon   4
  Thai   3
dances
  social   19
  traditional   33
deaf culture and arts   80
development, language-based   29
drama   73, 81, 94, 135, 143, 144, 148
drumming   33
dualism   192

E

early church   88
economic opportunity   83
education   80
educational curricula   232
emotion(s)   48, 72, 91, 122, 143, 171
enactment(s)   42–43, 123–24, 145, 149–50, 165
  dance features   153
  dramatic features   152
  musical features   151
  oral narrative   235
  oral verbal arts   154
  visual features   156
equipment   52
ethnoarts   x, 69, 234
ethnodoxology   x, 15, 31, 178–79, 208
ethnomusicologists   30
ethnomusicology   37

F

family 51
festival 20, 130, 204, 210, 213–15
fieldnotes 57
fusion(s) 13, 121, 163

G

gatekeepers 33, 185–86, 209
Genre Enactment Features 120, 129, 147, 149, 152–55, 157, 159
Global Ethnodoxology Network (GEN) ix, 15, 58, 277, 279
God, as artisan 180
God's image 36, 98, 183

H

healing 14, 32, 221
Heart Arts Questionnaire 189, 199
humility 28, 31–32

I

identity 27, 34, 68, 166, 168–69, 213, 278
  community 70
  markers 40
indigenous hymns 86
indigenous traditions 59
innovation 163
Inside-out approach 47
interview(s) 54
  ethnographic 54–56

J

jokes 49
justice 225

K

kingdom creativity 21
Kingdom Goals 19, 68
kingdom of Heaven 15, 19
kinship 50

L

labor 83
laments 72
language(s) 50, 165–66
learner
  analytical 54
  energetic 54
  relational 54
  structured 54
learning style(s) 54
linguistics 37

literacy 68, 81, 229–31
literacy materials 227
local genres 45
love song 121, 124

M

marriage 51
materials 133
meaning(s) 102, 122
media, use of 71
meditation 91
memorization 88
mentoring 210
meristem 206
minority communities 169
missiology 37
multimedia collection 216–17
music 7, 19, 73, 131, 139, 143–44, 148
  devotional 22

N

narration 144
new artistry 106
New Creation ix, 2, 4, 9–10, 15–16, 63–65, 105, 118, 175, 264
note-taking 56

O

object manipulation 143
oral engagement 28
oral narrative genre 236
oral verbal arts 137, 139, 143–44, 148, 154
Outside-in approach 46

P

participant observation techniques 52
phenomenology 102, 118–19, 121
photography 60–61
play 223
poetic devices 144
  meaning 156
  sound 155
  words 155
polycentrism 29
power relationships 51
power structures 169
powwow
  traditional 91
prayer 91
principle bridge 182–83
productivity 83
proverbs (collection of) 151

Subject Index

publications 211
publishing 218

Q

questions
  closed 55
  open 55

R

radio dramas 93
reconciliation 68, 73
recording
  analytical 59
  audio 57, 150
  audiovisual 59
  equipment 58–59
  integral 58
  metadata 59
  video 57, 149–50
relationships 52
research 36
rest and play 68, 75
rhythm 144, 155, 170
rites of passage 19
ritual 20, 192–93
Rogerian psychotherapy 30

S

Scripture
  application 93
  artistic forms of communication 184
  interpretation 181, 183
  oral 68, 85
Scripture Relevance Dramas 93
self-identity, positive 34
shalom 67
signifiers
  iconic 103
  indexical 103
  lexical 103
silence 50
social justice 68, 77
songs 86
  collection of 150
  hybrid 25
  multicultural 25
  multilingual 25
sparking activity 204, 206, 208
spiritual formation 68, 92
spiritual warfare 32
sports 148
stable 168

storyteller 135
storytelling 85, 94, 101
strategies 177
  multicultural 198
structures
  malleable 168
  stable 168
sustainability 68, 213
symbolism, visual 156
syncretism 31, 191

T

teaching children 70
therapeutic model 31
trade language 19
tradition 163
transcription 140
translation 233, 235, 261
  Bible 84–85, 233–35
  oral 233
  workshop 234
transmission 10, 111, 165, 220
  intergenerational 32
trauma 14
trauma healing 72, 74, 112, 222

V

video stories 148
violence (alternatives to) 223
visual arts 81, 137, 143, 148
vocal features 143

W

well-being 68, 72
witness 14, 22, 123, 175, 188
worldview 51, 193
  animistic 190
worldview patterns 66
worship 22, 277
  biblical 86, 195
  corporate 68, 86, 195
  multicultural 87, 167, 264
  through dramatic tableaux 201
  through the pen 201
Worship Wheel 195,–97
Worship Workshop 237, 239, 241

Worship and Mission for the Global Church: An Ethnodoxology Handbook

James R. Krabill, Frank Fortunato, Robin P. Harris, and Brian Schrag, editors

This book offers theological reflection, case studies, practical tools, and audiovisual resources to help the global church appreciate and generate culturally appropriate arts in worship and witness. Drawing on the expertise and experience of over one hundred writers from twenty countries, the volume integrates insights from the fields of ethnomusicology, biblical research, worship studies, missiology, and the arts.

Community Arts for God's Purposes: How to Create Local Artistry Together

Brian Schrag and Julia Rowe

Community Arts for God's Purposes highlights the CLAT (Creating Local Arts Together) method, a seven-step process that inspires artistic creativity and collaboration with local musicians, dancers, storytellers, actors, and visual artists. In this manual, the arts are treated as special kinds of communication systems, connected to specific times, places, and social contexts.

*Available in English, Spanish, Portuguese, French, Chinese, Korean, Russian, and Indonesian

visit us at missionbooks.org

www.ingramcontent.com/pod-product-compliance
Lightning Source LLC
Chambersburg PA
CBHW082150070526
44585CB00020B/2156